Red Hat® Fedora™ Linux® 3 FOR DUMMIES®

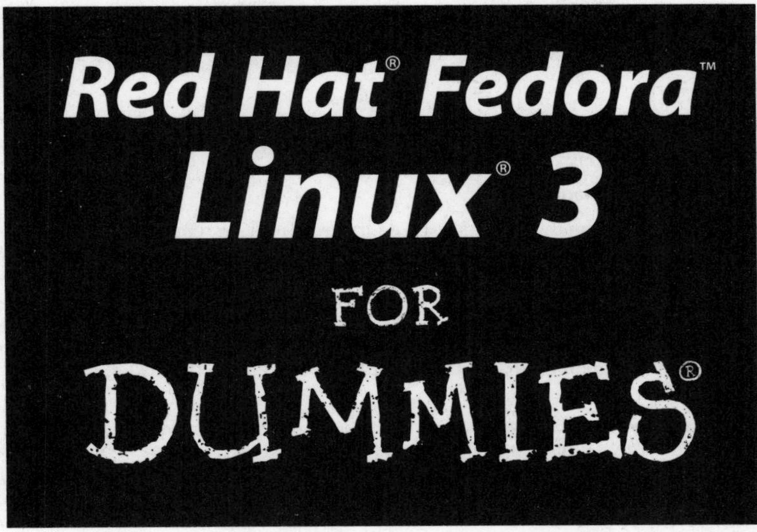

by Jon 'maddog' Hall and Paul G. Sery

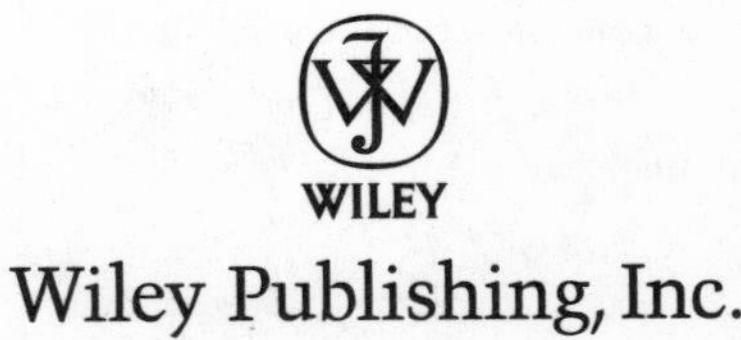

Wiley Publishing, Inc.

Red Hat® Fedora™ Linux® 3 For Dummies®

Published by
Wiley Publishing, Inc.
111 River Street
Hoboken, NJ 07030-5774

Published by Wiley Publishing, Inc., Indianapolis, Indiana

Published simultaneously in Canada

For general information on our other products and services, please contact our Customer Care Department within the U.S. at 800-762-2974, outside the U.S. at 317-572-3993, or fax 317-572-4002.

For technical support, please visit `www.wiley.com/techsupport`.

Wiley also publishes its books in a variety of electronic formats. Some content that appears in print may not be available in electronic books.

Library of Congress Control Number is available from the publisher.

ISBN: 0-7645-7940-1

Manufactured in the United States of America

1B/RW/RR/QU/IN

10 9 8 7 6 5 4 3 2 1

About the Authors

Jon "maddog" Hall is the executive director of Linux International, a vendor organization dedicated to promoting the use of the Linux operating system. He has been in the computer industry for more than a quarter of a century (somehow, that sounds more impressive than just "25 years"), the past 18 years of which have been spent using, programming, and admiring the Unix operating system. Jon works for Compaq Computer Corporation, where he is helping to shape Compaq's strategy with respect to Linux. Previously, Jon was the department head of computer science at Hartford State Technical College, where his students lovingly (he hopes) gave him the nickname "maddog" as he tried to teach them operating system design, compiler theory, and how to live an honorable life.

While working for Digital Equipment Corporation in May of 1994, "maddog" met Linus Torvalds, and was intelligent enough (his critics say "maddog" was just lucky) to recognize the potential of the Linux operating system. Linux changed his life, mostly by providing him with 22-hour workdays. Since "maddog" has started working with Linux, however, he has also started meeting more girls (in particular, his two godchildren). You can usually find Jon speaking at various Linux conferences and events ("maddog" just barks), and he has also been known to travel long distances to speak to local Linux user groups.

Paul G. Sery is a systems administrator employed by Sandia National Laboratories in Albuquerque, New Mexico. He is a member of the Computer Support Unit, Special Projects, which specializes in managing and troubleshooting Unix and Linux systems.

When he's not beating his head against stubborn computers, Paul and his wife, Lidia, enjoy riding their tandem bicycle through the Rio Grande valley. They also enjoy traveling throughout Mexico. Paul is the author of *Linux Network Toolkit* and the coauthor of several other books. He has a bachelor's degree in electrical engineering from the University of New Mexico.

Dedication

Jon 'maddog' Hall: To Mom & Pop™, whose aversion to things electronic is well known, and who can still call their son *Jon* rather than *maddog*.

Paul G. Sery: To my wife, Lidia Maura Vazquez de Sery.

Authors' Acknowledgments

I want to thank my wife, Lidia, for her patience, support, and good advice, all of which have made writing this book possible. Without her, I would still be the pocket-protector-wearing, busted-eyeglasses-fixed-with-tape-looking, "Star Trek"-costume-watching, wrinkled-shirt-suffering, spaghetti-in-the-pot-over-the-sink-eating, Saturday-night-hacking sorry sorta guy. Well, I was never into "Star Trek," and I *am* pecking at this keyboard on Saturday night, but my beautiful wife sure has made me a better man.

I want to thank the staff at Wiley Publishing, who make this book possible and provide outstanding support. Terri Varveris and Rebecca Whitney provided constant and essential assistance.

And, I also want to thank Anne Hamilton and Laura Lewin, who gave me the chance to write in general and this book in particular. Both showed great confidence in and patience with me. I am very grateful and wish them success in their ventures.

I want to acknowledge a total lack of assistance in writing this book from my dog, the infamous Oso Maloso: eater of many things that should have ended his long career early, including (but not limited to) ant poison, Advil (poisonous to dogs), many pounds of Tootsie Rolls one Halloween, several bags of chicken bones at one party, beer, and other assorted items; escaper of many fences and gates; and friend of the late, great Paunchy (whose name you see throughout this book) and other local dogs.

How useful was Oso? Well, one night while working on this book I got a phone call. Leaving my apple pie next to the keyboard, I went downstairs to take the call and passed him on his way up. I should have known something was up because he had a cell phone with him and no one answered when I picked up to take the call. I went up the stairs while he went down. The apple pie was gone. Oso 1, human 0.

Publisher's Acknowledgments

We're proud of this book; please send us your comments through our online registration form located at www.dummies.com/register/.

Some of the people who helped bring this book to market include the following:

Acquisitions, Editorial, and Media Development

Project Editor: Mark Enochs

Acquisitions Editor: Terri Varveris

Senior Copy Editor: Barry Childs-Helton

Technical Editors: Susan and Korry Douglas

Editorial Manager: Kevin Kirschner

Permissions Editor: Laura Moss

Media Development Specialist: Travis Silvers

Media Development Manager: Laura VanWinkle

Media Development Supervisor: Richard Graves

Editorial Assistant: Amanda M. Foxworth

Cartoons: Rich Tennant, www.the5thwave.com

Composition

Project Coordinators: Emily W. Wichlinski, Nancee Reeves

Layout and Graphics: Andrea Dahl, Lauren Goddard, Joyce Haughey, Barry Offringa, Heather Ryan

Proofreaders: David Faust, Dwight Ramsey, TECHBOOKS Production Services

Indexer: TECHBOOKS Production Services

Special Help

Christopher W. Morris

Publishing and Editorial for Technology Dummies

Richard Swadley, Vice President and Executive Group Publisher

Andy Cummings, Vice President and Publisher

Mary Bednarek, Executive Acquisitions Director

Mary C. Corder, Editorial Director

Publishing for Consumer Dummies

Diane Graves Steele, Vice President and Publisher

Joyce Pepple, Acquisitions Director

Composition Services

Gerry Fahey, Vice President of Production Services

Debbie Stailey, Director of Composition Services

Contents at a Glance

Table of Contents

Introduction

Red Hat Fedora Linux 3 For Dummies describes how to install and use this popular and powerful Linux distribution for fun and profit. Fedora Core is the successor to Red Hat Linux. Fedora Core 1 was essentially Red Hat Linux 10; if you *really* like numbers, think of Fedora Core 3 as Red Hat Linux 12.

Let's back up a little and mention that a Linux *distribution* is the combination of the Linux *kernel* (the core software, also known as an *operating system,* that controls your computer) and all its supporting applications, utilities, and installation-and-configuration software that helps you get work done and have fun with your computer. The word *Linux* has traditionally been used, depending on the context, as shorthand to mean a specific Linux distribution.

So why is *this* Linux distribution named Fedora Core?! What do a fedora and a core have to do with Linux? Well, the company Red Hat, Inc., recently decided it was time to concentrate on its core business, which is centered on its commercial product Red Hat Enterprise Linux. Red Hat merged its "free" Red Hat Linux distribution with the Fedora Linux Project to create the Fedora Core Project. (The Fedora Linux Project previously concentrated on developing third-party Linux-based applications and utilities.)

The Fedora Core Project is an open-source project. *Open source* describes all software published under the GNU Public License (GPL) and other similar licenses. Open-source software gives you (and everyone) access to the underlying source code and permits you to use, modify, and redistribute (for free or a fee) the code. The only restriction is that you cannot prevent other people from doing the same. Under the new arrangement, therefore, Red Hat maintains editorial control over — and provides resources for — the Fedora Core Project; the community of Fedora Core users and developers gets a larger role in technical development.

Less talk, more rock! *Red Hat Fedora Linux 3 For Dummies* will help you install and use the immensely popular Fedora Core 3 on your personal computer. We show you how to get work done and also do fun stuff. This book is also designed to be an effective doorstop or coffee-cup coaster. Whatever you use it for, we hope you have fun.

About This Book

Red Hat Fedora Linux 3 For Dummies is designed to be a helping-hands resource. It provides a place to turn for help and solace in those moments when, after two hours of trying to get your network connection to work, your dog bumps into your desk and knocks the book onto your computer, jiggling the network cable — and it magically starts working.

We tried our hardest to fill up this book with the things you need to know, such as how to do the following:

- Install Fedora Core 3.
- Get connected to the Internet, whether using broadband DSL, cable modems, or old-fashioned dial-up modems.
- Get connected to your local-area network (LAN).
- Build a simple-but-effective firewall.
- Build Internet and LAN services, such as Web pages and print servers.
- Use Red Hat Linux to play CDs and listen to Internet radio stations.
- Use the GNOME desktop environment. GNOME is the graphical system that makes your computer easier and fun to use. GNOME provides the look 'n feel of your computer plus many applications.
- Take advantage of useful and usable applications, such as the Open Office desktop productivity suite, Evolution desktop organizer and e-mail client, and streaming multimedia MPlayer.
- Work with the OpenOffice desktop productivity suite to satisfy your word-processing, spreadsheet, and presentation needs — or, install Wine (and possibly the commercial Wine enhancer CrossOver Office) so you can use Microsoft Office directly from your Fedora Core computer!
- Upgrade your computer and network security.
- Know where to go for help.
- Manage your Fedora Core workstation.

You also encounter troubleshooting tips throughout this book. Chapter 18 is, in fact, devoted to the subject. It's not that Fedora Core is all that much trouble, but we want you to be prepared in case you run into bad luck or unusual situations.

The instructions in *Red Hat Fedora Linux 3 For Dummies* are designed to work with the version of Fedora Core you find on this book's companion DVD; we also describe how to download several software packages not found on the DVD. Feel free to use other versions of Fedora Core, or even other Linux distributions, but be aware that our instructions may not work exactly as given, or (sometimes) even at all. O brave new world. Good luck!

Foolish Assumptions

You probably know what they say about people who make assumptions, but *Red Hat Fedora Linux 3 For Dummies* never would have been written if we didn't make a few. This book *is* for you if you

- **Want to build a Fedora Core workstation:** You want to use the Linux operating system to build your personal workstation. Surprise! The DVD in the back of this book contains the Fedora Core 3 distribution.
- **Have a computer:** It's just a technicality, but you need a computer because we describe how to install Fedora Core 3 on a computer.
- **Have no duct tape:** You want to put the Fedora Core operating system and the computer together, and using duct tape hasn't worked.
- **Don't want to be a guru:** You already have hobbies, and don't want to become a Fedora Core guru — at least not yet.

However, *Red Hat Fedora Linux 3 For Dummies* is *not* for you if you're looking for

- **An all-encompassing reference-style book:** We simply don't have enough space, or permission from the publisher, to provide a comprehensive range of topics. We concentrate on providing help with getting popular and useful programs up and running. We devote more space, for example, to getting your DSL or cable modem working than to describing the theory that makes them work.
- **A system-administration book:** Again, we don't have enough space to do the subject justice. We provide instructions on how to perform certain essential administrative tasks, like adding users, packages, and network connections. We select certain topics to focus on and leave the rest for other books.

Conventions Used in This Book

At computer conventions, thousands of computer people get together and talk about deep technical issues, such as the following:

- Could Superman beat Batman?
- Could The Punisher beat Superman?
- Could The Punisher, Superman, Batman, and Spiderman together beat Linus? (No way!)

But these late-night, coffee-induced conventions aren't what we mean. Our conventions are shorthand ways of designating specific information or tasks.

Typing code

Fedora Core provides various graphical user interfaces (GUIs) to help you do most of the tasks you want to do. However, many people still find that performing many tasks "manually," by typing a command, is easier; in some circumstances, it's the only way to get a job done.

Therefore, we show you in Chapter 4 how to use a text-based terminal-emulator window to run a command. In anticipation of manually running commands, we describe several conventions in this section.

When you see URLs (Uniform Resource Locators), filenames, directories, commands, and parameters in a paragraph, they're formatted `in monospace type`. That helps differentiate those items from the general text.

When you see words in boldface, they indicate something you should type; for example:

> Type **man chown** at the command prompt and press Enter.

That line tells you to enter the command `man chown` and press the Enter (or Return) key. The command is then executed. (Throughout this book, we say "press the Enter key" or "press Enter" whenever we want you to execute a command; the Enter key is synonymous with the Return key.

Commands set off by themselves, rather than shown in the text, look like this:

```
pwd
```

Here's a rundown of the command *syntax* (how you string 'em together) in Linux:

- Text *not* surrounded by `[ ]` or `{ }` brackets must be typed exactly as shown.
- Text inside brackets `[ ]` is optional.
- Text in *italics* indicates the part of a command that must be replaced with appropriate text. You should not type verbatim the italicized part of a command. If we say "Enter the command **more *somefile***," we mean for you to replace *`somefile`* with the name of the file you're interested in. For example, you may end up entering the command **more /etc/passwd**, where you substitute `/etc/passwd` for *`somefile`*.
- Text inside braces `{ }` indicates that you must choose one of the values inside the braces and separated by the `|` sign. For example, you should

enter either **echo "one"** or **echo "two"** or **echo "three"** if you see a command such as **echo "{one | two | three}"** show up in the book.

- An ellipsis (. . .) means "and so on," or to repeat the preceding command line as needed.

Don't concern yourself much with these conventions for now. In most chapters in this book, you don't need to fuss all that much with these details. When you do need to know something about a particular syntax, come back to this introduction for a refresher course.

Keystrokes and clicks

Some instructions require that you press a specific key or keys to execute the desired result. If you need to press a single key, we say, for example, "press the A key." We use a plus sign to indicate multiple keys. For example, Ctrl+Alt+Delete means that you should press the Ctrl key, Alt key, and Delete key all at the same time.

Most applications and utilities we describe in this book use a graphical user interface (GUI), such as the Fedora Core display or network configuration utility, which allows you to control your computer by pointing and clicking with your mouse. When we tell you to "click" something, we want you to press the left button on your mouse. Some actions require that you use the right button; in those cases, we explicitly say "right-click."

How This Book Is Organized

Like all proper *For Dummies* books, *Red Hat Fedora Linux 3 For Dummies* is organized into independent parts. You can read the parts in any order. (Heck, if you have ever seen the movie *Memento,* you may want to read the parts in reverse.) Basically, this book isn't meant to be read from front cover to back; rather, it's meant to be a reference book that helps you find what you're looking for when you're looking for it. Between the Contents at a Glance page, the table of contents, and the index, you should have no problem finding what you need.

If you do read the chapters in this book in order, you encounter the useful and interesting things first and the more technical items last. For example, after installing Fedora Core in Part I, you may want to proceed immediately to Part II to see how to connect Linux to the Internet or your local network. From there, you can use your new workstation to surf the Internet and use e-mail.

The following sections describe each part.

Part I: Installing Fedora Core

In Part I, we introduce the Linux operating system, a dash of its history, and some things you can do with the Fedora Core distribution. We also describe how to prepare your computer to install Fedora Core; because many, if not most, computers come with *another* (ahem) operating system installed, we describe how to reorganize your computer's hard drive so you can install Linux. You find out what Linux is and how to prepare your computer to install Fedora Core. We then walk you through the installation and show you the basics of working with Fedora Core.

Part II: Got Net?

In Part II, you find out about connecting to the Internet and local networks. You see how to jump on the Internet with your everyday modem, high-speed (broadband) DSL connection, or cable modem. We also show you how to connect to an existing network. If that local network has a high-speed Internet connection, you can use it as your portal to the wonderful world of surfing. The Internet can be dangerous, so we include instructions for creating your own firewall.

Part III: Linux, Huh! What Is It Good For? Absolutely Everything!

Part III guides you through the particulars of *doing* something with Fedora Core. This part introduces you to the GNOME desktop window environment and takes you through its paces by finding out how to move, resize, hide, and close windows and how to use the file manager and much more. Two chapters are devoted to using the Fedora Core multimedia capabilities, such as listening to CDs and MP3s, in addition to how to rip and record them. The world's online radio stations are now available to you with streaming-media technology. We introduce you to the Mozilla browser so you can surf the Net and use the Evolution organizer to read your e-mail, use your calendar, and perform other tasks. We also describe in detail the full-featured OpenOffice desktop-productivity suite. You can use OpenOffice with your Fedora Core machine to do all your writing and other work-related functions. You can even write a book with it!

Part IV: Revenge of the Nerds

In Part IV, we guide you through the use of your Fedora Core computer's network capabilities. It's Nerd City, but it's also fun and useful. We start by showing you how to build a simple network. After your network is up and running, we describe how to build network services, such as the Apache Web server, Samba, and printer servers. The last two chapters in this part are devoted to exploring the art of network computer security and troubleshooting network problems. Insert your pocket protector, strap the old Hewlett-Packard calculator to your hip, retape your glasses, and get ready for Saturday night!

Part V: The Part of Tens

A *For Dummies* book just isn't complete without The Part of Tens, where you can find ten all-important resources and answers to the ten most bothersome questions people have after installing Fedora Core. (The folks at Red Hat Software provided these questions; they'd know.) We introduce the ten most important security concerns too.

Part VI: Appendixes

Ah, the appendixes. Appendix A outlines the Fedora Core systems administration utilities. Appendix B describes how to find out about the details of your computer's individual pieces of hardware; this information is sometimes helpful when you're installing Fedora Core. Appendixes C and D introduce you to using and managing the Linux file system. Appendix E shows how to use the Red Hat Package manager (RPM). Appendix F completes this book by describing what you can find on the companion DVD.

What You're Not to Read

Heck, you don't have to read any of Red Hat Fedora Linux 3 For Dummies if you don't want to, but then, why did you buy it? (Not that we're complaining.) Part I has background information. If you don't want it, don't read it. Also, the text in sidebars is optional, although often helpful. If you're on the fast track to using Fedora Core, you can skip the sidebars and the text next to the Technical Stuff icon, as described in the following section. But we suggest instead that you slow down a bit and enjoy the experience.

Icons in This Book

This section describes the icons you see in this book. Icons amplify the discussion by calling attention to interesting or important information.

Nifty little shortcuts and timesavers appear next to this icon. Fedora Core is a powerful operating system, and you can save unbelievable amounts of time and energy by using its tools and programs. We hope that our tips show you how.

Don't let this happen to you! We hope that our experiences with Fedora Core can help you avoid the mistakes we have made.

This information helps you to recall information presented elsewhere in the book.

This information is particularly nerdy and technical. You can skip it, but you may find it interesting if you're of a geekier bent.

Where to Go from Here

You're about to join the legions of people who have been using and developing Fedora Core and Linux. We have been using Unix for more than 20 years, Linux for more than 10 years, and Fedora Core (and Red Hat Linux) for almost 10 years. We have found Fedora Core to be a flexible, powerful operating system, capable of solving most problems, even without a large set of commercial software. The future of the Linux operating system — Fedora Core in particular — is bright. The time and energy you expend in becoming familiar with it will be worthwhile.

Part I
Installing Fedora Core

"Jerry, were they up there before you passed the installation's point of no return?"

In this part . . .

You're about to embark on a journey through the Fedora Core installation program. Perhaps you know nothing about setting up an operating system on your computer. That's okay. The Fedora Core installation system is easy-going by nature and straightforward to use. Plus, we help guide you through the installation process.

In Chapter 1, you get a handle on what Fedora Core is all about and what it can do for you. Chapter 2 helps you get ready to install Fedora Core and repartition your hard drive, if necessary. The real fun begins in Chapter 3, when you install your own penguin. (Linus Torvalds, the inventor of Linux, loves penguins, and they have been adopted as the Linux mascot.) Chapter 4 gives you a brief, but important, introduction to working with Fedora Core.

Chapter 1

And in the Opposite Corner . . . a Penguin?

In This Chapter

- Napping through Linux History 101
- Finding out what Fedora Core can do
- Using Fedora Core as a workstation
- Using the Fedora Core network functions

We see a penguin in your future. He's an unassuming fellow who's taking on a rather big competitor — that *other* operating system — in the battle for the hearts, minds, and desktops of computer users. Fedora Core, the successor to Red Hat Linux, is undeniably one of the driving forces behind the Linux revolution — and is the most popular Linux brand.

This chapter introduces you to the latest and greatest Fedora Core release, Fedora Core 3. This book covers all the bases (a good number of them, at least) about how to use Fedora Core as a desktop productivity tool, Internet portal, multimedia workstation, and basic network server. You can do lots of things with Fedora Core; this chapter gives you an overview of the possibilities — in addition to a brief look at the history of Linux.

History of the World, er, Linux: Part II

In the beginning of computerdom (said in a booming, thunderous voice), the world was filled with hulking mainframes. These slothful beasts lumbered through large corporations; required a special species of ultra-nerds to keep them happy; and ate up huge chunks of space, power, and money. Then came the IBM PC and Microsoft, and the world changed. Power to the people, sort of.

In 1991, a student at the University of Helsinki named Linus Torvalds became dissatisfied with the standard PC operating system. He thought that the Unix operating system might be better suited than MS-DOS or Windows to help him accomplish his work. Unix was invented in the 1970s and, although powerful, it was expensive, so he began writing his own version of Unix. Now, writing your own operating system is a simple task — not! After formulating the basic parts, Torvalds recruited a team of talented programmers through the Internet, and together they created a new operating system, or kernel, now named Linux.

One of the most important decisions that Torvalds made in the early days of Linux was to freely distribute the Linux kernel code for anyone and everyone to do with as they wanted. These free Linux *distributions* were (and still are) available in several forms, mainly on-line.

The only restriction Linus imposed on the free distribution of his creation was that no version of the software can be made proprietary. (*Proprietary* software is owned and developed by private companies in places that often rival Area 51 in security. However, *open-source* code is for "the people" — anyone can use and develop it without fear of violating copyrights or patent restrictions.) You can modify it to your heart's content and also distribute it for fun or profit. What you *can't* do is stop anyone else from using, modifying, and distributing the software you have modified.

Think of open-source software as a path. Linus and others started building the path, and many people came along and found it useful. Some people began adding to the path, while others used it as is. You can use the path, make it wider, and add another branch, if you want — but you can't stop anyone from using the original path or the section you added; neither can you prevent people from adding their own branches.

The lack of traditional proprietary software restrictions on Linux has led to continued improvements and innovations in its technology — and subsequently its immense popularity. Open-source software, and Linux in particular, is transparent to all users and developers. That transparency allows people throughout the world to rapidly improve Linux and its associated subsystems. In contrast, proprietary operating systems are like a sealed, black box where no one except a small group of privileged insiders knows what goes on inside. Only that select group can make modifications, and that limits innovation and improvements.

Return to our brief history lesson: In early spring 1994, the first real version of Linux (Version 1.0) was made available for public use. It was very exciting. Even then, it was an impressive operating system that ran smartly on computers with less than 2MB of RAM and a simple 386 microprocessor. Linux 1.0 also included free features for which other operating systems charged hundreds of dollars. Nowadays, tens of millions of users enjoy Linux at home and work.

Free Software?

The Free Software Foundation (FSF), the brainchild of the great Richard Stallman, contributes much of the utilitarian software that makes using Linux much easier. Most of its bread-and-butter utilities and commands, such as `ls` and `cat`, come from the FSF. Stallman is considered by many to be the originator of the open-source movement.

By the way, if you're wondering about the whole penguin thing, the answer is simple: Linus loves penguins. The Linux world naturally started using the bird as its symbol. The friendly and familiar penguin (whose name is Tux, by the way) now symbolizes All Things Linux.

Knowing What You Can Do with Fedora Core

Fedora Core combines all those pieces, plus some additional applications, and then goes another step to add a few of its own — to create an *integrated product.* The Fedora Core Project combines the basic Linux operating system with software (some made by other companies and some made by Red Hat) to produce a package with a value that's greater than the sum of its parts. That combination is known as a *distribution,* or *flavor,* of Linux.

To get you up and running as quickly as possible, we have bundled the Fedora Core 3 distribution on the DVD in the back of this book.

If your computer cannot use DVDs, you can get the full Fedora Core 3 distribution on CD-ROMs by sending in the coupon in the back of this book.

Fedora Core (and in its previous life, Red Hat Linux) was initially used almost solely to provide network-based services such as Web pages. However, the company Red Hat, Inc. — along with many open-source developers (such as the GNOME Project) — started working hard to make Linux suitable for the desktop. The result is that Fedora Core is now used in both server and desktop environments. And it's used by individuals, businesses, and governments to cut costs, improve performance, and just plain get work done.

You can use Fedora Core as a desktop workstation, a network server, an Internet gateway, a firewall, the basis of an embedded system (for, say, a smart VCR or refrigerator), or even as the brains of a multiprocessor supercomputer. And, thanks to the many, many people who continually make refinements and innovations, Fedora Core continues to become more flexible and capable with each release.

This list shows some of the features that Fedora Core provides:

- **Desktop productivity tools:** Red Hat and now Fedora Core have successfully worked overtime during the past few years to make Linux work on your *desktop* (that is, the single-computer system that most people use for everyday tasks such as word processing or Web browsing). Fedora Core bundles software — such as the OpenOffice suite of productivity tools and the Mozilla browser — with the operating system so you can get everyday work done. The OpenOffice suite has a full-function word processor plus spreadsheet, presentation, graphical drawing, and Web-page-creation tools. Its word processor can read and write all Windows Office formats, plus many others (such as WordPerfect). Mozilla is a full-featured browser on a par with Microsoft Internet Explorer.
- **Multimedia stuff:** Fedora Core packs numerous multimedia tools for you to use. You can play, record, and rip audio tracks from CDs and DVDs. You can listen to streamed media sources (such as radio stations) over the Internet with Rhythmbox. Linux also lets you transfer photos and other items from your own cameras and MP3 players.
- **Network services:** Fedora Core's traces its roots to providing network-based services. Linux found its initial popularity in performing jobs like Web serving, file serving, and printer sharing — and hasn't missed a beat. We show you how to create several network services with Fedora Core in Part IV of this book.

Boosting Your Personal Workstation

We can't emphasize enough how well Fedora Core functions as a personal computer. With Fedora Core, you can easily create your own inexpensive, flexible, and powerful workstation. Fedora Core provides the platform for most of the applications you need to get your work done. Many applications, from desktop productivity suites to Web browsers and multimedia systems, come bundled with Fedora Core. For example, the following list describes just a few major categories of free software available for Linux, along with some examples of popular programs:

- **Office suites:** OpenOffice provides a complete desktop productivity suite that includes (for openers) an advanced word processor, a spreadsheet, and a presentation editor. The OpenOffice word processor can read and write Microsoft Word, HTML, spreadsheet, and graphics files.

OpenOffice provides its own file format and also reads and writes Microsoft Office 97, Office 2000, Office XP, and Office 2003 files. It can use other formats as well, such as Rich Text Format. Check out the site at `www.openoffice.org`.

- **Multimedia players:** Fedora Core packages and installs the open-source Rhythmbox player. You can use Rhythmbox to play downloaded Ogg/Vorbis files or Ogg/Vorbis streams; Ogg/Vorbis is a new open source multimedia format that is discussed in chapter 12. You can also download the excellent open-source MPlayer audio and video player. MPlayer lets you watch DVDs and listen to or view Windows MediaPlayer audio/video streams. You can, alternatively, download a free version of the proprietary RealPlayer, from RealNetworks, to listen to RealAudio streams. The Internet is going nuts with multimedia, and these multimedia players let you get in on the action.
- **Running Microsoft Windows applications and environments:** You can use Fedora Core to run Windows programs. The WINE (Wine Is Not an Emulator) system facilitates running Windows programs directly under Linux. WINE builds a bridge between the Linux and Windows world giving you the best of both worlds. (The commercial product VMware Workstation builds a different kind of bridge between those worlds by creating a virtual computer *within* your Linux PC. From the software's point of view, this *virtual machine* looks, acts, smells, and performs just like a "real" Windows computer (its normal environment), but it's really just a program running under the Linux operating system.)
- **Web browsers and e-mail clients:** Fedora Core includes the open-source browser Mozilla to provide a powerful, reliable, and secure browser to surf the Web with. You also get Ximian Evolution personal organizer — which includes an e-mail client, calendar, and other functions like those of Microsoft Outlook — to help with your messaging and organizational needs.

Using Linux Network Tools and Services

Linux computers can provide many powerful and flexible network services. Your Fedora Core 3 DVD comes packed with the tools to provide these services:

- **Apache Web server:** The open source Apache Web server runs the majority of all Web servers on the Internet. You can start a simple Web server by simply installing the bundled Apache software from this book's companion DVD.

- **OpenSSH:** The open-source version of Secure Shell (SSH) enables you to communicate securely across the Internet. Secure Shell is much safer than Telnet because Secure Shell encrypts your communication when you log in (even when you log in to other computers), significantly reducing the chance that unauthorized others can discover your passwords and other sensitive information. OpenSSH also provides other authentication and security features, and enables you to copy files securely from machine to machine. With OpenSSH, you can prevent people from listening to your communication.
- **Internet-access utilities:** Fedora Core provides several configuration utilities that help you connect to the Internet. The utilities help you to configure DSL, cable modems, and plain old telephone modems to connect to the Internet. They also help you to connect to local-area networks (LANs) that use Ethernet adapters.
- **Firewalls:** A *firewall* is a system that controls access to your private network from any outside network (in this case, the Internet) and controls access from your private network to the outside world. To keep the bad guys out, Fedora Core provides protection by giving you the tools to build your own firewall. Fedora Core is flexible in this regard, and many software packages are available, including the popular and simple-to-use netfilter/iptables filtering software, which is included on this book's companion DVD. Chapter 8 covers using and modifying the default Fedora Core firewall.

This list is just a sample of the network-y things you can do with Fedora Core. We describe many of them in this book.

Chapter 2

Paving the Way for Fedora Core

In This Chapter

- Preparing to install Fedora Core
- Determining whether your Windows partition is FAT or NTFS
- Defragmenting your hard drive
- Resizing FAT partitions
- Resizing NTFS partitions

All major personal computer (PC) manufacturers install Microsoft Windows on their machines by default. However, you can purchase computers *sans* operating system via mail-order or from local, non-brand stores.

What does that mean? Basically, you can skip this chapter if you have a "bare" PC without a preinstalled operating system. You can also skip this chapter if you want to remove Windows from your PC or if your Windows computer has a second partition on which you can install Linux.

A *partition* is a portion of a disk drive used to organize files and directories. For example, the famous Windows *C* drive is installed on its own partition. A partition can use all or part of a disk. Most computers now partition the entire hard disk for drive C, although some include a second partition for drive D. However, if you have Windows installed on your PC and want to keep it, you have to make accommodations for Fedora Core. Fortunately, Linux is an easy-going fellow who gets along well with others. You can install Fedora Core next to Windows on the same drive in a configuration called a "*dual-boot" system:* You choose which operating system to use when you power up, or *boot,* your computer.

This chapter shows you how to prepare your hard drive so that Linux and Windows can live in harmony worthy of a schmaltzy soda commercial. What the world needs now is dual-boot, sweet dual-boot — oh, never mind.

Preparing Your Windows Computer for Fedora Core

Before you install Fedora Core alongside an existing Windows installation, you need to get your hard drive ready. This list of steps provides an overview of the disk preparation process:

1. **Put on a red fedora.**
2. **Back up everything that's on your Windows computer.**

   The processes we describe in this chapter should not affect your existing Windows installation. However, you can never be too safe in dealing with your precious files, so you should back them up. A description of how to back up the contents of a Windows computer is beyond the scope of this book. Numerous commercial and freeware (not to be confused with open-source) backup systems are available.
3. **Determine how your Windows computer's hard drive is formatted.**

   Microsoft Windows uses two types of disk formats: FAT (File Access Table) and NTFS (NT File System). FAT is older and less advanced than NTFS. Open-source utilities are available for resizing FAT-based disks to make room for Linux, but you have to purchase commercial software to repartition NTFS systems. (The next section tells you how to know which format you have.)
4. **Defragment your disk.**

   All resizing programs require you to *defragment* your disk before proceeding. Over time, the bits and bytes that make up your files tend to get scattered around your hard drive. If too many of these fragments are left floating around, resizing may not work — or may even cause problems. Tidy them up; the next section covers defragmenting.
5. **Repartition your computer's hard drive to make room to install Fedora Core if you want to install it alongside Windows (or another operating system).**

   You can use destructive or nondestructive resizing to make room for Linux. *Destructive* resizing wipes everything, including Windows and your data files, off your hard drive and starts fresh. *Nondestructive* resizing uses Windows utilities to dynamically shrink the existing partition and then uses the freed space to make a new Linux partition. (Resizing is covered later in this chapter.)

The open-source FIPS (First nondestructive Interactive Partition Splitting) program comes with the full Fedora Core distribution to repartition FAT disks. To repartition NTFS disks, you have to use a commercial utility such as Norton PartitionMagic 8.0 or Norton Ghost 2003; both these programs also work on FAT systems.

"Am I FAT or Just NTFS?"

The process of determining your partition type is straightforward. These instructions describe how to use the tools provided by Windows (Windows 9*x*, Windows Me, Windows NT, Windows 2000/2003, and Windows XP) to show the partition type.

Follow these instructions on all Windows systems:

1. **Start your computer.**
2. **Open the My Computer icon.**
3. **Right-click the drive C icon.**
4. **Click the Properties button.**

   You should see information displayed about the partition, as shown in Figure 2-1.

Figure 2-1 shows the information about drive C (the partition). The upper-middle part of the figure shows (in this case) that the partition uses NTFS.

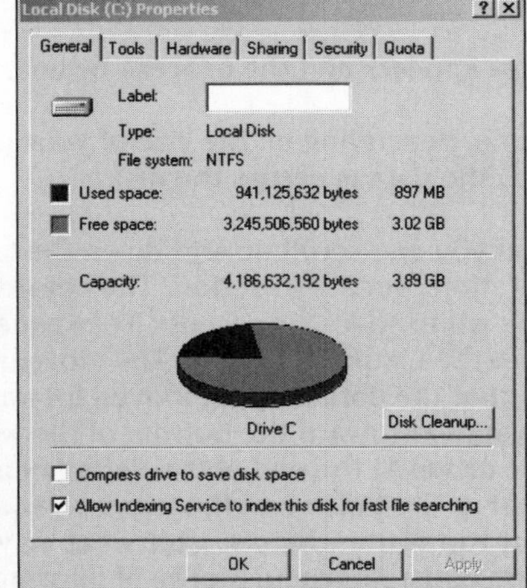

Figure 2-1: The Properties window shows an NTFS partition.

Defragmenting Your Hard Drive

When you know how your hard drive is partitioned, it's time to defragment. This section describes how to defragment both FAT and NTFS partitions.

Defragmenting consolidates all files on your hard drive into contiguous portions. This task is necessary because Windows is a slob as operating systems go, scattering data all over the hard drive faster than a nerd chasing autographs at a *Star Trek* convention.

These steps show how to defragment your Windows partition:

1. **Close all programs and windows on your computer, leaving just the desktop and icon bar.**
2. **Double-click the My Computer icon on the desktop.**
3. **Select drive C by clicking it, and then choose File⇨Properties⇨Tools.**
4. **Click the Defragment Now button.**

   The defragmentation program looks at the drive to determine whether it needs defragmentation.

   You may get a message telling you that you don't need to defragment because your hard drive is not very fragmented; don't believe it. Under ordinary circumstances, this statement may be true. But resizing a disk is a tricky affair; you must fully defragment your hard drive because you're going to move the end of the partition file system and make the partition smaller, erasing everything outside that barrier.
5. **Click Start.**

   The defragmentation window appears and the process begins.

Defragmenting can take a long time, depending on the size of your hard drive and how spread out (fragmented) the data is across the disk.

Click the Show Details button and you can scroll up and down the large window to watch the defragmentation process in action. The colored blocks represent programs and data; the white space represents free space on your hard drive that FIPS can allocate to the Linux file system. The movement of the blocks around the screen shows that the data is being moved forward on the drive. Expect to see white space appear toward the bottom of the window, which represents the end of your drive. At the end of the defragmentation process, no colored blocks appear at the bottom of the window, and all the blocks are compressed toward the top of the window. After what may seem like quite a long time, defragmentation ends. All useful blocks of information are now at the beginning of the drive, making it ready for the resizing program.

These instructions describe how to defragment your computer if you're running Windows NT, Windows 2000/2003, or Windows XP (NTFS):

1. **Close all programs and windows on your computer.**
2. **Click Start⇨Programs⇨Accessories⇨System Tools⇨Disk Defragmenter.**

3. **Select the partition you want to defragment.**

   Most computers use a single partition labeled C:\ (the ubiquitous "C drive").

4. **Click the Defragment button and the process starts.**

   Figure 2-2 shows the defragmentation process for an NTFS partition.

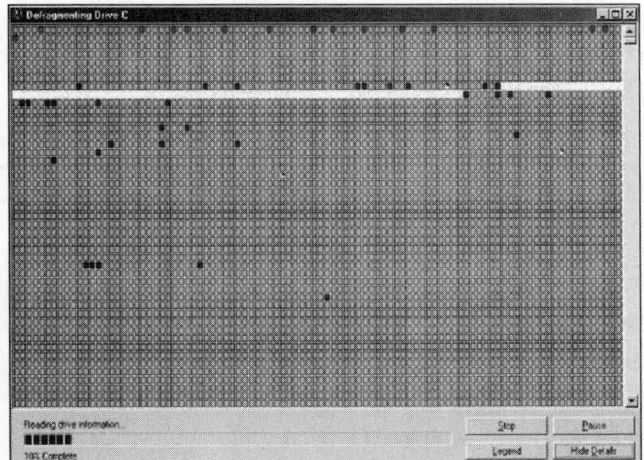

Figure 2-2: Defragmenting an NTFS partition.

We're Moving on up, to the Linux Side

After you've defragmented your hard drive, you need to make room for Linux. This section describes how to repartition your Windows computer to make the necessary room. You can use the open-source FIPS program to repartition FAT partitions. FIPS doesn't work on NTFS partitions, so you need to purchase a commercial tool, such as PartitionMagic. The next section is dedicated to using FIPS on FAT. The subsequent section describes using PartitionMagic on NTFS partitions.

We strongly suggest backing up your entire hard drive before proceeding. If that's impractical or impossible, you should back up all your important files. You can generally reinstall your operating system and applications from distribution discs, but you can't do that for your data. You don't want to lose any files or programs that you worked hard to create. Refer to your system's owner's manual to find out how to back up your system — and how to restore the data if necessary.

Resizing FAT partitions with FIPS

FIPS resizes your FAT-based Windows partitions. Newer versions of Windows (some versions of Windows 95, Windows 98, and Windows Me) use a 32-bit file-allocation table (called FAT32) and drive-management tools that provide for single-drive configurations larger than 2GB. Older versions of Windows 95 use a 16-bit FAT (called FAT16, oddly enough); to use space over and above 2GB, the hard drive has to be partitioned into logical drives of 2GB or less. Newer computers have hard drives much larger than the old 2GB limit. If the drive is repartitioned, the large drive-management system is disabled, and DOS and Windows partitions are again limited to 2GB.

To get this job done, you have to use the ancient MS-DOS (Microsoft Disk Operating System) operating system — and yes, one way or another, all of Windows-dom owes its existence to MS-DOS. The following instructions describe how to create an MS-DOS boot floppy disk, which you use to run FIPS:

1. **Insert a floppy disk and click the My Computer icon.**

   Please be aware that these steps *permanently erase* all information from the disk.

2. **Right-click the 3½ Floppy (A:) icon and choose the Format option.**

   The Format A:\ window appears.

3. **Click the Make a bootable disk option and then the Start button.**

   A confirmation window, labeled Format A:\, opens again.

4. **Click the OK button and your floppy is formatted.**

The Fedora Core distribution, bundled on a single DVD included with this book, unfortunately doesn't include the FIPS utility. However, you can download FIPS to the floppy disk you just created:

1. **Open your browser and go to the following Web site:**

   ```
   http://download.fedora.redhat.com/pub/fedora/linux/core/
         1/i386/os/dosutils/fips20.
   ```

2. **Download** `fips.exe`, `restorrb.exe`, `errors.txt`**, and (optionally)** `readme.1st` **and** `fips.faq` **to your floppy disk.**

3. **Boot your computer from the floppy disk.**

   The computer restarts in MS-DOS mode.

4. **Type** fips **at the prompt and press Enter.**

   Some messages appear and flash by, but you can ignore them all except the last one, which asks you to `Press any key`.

5. **When you see the** `Press any key` **message, do so.**

   You see all existing partitions on the hard drive.

6. **When you see the** `Press any key` **message, do so again.**

   You're getting good at this! A description of the drive and a series of messages flash by. Then FIPS finds the free space in the first partition.

7. **When you're asked whether you want to make a backup copy of sectors, press** y **for yes.**

   The screen asks whether a floppy disk is in drive A.

8. **Remove the boot floppy, place a formatted floppy disk in drive A, and then press** y.

   A message similar to `Writing file a:\rootboot.000` appears, followed by other messages and ending up with the message `Use cursor key to choose the cylinder, enter to continue.`

   Three columns appear on-screen: `Old Partition`, `Cylinder`, and `New Partition`. The `Old Partition` number is the number of megabytes in the main partition of your hard drive. The `New Partition` number is the number of megabytes in the new partition that you're making for the Fedora Core operating system.

9. **Press the left- and right-arrow keys to change the numbers in the** `Old Partition` **and** `New Partition` **fields to create the space you need for both the Windows operating system and Linux.**

   See Chapter 3 for installation requirements.

10. **When you have the correct amount of hard drive space in each field, press the Enter key.**

    The partition table is displayed again, showing you the new partition that has been created for the Linux operating system. This new partition is probably `Partition 2`; drive C is probably `Partition 1`.

    You also see a message at the bottom of the screen, asking whether you want to continue or make changes.

11. **If you're satisfied with the size of your partitions, press the C key to continue (if you *aren't* satisfied, press the R key, which takes you back to Step 10).**

    Many more messages about your hard drive flash by. Finally one appears that tells you the system is ready to write the new partition scheme to disk; it asks whether you want to proceed.

12. **Press the Y key to make FIPS write the new partition information to the hard drive.**

    The partitioning process begins.

    REMEMBER

    If you press the N key, FIPS exits without changing anything on your hard drive — leaving your hard drive exactly the way it was after you defragmented it.

13. **To make sure the nondestructive partitioning worked properly, remove the boot floppy disk and reboot your system by pressing Ctrl+Alt+Delete.**
14. **Allow Windows to start, and then run ScanDisk (click the Start button and choose Programs⇨Accessories⇨System Tools⇨ScanDisk).**

    ScanDisk indicates whether you have all the files and folders you started with and whether anything was lost. Even if everything is found to be okay, consider keeping any backup files around for a while, to be on the safe side.

You're ready to install Fedora Core 3, which we explain how to do in Chapter 3. The Fedora Core installation process can use the newly created space to create its own partitions. Chapter 3 describes how to use the new space without stepping on the existing Windows partition.

Resizing NTFS partitions with a little PartitionMagic

Resizing NTFS requires the use of commercial tools, such as Norton Ghost (`www.norton.com`) or PartitionMagic (`www.symantec.com/partitionmagic`). PartitionMagic works by shrinking the Microsoft Windows partition, leaving free space for a new partition. Norton Ghost 2003, however, doesn't dynamically modify your existing NTFS file system. Instead, it backs up your existing Windows partition (takes a "snapshot") and then creates one or more new partitions over the original. Finally, it writes the original Windows image to the new partition. Ghost requires a storage device on which to save the snapshot image. If your Windows installation is relatively small (less than 4GB), you may be able to use a writable DVD or (for a snapshot of less than 1GB) even a writable CD-ROM as a storage device. However, you have to use a second hard drive, tape backup, or other backup mechanism for larger installations.

We describe in this section how to use PartitionMagic. We don't use Norton Ghost, even though it's an excellent tool, because we can't assume that you have large enough backup resources to use it. (If you want to use Ghost, you need a backup medium that's large enough to store your entire Windows installation.) PartitionMagic doesn't give you all the warm fuzzies of getting a backup along with your resizing, but it still works very well. We have used it a number of times with good results.

These steps describe how to install PartitionMagic:

1. **Get out your credit card, go to your friendly nearby computer store (or online to your friendly Internet store), and buy PartitionMagic 8 from Symantec.**

This statement is a bit uncomfortable to make in a book devoted to the free, open-source Linux operating system. However, the name of the game is getting the job done — and in this case, we have no noncommercial alternative. (An open-source application *is* on the horizon. We will evaluate and report as soon as possible.) Until an open-source NTFS resizing utility breaks out into the light, your best bet is to make the purchase.

Three NTFS variations are available. Older Windows 9*x* systems used one type, Windows NT used another, and the third version serves current Windows versions. For this job, you must use PartitionMagic 8 (the current version) because it can recognize and handle all three NTFS versions.

2. **Start the PartitionMagic installation by inserting the disc into your CD-ROM drive.**

   The installation window opens.

3. **Click the PartitionMagic button.**

   Another dialog box opens, asking whether you want to install the program.

4. **Click the Install option.**

   An installation wizard starts.

5. **While the wizard runs, answer its questions according to how your computer is configured.**

   You should generally be able to use the default options.

6. **Create a rescue disk.**

   The installation wizard guides you through this process.

After you install PartitionMagic, you can use it to repartition your drive. The following instructions show how to select an existing partition, shrink it, and then create a second one from the new space:

1. **Start PartitionMagic.**

   You see a screen like the one shown in Figure 2-3.

2. **Click to select the partition you want to reallocate.**
3. **Click the Create a new partition option in the upper-left corner of the screen.**

   The Create New Partition dialog box opens. This wizard guides you through the process of shrinking the existing partition and creating a second one from the new space.

4. **Click the Next button.**

   The Where to Create dialog box opens.

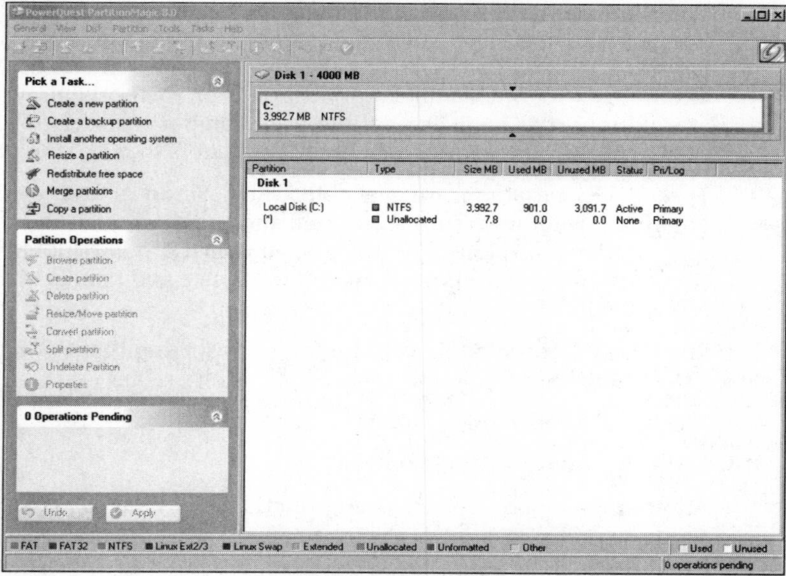

Figure 2-3: The initial PartitionMagic screen.

5. **Tell PartitionMagic which partition to repartition.**

   In this example, we assume that you have the typical single-partition Windows computer (the ubiquitous drive C), as shown in Figure 2-4.

Create New Partition

Where to Create

Select the location on the disk where you would like the new partition to be created.

In the list below, indicate where you want the new partition to be created. The wizard will move and/or resize other partitions to make room for the new partition if necessary.

C:
3,992.7 MB NTFS

Location for new partition	Can Create As
Before C:	Primary or Logical
After C: (Recommended)	Primary or Logical

Tips... | < Back | Next > | Cancel

Figure 2-4: The Where to Create dialog box.

6. **Click the Next button.**

   The Partition Properties window appears (as shown in Figure 2-5), offering these options for your new partition:

   • **Size:** The size of the partition depends on the size of your disk.

- **Label:** The label is optional and arbitrary. Use any description you want.
- **Create as:** You can choose either Logical and Primary. PC drives can have as many as four primary partitions and any number of logical ones.

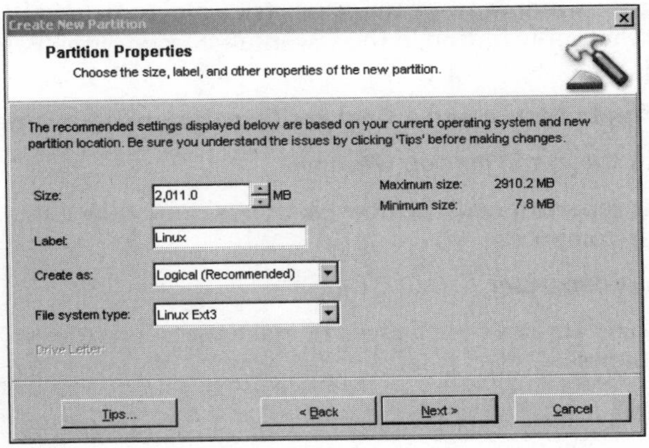

Figure 2-5: The Partition Properties window.

7. **Specify the options you want to apply to the new partition.**

   Figure 2-5 shows the settings we entered: Our new partition has a 2GB size, a `linux` label, is a Logical partition, and uses the `ext3` file system.

8. **Click the Next button.**

   The Confirm Choices dialog box opens, as shown in Figure 2-6. (PartitionMagic wants you to be sure about the new partitions you're about to create, so it summarizes the potential new configuration.)

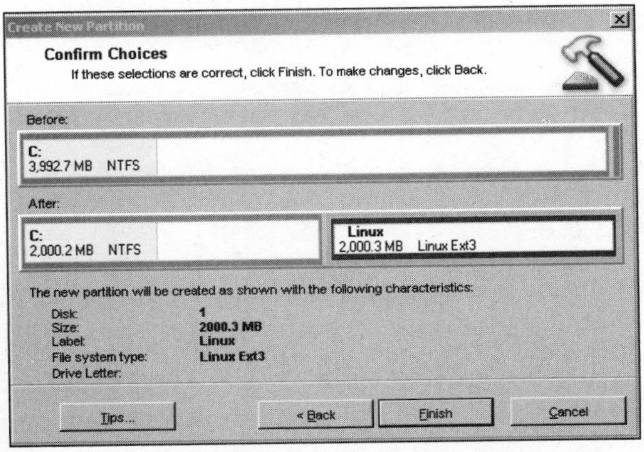

Figure 2-6: The Confirm Choices dialog box.

9. **Inspect the summary information and click the Finish button if you're satisfied with the selection.**
   - If you don't want to repartition with the current choices, click the Back button to return to the preceding window, where you can make new choices.
   - If you click the Finish button, the new partition-to-be displays in the main window. However, your disk isn't repartitioned until you click the Apply button in the lower-left corner of the PartitionMagic window.
10. **Click the Apply button and a final confirmation window opens.**
11. **Click OK in the confirmation window.**

    Your disk is repartitioned; the new partitions don't take effect until you reboot your computer.
12. **Reboot your computer.**

    PartitionMagic applies the changes to make the new partition while your computer boots.

Chapter 3

Ready, Set, Install!

In This Chapter

- Deciding which Fedora Core installation type to use
- Starting the Fedora Core installation process
- Automatically selecting Linux partitions
- Configuring your network
- Configuring your system options
- Finishing the installation and rebooting
- Configuring your display
- Using the Setup Agent to complete post installation

Installing Linux isn't rocket science — it's more like astrophysics. (Well, maybe it's not *quite* that complicated.) Although installing Fedora Core may seem at first like a difficult job, it's actually pretty simple. The installation process requires that you answer a few questions, and then the process takes care of itself.

When you're done, you have a powerful computer that's capable of performing most, if not all, of your daily computing chores — all for the cost of this book! That's pretty amazing when you think about it: For a few bucks, you get the same amount of operating power that would have cost a ton just a few years ago.

This chapter walks you through the process of installing Fedora Core 3. The process involves inserting the companion Fedora Core 3 DVD disc, powering on your computer, and answering some questions.

This book comes with a companion DVD disc that contains the entire Fedora Core 3 distribution. The single DVD replaces several CD-ROMs so you don't have to continually swap CD-ROMs during the installation process. It also makes installing the software easier; you don't have to find the particular CD-ROM that contains a specific package. If your computer cannot handle DVDs, however, you can obtain the Fedora Core 3 distribution on CD-ROMs by mailing in the coupon in the back of this book. You can also download directly, and for free, from fedora.redhat.com/download if you have a broadband connection or a dial-up and a lot of patience.

For installation purists only

You can run the Fedora Core installation system from either a graphical or text-based interface. If the installation process successfully detects your graphics hardware, the graphical method is selected automatically, and that's the system we discuss in this chapter. In addition to the ease of using a mouse to point and click, the graphical method groups similar configuration choices. For example, the keyboard and mouse selections are presented within one window, not two, as in the text-based installation.

You may have to use the text-based installation, for these reasons:

- Your mother told you never to point and click.
- In an unlikely (but possible) turn of events, the Fedora Core installation system found it couldn't use your graphics adapter. Occasionally the installation system cannot start the graphics interface; in that case, it defaults to text mode. Using the text-mode interface, you use the keyboard to enter information and the cursor (arrow) keys to move you from step to step.

You can select the text-based installation method by typing **linux text** at the `boot:` prompt.

The Fedora Core installation process has a point of no return. That time comes toward the end of the configuration process, after which your disk is partitioned and the software is installed (see the section "Installation Stage 5: The Point of No Return," later in this chapter). If you stop at or before that point, you keep intact the old operating system and data on your computer.

Choosing an Installation Type

Fedora Core provides several installation types to choose from. Although we think that you can probably get away with having less space on your system, we decided to give you the minimum disk space requirements that Fedora Core suggests for each installation option:

- **Workstation:** This option adds software-development tools, such as the gcc (Gnu C Compiler) compiler, to the Personal Desktop installation process described next in this list. You need at least 3GB of disk space to use this option. We use the Workstation installation option in this book not because we're programmers but, rather, because the tools often come in handy when you're installing certain applications. We encourage you to use the Workstation installation type for your Fedora Core installations.
- **Personal Desktop:** This option installs the software necessary to use your computer as a personal workstation. Applications such as Mozilla, OpenOffice, and Evolution plus the GNOME graphical environment give you all the tools you need to enjoy the Internet and get your work done. This installation type requires at least 2.3GB of free space.

- **Server:** Using this option creates an operating-system environment for computers that provide services, such as hosting Web pages. This installation requires at least 1.1GB of free space if you want the minimum number of bells and whistles; at least 1.4GB of free space if you want to install all the bells and whistles but not the graphical X-Window System; and at least 2.1GB to install all the bells and all the whistles, and to throw in the Acme Bell and Whistle Factory.
- **Custom:** This installation type provides two options: minimal and everything. The minimal option installs the bare essentials and nothing more; this option requires only 620MB of space. The everything option installs, as you may have already guessed, every piece of software plus the kitchen sink; you need at least 6.9GB for this option.
- **Upgrade:** Updates the Fedora Core software that's already installed on a computer and leaves all existing settings, users, and data alone. You can optionally choose to install additional packages. Your disk space use should stay roughly the same as your existing installation. Additional packages require additional space, of course.

Both the Workstation and Personal Desktop installation options create a computer you can use for your daily work. In either case, the installation includes the GNOME graphical user interface (GUI) and all the tools that an average computer user (that's you) needs to survive. If you want software that the installation doesn't provide, you can always add packages later.

Installation Stage 1: Beginning the Journey

Before you install Fedora Core, you need to insert the companion DVD into the DVD/CD-ROM drive and boot or reboot your computer. The instructions in this section describe how to start installing Fedora Core on your computer.

This section gets you started with the Fedora Core installation process. Use these initial steps to start the installation and perform some basic configuration:

1. **Insert the companion DVD and boot (start) your computer. (If your computer can't boot from a DVD, use the coupon at the back of this book to obtain Fedora Core CD-ROMs.)**

   After contemplating the meaning of life, your computer displays the first installation screen, which includes the `boot:` prompt.

2. **Press Enter.**

   A series of messages scrolls by, indicating the hardware that the Linux kernel detects on your computer. Most of the time, particularly with newer systems, Fedora Core detects all the basic hardware. Then the Fedora Core installation process starts and the Welcome to Fedora Core window opens.

If the installation process crashes at this point, reboot your computer and add the `nofb` option after the `boot:` prompt (for example: **boot: nofb**). If that fails, reboot and use the text installation mode: **boot: linux text**. Also, Sony Viao notebook users may need to enter the option `pci=off ide1=0x180,0x386` at the `boot:` prompt to make their CD-ROM drive work correctly.

3. **If prompted with the CD Found screen, you can select to verify that your DVD or CD-ROMs are error-free. (Refer to the sidebar "Checking your discs.") Otherwise, press Tab to select the Skip option and then press Enter.**
4. **Click the Next button.**

   The Language Selection window opens.

You can view information about Fedora Core by clicking the Release Notes button, in the lower-left corner of the screen. Additional information about where to find more information is displayed on the informational sidebar on the left side of the information window.

5. **Select a language (if you don't want the default of English) and click Next.**

   Choose the language you speak — or, if you're feeling adventurous, one you don't (not recommended).

   The Keyboard Configuration window appears.
6. **Select your keyboard configuration and then click Next.**

   Usually Fedora Core detects and configures your mouse, but if it doesn't, the Mouse Configuration window opens.
7. **If prompted (unlikely), select your mouse (squeak!) and click Next.**
   - If you have a PS/2 mouse, all you have to do is select the manufacturer and the number of buttons.
   - If you have the older style of mouse that connects via a serial port, you have to select the manufacturer, number of buttons, and serial port to which it's connected; you have only four serial ports to select from (in many cases, only two: either `ttyS0` or `ttyS1`).
   - If you have a two-button mouse (either serial or PS/2), you can choose to have it emulate three buttons by selecting the Emulate 3 Buttons option. You emulate the third (middle) button by pressing both mouse buttons at one time.
8. **In the Installation Type window, select the Workstation option and click the Next button.**

Checking your discs

Fedora Core provides a validation mechanism for checking its DVD (or CD-ROMs). If your distribution disc is a DVD, Fedora Core uses numeric keys to help verify that it isn't corrupted: You can enter **linux mediacheck** at the `boot:` prompt, at the beginning of the installation process, to verify the disc's integrity. Follow these steps to verify that your DVD is in working order:

1. **Select the OK option by pressing the Enter key if you want to verify that your DVD (or CD-ROM) is okay.**

   If you don't want to verify your disc — perhaps you have already checked them during an earlier installation, or you trust us (d'oh!) — you can select the Skip option to return to the Fedora Core installation process without checking the medium.

   If you choose to verify, the Media Check window opens.

2. **Press the Tab key to select the Test option and press the Enter key to start the integrity check.**

   The media-check system displays a progress meter and then shows the result in the Media Check Result window when it's finished. The possible results are PASS and FAIL.

3. **Select the OK button (the only option) in the Media Check Result window.**

   The Media Check dialog box opens and the disc ejects.

4. **Assuming your DVD passed, re-insert the DVD and select Continue.**

   The installation process continues.

5. **If you're testing CD-ROMS, insert the second or third CD-ROM and repeat Steps 2–4 for each CD-ROM. You're finished after testing the third CD-ROM.**

Obviously, if the DVD (or any of the CD-ROMs) fails the test, you shouldn't use it. You should buy another copy of this book. (No, no — just kidding.) Contact the Wiley Product Technical Support department, at `www.wiley.com/techsupport`, to find out how to get a replacement DVD (or CD-ROM).

Installation Stage 2: Slicing and Dicing the Pie

You must decide where on your hard drive to install Fedora Core. This process, called *disk partitioning,* divides the disk into multiple sections. Fedora Core is then installed on its own partitions.

Fedora Core provides both automatic and manual methods for creating disk partitions. We use the Fedora Core automatic method because it's easy. The automatic method erases any existing Fedora Core partitions, but doesn't touch any existing Windows partitions. If you don't have any existing Fedora Core partitions or unused space on your disk, you have to make some free space. Refer to Chapter 2 for instructions on how to shrink Windows partitions to make space for Linux.

Confidential for Windows users

If you're installing Fedora Core in a dual-boot configuration with Windows NT, Windows 2000, or Windows XP, your NT boot record is temporarily overwritten, which means you cannot boot Windows NT. Don't panic: Your NT partition — C drive — isn't erased, it has just been rendered temporarily unbootable. (An NT *boot record* is what enables a Windows NT system to start automatically whenever you start your computer.)

You can install Fedora Core without overwriting the NT boot partition if you click the Change Boot Loader button and select the Do Not Install a Boot Loader radio button. When you click the Next button, the Advanced Boot Loader Configuration window opens. Select the First Sector of Boot Partition option and then click the Next button. Your Windows boot configuration continues to operate as before.

Linux disk partitions are analogous to Windows disk partitions. The well-known C drive uses a single disk partition. The Linux equivalent is the `root` (/) partition. The two operating systems use different terminology, and the analogy isn't perfect, although the concept is the same.

The Fedora Core installation system must partition your hard drive in order to install its software. Partitions divide a hard drive into one or more parts. The divisions are used to organize the software and data (the operating system, user files, and so on) that make up the operating system.

Fedora Core provides two partitioning methods: automatic and manual. Using the manual method requires you to make numerous decisions about how to divide your hard disk into individual partitions. The automatic method makes the whole process much simpler, and we recommend it unless you're feeling lucky (or want to experiment or have the experience of manually partitioning your hard drive). We use the automatic method in this book.

1. **We suggest using the `Automatically partition` option (the default selection), so click the Next button.**

   If you're using a new disk that has never been partitioned (or your existing disk's partition table has become corrupted in some way), a Warning dialog box appears.

2. **If prompted, click the Yes button in the Warning dialog box.**

   The Automatic Partitioning window appears. You have three options:

- **Remove all Linux partitions on this system:** This option leaves any Windows partitions (FAT, VFAT, and NTFS) unmodified while erasing any existing Linux partitions. Use this option if you're reinstalling Fedora Core (in either a dual-boot or solo configuration).
- **Remove all partitions on this system:** This option is the most dangerous one because it erases everything on your hard drive. Use this option only if you're absolutely sure that you don't have, or don't want to save, anything on your disk. Your new Fedora Core installation becomes the only operating system on the hard drive if you use this option.
- **Keep all partitions and use existing free space:** Use this option if you used the nondestructive repartitioning we describe in Chapter 2 to shrink your Windows partition and free up space to install Fedora Core alongside Windows; this is a *dual-boot* configuration.

Danger, Will Robinson — Danger! Never select the Remove all partitions on this system option unless you want to erase everything on your hard disk! Use extreme caution because this action destroys all installed operating systems (Windows and any earlier version of Fedora Core) along with all data. You may use this option, for example, if your computer had Windows preinstalled and you want to convert it to a Fedora Core-only workstation.

3. **Select the partitioning option — in the Automatic Partitioning window — most appropriate for you and then click the Next button.**

   Before you select a partition type you should consider the following:

   - If you repartitioned your Windows disk (as described in Chapter 2) to make room for Linux, click the button labeled `Keep all partitions and use existing free space`. The Fedora Core installation system puts Fedora Core on the extra space on the disk.
   - If you're installing Linux over an old Linux installation, click the `Remove all Linux partitions on this system` button.
   - If you want to erase any existing operating system (along with all programs and data on the disk) and start fresh with Fedora Core, click the `Remove all partitions on this system` button.
   - To see how your disk will be partitioned before you give the go-ahead, you can select the option labeled Review (and modify if needed) the partitions. Selecting this option lets you review and also modify your partitions.

4. **When a Warning dialog box opens, describing the consequences of your selection, choose one of these options:**

   - Click Yes to continue the installation.
   - Click No to return to the Automatic Partitioning window in Step 3.

   If you click Yes, the Boot Loader Configuration window appears, as shown in Figure 3-1.

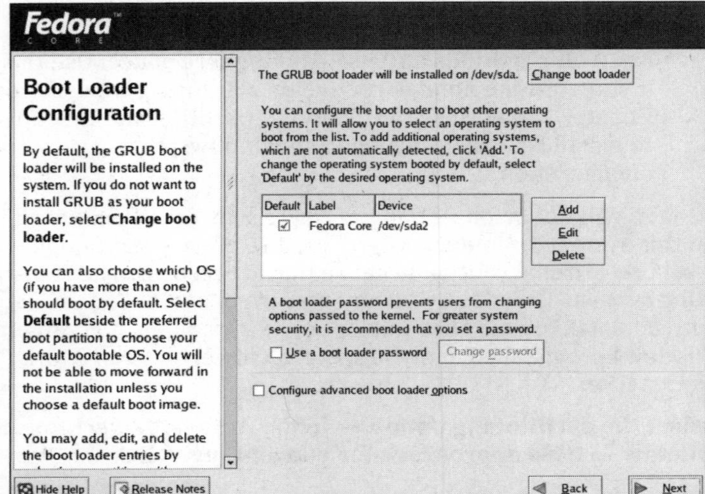

Figure 3-1: The Boot Loader Configuration window.

5. **The boot-loader defaults should work just fine for you, so click Next.**

   The boot loader helps start your operating system when you start your computer; if you create a dual-boot computer, the boot loader allows you to select one operating system or another. The standard Fedora Core boot loader is GRUB, a powerful program that can do more than just load an operating system. However, the GRUB default options should be all you need (and a description of its advanced features is beyond the scope of this book).

If your computer has a network interface card (NIC), Fedora Core detects it and the Network Configuration window appears, as shown in Figure 3-2. You should proceed to Step 1 in the next section and configure your network. However, if you don't have an Ethernet NIC (or are using a wireless device that Fedora Core doesn't detect), the installation process skips the network configuration and continues at Step 9 in the following section Installing Stage 3: Configuring your Network.

Figure 3-2: The Network Configuration window.

Installation Stage 3: Configuring Your Network

If you're ready to configure your network and your computer has an Ethernet adapter or a Wi-Fi (a wireless network interface using the 802.11b standard) adapter, enter the appropriate information, as described in the following steps. If you have a network adapter but don't have a (wired or wireless) network to connect to, you should still enter a host name in Step 6. Entering a host name makes life easier if and when you eventually connect to a network.

If you have a NIC, the Network Configuration window appears and you can follow this next set of steps to configure your system for a network; if you don't have a NIC, skip to Step 9 in the following steps:

1. **If you're connecting to a network that uses the Dynamic Host Configuration Protocol (DHCP), you don't have to do anything more to configure your network connection. Click the Next button and skip to Step 9.**

   You may need to consult with your LAN's administrator to find out whether the LAN (local-area network) uses DHCP. If you constructed your own LAN and don't know whether you're running DHCP, you're not. (Go to Chapter 15 to find out how to install and configure a DHCP server.)

2. **Click the Edit button.**

3. **Toggle off the DHCP option by clicking the button labeled** `Configure using DHCP`.

4. **Enter your IP address and netmask in the subwindow labeled** `Edit interface`.

   The following list briefly explains IP addresses and netmasks:

   - **IP address:** This string of numbers is the numeric network address of your Fedora Core computer — address by which your computer is known on your local-area network (and, in many cases, on the Internet). If you haven't registered your private network's address space with InterNIC (the organization in charge of distributing IP addresses), you can use the public address space that contains a range of addresses from 192.168.1.1 through 192.168.254.254.

     If you're connecting to an existing LAN, consult its administrator to get an IP address that isn't already being used. You have to keep track of unused IP addresses if you're running your own LAN.

   - **Netmask:** Private networks based on the Internet Protocol (IP) are divided into subnetworks. The netmask is a string of binary bits that divides the IP address into two parts: a network address and a host address. For IP addresses, such as the example in the preceding bullet (192.168.1.1), the most common netmask is 255.255.255.0. This mask creates a network address of 192.168.1 and a host address of 1.

5. **Click the OK button.**

6. **In the Hostname text box (next to the button labeled** `manually`**), type your computer's network name — including the host and network (domain) name — in the text box.**

   For example, if you want to name your computer `cancun` and your network name is `paunchy.net`, you type **cancun.paunchy.net**.

   If you don't give your computer a name and domain name during the network configuration process, it's referred to as `localhost.localdomain`. Otherwise, the Welcome screen refers to whatever name you gave it. For example, in the preceding example, you would see `Welcome to cancun.paunchy.net`.

7. **Enter your gateway and primary DNS (and, optionally, the secondary and tertiary DNS) IP addresses in the appropriate text boxes in the Miscellaneous section, at the bottom of the screen.**

   These parameters have distinct functions:

   - **Gateway:** The *gateway* is the numeric IP address of the computer that connects your private network to the Internet (or to another private network). Fedora Core uses the address `192.168.1.254` by default. You can accept this address, but leaving it blank is a better option, unless that address is really your gateway. Chapters 5, 6, and 7 describe how to configure your Linux computer to connect to the Internet via a telephone, broadband (DSL or cable), and existing LAN connections, respectively. If you do that, setting a default route now can interfere with your connection.

- **Primary DNS:** The Internet Protocol uses the Domain Name Service (DNS) system to convert names such as `www.redhat.com` into numeric IPs. A computer that acts as a DNS server is a *name server.* We suggest leaving this box blank, however, unless you're on a private network with a name server or are connected to the Internet (your ISP supplies a DNS). When you designate a nonexistent name server, many networking programs work very slowly as they wait in vain for the absent server to do something.
- **Secondary and tertiary DNS:** The secondary and tertiary DNS back up the primary DNS server. If your computer cannot find the primary DNS server, it may find the secondary. If not, it should find the tertiary. Best of luck!

If you're connecting to someone else's LAN — if you're building a Fedora Core computer at work, for example — you should obtain this address from your system administrator. If you're connecting to your own LAN at home, consult yourself because you're probably the administrator.

8. **When you complete the Network Configuration form, click the Next button to continue.**

   The Firewall Configuration window opens.

9. **In the Firewall Configuration window, click the Remote Login (SSH) button.**

   The firewall is turned on by default. You can turn it off if you want, but we recommend leaving it turned on.

   Fedora Core 3 also includes the new and powerful SELinux option. SELinux provides mandatory access controls (acls) that greatly increase the security of your computer. We introduce SELinux in Chapter 17. We recommend leaving SELinux active (the default).

10. **Click the Next button.**

Fedora Core creates for your computer a firewall designed for use by a workstation. The firewall is *stateful,* which means that it keeps track of which connections the network traffic (both incoming and outgoing packets) belongs to. It provides good protection, and we use it for the personal workstations and network servers we describe in this book.

The next section shows you how to finish the configuration of your Fedora Core workstation.

Installation Stage 4: Configuring Your Options

This section describes the basic configuration steps for your Fedora Core computer. We describe how to set your time zone and the `root` user password. You also choose to install extra software in addition to the default packages. The following steps describe how to perform these basic tasks.

Follow these steps:

1. **The Additional Language Support window opens. Make your selection, if necessary, and click the Next button.**

   The Time Zone Selection window appears.

2. **To select your time zone, click the dot representing a city closest to where you live.**

   You can use the map to point and click your way to time-zone bliss. When you click one of the thousand points of light, the represented city and its time zone appear in the subwindow below the map. You can also click the slider bar at the bottom of the screen to locate the name of your city or time zone. After you find it, click the text to select your time zone.

3. **Click Next.**

   The Set Root Password window appears.

4. **Type your `root` password in both the Root Password and Confirm text boxes.**

   The password is for the `root` user account. Whoever has this account is also known as the *superuser,* and has access to the entire system and can do almost anything — good and bad.

   The `root` user is the only user who can access all resources on your computer. All files, processes, and devices are controlled by `root`. You should log in as the `root` user only to perform system maintenance or administrative tasks. To avoid making unwanted changes or deletions to these important files, you should normally log in as a regular (non-`root`) user. See Step 2 in the section "Post-Installation: Using the Setup Agent," later in this chapter, to find out how to add a user.

   You have to type the password twice to make sure you typed it correctly. The password appears on-screen as asterisks as you type it. ("Holy breach of security, Batman!" You wouldn't want someone to be able to look over your shoulder and get your password, would you?)

5. **Click Next.**

   The Package Installation Defaults window opens and displays a summary of the important software to be installed. You're given the choice of selecting either the Install default software packages (the default) or the Customize software packages to be installed options.

In this book, we use the default packages from the Workstation installation environment.

If you select the Customize the software packages to be installed option, the Package Group Selection window opens. You can select additional packages to be installed individually or by group. For example, if you want to install the KDE environment, simply click the button next to the KDE Desktop Environment menu and all the necessary packages are then selected. Select individual packages by clicking the Select individual packages radio option. After you make your selection, click the Next button and proceed to Step 6.

6. **Click the Next button.**

   The About to Install Window appears. A loud voice reverberates, announcing that this is The Point of No Return! Not exactly. No loud voice says anything, except in our heads (it's so annoying), but this *is* the point of no return. If you click the Next button, your disk is reformatted in whatever way you selected in the preceding section — and Fedora Core is then installed. The following section describes how that process goes.

Introducing password etiquette

To be effective and keep the operating system happy, your password must be at least six characters long — but you should use at least eight characters: The more characters you use, the harder the password is to break. If you're concerned about security, we recommend that you use a combination of uppercase and lowercase letters, symbols, and numbers to make your password as difficult as possible to compromise. In addition, don't choose anything you can find in a dictionary, or names or items that are easy to associate with you. In other words, your name, your name spelled backward, your birthday, your dog's name, or any word in any language (including the "unprintable" ones) are all poor choices. `Beer`, for example, is a poor selection for Jon's password, even though it has both uppercase and lowercase letters, because Jon and beer are usually seen in close proximity to each other.

A good way to come up with a good password is to select a phrase and garble it. For example, make "I am not a number" into something like `imNOtun#`. Even though the result doesn't spell out the phrase in any real way, it gives you all the cues to remember the essentially random characters ("I am" = `im`, "not" = `NOt`, "a" = `un`, and number = `#`). Other common substitutions are @ for *a*, 3 for *e*, 9 for *g*, 1 for *l*, 6 for *b*, and 5 for *s*. But remember: Those are *common*.

If you record your password, store it where it won't get lost and cannot be easily found or stolen. For example, save your work passwords at home or store them in a locked desk or safe. You can store passwords in a PDA (personal digital assistant) as long as you use the little gadget's password-protection capability; you can also use encryption software to store passwords on PDAs. Do not, however, write your password on a sticky note and attach it to your computer monitor. (D'oh!)

GNOME is the default Fedora Core graphical environment for Fedora Core 3, and it's what we use throughout this book. However, many people prefer the KDE environment. The choice is yours; you can use either environment or both, if you want. (If you install both GNOME and KDE on your computer, you can select one or the other as your desktop environment when you log in.) To install KDE, select the Customize software packages to be installed option, as described earlier, in Step 5. Click the check box next to the KDE package group and then click the Next button.

Installation Stage 5: The Point of No Return

The installation process described so far in this chapter hasn't yet resulted in making any permanent changes to your computer. Your selections haven't been written in stone, so to speak. Nothing has been erased. No Fedora Core packages have been written to your hard drive, either. You can stop the installation process and go back to your good old computer by clicking the Back button.

Make your decision whether to proceed. Then, if the answer is yes, take a deep breath and follow these instructions to install Fedora Core on your computer:

1. **Click the Next button in the About to Install window.**

   The Required Install Media dialog box opens. (If you're using CD-ROM discs, you're told which discs you need.)

   You can click the Reboot button if you want to abort the installation process. In that case, no changes will be made to your computer.

2. **After you hold your breath for a second (don't turn blue!) and then decide to take the plunge, click the Continue button.**

   Your disk partitions are created and formatted, and then the Fedora Core distribution is written to them. The Installing Packages window (see Figure 3-3) tells you which package is being installed in addition to how many have been installed, how many remain to be installed, and the estimated time remaining.

3. **(Optional) If you're using CD-ROMs, insert the second or third discs when prompted and click the Yes button.**

   A congratulations window opens.

   The installation process takes only a few minutes if you have the latest, greatest high-speed computer with a fast DVD or CD-ROM drive. Otherwise plan to spend 20 minutes — or longer — when you're using older equipment.

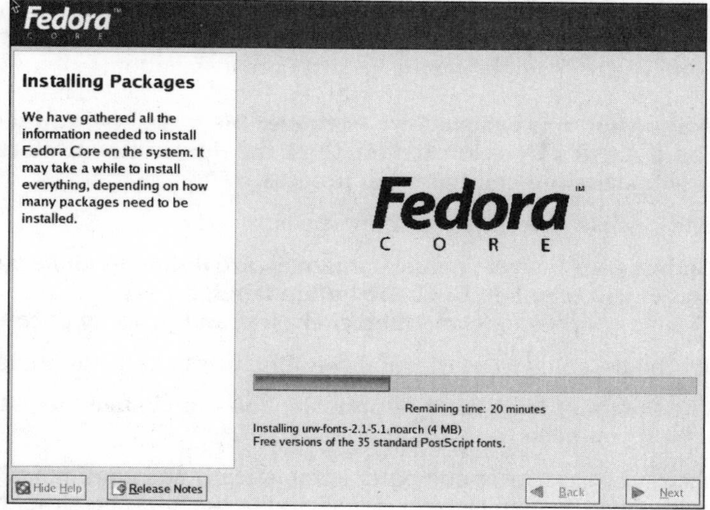

Figure 3-3: The Installing Packages window.

4. **Click the Reboot button when prompted, and remove the companion Fedora Core 3 DVD (or CD-ROM) from the computer.**

   Your computer reboots and the Display settings window opens. If you want, you can reconfigure your display settings and video card; you can also configure them for a dual head (two side-by-side) display.

5. **Click OK.**
6. **Click Next in the warning dialog box that opens.**

Fedora Core is installed! The following section helps to finish various post-installation tasks that will make your Fedora Core computer easier to use.

Post-Installation: Using the Setup Agent

After your computer reboots and the Display settings window closes, the Setup Agent opens. The Setup Agent simplifies the installation process by pushing some configuration work to the post-installation phase. Your new Fedora Core computer will work just fine whether or not you run the Setup Agent — but a little fine tuning makes it work better.

The Setup Agent automatically runs the first time you boot your computer after installing Fedora Core. The agent asks you to read and accept the Fedora Core license, reconfigure your monitor (optional), create a user login account, (recommended; use the `root` account for system administration), set the date and time, test your sound card, and install any optional software packages.

The process of configuring these individual systems is described throughout this book. However, the following steps describe how to use the Setup Agent immediately after completing the Fedora Core installation:

1. **When your new Fedora Core computer boots (starts), you see the Setup Agent's Welcome screen. Click the Next button to start the post-installation configuration process.**

   The License Agreement window opens.

2. **Gather your lawyers (guns and money are optional) and read the agreement together. Click the button labeled** `Yes, I agree to the License Agreement` **and then click Next and proceed to court.**

   Truthfully, going to court is unlikely. But, just in case, deny everything.

3. **The Date and Time window appears. You can change the date and time if you need to.**

   You can also let your computer automatically and continuously update your clock. If you plan to be connected to the Internet, either through a LAN (local area network) or a broadband modem (DSL or cable), click the Network Time Protocol tab and select the Enable Network Time Protocol (NTP) option. Select an NTP server from the drop-down menu of NTP servers and click the Add button. The default choices `clock.redhat.com` and `clock2.redhat.com` work well, but you can enter any one you want. Alternatively, you may have access to an NTP server not on the list and can enter it manually. Click the Forward button to continue to the Sound Configuration screen.

   We recommend that you use the NTP option if your computer is connected continuously to the Internet on an Internet-connected LAN, a DSL connection, or a cable modem. PC clocks tend to drift from seconds to minutes per day. It's better to be up to date than not.

4. **Click the Next button.**

5. **The Display window opens. Change your monitor type, display resolution and the colors depth, if you want.**

   You can change the monitor type by clicking the configure bar and selecting from the drop-down menu that opens. Change the resolution and/or color depth by clicking on the appropriate bar and selecting a value.

6. **Click the Next button.**

   The System User window opens. Only the `root` user account was created during the installation process, but you have the chance here to create one or more user accounts.

7. **Enter an account name, the name of the account owner, and its password. Click the Next button to continue.**

   If you're connected to a LAN that provides a network login (such as a Kerberos network), click the Use Network Login button and select the appropriate option. You most likely encounter a network login only when you're connected to a large corporate network. It's beyond the scope of this book to describe this particular plethora of situations. Consult your system administrator.

8. **Fedora Core does a good job of detecting hardware, such as sound cards, and should detect yours. Click the Play test sound button to test your audio system.**

   A dialog box opens, asking whether you heard the music.

9. **Click Yes if you hear the penguin playing the guitar.**

   An Error dialog box opens if you click No.

10. **Click OK to continue.**

    If the sound test fails, consult the section in Chapter 12 for help with setting up your sound system. Click the Forward button to continue.

11. **Click the Next button.**

    The Additional CDs window opens. The companion Fedora Core DVD doesn't include any additional software, so you have nothing to do here.

12. **Click the Next button.**

    The Finish Setup window opens.

13. **Click the Next button. The Setup Agent closes and your Fedora Core computer is ready to use.**

You can run Setup Agent whenever you want. The Setup Agent is a script named `firstboot`. You can run the Setup Agent by running the `firstboot` script with the `reconfig` option. Just log in as as `root` and run the following commands from a GNOME Terminal window:

```
rm /etc/sysconfig/firstboot
/usr/sbin/firstboot
```

That's it! You have built yourself a Fedora Core computer. After your computer reboots itself, you can then use it as your personal workstation.

Chapter 4

Getting to Know Fedora Core

In This Chapter

- Booting your Fedora Core computer
- Logging in to your Fedora Core computer
- Using graphical and text-based applications and utilities
- Setting up your monitor and video card
- Getting to know the Fedora Core file system
- Making user accounts for the first time
- Logging out of your Fedora Core computer

If you have installed Fedora Core, you should spend a few minutes studying some basics before you start using it. This chapter covers just enough, but no more, of the Linux fundamentals needed to get you started. We cover topics such as starting and stopping your Fedora Core computer, understanding the difference between graphical and nongraphical applications, and how Linux uses files.

We start by describing how to start your new Fedora Core computer. This process is simple, but it's helpful to know more about it.

Booting Your Fedora Core Computer

To *boot* a computer means simply to start it or turn the power on; to *reboot* a computer means to restart it. The following steps describe how to boot your Fedora Core computer:

1. **Make sure that your computer is turned off.**
2. **Turn on the power to your computer.**

After a short time, the Fedora Core boot menu appears on your screen. If you have only Fedora Core installed on your computer, you're given only one choice of operating systems to boot: Linux (see Installation Stage 2: Slicing and Dicing the Pie in chapter 3 for more information about dual-booting).

Fedora Core runs in three different states (referred to as *run levels*): 1, 3, and 5. Each run level is used to perform different functions. At Level 1 (also called *single-user mode*), Linux operates with a minimum of processes so that you can make configuration changes and troubleshoot problems. In Level 3, the computer runs without a graphical interface, so you have to interact with the computer by typing commands; you typically use Level 3 to run servers that provide only network services that don't need graphical interfaces. When your Fedora Core computer is running in Level 5, it runs with the graphical X interface; it's the default run level. You can use GRUB (Grand Unified Bootloader) to select a different Linux run level. When GRUB appears, press **e** for edit. Three lines appear. Press the down-arrow key to select the line that begins with `Kernel`. Press the **e** key again, add a space, and then press **1**, **3**, or **5.** Press the Enter key and then press the **b** key. Your computer boots into the selected mode.

3. **Press the up- and down-arrow keys to highlight the word** `Linux` **(if it's not highlighted already) and then press Enter.**

   - If you don't press any of the keys, the default operating system (that is, Fedora Core, which sets itself as the default when you install it) starts automatically after a 10-second delay.
   - If you're running more than one operating system (for example, Fedora Core and Windows), you can select any of the listed operating systems to boot; we assume here that you choose Linux.

   After you press Enter, Fedora Core boots. During this process, a graphical progress window shows how far along the boot process is. You can (optionally) display lots of technical information by clicking the Show details button. The optional information is what Linux is learning about your computer and its hardware (disk drives, networks, and memory, for example).

Logging In to Your Fedora Core Computer

When you use Fedora Core (or any Linux distribution), you must log in as a particular user with a distinct login name. Why? Because Linux is a multiuser system — therefore it uses different accounts to keep people from looking at other people's secret files, erasing necessary files from the system, and otherwise (intentionally or unintentionally) doing bad things.

The use of unique identities helps to keep the actions of one person from affecting the actions of another because many people may be using the same computer system at the same time (for example, over a network). A benefit of this strategy is that Linux computers are essentially invulnerable to viruses simply because no user's files and directories can be used to corrupt the system as a whole.

As Fedora Core boots, you see all sorts of messages scrolling by on the screen. After the scrolling stops, the login screen appears.

If you chose (during installation) not to have the X Window System start automatically whenever you boot your system, you see the `login:` prompt.

If you make a mistake while typing the password or your login, the system asks you to retype it.

We strongly recommend that you do most of your experimentation with Fedora Core as a nonprivileged user — and that you log in as the `root` user only when necessary. If you operate as `root`, you can delete or change anything and everything — and you run the risk of corrupting your system, having to reinstall the operating system, or losing data. When you're logged in as a regular user, you can accidentally erase your own files and data, but you cannot erase someone else's files or system files.

Fortunately, Fedora Core provides many graphical administration utilities you can start as a nonprivileged user. Each Fedora Core administrative utility prompts you to enter the root password as it starts and then performs its specific function, but only that function, with root privileges. You're prevented, therefore, from doing unintended damage to other systems. (See Appendix C for information about how file permissions work and how you can modify them.)

Using Graphical and Text-Based Applications and Utilities

Fedora Core installs the graphical X Window System (also known simply as X) by default. You can perform most administrative tasks with the GUI-based tools (GUI stands for *g*raphical *u*ser *i*nterface) that Fedora Core provides. Most of the how-to instructions in this book use the X-based applications and utilities. We do that because they're generally easier to use — and because this book wasn't written for techie systems administrators.

Occasionally a utility or program doesn't run graphically. Believe it or not, some geekier users *prefer* to use a text-based system. If you're not familiar with doing some basic administrative tasks with a text-based system, we don't recommend using one just because you can. Not being a geek is okay. We still like and respect you. On the other hand, it makes good sense to know some basics, just in case you have to wing it someday with the text-based interface.

Text-based interfaces are generally run from a *shell,* which acts as a text-based interface between the Fedora Core operating system and you. The `bash` shell, which Fedora Core uses by default, displays a prompt, like this: `[lidia@cancun lidia]$`. You enter commands at the shell prompt, and the result is displayed. That's where the term *command-line interface (CLI)* comes from.

Bash stands for Bourne-Again Shell. Bash has nothing to do with Ludlum movie sequels but is technically a command language interpreter. Bash can work interactively or receive its input from a file or pipe.

You can start a shell from within the GNOME interface by starting a GNOME Terminal session (also known generically as a terminal emulator). Click the GNOME Applications button (the red hat, er, red *fedora* in the upper-right corner of the screen); we'll refer to this as simply the GNOME Menu. Then choose System Tools➪Terminal (or right-click anywhere on the GNOME Desktop and choose Open Terminal) to start a terminal session, as shown in Figure 4-1. (You can find out more about the GNOME environment in Chapter 9.)

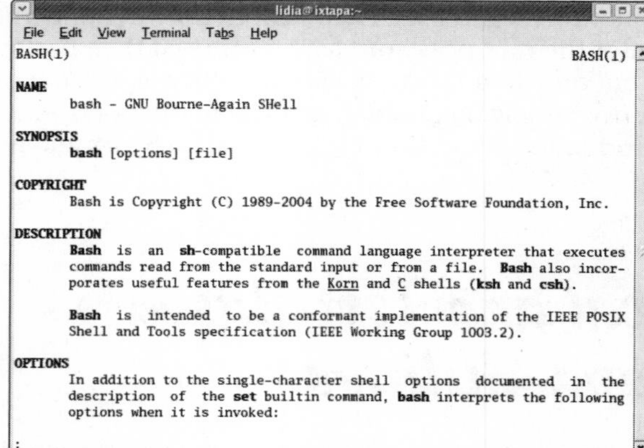

Figure 4-1: A GNOME Terminal session.

The GNOME Menu button is similar in function to the Windows Start button.

If you want to run individual programs without starting an interactive shell, you can use the GNOME Run Program menu: Click the GNOME Menu button and choose Run Application. When the Run Application window opens, type the name of any program in the text box. The program then runs, if it's graphically oriented. You don't see the output if the program is designed to interact with the terminal screen (the technical term is *standard output*), unless you click the Run in Terminal button. Entering **xclock**, for example, displays a graphical clock on-screen. Running the simple `ls` command after clicking the Run in terminal button displays a list of files.

The GNOME Terminal is similar to the MS-DOS window in Windows in the way it interacts with you. Opening an MS-DOS window provides a text-based window in which to enter DOS commands. The underlying technology of a Windows CLI is different from that of a Linux CLI, but the Linux CLI provides far more capabilities.

Configuring Your Monitor and Video Card

The Fedora Core installation process is good at automatically configuring itself to use your video hardware and monitor. Linux uses the X Window System (X, for short) to display graphics. However, occasionally the X configuration process fails, or you may want to reconfigure it. Either way, Fedora Core gives you access to the same configuration tool it uses during the installation process.

The Fedora Core X configuration utility is the system-config-display. We refer to it as simply the *Display Configurator.* Generally, the Display Configurator automatically detects your monitor (display) and graphics card. After they have been detected, you can set your display's resolution and color depth.

Starting the Display Configurator

You can start the Display Configurator even if you're not running X (if you're running in nongraphical mode; you're at Run Level 3):

1. **Log in as `root`.**

   You automatically see a command-line interface.

2. **Enter this command at the Bash prompt:**

   ```
   system-config-display
   ```

   The Display Configurator window opens. The utility runs within a graphical interface.

You can, of course, start the Display Configurator if your computer is running X. You may want to reconfigure your system, for example. Follow these instructions to start the utility:

1. **Click the GNOME Menu.**
2. **Choose System Settings⇨Display.**

3. **Enter the** `root` **password if you're prompted.**

   The Display Configurator opens the Display settings window. Use the set of steps in the next section to configure your graphical X interface.

The X Window System (*X,* for short) was invented at the Massachusetts Institute of Technology (MIT) to display graphical applications across a wide range of machines. It was originally built to run on Unix platforms, but has been adapted to Linux and other platforms.

Old monitors that lack multiscanning capability can be damaged if you try to use them at a resolution higher than VGA, which is 640 x 480 and 60Hz (a multiscanning monitor can switch to the same signal frequency that a video card generates). Monitors manufactured in this century, and most since the mid-1990s, have built-in protection mechanisms to keep them from burning up in what is known as *overdriving,* but older monitors don't have this type of protection. Older monitors can literally catch on fire. If you hear weird noises from your monitor or smell burning components, turn off your monitor immediately!

Configuring the display

The Display Configurator allows you to configure your display's resolution, color depth, monitor type, video driver, and dual monitors. A description of the use and configuration of dual monitors is beyond the scope of this book. Here we describe how to configure the other options. After you start the Display Configurator, as described in the preceding section, it defaults to the Settings tab.

Follow these steps to reconfigure your monitor:

1. **Modify the display resolution and color depth, if you want.**

   You can always return to a previous setting, so don't hesitate to experiment here.

2. **Click the Hardware tab to modify your monitor and video-driver settings.**

   Figure 4-2 shows that you can configure the monitor or the video card.

3. **Click the Configure button next to the Monitor Type option.**

   The Monitor window opens. You can use this window to configure the exact, or nearly exact, settings for your monitor.

4. **Try to locate and select your particular monitor.**

   You can choose from among dozens and dozens of monitors; you have at least as good a chance of finding yours as winning PowerBall — well, actually a much better chance.

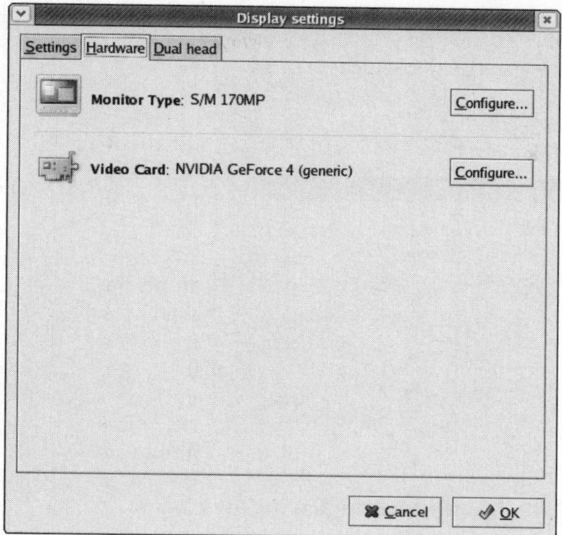

Figure 4-2: The Display Settings dialog box.

5. **If you find it, select your monitor's manufacturer and model, click OK, and skip to Step 8.**
6. **If you don't find your monitor, your best bet is to rummage around in one of the two generic submenus.**

   The Generic CRT Display submenu has generic settings for several resolutions for old-fashioned heavy, glass (monster) monitors; CRT is short for *c*athode *r*ay *t*ube. The Generic LCD Display submenu provides settings for flat-panel displays using a *l*iquid *c*rystal *d*isplay. If you don't know which type fits your monitor, take a guess and try one. Keep trying different generic monitors if your first choice doesn't work.
7. **Select the generic setting that most closely matches your display, click OK, and return to the advanced settings window.**
8. **Click the Configure button next to the Video Card label.**

   The Video Card window opens, as shown in Figure 4-3.
9. **Select your video card from the long list of choices. If you cannot find your specific make and model of video card, select the VESA driver (generic) option.**

   The lowest-resolution (8-bit) option allows only 256 colors on the window at one time. The 16-bit option allows 65,535 colors, and 24-bit allows more than 16 million colors (that's why it's also called *true color*).
10. **Click OK to return to the Display Settings window.**

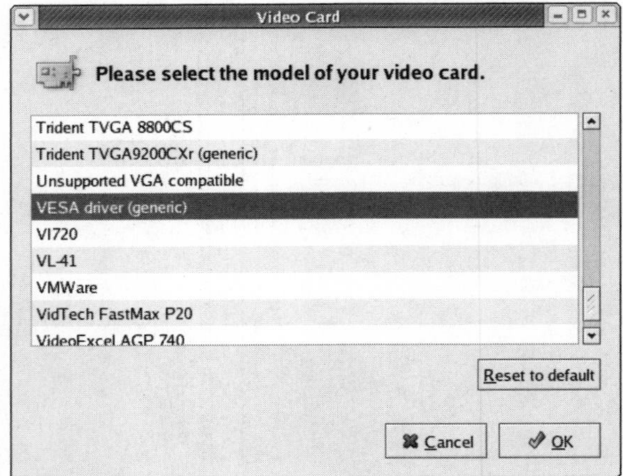

Figure 4-3: The Video Card dialog box.

11. **Click OK and the Display Settings window closes.**

    An Information window opens, informing you that you need to log out and then log back in to make the changes take effect.

12. **Click OK to leave the Information window.**

13. **Log out and then log back in to make the changes take effect.**

    Alternatively, you can reboot your computer to enforce the changes.

You can also restart X unceremoniously, but quickly, by pressing Ctrl+Alt+Backspace. Your current X session is stopped and eventually restarted. You can then log back in.

Delving deep into color depth

Color depth, the number of colors your system can have active on the window, is loosely a function of both the amount of video memory contained by your system and the window resolution.

If your system has a small amount of random access memory (RAM), your screen can have a resolution of 1024 x 768 pixels (dots) with 256 colors (8 bits) on the screen at one time. If your system has 2MB of memory, you can have 64 thousand colors (16 bits) on the screen at the same time at the same resolution. The more memory you have, the more colors you can display for any given resolution.

When you want to display an image and the color depth isn't correct, nothing drastic happens. The picture may look lackluster or not quite normal. That's because X has an interesting capability that allows the use of *virtual color maps*: the active window can utilize all the colors of the bits of color depth, even if other windows are using different colors.

Introducing the Linux File System Tree

Linux, like Windows, uses files and directories to store and organize information and applications. This section introduces the Linux file system.

Linux sees all its parts, except its network, as files. No surprise that Linux accesses files, directories, and devices as *file addresses*. To figure out where everything is, Linux uses a system of letters and numbers to refer to drives and drive partitions — for example, `/dev/hda` may be the name of the first IDE hard drive in the system, and `/dev/sdb` may be the name of the second SCSI hard drive.

You can compare the Linux file system to an upside down tree. The trunk of the tree is the root directory — represented by a / (slash). A series of limbs, branches, and leaves extends below the root: Limbs are mount points, the branches that extend from the limbs are directories, and the leaves on those branches are your files. Figure 4-4 shows the root, several directories, including etc, and a couple of files in etc.

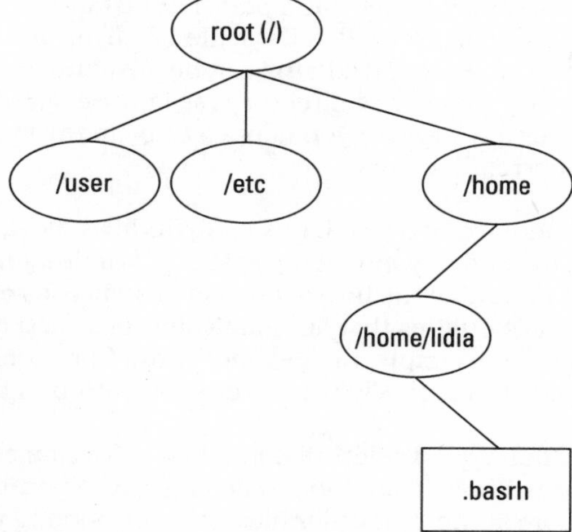

Figure 4-4: The Linux file system resembles an upside-down tree.

Each mount point is a drive partition or a remote file system (such as your DVD or CD-ROM drive) that is mounted to— identified and made visible as a directory of the limb "above" it on the imaginary tree. Whenever a disk partition or remote file system is mounted on the directory branch, it turns that branch into another limb — allowing even more branches to be positioned and attached below the mount point.

Fedora Core needs at least a `root` partition in your directory structure and a swap space partition. The `root` partition stores all personal and system files and directories; Linux uses *swap space* to extend memory capabilities temporarily beyond the limit of your random-access memory (RAM). If you have 512MB of RAM and 512MB of swap space, for example, you can run a program that uses almost 1GB of memory. Part of it is stored in memory and the rest sits in swap space.

This configuration isn't much different from the Windows and MS-DOS file systems — Windows, after all, uses the concept of a hierarchical directory tree — but the syntax is somewhat different. The top-level directory in Fedora Core, `root`, is designated with a forward slash (/). Every subsequent subdirectory name follows that initial slash. For example, the `home` directory is a subdirectory of `root` and is shown as `/home`. In the Windows world, the equivalent of the `root` directory is designated with an initial backslash (\). The famous `C:` prompt is synonymous with `C:\`. The theme for both operating systems is carried forward when dividing subdirectories: Linux uses forward slashes and Windows uses backslashes. For instance, a directory can be shown as `/xyz` in Linux or as `C:\xyz` in Windows. Both operating system can have subdirectories, such as `/xyz/abc` in Linux or `C:\xyz\abc` in Windows.

The location of a file or directory is given as a *path*. For instance, `/xyz/abc` describes the path to the subdirectory `abc`; if the file `123` lives in subdirectory `abc`, then its path is `/xyz/abc/123`. Paths can be absolute or relative. Absolute paths always refer to the `root` directory (as in the examples just given). Relative paths refer to wherever you happen to be in the system; they're relative to your current location.

Another fundamental difference between Linux and Windows file systems is that Linux requires you to explicitly mount file systems. Windows does so automatically. Explicitly mounting the file system isn't as onerous as it sounds. Fedora Core installs utilities that automatically sense and mount file systems when necessary. For example, the default Fedora Core configuration mounts a DVD or CD-ROM automatically whenever you insert it in the drive.

The Workstation installation type we describe in Chapter 3 automatically sets up your root and swap partitions in addition to an extra boot partition used for storing the Fedora Core kernel and other files used for booting your computer. (The Personal Desktop installation type uses the same partitioning scheme as the Workstation installation type.)

Creating User Accounts

Because Fedora Core is a multiuser system, more than one person at a time can use it. For example, you can be logged in at the computer console (the attached keyboard and monitor) while someone else is logged in via a network connection. Therefore you — and every other user — must have an individual user account in order to use the computer. Each account requires an individual account name and password to protect your information and keep your tasks separate from other people's tasks.

If you have cause to add new users (if you have a home network, for example) or you forgot to create a nonroot user account during installation, this section shows you how. Fedora Core offers both graphical and text-based user account creation and modification tools for your convenience. The following two sections describe how to use both types of utilities.

You can use the Fedora Core User Manager to modify an existing user account. Click the user name and then the Properties button, and a window similar to the Create New User window opens. You can then modify any aspect of the account.

Using the Graphical User Manager

The Fedora Core User Manager is an excellent administration tool that can make your life easier. It provides an easy-to-use interface that simplifies your system administration job. Use the User Manager to create a new account by following these steps:

1. **Open the User Manager by clicking the GNOME Menu button and then choosing System Settings⇨Users and Groups.**

   This is a job for superuser. If you're not logged in as the `root` user, you're prompted to enter the `root` password.

   The Fedora Core User Manager window appears.

2. **Click the Add User button in the upper-left corner of the screen.**

   The Create New User window appears, as shown in Figure 4-5.

3. **Enter your user name, real-life name (full name), and password twice (to confirm that it's correct); accept the Login Shell default of** `/bin/bash`.

   The Fedora Core User Manager also creates a home directory by default.

   Most of these items are self-explanatory, but here's some additional information:

   • Your user name (also known as a *login name*) is the name you use to log in to your computer. Make your user name easy to remember and use all lowercase letters. Cute names may not seem appropriate later. Avoid choosing a name that is too long because you may have to type it several times a day. You may also end up using your user name as your e-mail address and have to give it over the telephone, so a login name such as `phool` results in missent messages, leaving you feeling phoolish.

Create New User

User Name:

Full Name:

Password:

Confirm Password:

Login Shell: /bin/bash

Create home directory

Home Directory: /home/

Create a private group for the user

Specify user ID manually

UID: 500

Cancel OK

Figure 4-5: The Create New User dialog box.

- You can enter your full name if you want. That information is saved in the `/etc/passwd` file, which anyone with an account on your system can read. This information is generally useful to system administrators because it allows them to connect a person with each account. (Well, okay, it's probably superfluous if you're configuring your personal system.)
- The new password should be different from the one you use for `root`.

  As you type the password, a line of asterisks (rather than the actual password) appears on-screen in case someone is looking over your shoulder as you type. (Fedora Core is showing its paranoid side here.) In text mode, you don't get any feedback, such as asterisks or other characters.
- Among your many choices for a default shell, `/bin/bash` is a good choice (`bash` is a popular shell that is the default for Fedora Core).

4. **Click OK.**

   Your account is created.

Fedora Core uses the Pluggable Authentication Module (PAM), which prevents you from entering trivial or otherwise dangerous passwords; don't use that as assurance, however, that your new password is a good one. A good password cannot be found in any dictionary because password crackers have programs that automatically try all dictionary words to crack your password. Avoid birthdays and anniversaries or anything someone could associate with you. For ideas about good passwords, check out Chapter 3. Just don't forget it, and *don't* write it on a sticky note and put it on your monitor!

You can also use the Fedora Core User Manager to delete an existing user account. Click the user name and then the Delete button, and the account is immediately removed. Be careful and be sure of what you want to do — Fedora Core doesn't ask you to confirm the account deletion. Fortunately (in this case), the account's `home` directory is left intact (not deleted); you can go back and re-create the account if necessary.

Using the text-based useradd command

Many system administrators prefer using text-based (CLI) tools and utilities. Text-based tools are relatively easy to use after you become familiar with them. They also tend to save time if you're doing numerous administration jobs simultaneously, because you don't have to work between multiple windows — instead, you just type a series of commands.

These steps describe how to use the `useradd` program to create a user account:

1. **Open a GNOME Terminal window by clicking the GNOME Menu button and choosing System Tools➪Terminal.**
2. **Log in as root by entering this command:**

   ```
   su -
   ```

3. **Enter the** `root` **password when prompted.**
4. **Type** useradd *name* **at the command prompt, where** *name* **is the login name for the new login account.**

   To change the system assigned password for the account you've just created, enter the following command:

   ```
   passwd name
   ```

5. **Type a password when you're prompted and press Enter.**

   This step changes the password of the new account, which had a default password assigned to it by the `useradd` command in Step 4. (What good is a password if you use the default?)

6. **Type your password again.**

   Fedora Core asks you to retype your new password to ensure that the password you typed is the one you thought you typed. If you don't retype the password exactly as you did the first time (which is easy to do because it doesn't appear on-screen), you have to repeat the process.

   Fedora Core updates the password for the new login.

Ending Your First Session

Logging off the system and restarting the login process is simplicity itself. To do so, click the GNOME Action button and choose Log Out. The Are You Sure You Want to Log Out? window appears, and you're asked to confirm that you want to log out. If you do (do you *really?*), click the OK button and you're outta there. Click No if you change your mind and want to play around with your new operating system a while longer.

You can also choose to reboot — or halt — your computer from this window by clicking the Shutdown button or the Reboot button and then clicking OK to confirm your decision. Depending on which you choose, your system stops completely or reboots. You can also press the Ctrl+Alt+Backspace keys to shut down your current session. This method is less graceful but still effective, especially in case some renegade process freezes your X session.

Part II
Got Net?

"Just as I thought, Sergeant! When are people going to learn that dial up kills?"

In this part . . .

After you have created your Fedora Core workstation, it's time to get to work. The chapters in this part show three different ways to connect to the Internet: the traditional, slow but ubiquitous dialup (analog) modem; a cutting-edge and blazing broadband DSL or cable modem; or an existing local-area network (LAN) connected to the Internet.

Chapter 5 concentrates on telephone-based modems. Modems are much like old, reliable pickup trucks: They may not be the fastest way of getting somewhere, but they still get you there. In fact, modems still provide the simplest and most economical Internet connection available.

Chapter 6 introduces broadband Internet connections. Telephone, cable, and companies in between provide broadband service to many communities. For not-altogether-unreasonable prices, you can get high-speed, always-on service.

Many people have access to existing local-area networks (called LANs) that link computers at work, school, and home. Chapter 7 shows how to connect your computer to a LAN — and if your LAN has an Internet connection, you can find out how to configure your workstation to use it.

Your computer becomes vulnerable, however, after you connect to the Internet. This statement is especially true if you use a service (such as DSL) that is constantly connected. The difference is similar to living on a quiet street versus a busy one. You're more vulnerable on the busy street. That's why we show you (in Chapter 8) how to build a firewall to reduce your online vulnerability.

Chapter 5

Dull Dial-Up Modems Still Get the Job Done

In This Chapter

- Finding an Internet service provider (ISP)
- Configuring your Internet connection
- Configuring your modem
- Connecting to your ISP

Surfing the Net is lots of fun and sometimes a useful activity. Come on, admit it: You know you tie up the phone line for hours just to annoy your family or roommates, browse sites with silly addresses such as `www.theonion.com`, and chat with people you'd never dream of speaking to in person. The catch is that before you join the chaos of the online universe, you have to connect to the Internet.

Since prehistoric times, the simple modem has been used to make that connection. Okay, now that high-speed "broadband" Internet connections have become popular, describing how to use an old, slow modem may seem, well, so '90s. But many (if not most) people use modems, so this chapter describes how to set one up to connect to an Internet service provider (ISP).

This chapter assumes that you're connecting to the Internet using a standard dial-up modem. We describe how to configure your Fedora Core computer to use faster Internet connection technologies, referred to as *broadband connections,* in Chapter 6.

Many people have access to Internet-connected networks at work and school. (Or maybe your five-year-old has constructed an Internet-connected home network.) Chapter 7 describes how to connect your Fedora Core computer to an existing private network and gain access to the Internet through its connection. You can then surf at lightspeed until the cows come home.

If you're buying a modem

Dial-up modems are an old technology, but still the most common method for making personal or small-business Internet connections. This statement may not be true much longer because the number of users with broadband connections is rising fast, and most large businesses also use broadband services.

An *internal modem* plugs into a PCI or ISA slot on your computer's motherboard, or a PCMCIA slot on laptops, and receives power from the computer. An *external modem* comes in its own enclosure, requires its own power supply (those electrical plugs sticking out of clunky black boxes), and connects to the computer via a serial (sometimes referred to as RS232) connection. Both types of modems use your phone jack to connect to the Internet.

Internal modems are generally less expensive than external ones, but external modems have several advantages. You can easily turn them on and off, you can connect them to a computer without opening the computer case, and if your telephone line is struck by lightning, the charge passing through the modem doesn't damage your computer. On the other hand, internal modems need only a telephone line cable — whereas external modems require a telephone line, a serial connection, and power-supply cables.

Desperately Seeking ISP

To get connected using a dial-up modem, you have to hook up a modem to your computer and then find a good Internet Service Provider (ISP) to dial up to. Odds are that you have an internal modem that came installed with your computer. If not, you have to purchase one, either internal or external. Once you have the modem you may want to check out *Upgrading & Fixing PCs For Dummies,* 6th Edition, by Andy Rathbone (Wiley) to find out how to install it.

The best way to find a good ISP is by word of mouth. Getting personal recommendations is a good way to find out both the good and bad points of an ISP that don't show up in advertisements. Before you sign on with an ISP, make sure that the company supports Linux.

If you don't have any friends and your acquaintances don't speak to you, try finding a local Linux user group (LUG) to ask. You can look up LUGs at the Fedora Core community Web page, at `www.redhat.com/apps/community`.

Table 5-1 lists some major ISPs that support Linux.

Table 5-1 Large ISPs That Support Linux

ISP	*Toll-Free Phone Number*	*Web Address (U.S. Only)*
Access4Free	866-MyFreei/ 770-349-3430 (free)	www.access4free.com
AT&T WorldNet	800-967-5363	www.att.net
CompuGlobalMega HyperNet Network	555-867-5309	www.compuglobal megahyper.net
CompuServe	800-336-6823	www.compuserve.com
Earthlink	800-EARTHLINK	www.earthlink.net
Prism Access	888-930-1030	www.prism.net
SprintLink	800-473-7983	www.sprint.net

Whichever one you want to use, be sure to ask your potential new ISP whether it offers a dialup PPP service. PPP (which stands for *P*oint-to-*P*oint *P*rotocol) is what Linux uses to connect to the Internet. If the person you talk to gives you the verbal equivalent of a blank stare, you may want to move on.

After you choose your Internet service provider and arrange payment, the ISP provides certain pieces of information, including the following:

- Telephone access numbers
- A username and password
- An e-mail address (typically, your username added to the ISP's domain name)
- A primary and secondary *Domain Name Server (DNS)* number, which is a large number separated by periods into four groups of digits
- An SMTP (mail) server to handle your outgoing messages
- A POP3 or an IMAP server name, used to download e-mail from the ISP's server to your machine

Access4Free provides a nice combination of free and subscription Internet service. After you register, you get your first 10 hours of service per month free. You're charged on an hourly basis up to $9.95 over 10 hours. You can also subscribe for unlimited dialup access for $9.95 per month; subscribing gives you telephone support (866-693-7334) that costs $5 per call otherwise. (That's not bad, either!) Access4Free also provides local dialup and PPP access in many U.S. cities.

Configuring Your Internet Connection

You need to configure your modem so that Fedora Core can use it to connect to your ISP. The Dialup Configuration utility does a good job of detecting, and then configuring, your modem. It also sets up a dial up account to connect your computer to your ISP (and, therefore, to the Internet). When you have the ISP and modem in place, the next step is to create a modem configuration:

1. **Click the GNOME Menu button (the red hat in the upper-right corner of your screen) and choose System Tools➪Internet Configuration Wizard.**

2. **Enter the `root` password in the Query dialog box, if you're prompted.**

   You must have root (that is, the highest level of) access to configure your modem.

3. **When the Add new Device Type window opens, click the Modem connection and then the Forward button.**

   The Searching for Modems dialog box appears briefly while the Internet Configuration Wizard scans your computer for modems.

4. **If no modem is detected or recognized, the Warning dialog box opens.**

   If the modem is found, the Select Provider window opens and you should skip to Step 8.

5. **Click the OK button.**

   The Select Modem window appears, as shown in Figure 5-1.

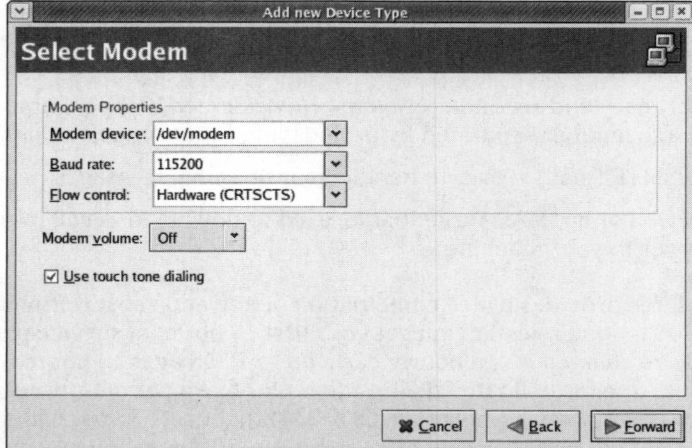

Figure 5-1: The Select Modem dialog box.

When the Internet Configuration Wizard doesn't find a modem, it guesses that one is attached to a serial port: `/dev/modem`. (A *serial port* is the mechanism your computer uses to communicate with a serial device, such as a modem; Universal Serial Bus (USB) is the modern equivalent of a serial port.)

6. **You cannot be sure that the `/dev/modem` device exists, so select `/dev/ttyS0`; select `/dev/ttyUSB0` if you're using an external USB modem.**

   - The `/dev/ttyS0` device is the first serial port on your computer; `/dev/ttyUSB0` is the first USB device.
   - You can also modify the modem settings, if you want, in the Select Modem window.

7. **Click the Forward button.**

   The Select Provider window appears.

8. **Select the appropriate preset configuration if you live in one of the listed countries.**

   You can, of course, choose to select another unlisted ISP — and you can click the T-Online button if you use that ISP. The German ISP T-Online also provides English service. If you select this service, enter your information in the dialog box that opens.

9. **In the Select Provider window, enter your ISP's phone number, the name of your ISP, your login name, and your password in the appropriate boxes.**

   You should also enter your ISP's prefix and area or country code (if necessary) in the appropriate text boxes.

10. **Click Forward after you enter the information.**

    The IP Settings dialog box opens, as shown in Figure 5-2.

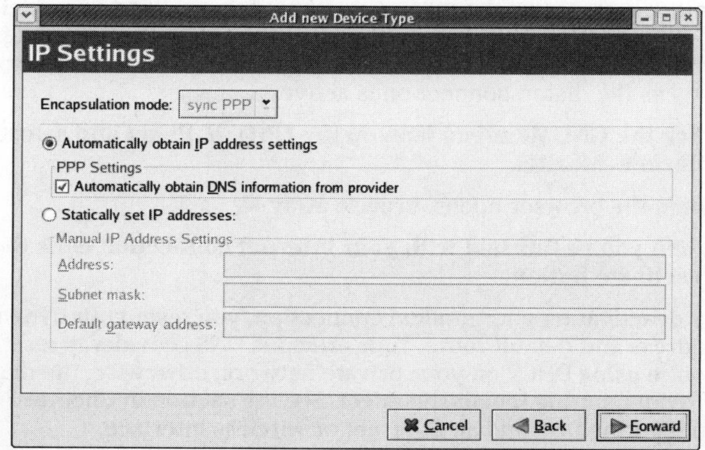

Figure 5-2: Configuring your dialup IP settings.

You have two default options in the IP Settings dialog box:

- `Automatically obtain IP address settings`
- `Automatically obtain DNS information from provider`

The default options permit your ISP to use PPP (Point-to-Point Protocol) to create an Internet connection across your telephone line and to use your ISP's DNS service to look up Internet names.

11. **These settings should work with your ISP, so click the Forward button.**

    The Create Dialup Connection window opens, showing a summary of the information you just entered.

12. **Click Apply.**

    The Network Configuration window opens. You see your new modem and any other network device, such as an Ethernet interface, in the window.

When you've finished creating the modem configuration, you can activate it and get connected to the Internet. Here's the drill:

1. **In the Network Configuration window, click the File⇨Save menu option to save your modem configuration.**
2. **Click the OK button when the Information window opens.**
3. **Click the Modem device to select it.**

   The Modem line is highlighted in blue.

4. **Click the Activate button to fire up the modem and connect to your ISP.**

   The Network Configuration tool dials up your ISP, authenticates your connection, and provides your computer with an Internet connection. Your ISP then uses the PPP protocol to set your IP address, default route, and DNS provider — automatically. Those numbers take precedence over any existing parameters (such as an Ethernet interface) as long as the dialup connection is active.

5. **Click the GNOME menu icon on the GNOME Panel and select Internet⇨Mozilla.**

   When the browser opens, browse away.

6. **When you're finished with your Internet connection click the Deactivate button.**

   By deactivating your modem connection, you reset your dynamic IP address and default route. Your previous DNS provider is reset only if you're using DHCP on your private network; otherwise, the dial-up DNS provider setting remains in effect. See the section in Chapter 7 about configuring DNS and an Ethernet or wireless interface.

Linux uses *device files* to communicate with peripherals. Device files are found in the `/dev` directory and are roughly equivalent to Windows drivers: the Linux kernel uses them to communicate with your hardware.

You can connect your modem to one of four serial ports or one of many USB ports available on your PC. An external serial modem is generally connected to port `/dev/ttyS0`, and sometimes to `/dev/ttyS1`, or even `/dev/ttyS2` or `/dev/ttyS3`; USB modems are connected to `/dev/ttyUSB0`, `/dev/ttyUSB1`, and so on. If you have an internal modem, it can be any one of the `tty` devices.

Firing Up Your Internet Connection

Fedora Core provides a PPP dialer utility to help you establish a PPP connection. You establish this connection by using the PPP configuration you set up with the Dialup Configuration tool (which we describe earlier in this chapter, in the section "Configuring Your Internet Connection").

To connect to the Internet with the PPP dialer, follow these steps:

1. **Click the GNOME Menu button and choose System Tools⇨Network Device Control.**

   The Network Device Control window appears, displaying all the network interfaces you have.

2. **Click the name of your modem (for example,** `Myconnection`**) and then click Activate.**

   The Network Device Control utility dials and connects to your ISP.

3. **When you finish using the Internet, click the Deactivate button in the Network Device Control window.**

   Your connection terminates.

Chapter 6

Broadband Rocks!

In This Chapter

- Understanding broadband Internet connections
- Using a cable modem connection
- Using a DSL modem connection

You're probably familiar with the ubiquitous dial-up Internet connection: You log on to the Internet, hear that screeching modem sound and — Presto! Whammo! — you're online. If you're lucky, the entire dial-up process takes less than a minute, but it can take longer. And then there are those Web pages that take so-o-o lo-o-ong to finish downloading. There is a better way to get connected — it's called *broadband,* a generic term for high-speed connections via cable TV and digital subscriber lines (DSLs). Cable connections are provided by cable television companies, and DSL by your telephone company. Both are much faster than dial-up connections, and both have their advantages and disadvantages.

The *broad* in broadband means that wires and cables that connect a modem to the Internet have a wide *bandwidth;* they can handle more data at faster speeds and with greater reliability. Plain old telephone service (POTS) was created for transferring analog voice data. Needless to say, POTS just doesn't do as well as broadband when it comes to the Internet.

The two most popular broadband types are cable modems and DSL. Cable modems connect through your cable television lines while DSL use POTS lines. Broadband connections work from roughly 100 kilobits per second (Kbps) to several million bits per second (Mbps). A *kilobit* is a thousand bits per second; a *megabit* is a million bits per second. That's enough speed to transfer graphics-rich Web pages in a few seconds; it's also enough to listen to several audio streams or to watch a low-resolution video stream.

We're on the verge of wireless broadband. The idea is to connect directly to an ISP without wires or cables of any kind. Some companies (such as Starbuck's) already offer such service on the small scale. On the larger scale, towns such as Rio Rancho, NM are about to become their own ISP. In the future, ISPs will offer wireless coverage similar to wireless telephone service. Stay tuned.

If you're ready to make the switch to a DSL or cable Internet connection, believe us when we tell you that you'll never want to go back to a dial-up modem. This chapter describes how to obtain and configure a broadband connection.

We recommend avoiding ISDN (Integrated Services Digital Network), satellite, and mental-telepathy-based broadband Internet connections. ISDN technology is old, and cable and DSL are better. Satellite Internet connections, just now being introduced, suffer from intrinsic problems such as transmission delays *(latency)* that wreak havoc with your communications; unfortunately, you can't upgrade to the speed of light. Some people say that mental telepathy (MT) works great, but we've found it scrambles our data.

DSL and Cable Connections: The Difference Is the Wiring

Although the voice-based telephone network is now modern in many ways, its underpinnings haven't fundamentally changed over the last century. The telephone network consists of pairs of copper wires, twisted into cables that connect homes and businesses to a telephone company's central offices (CO). The phone company uses switches in its COs to connect you to your destination when you make a call. The switches are designed to limit the range of frequencies (called *bandwidth*) that a phone call can use. The bandwidth is enough to recognize a voice, but not much more. Those limits prevent today's analog modems from pushing more than approximately 56,000 bits per second, or 56 Kbps, through the telephone network. (That 56 Kbps speed varies, mostly downward, depending on the condition of the copper wires you're connected to.)

Two of the most commonly used broadband systems are

- **Digital subscriber lines (DSL):** DSL is designed to avoid the restrictions of the traditional telephone system by circumventing the low-speed voice switches at the Central Office (CO). DSL uses the existing telephone wires, which connect your home to the nearest CO, to carry your Internet communication. After you're connected to the CO, however, your Internet communication is routed through a high-speed digital switch rather than through the voice equipment. By avoiding the voice equipment, you can achieve many times the speed of a dial-up modem.

  The main limitation of DSL is that traditional copper wire can carry a high-speed connection for only a few miles. Your telephone company can tell you whether it can provide you with DSL service.

- **Cable television networks:** Although Cable television (CATV) companies don't provide service to as many residences and businesses as the telephone companies do, their networks are not limited by historical constraints and are generally much faster than DSL. CATV networks also don't have the 3- to 4-mile limits that DSL has. Typically, you can get an Internet connection through your CATV company if the company offers it — and only if the company serves your neighborhood.

The Cable-Modem Option

Cable television companies have invested lots of capital to upgrade their networks in order to gain Internet market share. Their effort has paid off for consumers, and many places in the United States now have access to high-speed Internet connections at fairly reasonable prices.

However, you have to consider some downsides:

- Unfortunately, not all cable companies have caught up with 21st-century technology. Some CATV companies provide TV service but no Internet connections.
- Many people don't live in areas served by cable TV. Internet cable is also not a good medium for providing services such as Web page hosting.
- Your cable company may require you to connect to its ISPs (or use an independent ISP that it approves of). Many people like to use an independent ISP because they're familiar with it or it provides better service. Using your own ISP also makes it easier to set up your computer (or network) to provide services going out to the Internet. Cable companies cannot prevent you from using a different local ISP, but they don't charge you less — so you end up paying for two services, one of which you're not using.
- Relatively few cable companies directly support Linux. You may get a connection, but you're on your own if you need to troubleshoot problems, even problems that have nothing to do with Fedora Core but still affect your machine.

If you decide that cable access is the right choice for your Internet access needs, here's an overview of the process for connecting your Fedora Core computer to the Internet via a cable modem:

1. **Do some research and subscribe to an ICP service.**

   Locate an Internet cable provider (ICP) — usually that means your existing cable TV company — and subscribe to its ICP service.

2. **Make a hardware commitment.**

   Obtain an Internet cable modem through your ICP. Many ICPs provide cable modems as part of their service. Otherwise you can purchase a modem from the ICP or a consumer-electronics store.

3. **Get registered.**

   Register the cable modem with your ICP. You do have to register your modem with your ICP.

   You register your modem by giving your ICP the modem's Media Access Control (MAC) address. The ICP generates an IP address by using the MAC address as its reference. You don't need to do anything to your cable modem. Your ICP does the registration process and automatically assigns your modem an IP address. You're ready to use your Internet cable modem to connect to the Internet. Woo-hoo! Blazing speed is yours now!

4. **Set up the cable modem.**

   Cable modems have two connectors: a 75-ohm coaxial port and a twisted-pair (RJ-45) connector (the coaxial connector is the same type that's used for cable TV; the RJ-45 connector looks like a large telephone plug):

   - Connect a coaxial cable from the cable modem's coaxial port to the cable jack on your wall, just like you would do with a TV set.
   - Connect a network cable from the RJ-45 modem port to your Fedora Core computer. Normal network cables (referred to as Category 5 cables) may not work, depending on how the modem uses a single Ethernet connector rather than multiple Ethernet ports that are part of a switch. If yours uses the former, you need to use a *crossover* cable if you want to directly connect a computer to a cable modem. You can use normal Category 5 cables if the cable modem incorporates a network switch or if you connect the modem through a separate Ethernet hub or switch.

5. **Set up your Internet protocols.**

   Configure your computer to use DHCP on the network interface that connects to the modem. Restart your computer's network interface, and you should be good to go.

The following sections take you through the process of finding a cable provider and setting up your access.

Finding an Internet cable provider

Finding an *Internet cable provider* (ICP) is as simple as calling your cable television company. Not all cable TV systems carry Internet traffic, but many do.

Locating a cable television company that provides broadband Internet connections is, unfortunately, quite easy. It's unfortunate because little competition exists within the cable industry. Federal law effectively restricts competition within municipalities and creates the environment for monopoly-like companies. The result, of course, is that prices remain higher than necessary. Oh, well, at least many cable companies are offering Internet connections.

Your ICP is your default Internet service provider (ISP). Most cable companies give you one or more e-mail addresses. However, cable companies don't generally provide login accounts (as other ISPs do).

Login accounts are used for launching applications and storing information. They aren't essential, but they're useful. Of course, nothing stops you from maintaining a regular ISP and using its login account. You then have a high-speed Internet connection you can use to log in to any account you have.

We don't run you through the process of signing up for cable Internet service because it varies from ICP to ICP. In any case, the process should be simple enough. A good portion of the sign-up process involves waiting on hold and listening to Muzak. One suggestion, though: Make sure that you have pertinent information about your system and that the cable company knows you're using Linux.

Dealing with the hardware

One great thing about Internet cable is that you can buy the cable modems from your local electronics store or an Internet store. (By way of comparison, you generally have to lease or purchase DSL equipment through the DSL provider.) Cable modems are generally priced the same whether you purchase through your provider, the Internet, or a bricks-and-mortar store. (Cable companies sometimes run promotions where they return by rebate most, if not all, of the price of the modem.) But the convenience of running to a local store is significant, especially if your cable modem breaks on a Saturday night and you just *have* to download the latest game patch.

Before you purchase a cable modem, make sure that you

- Ask whether you have to buy your modem through the cable provider. If not, you can shop around for the best price.
- Make sure that the modem you buy is compatible with your service provider. The cable industry is converging on using the Data Over Cable Service Interface Specification (DOCSIS) as its Internet hookup standard. DOCSIS modems are quite easy to configure, so keep your fingers crossed that your service provider uses them.

  In the unlikely event that your provider doesn't use DOCSIS, you'll probably have to obtain your modem through your provider.

How cable modems work

Modern cable modems do more than just transmit and receive Internet Protocol (IP) packets. Yes, they do the basic modem job — transmit and receive IP packets by modulating and demodulating electrical signals over the cable TV wires (thus the name *modem*, from *mo*dulate/*dem*odulate). But cable modems now use the industry-standard Data Over Cable Service Interface Specification (DOCSIS) protocol to deliver electrical signals across the cable network. Those signals carry the actual bits and bytes that make up network packets. A good analogy is an AM or FM radio. The DOCSIS-based signals transmit bits and bytes just like radio waves transmit speech or music.

The instructions we provide later in this chapter are designed for DOCSIS modems.

Setting up your cable modem is usually a straightforward process. DOCSIS cable modems act as network bridges. A *network bridge* simply transfers your network packets from one side to the other, and vice versa. One side of the bridge connects to the cable TV company. The other side connects to your computer through your Ethernet NIC through a Category-5 crossover cable; you can also connect through a network switch or hub (LAN). If your modem is the bridge type — most cable ISPs in the United States use that system — then it doesn't require any configuration.

Setting up Internet protocols

You don't have to configure your DOCSIS cable modem for it to work. What you *do* need to do, however, is register your modem's Ethernet address with your ICP and tell your Fedora Core computer how to connect to the modem. Cable modems typically connect to your computer via an Ethernet network interface. Therefore, you need to connect the cable modem to your computer using an Ethernet-based network.

You need to configure your Fedora Core computer's Ethernet adapter using the Dynamic Host Configuration Protocol (DHCP); you need an Ethernet adapter, of course, installed on your computer. Your cable modem sets the IP address of your Ethernet NIC by using DHCP. These instructions show you how to do that:

1. **Log in to your computer.**
2. **Click the GNOME Menu button and choose System Settings⇨Network.**
3. **Enter the** `root` **password if you're prompted, and then click OK.**

4. **Click the New button.**

   The Select Device Type window opens.

5. **Select the Ethernet connection option and click the Forward button.**

   The Select Ethernet Device window opens, showing the Ethernet device (or devices) that the Network utility found.

6. **Select Ethernet connection and click the Forward button.**

   The Select Ethernet Device dialog box opens.

7. **Select the appropriate devices and click the Forward button.**

   The Configure Network Settings window opens, as shown in Figure 6-1. By default, the option labeled `Automatically obtain IP address settings with DHCP Settings` is selected; the `Automatically obtain DNS information from provider` button is activated too. These are indeed the settings you need to use with DOCIS cable modems. However, you can choose a name for your computer.

8. **Pick a name for your computer and enter it in the Host name (optional) text box.**

   This step is optional; you can skip it and go to Step 9 if you want.

9. **Click the Forward button.**

   The Create Ethernet Device window opens, showing a summary of your Ethernet interface's configuration.

10. **Click the Apply button and control returns to the original Network Configuration window.**

    The Network Configuration window shows your new Ethernet device. However, you still need to save your changes before exiting the configuration system.

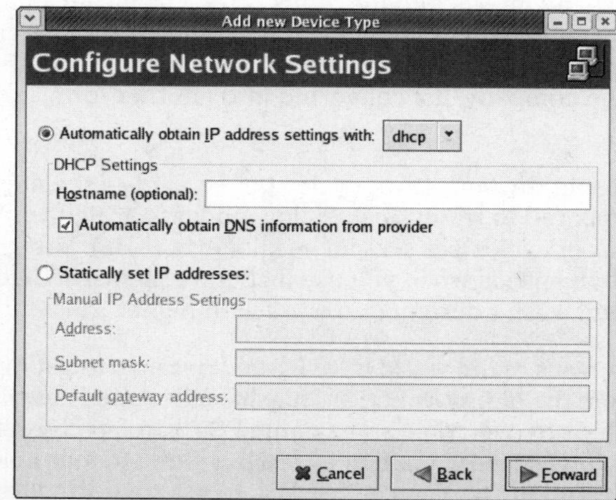

Figure 6-1: The Configure Network Settings dialog box.

11. **Choose File➪Save and click the OK button.**

    Before you click OK, an Information window pops up, telling you that your changes have been saved and that you need to restart your network or computer to make them take effect. Then you return to the Network Configuration window.

12. **Click the Activate button and your new Ethernet NIC turns on.**

13. **Choose File➪Quit to close the Network Configuration window.**

    You have created and saved the configuration necessary to use your cable modem. You have also activated that connection. You can start using your broadband Internet connection. Open Mozilla, for example, and start browsing at lightning speed.

We strongly advise protecting your Internet connection with either the default firewall — installed automatically during the general installation process — or the one we describe in Chapter 8. The default firewall is automatically configured and run unless you choose not to install it (as described in Chapter 3) or explicitly turn it off. We prefer to install and use the more secure firewall from Chapter 8; nothing is wrong with the default firewall, but it's less protective than ours. You can verify that your firewall is active by running the command **service iptables status** as `root`.

The DSL Option

We're all wired — wired for telephones, that is. DSL modems take advantage of this old, common, appropriately named Plain Old Telephone Service (POTS) to provide a high-speed Internet connection to consumers. The DSL option uses special equipment to pump much more data through the POTS lines than a traditional analog modem does.

DSL provides high-speed Internet connections by electronically converting your computer's digital network communications into a form that can be transmitted over the telephone company's POTS. When your data finds its way to the telephone company, it's converted into another form and forwarded to your ISP.

DSL uses frequencies in the *millions* of cycles per second — the megahertz (MHz) range — compared to traditional analog modems, which work with signals in the *thousands* of cycles per second — kilohertz (KHz). You get much higher communication speeds when you use higher frequencies. Unfortunately, the telephone system wasn't designed to work with higher frequencies.

Fortunately, the brainiacs of the world have figured out how to get high-speed DSL connections from the old, slow POTS. They have designed new digital signal-processing chips to overcome some of the POTS architecture limitations. The result is that if you live close enough — roughly three to four miles — to your DSL provider's equipment, you can use DSL to get connected to the Net.

Facing DSL configuration woes head-on

This section describes the basic DSL modem-configuration issues. We take the time to give you an overview because it's easy to focus on the trees at the expense of the forest. Please check out and get familiar with the following list. Getting your DSL modem working is easier after you do so.

Most consumer DSL providers now use the asymmetrical DSL (ADSL) type of connection. The following list describes the process for getting an ADSL connection working. (Please note that we use the generic acronym DSL interchangeably with ADSL. Most consumer DSL connections are really ADSL, and that's the type of connection we describe in this chapter.) Follow these steps to set up DSL service:

1. **Find a DSL provider.**

   You need to find out whether you live or work close enough to the DSL provider's equipment to get a connection. DSL providers check your address and tell you whether they can take your business. You can often check your proximity on the DSL provider's Web site.

2. **Connect your DSL modem to your telephone jack and your computer.**

   Your DSL modem acts as the intermediary between your computer and your DSL service provider. You must connect one side to the phone jack and the other to your computer's Ethernet NIC.

3. **Configure your Fedora Core computer to communicate with the DSL modem.**

   Your Fedora Core computer connects to the DSL modem via an Ethernet NIC. You must configure your Ethernet NIC to work with the modem.

4. **Configure the DSL modem with your PPP account name and password from your ISP.**

   You must authenticate your DSL modem to your ISP. DSL connections get logged on to your ISP, just as those from traditional analog modems do. You configure your DSL modem with your ISP user name and password.

5. **Configure the DSL modem's internal (private) network interface.**

   Your DSL modem must be able to communicate with a Fedora Core computer over an Ethernet connection. You must configure the DSL modem so that it uses the same network parameters as your computer.

6. **Configure the DSL modem user and administrative passwords.**

   DSL modems provide a reasonable level of security. You should take advantage of this security by assigning your own password to the modem. That action prevents hackers from breaking into your modem and causing problems.

7. **If necessary, configure the modem's network address translation (NAT) settings.**

   Many, if not most, DSL modems come configured to use NAT by default. This is a good thing because NAT effectively works as a firewall. There's no such thing as too much protection.

   The Internet was designed to send — or *route* — information as quickly as possible to its destination. Internet Protocol (IP) addresses are used to designate where the information is coming from and where it's going. IP addresses can be routable or nonroutable. Nonroutable addresses can be reused; you can use the same nonroutable addresses that your neighbor uses without interfering with one another.

   NAT converts nonroutable IP addresses into routable ones, which is useful when you're connecting your private network to the Internet by translating your internal IP addresses into one of your ISP's routable IP addresses. You need to configure your DSL modem to convert your computer's private and nonroutable address (for example, `192.168.1.1`) into an address assigned to your DSL connection by your ISP.

8. **Save the settings to nonvolatile memory and restart the modem.**

   You need to save your DSL modem's settings after you have them working. You don't want to enter the configuration every time you turn on your modem.

Finding a DSL provider

You must obtain both DSL and ISP services to make your broadband connection. Some companies — notably, the regional Bell telephone companies — can provide both services. However, in our case, we preferred our ISP to the ISP that was aligned with the DSL provider. (We were fortunate enough to retain our existing ISP when we purchased our DSL service.)

The DSL provider market is still quite fluid. Research the DSL service providers in your area carefully before choosing one — and remember that longevity is as important as a low price. Regional Bells are more likely to provide long-term service than many of their competitors.

Usually, you have to select an ISP after you choose a DSL provider. DSL providers either provide their own ISP or allow you to choose from several independent ones (the DSL provider makes the arrangements and works directly with the third-party ISP).

The many faces of DSL

DSL comes in a variety of flavors. Most consumers end up using ADSL because it offers inexpensive Internet connections at reasonably high speeds. ADSL serves an individual computer user's Internet needs very well; it even provides a small business with adequate service. ADSL is, not surprisingly, the most available of all DSL flavors.

The other types are more suited for business use. Most locales probably have access to only two or three of these services. DSL comes in a range of variations:

- **ADSL (asymmetrical DSL):** The ADSL download *(downstream)* speed isn't the same as its upload *(upstream)* speed. (That's why it's asymmetrical.) The maximum ADSL speed is 8 Mbps, but it's usually limited to less because of the POTS infrastructure limitations.
- **G.Lite:** Also known as Universal DSL or *splitterless* ADSL, G.Lite is a low-speed version of ADSL that doesn't require filtering out the POTS signal. It provides as much as 1.5 Mbps downstream and 512 Kbps upstream.
- **HDSL (high-bit-rate DSL):** HDSL is a symmetrical protocol with equal upstream and downstream speeds. You can use HDSL as a substitute for T1 connections because it provides the same data rates of 1.544 Mbps.
- **HDSL2 (high-bit-rate DSL 2):** HDSL2 provides the same specifications as HDSL, but works over a single twisted-pair connection.
- **IDSL (ISDN digital subscriber loop):** IDSL, the successor to the current ISDN technology, uses the same line encoding (2B1Q) as ISDN and SDSL. IDSL is used mostly to provide DSL service in areas where the more popular forms, such as ADSL and SDSL, aren't available. IDSL is capable of providing upstream and downstream rates of 144 Kbps.
- **SDSL (single-line DSL):** SDSL is commonly called *Symmetric DSL* because SDSL upstream and downstream speeds are the same.
- **VDSL (very-high-bit-rate DSL):** VDSL provides as much as 50 Mbps over distances up to 1,500 meters on short loops. VDSL is particularly useful for campus environments — universities and business parks. VDSL is now being introduced in market trials to deliver video services over existing phone lines. You can also configure VDSL in symmetric mode.
- **xDSL:** *x*DSL is a generic term for all the DSL flavors (the *x* means "whatever").

A real-world example: Configuring an ActionTec DSL modem

Writing explicit configuration examples is always difficult and liable to leave some readers disappointed. But the DSL world appears to be consolidating around modems with Web-based configuration interfaces. Therefore we can provide an example here that should be useful to you, regardless of whether you have the same type of modem. Good luck!

This section shows you how to use one of the more common DSL modems. Qwest, which is a "baby Bell" and one of the larger DSL providers, uses this equipment. Our modem router is the Qwest-recommended equipment. You configure it by editing Web-based menus.

The following instructions describe how to configure your ActionTec DSL modem. Remember that we're including these instructions only to provide an example of what a DSL configuration looks like. If you're using a different modem or service provider, or both, your configuration looks somewhat different.

1. **Connect your ActionTec modem to your telephone line by plugging the supplied cable from the modem's Line port to a telephone jack.**
2. **Connect your Fedora Core computer's Ethernet to the DSL modem's Ethernet port.**

   If your computer is connected to a private network, connect the DSL modem's Ethernet to the same network. This step usually requires that both the computer and the modem connect to the same Ethernet switch or hub. See Chapter 7 for information about connecting to private networks (also referred to as *local-area networks,* or LANs).
3. **Start Mozilla on your computer and type** http://192.168.0.1 **in the Location text box, at the top of the window.**

   This address happens to be the one that the ActionTec modem uses. Your mileage may vary.
4. **Click the Setup/Configuration button.**

   The Setup/Configuration window opens.
5. **Click the Basic Setup button.**
6. **The Setup window opens, reminding you to connect your modem to a telephone connection and your computer(s).**
7. **Press the Next button.**

   The Broadband Connection window opens.
8. **Keep the default PPPoA option and click the Next button.**

   PPPoA stands for PPP over ATM, where PPP is the Point-to-Point Protocol and ATM is Asynchronous Transfer Mode; ATM does *not* stand for All The Money you want! PPPoE is PPP over Ethernet. Don't worry about the acronyms; the important thing to know is that PPPoA is the most common method used to connect DSL modems to broadband service providers.
9. **When the Broadband Connection–PPP window opens, enter in the appropriate text boxes the user name and password that your DSL provider gave you.**

   Enter the static IP only if you asked for and received one from your DSL provider. The only time you need to use a static IP is when you want to provide some network service to the Internet.

10. **In the Save and Restart window, press the Save and Restart button.**

    The Congratulations! Just as it says, the modem connects itself to your DSL provider and stops blinking when it's ready.

11. **Click the Status tab to see information about your connection.**

Securing your DSL modem

After you set up a connection to the Internet through your DSL modem, you have the same need as everyone else who does that: to make it more secure. The following steps describe how to set a password (please see Chapter 3 for advice about choosing good passwords):

1. **If you're continuing from where you left off in the preceding section, click to select the Setup tab.**
2. **Click the Change Admin Password button.**
3. **Enter your password in the first text box and repeat it in the second.**
4. **Click the Save and Restart button.**

   The Save and Restart window opens.

5. **Click the Save and Restart button again.**

   Your new password is saved. You're prompted to enter a user name and password the next time you try to view or modify the DSL modem. The user name is `admin`, and the password is whatever you just set it to.

The exact way to accomplish each of these steps varies between manufacturers. The general idea is still the same — and many steps should be quite close to what we describe here. All DSL modems require the same basic information: ISP user name, password, and so on. You should always set your DSL modem to use NAT because it acts as a firewall. Consult your modem's user guide for detailed configuration information.

Chapter 7

Connect Locally, Communicate Globally: Connecting to a LAN

In This Chapter

- Networking with an Ethernet or wireless NIC
- Using the Fedora Core Network utility
- Starting and stopping your local network connection

This chapter shows how to connect your Fedora Core computer to an existing local-area network (also called a LAN or a *private network*). It's different from connecting directly to the Internet with a dialup modem or broadband connection as described in Chapters 5 and 6; those chapters show you how to connect a single, stand-alone Fedora Core computer directly to the Internet. In this case, you connect your Fedora Core computer to a LAN, which might have its own Internet connection.

You may be building your Fedora Core computer to use at home, work, or school. It doesn't matter what the venue is: You can use the information in this chapter to connect your computer to any existing LAN.

Don't get discouraged if you don't have access to a LAN. You can make your own! Chapter 15 describes how to build one.

In this book, the terms *LAN* and *private network* are used interchangeably.

If you configured your Ethernet card to connect to your LAN during the installation process we describe in Chapter 3, that's great! You can skip this chapter or just browse through it for fun. Otherwise, you can use this chapter to connect your computer to a LAN.

Introducing Local-Area Networks

The invention of Linux revolutionized computer networking. Creating a LAN before Linux existed was expensive and complicated. LANs were the nearly exclusive domain of big corporations, universities, and such.

But networking was built into Linux, in the form of the TCP/IP networking protocols, from the beginning. In the mid-1990s, if you could afford a couple of PCs, a cheap piece of coaxial cable, and a couple of Ethernet adapters, a LAN was born. Ethernet adapters, also commonly known as *network interface cards* (NICs), cost about $150 or more at the time. Prices, fortunately, have crashed since then, falling to earth faster than a middle-aged rock star: A 100Mbps NIC now costs as little as $10, and you can buy an 11Mbps wireless NIC for less than $50 (54Mbps 802.11g cards sell for not much more than $50).

To get your Fedora Core computer connected to a network, however, you do have to configure a handful of networking subsystems. Here are the tasks that have to be done for your network to work:

- Install your wireless or Ethernet NIC. Most computers, laptops and desktops, include preinstalled Ethernet NICs. Many laptops also come equipped with wireless NICs. If you need to retrofit a NIC, follow the instructions that come with the device.
- Load your wireless or Ethernet NIC kernel module. Fedora Core generally detects your hardware and automatically loads the correct kernel modules.
- Configure your NIC's IP address, netmask, and gateway.
- Configure your Domain Name Service (DNS), which converts Internet names into Internet Protocol (IP) addresses.

Wireless networking (or Wi-Fi, as explained in an upcoming sidebar) suffers from some security vulnerabilities. Consult the "Wireless network warning" sidebar, later in this chapter.

Performing these steps requires some "heavy lifting." Your load is eased considerably by using the graphical Network Configuration Utility, a system-administration tool that comes with Fedora Core. Have fun!

Configuring Your NIC with the Fedora Core Network Utility

To use your Fedora Core computer with an existing local-area network (LAN), you need at least two pieces of hardware:

- A wireless or Ethernet NIC (network interface card) installed on your computer
- A network hub, switch, or wireless access point to connect to the NIC

After you set up the hardware, the next step is to configure your Fedora Core network settings.

Preparing to configure your wireless NIC

Before you can configure your wireless NIC, you need to figure out two things:

- The type of wireless NIC you have (or need)
- How your wireless NIC should connect to your network

The two most widely used types of 802.11b (11Mbps) wireless electronics (or *chip sets*) are by Wavelan (built by Lucent Technologies) and Prism2 (designed by Intersil). Fedora Core supports both types. Here are some details (manufacturers and so on) to help you figure out what kind of chip set your device uses:

- **Wavelan:** Orinoco is the leader here; other (less popular) models include Apple Airport Enterasys RoamAbout 802, Elsa AirLancer 11, and Melco/Buffalo 802.11b.
- **Prism2:** D-Link DWL-650, LinkSys, Netgear, WPC11, and Compaq WL110; other, less popular models include Addtron AWP-100, Bromax Freeport, GemTek WL-211, Intalk/Nokia, SMC 2632W, YDI, Z-COM X1300, and Zoom Telephonics ZoomAir 4100

At the time this book was written, the newest available wireless protocol was 802.11g. Technology built to this standard can run at up to 54 Mbps, roughly five times the speed of an 802.11b system. However, there are not many Linux drivers available for this technology yet. The Prism54 project is busy developing open-source Linux drivers for the 802.11g protocol, so please look at `www.prism54.org` to see whether your wireless card has a driver (by the time you read this chapter). One company, Linuxant, sells software that allows your Linux computer to use Microsoft drivers. Consult their Web site `www.linuxant.com` for more information about their product.

IEEE, Wi-Fi, and wireless networks

IEEE (pronounced "eye-triple-e"), or Institute of Electrical and Electronic Engineers, is a worldwide professional society of nerds (specifically, those nerds who care enough about technical matters to set consistent standards) The IEEE, the "triclops" of wireless networking (one eye, three Es, get it?), concerns itself with issues such as which frequency wireless networking devices should use. Fortunately, this group has devised this wonderful standard that now enables everyone who's interested to communicate without stringing wires between machines.

The dominant wireless standard is a combination of ingredients. It's based partly on the IEEE 802.11b standard (also called Wi-Fi, short for *wi*reless *fi*delity) — and also two older standards (802.11a and the more recent 802.11g). Hey, call it shorthand: If you hear people talking about a Wi-Fi NIC, they're just talking about wireless NICs.

The first order of business is to figure out how your wireless NIC (or network adapter) should connect to your network. Wireless NICs connect to a LAN in two ways:

- **Adapter to adapter:** This type, referred to as an *ad-hoc* connection, is useful if you have two or more computers that you want to talk and form their own, exclusive private network.
- **Adapter to wireless access point:** This type, called *infrastructure,* provides a single entrance (an access point) into a LAN. An *access point* allows one or more computers to be connected to a network. However, unlike an ad-hoc network, the individual computers can connect to any access point that allows them to.

The wireless-configuration instructions we provide work with either the infrastructure or ad-hoc connection methods. Your wireless NIC can connect to either the access point or other computers (Linux and Windows) as long as you correctly configure your network ID (ESSID) and your encryption key.

Why ad-hoc is better than infrastructure

Using ad-hoc mode provides several advantages:

- **Lower costs:** You don't have to purchase an access point; access points starts at around $50. Computers using wireless NICs running in ad-hoc mode communicate directly with each other, eliminating the need for a common access point.

- **Simpler configuration for Linux users:** Older access-point devices could be configured using only Windows-based software — using the simple network-management protocol (SNMP), to be exact. You had to physically connect a Windows computer to the access point via a wired Ethernet network, and then use the software supplied with the device. That was difficult if you didn't have any Windows-based computers. Newer access points tend to use Web-based configuration tools, so you can use Mozilla to configure these newer devices.
- **Ad-hoc networks eliminate the need to configure any access points:** You configure only the wireless NIC in each computer on your network. You can use the Fedora Core Network Configuration utility to configure a wireless NIC, which simplifies the process. Each NIC must have the same network ID and encryption key.

Ad-hoc networks can also provide a bit more security because they connect to other networks — and the Internet — through a network router. Access points work as network bridges. Routers examine IP addresses and then decide where to direct network traffic from one network to another. Bridges automatically pass on all traffic. Ad-hoc networks can be configured to more tightly — but not completely — control network traffic than access-point-based networks. Ad-hoc networks with firewalls are easier to configure than networks that use access points. (Many current access points now provide NAT and firewall support; using NAT effectively creates a firewall.)

Configuring your Ethernet or wireless NIC

To get your Fedora Core computer working on a LAN, you must first configure its network interface card, or NIC. The *NIC* is the device that electronically connects your computer to your LAN. To work with the other computers on your network, your Ethernet or wireless adapter must be given a network address and a few other pieces of information.

We have divided the configuration instructions between Ethernet and wireless NICs. The instructions start by showing you how to start the Fedora Core Network Configuration Utility. We then devote a subsection apiece to describing the particulars of configuring Ethernet and wireless devices. After we cover the device specifics, we discuss general configuration issues. The overall configuration process is outlined in these steps:

1. **Start the Network Configuration Utility.**
2. **Configure your Ethernet or wireless NIC.**
3. **Configure your computer's host name.**
4. **Configure your computer's domain name service.**
5. **Restart your network.**

Wireless network warning

Wi-Fi, the standard for wireless technology, uses an encryption system named *wireless equivalent privacy (WEP)* to provide security. WEP encrypts communication between wireless devices to prevent someone with the right equipment from listening to and using your wireless network. But WEP is flawed and can be broken using widely available tools. If a hacker breaks in to your Wi-Fi network, he can read your communications. But your problems don't end there. Hackers can use your wireless network to connect to the Internet; you give the bad guys a free lunch *and* a launch pad to the Internet.

On the other hand, wireless networking is so useful that many people make accommodations for the risk. The logic? If you assume that your wireless network is open to the public, you can take other precautions to keep your communications private.

You should use OpenSSH, Secure Sockets Layer (SSL), and virtual private networking (VPN) — all bundled with Fedora Core — to conduct all your internal and external communication. Keep in mind that using SSH, SSL, and VPN protects your information, but doesn't prevent someone from connecting to your network. The next generation of wireless security is supposed to fix the WEP weakness. Until the WEP problems are solved, be aware of the risks.

Starting the Network Configuration utility

Follow these steps to start the Network Configuration utility:

1. **Click the GNOME Menu button and choose System Settings⇨Network.**
2. **Enter the** `root` **password if you're prompted to do so.**

   Figure 7-1 shows the initial configuration window; a NIC may or may not be displayed there. The NIC is displayed only if you configured your networking during Fedora Core installation.
3. **Click the New button if no NIC is displayed on the Devices tab (or if you want to configure an additional NIC).**
   - If you're working with an Ethernet device, skip to Step 3 in the "Configuring an Ethernet NIC" section that follows.
   - If you're working with a Wi-Fi NIC, skip to Step 1 in the "Configuring a wireless NIC" section, later in this chapter.

   The Select Device Type window appears.
4. **Select the appropriate type of device from the list and click the Forward button.**

   For example, select Ethernet if you're using that type of interface. If you're using a Wi-Fi device, select Wireless connection.

What you do next depends on whether you're configuring an Ethernet NIC or a wireless NIC. The following two sections are devoted to Ethernet and wireless NICs, respectively.

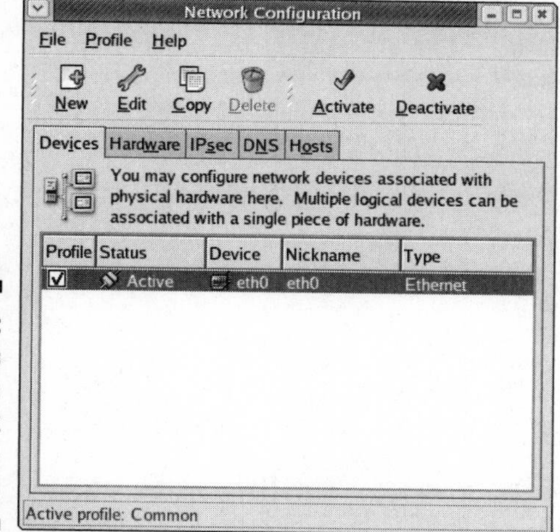

Figure 7-1: The Devices tab in the Network Configuration window.

Configuring an Ethernet NIC

If you're using an Ethernet NIC, follow the steps in this section to configure its parameters (if you're using a wireless NIC, go to the following section):

1. **Follow the steps in the preceding section, "Starting the Network Configuration utility."**

   When you select Ethernet from the drop-down list in Step 4 of the preceding steps, the Select Ethernet Device window appears.

2. **Select the appropriate Ethernet device and click the Forward button.**

   The Network Configuration utility detects all the Ethernet devices attached to your computer. Most PCs have only one Ethernet device, so you shouldn't have to decide which one to select.

   The Configure Network Settings window opens (refer to Figure 7-2).

3. **Configure your TCP/IP address settings.**

   The Network Configuration utility selects DHCP (Dynamic Host Configuration Protocol) as the default method for determining your machine's IP address. (DHCP dynamically assigns an IP address and other parameters to your Ethernet NIC, and you're finished configuring your NIC.) If you're connecting to a network that provides DHCP service, type your computer name in the Hostname (optional) field (for example, **Cancun**), click the Forward button, and go to Step 9.

   If your network doesn't use DHCP, you need to manually configure your IP address. Proceed to Step 4.

Figure 7-2: Entering your static (non-DHCP) IP address settings.

4. **Click the Statically Set IP Addresses radio button.**

   You should ask your friendly local system administrator (unless you're the administrator, in which case you may want to avoid talking to yourself) which system your network uses.

   Life is a bit more complicated if you have both a wireless NIC and an Ethernet NIC on your computer. You can run both devices at once, but the configuration is more difficult. You can solve the problem by clicking the Automatically Obtain IP Address Settings With radio button so the dot disappears. This simple mouse click prevents the Ethernet NIC from starting automatically.

5. **Assign an IP address to your computer by typing it in the Address text box.**

   IP addresses are analogous to street addresses: They provide a number that uniquely distinguishes your machine from all others. Private IP addresses don't require any registration with the powers that be — the InterNIC organization that distributes IP addresses. Private IP addresses aren't routed on the Internet so you can use these on your private network.

   If you're on a network with registered IP addresses, be sure to get an IP address from your system administrator. Otherwise use a private IP addresses. You could use (for example) any Class-C address between `192.168.1.1` and `192.168.254.254` — such as `192.168.1.20` or `192.168.32.5`. Private IP addresses in this range are designated for use by private networks. By design, private IP addresses don't get *routed* (sent from one network to another) through the Internet.

6. **Type** 255.255.255.0 **or the netmask for your IP address in the Subnet Mask text box.**

7. **In the Default Gateway Address text box, type the IP address of the Internet gateway for your LAN.**

   The Internet gateway is the device (router or computer) that connects your network to your ISP and the Internet. Obtain the address from your system administrator if you're at work and have one. If you're a home user, a typical convention is to assign the highest address, 254, of a Class C subnetwork as the gateway. For example, type **192.168.1.254.**

   Your TCP/IP Settings should look similar to the ones in the dialog box shown in Figure 7-2.

8. **Click the Forward button.**

   The Create Ethernet Device dialog box opens, indicating that you have finished the configuration process. The dialog box shows a summary of the information you entered in the preceding steps.

9. **Review the summary and click the Apply button.**

   You return to the Network Configuration window, which now displays the newly configured Ethernet NIC.

10. **Save the new configuration by choosing File⇨Save.**

    A dialog box opens, informing you that your changes have been saved. Click the OK button to continue.

11. **Start the NIC by clicking the Activate button.**

    This step completes your Ethernet NIC configuration.

Your Ethernet NIC is now active. But you still need to configure your domain name service (DNS) if you aren't using DHCP. Proceed to the section "Configuring DNS," a little later in this chapter.

Kernel modules are the Linux equivalent to Microsoft Windows device drivers. Usually, Fedora Core detects your Ethernet adapter and automatically loads the correct module. However, if Fedora Core cannot find your Ethernet adapter, you can try to find the correct one on the supplied list.

Configuring a wireless NIC

This section describes how to configure the parameters for a wireless NIC, also called a Wi-Fi NIC. (Skip this section if you don't have a wireless NIC.)

The following steps describe how to configure your wireless device.

1. **Follow the steps in the section "Starting the Network Configuration utility," earlier in this chapter.**

When you select Wireless from the drop-down list in Step 4 on the earlier list, the Select Wireless Device window appears.

2. **Select the appropriate wireless device.**
3. **Click the Forward button.**

   The Configure Wireless Connection window opens, as shown in Figure 7-3.

4. **Select either Managed or Ad-Hoc from the Mode drop-down list.**

   You use Managed mode when you're using an access point. Use Ad-Hoc mode if you configured a wireless network without an access point.

5. **Type** any **in the ESSID (Network ID) text box if you use an access point. Type the specific ESSID name for an ad-hoc network.**

   All machines connected to an ad-hoc wireless network must share the same ESSID. For example, you may choose the string `mynetwork` as your ESSID. In that case, you must enter **mynetwork** as the ESSID for all machines connected to your ad-hoc network.

6. **Enter the encryption key in the Key text box and then click the Forward button.**

   You should obtain the encryption key from your network administrator. If you have set up your own wireless home network, you can generate the key yourself. An *encryption key,* similar to a password, protects your wireless network from casual eavesdropping. In the Key text box, enter a key no more than 13 characters — for example, **this_is_a_password** uses all 13 of the allowed characters — and the more characters (as a rule), the more effective the encryption key.

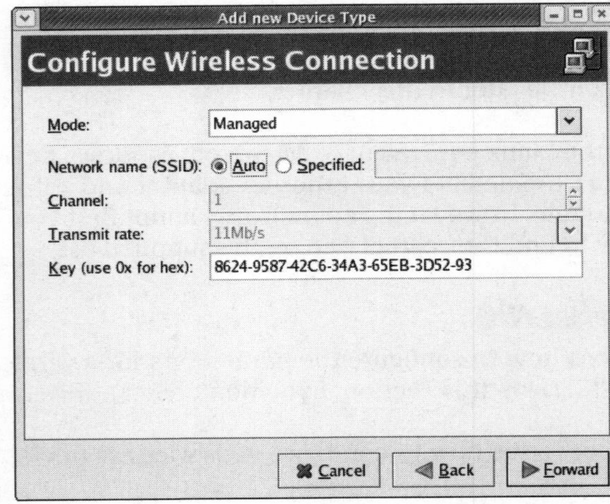

Figure 7-3: The Configure Wireless Connection dialog box.

Encryption keys are 40- or 128-bit binary numbers. They can be represented as text strings (as described in Step 6) or as a string of hexadecimal (hex) numbers. Hex numbers are commonly used in computer science to represent the longer, more ungainly binary numbers. For your purposes, it's sufficient to know that a hex number is represented by 16 characters: 0 through 9 and A through F. For example, hex 0 is represented as decimal 0; hex 3, as decimal 3; and hex 9, as decimal 9. But decimal 10 is hex A, and the decimal 16 hexadecimal value is F. The hexadecimal value of this sample key

```
this-is-a-password
```

is

```
746869735F69735F615F6B6579
```

You can enter the hex value in the Key field by prepending the string `0x` to the key. In the example, you enter this line:

```
0x746869735F69735F615F6B6579
```

After you enter your encryption key and click the Forward button, the Configure Network Settings window opens. The processes of assigning a host name, IP address, netmask, and gateway to your computer are the same as for an Ethernet interface. Consult Steps 3 through 9 in the preceding section, "Configuring an Ethernet NIC," for instructions on how to configure your wireless NIC TCP/IP parameters.

Your wireless NIC configuration is complete. You still need to configure your domain name service (DNS) if you aren't using DHCP. Proceed to the following section if that's the case.

Configuring DNS

If you're using domain-name service, you have to configure your computer to use from one to three DNS servers. You can use your LAN's DNS servers, if they're available. You can also use external DNS servers — regardless of whether any exist on your LAN. To configure your Fedora Core computer to use DNS, follow these steps:

1. **Click the DNS tab in the Network Configuration dialog box, which is where you leave off in the preceding list of steps.**
2. **Type the host name of your computer in the Hostname text box.**

   The host name is any name (for example, Cancun) that you want to use.

   If you're connecting to a network controlled by someone else (for example, at work), check with the system administrator before selecting a host name.
3. **Type the IP address of your DNS server in the Primary DNS text box.**

If your LAN provides a DNS server, you can use it as your primary name server (DNS).

4. **If you have one, type the IP address of your secondary name server in the Secondary DNS text box.**

   Most ISPs provide a backup DNS server address. If your LAN has its own DNS server, you can specify your ISP server as your secondary DNS server if you want.

5. **Type the domain name of your network in the DNS Search Path text box.**

   Figure 7-4 shows a sample DNS configuration screen.

   A *domain name* is a two-part name separated by a period. For example, `paunchy.net` is a domain name, which is the domain name of the sample LAN used in this book. You should replace the `paunchy.net` domain name, of course, with the name of your LAN.

6. **Choose File⇨Quit.**

   The Network Configuration Utility closes. Your settings are saved and are activated the next time you reboot your computer. Proceed to the following section to activate your settings immediately.

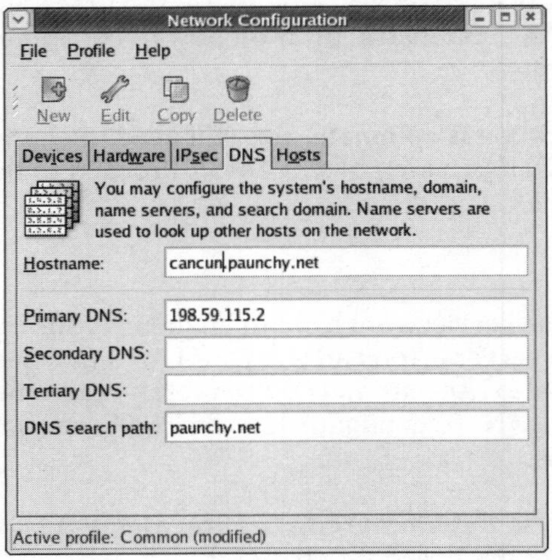

Figure 7-4: A sample DNS configuration.

Manually Starting and Stopping Your Network

Sometimes the Network Configuration utility configures your network stuff, but cannot activate it. Why does that happen? Who knows? It may be because the Network Configuration utility is still relatively young and should become better with age. In the meantime, you can start your networking systems another way, by following these steps:

1. **Click the GNOME Menu button, choose System Settings⇨Server Settings⇨Services, and then enter your** `root` **password if you're prompted.**

   The Service Configuration utility appears. Scroll down until you find the Network option.

2. **Select the Network option and then click the Restart button.**

   The Information window opens and confirms that your network has been restarted. Your new network settings take effect.

3. **If you're using a wireless NIC that doesn't communicate, you may have to restart your PCMCIA system:**

   a. Locate and click the PCMCIA service in the Service Configuration Utility.

   b. Click the Restart button.

   c. Repeat Step 3 to restart your network.

All networking is stopped and then started again.

Alternatively, you can log in as root in a terminal emulator and run this command: `service network restart`. (Or, to stop your network, run `service network stop`.)

Chapter 8

Only You Can Prevent Bad Firewalls

In This Chapter

- Introducing computer security
- Using the Netfilter/iptables firewall system
- Designing and viewing your filtering rules
- Automatically starting your firewall
- Automatically updating your computer software

After connecting to the Internet, you have to protect yourself from the bad guys. The bad guys wear black hats, just like in the movies (as opposed to red fedoras, which are a bit odd but good). You may also have heard them called hackers, crackers, black hats, and so on. Whatever their names and whatever their intentions, the Internet is getting more dangerous every day, so you have to take precautions.

No silver bullet exists when it comes to protecting yourself from computer mischief. You should not rely on any single method, or system, against hackers. The best defense is to create multiple lines of defense that overlap and provide extra protection. That's called defense-in-depth.

The first layer in your defensive shield is your firewall. A *firewall* is a device that enables you to use the Internet (or other network that's connected to it) while blocking the Internet from using you. Firewalls are one-way gates that allow your outgoing network connections while blocking incoming connections.

This chapter describes (not surprisingly) how to build a firewall. First, in case you doubt that you truly need a firewall, we explain why having a firewall is important. Then we introduce you to Netfilter/iptables, a Linux firewall system, and describe how to set up your firewall-filtering rules. After you set up your filters, we describe how to run the firewall automatically.

The firewall described in this chapter is designed to protect a single Fedora Core computer that's connected to the Internet or LAN. The firewall isn't designed to protect an entire LAN. Chapter 15 describes how to modify this firewall to protect your private network.

Understanding Why You Need a Firewall in the First Place

You may think there's safety in numbers — after all, millions of people, businesses, and organizations are connected at any given time to the Internet. What do you, an individual with a simple computer or small private network connected to the Internet, have to be concerned about? The bad guys are usually interested in big money or big publicity. I'm just the little guy and no one is interested in hacking little 'ol me, right?

That assumption sounds reasonable but can led to disaster. Many hackers use tools that automatically scan and attack thousands of computers in almost no time at all. Even a lazy hacker doesn't have to work hard to search large numbers of networks to find and exploit unprotected computers. (Don't forget that Internet worms propagate quickly too.)

Don't risk needlessly getting *owned* — the term used when a hacker breaks into and controls your computer. Fortunately, you can take some reasonable precautions and greatly increase your security. Linux provides effective tools for protecting yourself.

Using a firewall is one simple (but quite effective) way to protect yourself when you connect to the Internet. A firewall allows you to connect to the Internet while blocking unnecessary and unwanted connections from coming in.

Firewalls provide good bang-for-the-buck protection — but they're not the only security measure you should take. For example, locking your doors certainly helps to protect against burglars, but isn't 100-percent effective — they can still break through a window. Your best bet comes from using layers of security, such as locking your windows, using alarms, and keeping tabs on neighborhood activities. The idea is to have each layer reinforce the others. Chapter 17 describes how to add security layers to your computer. Layered security is your best protection.

Building an Effective Firewall

Fedora Core comes bundled with a simple but extremely effective firewall system named Netfilter/iptables. The Netfilter part refers to the firewall system built into the Linux operating system — the kernel, to be exact — and iptables is the interface that controls it. We refer to the overall system as iptables because that's the utility you work with.

The iptables system filters the IP packets that are the backbone of the Internet (IP stands for Internet Protocol). When you're connected to the Internet, all information (graphics and text) that you send and receive is sent in the form of IP packets. All information that enters and leaves your computer via the Internet is packaged in the form of IP packets. You can use iptables to accept or deny IP packets according to their destinations, source addresses, and ports.

Designing filtering rules: Permissive and restrictive methods

Filtering rules are like the bricks (or asbestos, if you prefer) used to build your firewall. Basically, filtering rules determine what network communication can go out of and come into your computer.

When you're designing firewall-filtering rules, you can choose between two philosophies:

- Allow all connections by default and then deny specific access.
- Deny all connections by default and then allow specific access.

If you allow all connections, you start by allowing all communication with your computer and then deny connections one by one. (This method is used by the Fedora Core firewall, which you create during the installation process.) The danger with this method is that you can unintentionally allow dangerous traffic to reach your machine. The alternative method is to start by *denying* all communication and then selectively *allowing* certain traffic. This more restrictive method is, from a security standpoint, the best way to create a firewall because you know exactly what access you're allowing. However, the restrictive method can also create problems; for example, you may unintentionally prevent needed or wanted network traffic from reaching your computer.

We explain how to use the restrictive method, for several reasons:

- **It's the safest method.** The restrictive method is safer because it minimizes all external contact with your Internet-connected computer. For example, it minimizes the information about your firewall that would otherwise be available to hackers through port scanning and other tricks.
- **It's easier to configure.** Because iptables provides stateful filtering, you have only two rules to configure as you create a safe firewall. By contrast, the permissive method requires you to configure numerous individual rules. Extra, unnecessary complexity reduces security.

The iptables system is effective because it uses *stateful filtering:* The firewall can keep track of the state of each network connection. It's a technical way of saying that iptables knows which IP packages are valid and which are not. For example, if you're browsing `www.dummies.com`, iptables keeps track of all packets that belong to that connection. The iptables utility can deny packets that are trying to reach your computer but don't belong to your connection, thus preventing any hackers from sneaking packets through your firewall.

Fedora Core installs an iptables-based firewall by default. The installation system configures a good level of protection during the installation process. You may recall from Chapter 3 that we advise you to use the default firewall configuration. However, the default firewall isn't as secure as we would prefer for connecting to the Internet. Therefore this chapter describes how to construct a more comprehensive and secure firewall.

Ports — the places where information comes into a computer or goes out — are essential to the Internet Protocol. Ports are used to organize the communication between clients and servers. For example, when you click a link on a Web page, your browser communicates with the Web server by using a port. That's a gross simplification, of course, but it describes the basic idea. Suffice to say that ports help control the internal workings of the Internet for such tasks as Web browsing.

Setting Up a Firewall

So you know that you need a firewall and want to create one. What's next? This section explains how to set up an iptables-based firewall, using the restrictive model. When you're done setting up your rules, see the section "Saving your filtering rules to a script," later in this chapter, so you don't have to enter these rules every time you turn on your computer.

In this section, you design an iptables-based firewall that turns off all incoming connections on an Internet connection (modem, LAN, or broadband) and still enables you to establish an outgoing connection to the Internet. You then back off the total restriction of incoming communication to allow incoming Secure Shell connection. (Secure Shell provides encrypted communications.)

Don't execute these instructions from a remote connection! You must run these commands from your computer's console. That is, you must be sitting at your computer and not be working on it from some other location over a network connection. The reason is simple: These firewall rules shut off external network connections before restoring them.

The steps that build your firewall, brick by brick, look like this:

1. **Log in to your computer as** `root` **and then open a GNOME Terminal window (right-click any empty part of the desktop and choose Open Terminal from the menu).**
2. **Type the following line to turn off the default Fedora Core firewall:**

   ```
   service iptables stop
   ```

   This firewall is the one created during the installation process we describe in Chapter 3. The iptables entries remove any existing filtering or Network Address Translation (NAT) rules. NAT rules are frequently used to make your computer appear to be coming from your ISP so that you don't have to register your computer for an official Internet Protocol (IP) address.
3. **Start building your firewall by entering the following rules that by filter out all network communication to, from, and through your computer:**

   ```
   iptables --policy INPUT   DROP
   iptables --policy OUTPUT  DROP
   iptables --policy FORWARD DROP
   ```

   These commands set the default policy of your firewall to not allow any network traffic into (the `INPUT` rule) or out of (the `OUTPUT` rule) any network interface; nor is any traffic allowed to pass between multiple network interfaces (the `FORWARD` rule) if you have them. At this point, you have an extremely safe firewall. So far, however, your computer is useless for network-related tasks. So the next step opens the firewall a little, giving you access to the Internet (or any network you're attached to) in a safe way.
4. **Enter the following rules to allow network traffic to pass through the loopback device:**

   ```
   iptables -A OUTPUT -j ACCEPT -o lo
   iptables -A INPUT -j ACCEPT -i lo
   ```

   Linux computers use a virtual internal network that you connect to via the *loopback interface* (`lo`). The loopback isn't a physical device, but rather is a virtual one. Linux uses `lo` for internal communications.
5. **To allow all outgoing communication from your computer, type the following two commands:**

   ```
   iptables -A OUTPUT -m state
     --state NEW,RELATED,ESTABLISHED -j ACCEPT
   iptables -A INPUT -m state
     --state RELATED,ESTABLISHED -j ACCEPT
   ```

These rules don't specify any particular network interface. However, because the filter is stateful, these rules effectively work on your Ethernet, wireless, or dialup Point-to-Point (PPP) interface.

The first filter rule permits all outgoing communication. The `--state NEW, RELATED, ESTABLISHED` option tells the firewall to allow packets of both new and already established connections to pass. (*Packets* are the basic building block of all network communication.) Also allowed are packets related to existing connections but using different ports, such as FTP data transfers.

The second filter rule controls the packets coming back from outgoing connections. When you connect to a Web site, for example, your browser sends out packets and the Web server responds to them. You can click a button on the Web site, and a new display pops up. Clicking a button sends a packet out, and the Web server sends packets back. You started out with blocking packets from the Internet; this rule creates an exception, allowing packets that belong to an existing connection — such as the one that represents you clicking a button — to return to your computer through the firewall. Note that we don't allow new incoming connections (`--state NEW`) to be established; doing so would defeat the purpose of this firewall.

6. **(Optional) Use the following rule to allow SSH connections to your Linux computer:**

```
iptables -A INPUT -p tcp -m state -state
   NEW,ESTABLISHED -j ACCEPT --dport 22
```

This rule permits SSH connections on Port 22 to enter into your computer.

The OpenSSH server is installed by default during the installation process we describe in Chapter 3. The service is also started automatically.

You can modify this rule to allow other types of incoming connections to your computer. For example, if you want to create a Web server and allow incoming connections to it, run this filter:

```
iptables -A INPUT -p tcp -m state -state
   NEW,ESTABLISHED -j ACCEPT -dport 80
```

Port 80 is used for Web server connections. (Chapter 16 shows you how to create a Web server.)

You have just created a simple, effective firewall that protects your computer from werewolves and hackers. Your firewall remains active until you turn the rules off or reboot your computer. The following section shows you how to display your new firewall rules.

Displaying Your Firewall Rules

After you configure your firewall, you naturally want to verify that the filtering rules are set up correctly. To display the firewall rules, follow these steps:

1. **Open a GNOME Terminal emulator window (right-click any empty part of the GNOME Desktop and select the New Terminal menu).**

   You can also open the GNOME Terminal by clicking the GNOME Menu and selecting choosing Tools➪Terminal.

2. **If you're not already the** `root` **user, enter the** `su -` **command in the GNOME Terminal window.**

3. **Enter the** `root` **password and type the following command to display the firewall rules:**

   ```
   iptables -L -v
   ```

After you complete these steps, you see the firewall-filtering rules displayed in the terminal window (use the verbose *-v* option in the preceding command to display extra information, including the network interfaces — for the sake of brevity, we don't use the option in this example):

```
Chain INPUT (policy DROP)
target prot opt in out source  destination
ACCEPT all --  lo any anywhere anywhere
ACCEPT all --  any any anywhere anywhere
     state RELATED,ESTABLISHED
ACCEPT tcp --  any any anywhere anywhere
     tcp dpt:ssh state NEW,ESTABLISHED

Chain FORWARD (policy DROP)
target  prot opt  in  out source    destination

Chain OUTPUT (policy DROP)
target  prot opt  in  out source    destination
ACCEPT  all  --   any lo  anywhere  anywhere
ACCEPT  all  --   any any anywhere  anywhere
        state NEW,RELATED,ESTABLISHED
```

iptables uses the concept of chains. A *chain* is a list of one or more interrelated rules. Each rule is a link in the chain. iptables has three built-in chains: `INPUT`, `OUTPUT`, and `FORWARD`. You can create custom chains to perform any filtering function you want. (For example, the default Fedora Core firewall filter creates a custom chain, called `RH-Firewall-1-INPUT`.) However, creating custom chains isn't necessary for this firewall, so we use only the built-in chains.

The first *chain,* `INPUT`, filters incoming packets. You can see that the default policy denies all packets. This policy makes for a perfect firewall — nothing can get in. However, the perfect firewall is also useless because your computer cannot see or interact with the network.

You can begin to make the firewall useful by creating a rule to allow all incoming packets on the logical loopback (`lo`) interface; the loopback interface is used for internal communication on your computer. The next rule allows the return packets, `RELATED` and `ESTABLISHED`, from outgoing connections to come back in. The last rule (which is optional) allows the incoming Secure Shell connections to your computer.

The next chain, `FORWARD`, prevents all packets from being forwarded through your Linux computer. Forwarding is necessary only if you use your computer for routing or other advanced networking functions.

The last chain, `OUTPUT`, defines which IP packets are allowed out of your computer. Again, the first rule allows unlimited traffic through the loopback (`lo`) interface. The second and last rule allows all packets to leave your firewall.

The following section describes how to save the rules you just created and displayed — in such a way that they can start automatically.

Firing Up Your Firewall

The preceding section describes how to display your firewall-filtering rules. However, you certainly don't want to manually enter these rules every time you reboot your computer. This section shows you how to automate your firewall. We show you how to make use of the Fedora Core utilities that save the rules you just created and start up the firewall whenever you boot your computer.

These instructions assume that you have configured the firewall as described in the preceding section — and that the configuration is still in effect.

Saving your filtering rules to a script

You need to save your rule set after you have created your firewall. Fedora Core provides a utility for doing just that. The `iptables-save` utility reads your current firewall rules and converts them into script-compatible form. Fedora Core also provides a script to start up your firewall whenever you start your computer. The /etc/init.d/iptables script runs whenever you start your computer and, thus, your firewall is started too. Follow these steps:

1. **Log in as** root **if necessary, and open a GNOME Terminal window (refer to Chapter 4) if necessary.**
2. **Type the following line to save the default Fedora Core firewall configuration:**

```
mv /etc/sysconfig/iptables /etc/sysconfig/iptables.bak
```

3. **Run this command and your firewall rules are saved to a script:**

```
iptables-save > /etc/sysconfig/iptables
```

Turning your firewall off and on

Fedora Core uses the /etc/sysconfig/iptables script to start Netfilter/iptables firewalls. The /etc/init.d/iptables script uses the filtering rules stored in the /etc/sysconfig/iptables file to implement the filtering rules.

You can start the Netfilter/iptables firewall by running this iptables script or by using the service utility:

```
service iptables start
```

You must be logged in as root, of course. Note that you can turn off your firewall by replacing start with stop:

```
service iptables stop
```

You can also use (from the graphical interface) the Fedora Core Service Configuration Utility. These next instructions show you how to use the utility to start or stop your firewall:

1. **Click the GNOME Menu button and choose System Settings⇨Server Settings⇨Services.**

   If you're not logged in as root, the Input window pops up and you're asked to enter the root password.

2. **Enter the** root **password you set during the Fedora Core installation process.**

   The Service Configuration window appears. This window controls all the Linux *daemons* (processes that provide services).

3. **Scroll down the Service Configuration window until you find the `iptables` service.**

   The check mark should be set in the check box.

4. **Click the Restart button in the upper-left corner of the window.**

   You could click the Start button, but we advise you to use the Restart function. The Start and Restart buttons give you the same result, but restarting works if the service is already running. Using the Start function doesn't work if the service is already running.

5. **Click the Stop button to turn off your firewall.**

   After the service restarts, you see a confirmation message.

6. **Click OK.**

   Your firewall is restarted, and you can exit from the Service Configuration window.

You can also prevent the iptables script from being automatically started when you boot the system. Click in the box immediately to the left of the service name to remove the check mark. Click the Save button, and the pointer (`/etc/rc.d/rc5.d/S08iptables`) to the startup script (`/etc/init.d/iptables`) is removed. You can restore the pointer by clicking in the box so the check mark reappears.

Part III

Linux, Huh! What Is It Good For? Absolutely Everything!

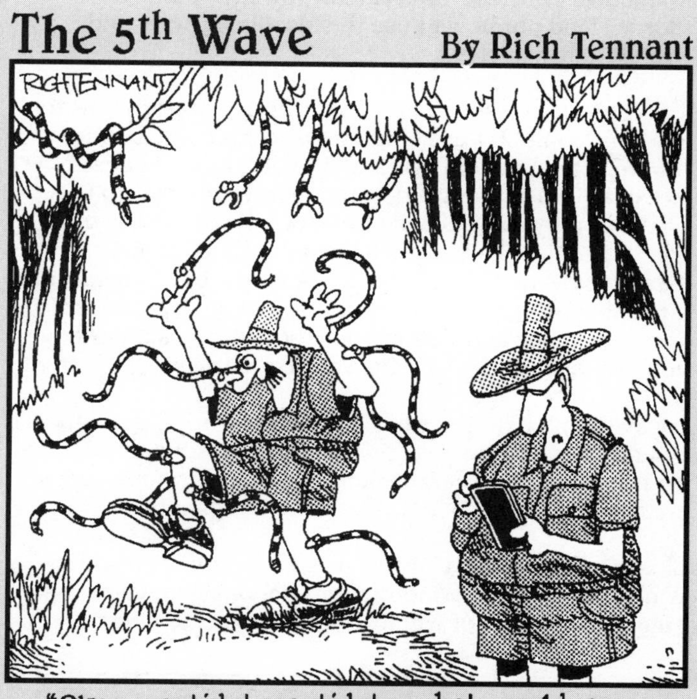

"Okay – antidote, antidote, what would an antidote icon look like? You know, I still haven't got this GNOME desktop the way I want it."

In this part . . .

One thing you can do with your computer is put up your feet and wait for the screensaver to kick in. You can confide to all your friends at the next party you attend that you have a "Fedora Core box." (That should make you wildly popular as they clamor to know when your stock options will mature.) Or you can use your new Fedora Core workstation to (gasp) get things done.

To that end, Chapter 9 introduces the friendly world of the GNOME windows environment. GNOME, a friendly li'l guy who likes to put a friendly face on Linux, can help you set up the "look and feel" of Linux so you feel comfortable and at home. Chapter 10 goes further and introduces cool things you can do with GNOME applications.

In Chapter 11, the fun starts. Can you say, "Par-*tay*"? (Sorry.) Find out how to use the Mozilla browser and Evolution e-mail client.

The fun continues in Chapter 12, where you learn how to use your computer as a multimedia center. It describes how to listen to audio CDs and files. It also introduces how to extract music from and burn music (and data) to CDs. The chapter then proceeds to show how to use the open-source multimedia players Rhythmbox and MPlayer to listen to flowing streams — no, not rivers, but rather, audio streams flowing from the Internet. You can listen to radio and audio clips and watch video too. With this knowledge, you may never have to leave your couch again.

Lucky Chapter 13 describes how to get work done with OpenOffice. Sorry — reality bites, and personal productivity suites (word processors and spreadsheets, for example) are a necessary evil. Gotta make the doughnuts.

Chapter 14 describes how to use the handy open-source Wine system to run Windows applications. Wine opens the humongous world of Windows applications to Linux users.

Chapter 9

Gnowing GNOME

In This Chapter

- Swooping over the X Window System
- Introducing the GNOME graphical environment
- Getting familiar with the GNOME desktop
- Introducing GNOME Menus
- Configuring MIME types
- Leaving your computer

Fedora Core provides two interfaces for you to use: the text-based command-line interface (CLI), described in Chapter 4, and the *graphical* (that is, picture-oriented) X Window System. The command-line interface is similar to the old MS-DOS (Microsoft Disk Operating System) environment; you type commands for the operating system to obey. The X Window System (also known simply as X) provides a graphical point-and-click environment in which most people prefer to work.

Fedora Core provides two desktop environments for you to use: GNOME and KDE (the K Desktop Environment). Both GNOME and KDE run on top of X; each includes a menu system to access utilities, applications, and shortcuts (in the form of icons), as well as numerous other enhancements. Both of these environments make Fedora Core simple and easy to use as a workstation.

GNOME is the default Fedora Core desktop environment. Fedora Core also gives you the option of installing KDE, an excellent system that many people prefer. However, because of the limited space in this book, we discuss only GNOME.

The excellent *Red Hat Fedora Linux 2 All-in-One For Dummies,* written by Naba Barkakati (from Wiley Publishing), describes KDE in more detail.

In this chapter, we introduce X and the basics for working with GNOME. You get a handle on how to work with the GNOME Panel and desktop (the *GNOME Panel* is similar to the taskbar in Windows computers). We show you some simple but effective maneuvers for managing your desktop.

Introducing the X Window System

Fedora Core gives you the option of using the GNOME and KDE desktop environments. GNOME and KDE, however, run on top of X, and X runs on Linux. *X* is the software that provides the low-level graphical bits and pieces that systems like GNOME use. X is the foundation that makes complex systems like GNOME possible.

X is composed of three parts:

- The X server
- Numerous graphics libraries
- A set of X client graphics applications

The *X server* is a program that communicates with the human-interactive hardware on your computer — such as the video card, keyboard, and mouse — acting as the liaison between the hardware and other graphics software. It uses the graphics libraries — software shared by many programs — to work properly with the graphics hardware.

X clients are the graphical programs (such as Mozilla and xclock) that you interact with. X clients display their graphical output through the X server; they also get their keyboard and mouse input through the X server. X clients can be run on the same computer that the X server runs on or across a network to any computer running an X server. For example, by using X, you can run an X client on a computer on the other side of the world and view it on the X server running on your home computer.

Suppose you're logged in remotely to a computer in Australia and you want to see what time it is there. You could run the text-based `date` command (from a CLI) to see the date and time, but that would be boring. Alternatively, you could run the xclock program on the remote machine and see a graphical clock displayed on your local computer. You can then verify that the Aussies use clocks that indeed run clockwise and have 24-hour days.

The X server program, often called simply *X*, isn't part of the operating system, as it is in some other operating systems. Instead, the X server is a *user-level* program — although it's special and complex.

The X Window System provides the foundation for these graphics-based systems:

- **Desktop environment:** A desktop environment is equivalent to a house where X is the foundation. GNOME and KDE are desktop environments that make using your computer easy, providing high-level functions such as menu systems, icons, and backgrounds.

- **Graphical applications:** Fedora Core installs numerous applications, such as games, system-administration utilities, the Mozilla browser, and OpenOffice.org, to provide the functionality that helps you use your computer (and the Internet) for work or play.

Introducing the GNOME Graphical Environment

GNOME stands for GNU Network Object Model Environment. GNU stands for GNU's Not UNIX, an acronym that pretends not to define itself (probably designed by guys who probably never went to the prom but did change the world). If you have trouble remembering acronyms, just think of GNOME as *g*reat graphics for *no* *m*oney, *e*h? However you remember it, GNOME is an open source graphical desktop environment. It provides a platform for completing your everyday tasks, such as word processing and Internet browsing, on your Fedora Core computer.

Log in to your Fedora Core computer and check out the GNOME interface. It should look something like Figure 9-1 and consists of these three major elements:

- **The desktop:** The *desktop* is what you see on your computer screen. It's the space where you do your work, equivalent to — ta-da! — the top of a desk. The desktop comes preconfigured with a neutral background and several icons (which include links to such places as your home directory and the trash bin). Icons are equivalent to the junk you pile on your desk: Some are useful and some aren't.

  When you double-click any of your Desktop icons, a Nautilus window opens and displays the contents of that corresponding object. *Nautilus* is a graphical shell (as opposed to a text-based CLI shell) for working with not only files and directories but also administration utilities and Web pages. See Chapter 10 for more information about Nautilus.

- **The Panel:** The menu bar that runs across the bottom edge of your GNOME screen is the Panel (there's more about the GNOME Panel later in the chapter). You can access every default GNOME and Fedora Core (or properly configured third-party application) from the Panel. The Panel is analogous to the drawers in your desk.

- **Applications:** These elements include user programs, system tools, and GNOME applications. User programs include applications such as Evolution and OpenOffice.org. System applications include the Fedora Core system-administration utilities (such as those for network configuration and user management) and GNOME utilities (such as the Help browser).

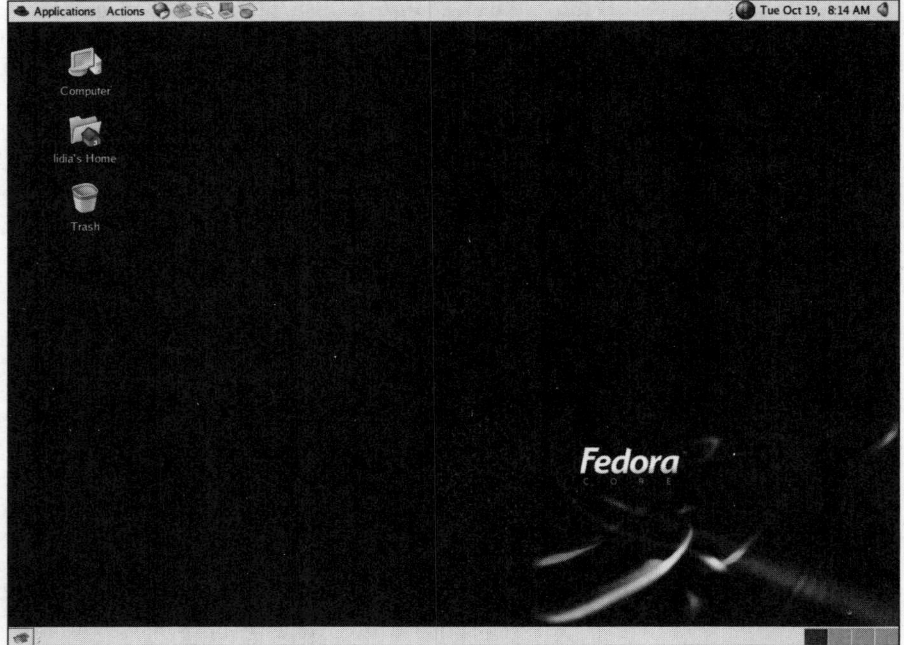

Figure 9-1: The GNOME desktop.

Introducing the GNOME Desktop

GNOME performs all the basic graphical functions you expect from a desktop environment. You can set the background and create icons, for example. This section shows how to perform some basic GNOME desktop maneuvers and configurations. After you master the basics, you can continue to explore on your own.

The default GNOME desktop, as installed by the Fedora Core installation, comes with several elements preinstalled. This section of the chapter takes a quick trip around the desktop.

Introducing the default desktop icons

In the upper-left corner of the desktop are four icons: Computer, your home directory, your hard drive (for instance, idedisk1), and Trash (refer to Figure 9-1). You'll also see an icon for each CD-ROM/DVD that you've inserted and any additional hard drives. The following list describes the function of each standard icon:

- **Computer:** This icon links to your local file system and network shares. Double-clicking the Computer icon opens a window showing four icons: Floppy, CD-ROM, Filesystem, and Network (you won't see the Floppy or CD-ROM icons if you don't have those devices). Double-clicking the Filesystem icon opens a window showing all your `root`-level directories (see Chapter 4) such as `/usr` and `/home`. Opening the Network icon allows you to browse the network file shares on your network. This network provides the same function as Windows Network Neighborhood.
- **Home directory:** This icon, which looks like a folder, represents your home directory. For example, if you create a user account named `lidia`, a directory named `/home/lidia` is created; the icon is labeled `lidia's Home`. When you log in as `lidia`, the home directory icon is linked to that directory. Double-click the home directory (or right-click and choose Open) and a Nautilus window opens, displaying the contents of the home directory.

  Double-click an icon to open the Nautilus window associated with the icon. For example, double-clicking your home directory opens a Nautilus file manager window linked to your home directory. You can also open an icon by right-clicking it and choosing the Open option.
- **idedisk1:** This icon is similar to your Home directory icon, except it shows the root-level view of your hard drive. Instead of showing the contents of `/home/lidia`, it shows / by default.

  Your hard drive icon name will most likely be idedisk1 because most PCs use IDE (Integrated Drive Electronics) hard drives. However, if your computer uses SCSI (Small Computer System Interface) disks, then the icon will be called scsidisk1.
- **Trash icon:** GNOME provides a method you can use to dispose of files and directories via the Trash directory. Click any icon, file, or directory and drag it to the Trash icon. Although Jesse James' Monster Garage-converted minivan trash truck doesn't come for your file, it's placed in the Trash directory. Like the trashcan in your home, the Trash directory sits in your home directory.

  Trashed items aren't really deleted until you right-click the Trash icon and choose Empty trash. You can undelete items by opening the Trash (double-clicking the icon) and then clicking the item and dragging it out onto the desktop or to an open Preferences window.

GNOME provides two methods for running programs from a text-based CLI. You can start a GNOME Terminal emulator window or use the GNOME Run Program function. The former opens a `bash` shell in a Terminal emulator window, from which you can launch applications. The latter opens a window in which you can enter the name of a program to execute. The primary difference between the two systems is that you can interact with an application more when you're using the terminal emulator. The Run Program system allows you to interact with an application only if it creates a GUI.

Changing GNOME's look and feel

GNOME gives you a way to change the look and feel of its elements — that is, their *theme:* the size, shape, texture, and color of the buttons, slides, menus, borders, and other pieces of an open window.

Changing themes

You can change your theme more easily and quickly than a politician after an election by choosing Preferences⇨Theme from the GNOME menu; alternatively, you can open the Start Here icon and select Preferences in the window that opens. Double-click the Theme icon when the Preferences window opens.

When the Theme Preferences window opens, the Application tab is activated by default. You can select any theme and all your open windows immediately adopt it. The application theme changes the tint and texture applied to each window. For example, selecting the Metal theme gives your windows a brushed surface appearance.

Click the Window Border tab. Click any of the themes and your window borders change. Window *borders* consist of the tint and texture of the strip that surrounds each window and the buttons on the strip.

Keep selecting different themes until you find one you like. Click the Close button when you're finished.

Changing desktop backgrounds

You can also alter the image that's displayed on your desktop. The image can be a picture, a pattern, or solid colors. Change the desktop to find one you like by right-clicking any blank (uncluttered) section of the desktop. Choose Change Desktop Background from the menu and the Background Preferences window opens. Select an image by clicking the Picture section or one of its variations. The Please Select an Image window opens. You can select any listed image or search for another image on your disk. Alternatively, you can select a solid color by clicking the No Picture button.

Open the Background Style menu and select either a solid color or a set of colors that change on the vertical or horizontal axis. You can then change the color (solid or gradient) by clicking the Color button. Select your color from the Pick a Color window. Repeat the process for the other color and you get a screen full of colors.

Right-clicking anywhere on a blank section of the desktop and then choosing Use Default Background resets the background. The default background is reactivated.

Toiling in your workplace

After using GNOME for a while, you find that as you start more and more applications, you create lots and lots of windows on the screen. You may even lose windows behind other windows. You start to suspect you'll have to strap together several monitors so you can display all the windows at once.

Monitors and flat panels are either heavy or expensive or both, so you're probably stuck using a single monitor. But you don't have to be stuck with one *screen.* GNOME lets you spread your work across multiple virtual monitors.

Imagine that you have a large GNOME desktop spread equally across four monitors. Life would be good if you could open windows on any of the monitors. You would have lots of real estate to spread out on.

However, because you probably don't *have* four monitors, GNOME subdivides the one you have into four virtual monitors called *workspaces.* Each workspace is equivalent to a real monitor, and you can spread out your work across it. The only limitation is that you can view only one workspace at a time.

Trading places on your Workspace Switcher

Switching between workspaces is easy. GNOME provides a utility, the Workspace Switcher, to select any workspace. The Workspace Switcher is on the GNOME Panel.

You use the GNOME Workspace Switcher to access each workspace. The Workspace Switcher is divided into four quadrants. Clicking any quadrant displays the corresponding desktop. Click the lower-right one (for example) and you enter that workspace.

You can force a window into any or all workspaces. Click the downward-facing arrow in the upper-left corner of a window. The menu that opens provides all the expected functions that close, minimize, maximize, and resize the window. However, toward the bottom of the menu are options for placing the window in any of the remaining three workspaces — or you can put the window in all the workspaces. You may want, for example, to put an application like Mozilla in all workspaces in order to use it no matter what you're doing.

Using GNOME Windows

Before you can do anything to a window, you have to get its attention. When you have a window's attention, it has *focus.* Depending on how you have set up GNOME, you can give a window focus with GNOME in several ways:

- Click the window's minimized icon on the GNOME Panel.
- Click the window's title bar, at the top of the window.
- Click a part of the window itself, which typically also makes the window the topmost one. This method is the default.

In this book, we stick with the Fedora Core and GNOME default setting that gives focus to a window when you click it.

Moving windows

To move a window, click anywhere on the window's title bar with the left mouse button (and hold it down). As long as you continue to hold down that button, the window moves anywhere that you move your mouse. Release the button and the window stays there.

Resizing windows

Sometimes a window is a little too big or a little too small, and life would be much easier if you could just nudge that window into shape. To do just that, position the mouse cursor on any border of the window. Click and drag the window's outline to the size you want. Release the mouse button and the window takes the new size.

Minimizing windows

Now that you have put lots of windows on the screen, how can you get rid of a few or all of them? You can *minimize* (or *iconify* — what a concept) a window by clicking the bold, underscored button toward the upper-right corner, which removes the window from the desktop and places it in a storage area of the GNOME Panel. If you're in a particularly devilish mood, you can be more drastic and *close* a window. You can see the icon on the GNOME Panel along the lower, central edge of the screen.

Here are a few ways to get rid of a window, starting with the least drastic and escalating to outright window death:

- Take advantage of any exit buttons or menu options that the window (or application in the window) gives you. For example, many applications allow you to choose File➪Exit to close the application.
- Click the X button in the upper-right corner of the window's title bar to close the window.
- Click the upper-left corner of the window (or right-click the title bar) and choose the Close option from the menu that opens.

You can return a minimized window to the desktop by clicking the icon that corresponds to the window on the GNOME Panel.

Maximizing windows

To make a window fill the entire screen, click the Maximize button in the upper-right corner of the window. Check out the buttons to the right of the title bar in a typical window: The Maximize button is the one in the middle; it looks like a square and works like the Cascade button in Windows.

Making GNOME Desktop Icons

You can create an icon on your desktop for any application on the GNOME menu. Just click the GNOME Menu button, find the menu item for the application you want an icon for, and then click the application's icon and continue to hold the mouse button. While holding the mouse button, drag the cursor to any open area on the GNOME desktop. Release the mouse button and an icon for that application is placed on the GNOME Desktop. You can then start the application by double-clicking the icon on the desktop.

With GNOME, you can enhance icons with *emblems* — additional information about what an icon is supposed to do. You can assign an emblem by right-clicking an icon and choosing Properties. The Properties window opens. Click the Emblems tab and select one of the emblems. For example, if you select the Cool emblem, a pair of Wayfarer sunglasses is displayed with the icon on the desktop — cool.

Another cool GNOME icon feature is the ability to stretch an icon's boundaries. Right-click an icon and choose Stretch. A dashed line and four square buttons bracket the icon. Click any button and you can stretch the icon image as much as you want.

Introducing the GNOME Panel

The GNOME *Panel* is the menu bar along the bottom of the desktop. The GNOME Panel, similar to the taskbar in Windows, provides a location to place common menus and applets for easy opening or viewing. The GNOME Panel also gives you a view of the virtual desktop and enables you to keep track of minimized windows.

By default, Fedora Core places icons on the GNOME Panel for accessing the GNOME menu, Mozilla, Evolution, OpenOffice (Writer, Impress, and Calc), a printer, the time, the up2date applet, and the GNOME Workspace Switcher. You can start any of these programs and utilities or use the Switcher by clicking its icon.

The most important element on the GNOME Panel is the GNOME Menu button on the far left side, which you use to access all standard GNOME applications and configuration tools. The GNOME Menu button, which looks amazingly similar to a red fedora, is in the lower-left corner of the screen. You can choose from any of the menus that are displayed when you click the GNOME Menu button. For example, the System Settings and System Tools menus contain many of the Fedora Core utilities you can use to administer your Fedora Core computer. The Sound & Video menu provides access to multimedia programs, and the Graphics menu provides access to applications that manipulate graphics. You get the idea.

You can right-click on any GNOME Panel icon to remove it, move it, lock it in place or change its launcher's properties. Changing the icon launcher's properties allows you to change the icon name, comment, command, type or icon graphics.

You can add icons to the GNOME Panel by right-clicking on any unused portion of the GNOME Panel and selecting Add to Panel... and then selecting the icon from the Add to Bottom Panel menu window. For instance, select Add to Panel... and the Add to Bottom Panel window opens. Select the Application Launcher option and then click the Forward button. Click on the Internet option, select Mozilla and click the Add button. The Mozilla blue globe and mouse icon is added to the GNOME Panel. Another interesting function of the GNOME Panel menu is the Custom Application Launcher utility. Open the Add to Bottom Panel window again. Select the Custom Application Launcher option and click the Add button. The Create Launcher Applet window opens. By entering the name and pathname of an application in the appropriate text boxes, you can add a new applet to the GNOME Panel that *launches* that application.

Give it a try. For example, if you frequently log into another computer using SSH, you can add a custom icon that simplifies the task as follows:

1. **Open the Create Launcher dialog window.**
2. **Add the name of the icon, for instance,** `SSH to mybox`**; you can optionally enter a generic name and comments.**
3. **Next, enter the command that the icon will launch:**

```
/usr/bin/ssh mybox
```

4. **In this case, we want to run this command in a terminal window, so click the Run in terminal button.**
5. **Optionally, click the No Icon button and select an image from the pages of icon images. For instance, we scrolled down and selected the red apple.**
6. **Click the OK button and your icon is born.**

Figure 9-2 shows the new icon.

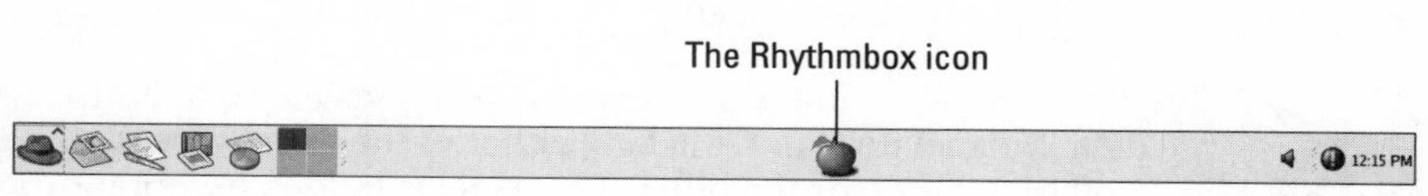

Figure 9-2: The GNOME Panel launcher applet is born.

After you finish editing the Create Launcher Applet window, click OK. The icon is added to your Panel. You can create a launcher for any application on your Fedora Core computer in the same way.

GNOME provides a file-searching utility, named Search Tool. Click the GNOME Menu button and choose Search for Files..., and the Search Tool opens. Enter the name of a file you want to find and click the Find button. Click the Advanced tab and you can conduct a more finely tuned file search.

Adding and Deleting Panels

You're not limited to the default GNOME Panel; you can create additional panels at will. Right-click anywhere on an unused portion of the GNOME Panel and choose New Panel.

The new panel is blank and doesn't contain any icons, like the default GNOME Panel does. The new panel does have a basic menu you can use to populate it with icons and other menus. Right-click the new panel and a submenu opens. You can use the Add to Panel menu to configure the new panel. For example, choose Accessories⇨Clock and a digital clock is added to the panel. Or you can click Amusements⇨Geyes. Keep adding icons until you're satisfied with the new system.

If the screen starts to look too cluttered, you can remove any panel you create — but you can't remove the default GNOME Panel. The process is simple: Right-click any unused section of the panel and choose Delete This Panel. Click the Delete button in the Delete Panel window that opens, and the panel is "depaneled."

You can make any panel hide when it's not in use. Right-click any unused section of the panel, choose Properties from the pop-up menu, and the Panel Properties window opens. Select the Autohide option and click the Close button. The panel disappears off the edge of the screen until you move the mouse cursor back to that edge. The panel then reappears.

Every new panel contains arrows at each end, called Hide buttons; the original default Panel does not. Clicking either of the arrows forces the panel to slide off to one side or the other. The panel is hidden except for those same arrows. Clicking the arrow uncovers the hidden panel.

Introducing GNOME Menus

You can access most Fedora Core and GNOME applications and utilities via the GNOME Menu. Individual applications are listed in Chapter 10 but the various menu categories listed are as follows:

- **Accessories:** Useful-but-extra applications that don't belong to any groups on this list are labeled as accessories. Applications such as the GNOME calculator, a text editor, and a dictionary are placed in this category. Just enter a word and its definition is displayed.
- **File Browser:** This utility allows you to browse Windows and Linux (via Samba) network file systems.
- **Games:** Because Linux was initially built to run services, it may not come to mind first as catering to game players. But it has lots of games. Open the Games icon and you see many of them. You can waste your life with Linux just as easily as with Windows! Ha!
- **Graphics:** You can view and manipulate images with several graphics utilities. Click the GNOME Menu and then the Graphics menu and you can run applications like The GIMP (an excellent tool for working with and editing images). You can use the Scanning tool to scan images into

the computer via a scanner, and use the digital-camera tool to upload pictures from your camera.

- **Help:** You can access a Nautilus window that displays GNOME help information.
- **Internet:** The new Fedora Core default e-mail client Evolution is in this folder. You also find the graphical chat application, Instant Messenger, here.
- **Network Servers:** You can view Samba servers on your network. The Network Servers option provides the same function as Microsoft Network Neighborhood does.
- **Office:** The open-source OpenOffice applications are stored in this folder. OpenOffice provides a word processor, spreadsheet, presentation manager, and drawing tool, all of which you access here. You can also find the OpenOffice repair and printer configuration utilities here. (Icons are automatically placed on the GNOME Panel.)
- **Preferences:** Choosing this menu option opens the same window as double-clicking the GNOME Desktop Start Here icon and selecting the Preferences icon.
- **Programming:** Linux provides a good programming environment. Fedora Core provides links, via this menu, to several programming utilities, such as Emacs, that many people use for editing source code.
- **Recent Documents:** Choosing this option opens a submenu of the most recent documents you have edited. Click any document to start editing it again.
- **Run Applications:** You can use this option to run an application manually. Just click the option and enter your command in the dialog box that opens. In effect, Run Applications is a shortcut around using the GNOME Terminal.
- **Sound and Video:** Fun stuff is stored here, such as the Rhythmbox, CD player, and XMMS audio applications. You also find in this folder more mundane items, such as the volume control and volume monitor utilities.
- **System Settings:** Fedora Core places many of its fabulous configuration utilities here. For example, the Fedora Core Network Configuration, X configuration, and sound-card-detection utilities are here. This menu also includes the Server Settings menu, which you can control various daemons.
- **System Tools:** You can access more of the Fedora Core system-administration utilities from this folder. The Preferences window also lets you configure items other than screensavers-with-maniacal-rantings. (We leave it to you to explore the wonderful world of setting your keyboard bell and other such items.)
- **Search for Files:** This function helps you search for files and directories on your computer. Selecting this function opens a window in which you can enter filenames to search for.

Configuring GNOME MIME Types

You can modify the look and feel of your desktop by using an assortment of GNOME configuration utilities. Double-click the Start Here icon on the desktop. When the window opens, double-click the Preferences icon. (You can access the same functions by clicking the GNOME Menu button and then opening the Preferences menu. A submenu opens, showing the same options as in the Preferences window.)

The following example shows how to associate the Ogg MIME type with the Rhythmbox player:

1. **Double-click the File types and programs icon in the Preferences window.**

   The File Types and Programs dialog box is displayed.

2. **Choose Audio⇨OGG audio and click the Edit button.**

   The Edit file type window opens. The Edit File Type window shows that Ogg audio files belong to the `application/x-ogg` MIME type. The window also shows that Ogg audio files use `.ogg` file suffixes.

3. **Click the Default action pull-down menu and choose Music Player.**
4. **Click the OK button and Rhythmbox ready to play Ogg files.**

The Preferences window also lets you configure items other than screen savers with maniacal rantings. We leave it to you to explore the wonderful world of setting your keyboard bell and other items.

Goodnight GNOME

You have two options if you don't want to turn your computer off but don't want to leave it open to anyone just walking by: locking the GNOME Desktop and logging out.

The following sections describe the processes.

Locking your computer

Locking your screen is one of the best security features you can use. To lock your screen, click the GNOME Menu button and choose Lock Screen. Your screen locks up and you must enter your password to get back in. Locking your screen is a good idea when you're going to be away from it for even a minute or two.

You can also configure GNOME to automatically lock your screen after a set time delay. This is useful if you're using your Fedora Core computer in a work environment. Setting the screen lock ensures that you won't leave your computer open indefinitely. Use the following instructions to set your screen lock:

1. **Click the GNOME Menu and select Preferences⇨Screensaver.**

   The Screensaver Preferences window opens.

2. **Click the Lock Screen After button.**
3. **Click the up or down arrows to select the time after which the screen lock takes affect.**

   A setting of ten to fifteen minutes is a good compromise.

4. **Click the Close button.**

Going home for the night

After you have finished for the day and want to go home (or just upstairs), you need to log out. Click the GNOME Menu button and choose Log Out. A dialog box labeled `Are you sure you want to log out?` opens. Click the OK button and — you guessed it — you log out. You also have the options to shut down or reboot your computer.

GNOME configures a random screensaver by default. You can select a single screen saver as follows:

1. **Click the GNOME Menu button and choosing Preferences⇨Screensaver.**

   The Screensaver Preferences window opens.

2. **Click the Mode: pull-down menu and select Only One Screen Saver.**
3. **Scroll up and down until you find a screensaver you like.**

   For example, you can switch from the default random screensaver to the Xjack screensaver (because all work and no play makes Xjack a dull Xboy). It's not a bad selection for those long winters spent at peaceful resorts with plenty of time to write Linux books!

4. **Click the Close button.**

eXterminating X

When you can't get your applications to respond to you, you can simply stop X, which kills all programs running under it. To do so, press the Ctrl+Alt+ Backspace keys all at once. If you started X manually, you can then log out of the account. If X is started automatically at boot time (as we assume in this book), you see the X login screen and you can log back in.

Chapter 10

Gnowing More Applications

In This Chapter

- Introducing Nautilus, the GNOME file manager
- Introducing Fedora Core/GNOME Applications

Many applications help make your Fedora Core computer useful. In this chapter, you find out how to use Nautilus, one of the central GNOME applications. Nautilus manages files and other objects. We also introduce all of the Linux and GNOME applications that are installed by default.

Navigating with Nautilus File and Internet Integration Manager

Being the boss doesn't necessarily make you a bad person. Does it? It's just a job. Right? Well, that little GNOME guy is a good worker, doesn't get paid much, and likes to get bossed around. Just press a key here and click a button there, and you can boss him around like any worthy pointy-headed *Dilbert* manager. GNOME even comes with its own file and integration manager that saves you work and makes time for those long lunches.

Nautilus is the graphical navigation system that GNOME uses to get you around your files and your network. Nautilus follows in the tradition of all good file managers, by showing you a display of the files and directories on your computer. You can copy, move, delete, and execute files by pointing and clicking — and it's a snap (okay, a click) to create directories and view file details. Nautilus even goes a step further: You can use it to configure your GNOME desktop. And that's not all! Nautilus can also navigate the Internet, access multimedia applications, and slice and dice! Not a bad deal, considering that it works for free.

Waking up Nautilus

Fedora Core installs a GNOME Desktop Nautilus icon that points to your home directory. The icon is in the upper, left corner of your Desktop. Double-click the icon and a Nautilus window opens, as shown in Figure 10-1. The window shows the contents of your home directory.

You see the Nautilus menu displayed along the top of the window. It follows a familiar menu format (File and Edit, for example) and does all the things you would expect a file manager menu to do.

Click View⇨Reload to update Nautilus's view of the current directory. The Reload function is useful if you create a new file. The file doesn't show up in the file manager until you move to another directory and return, or else reload.

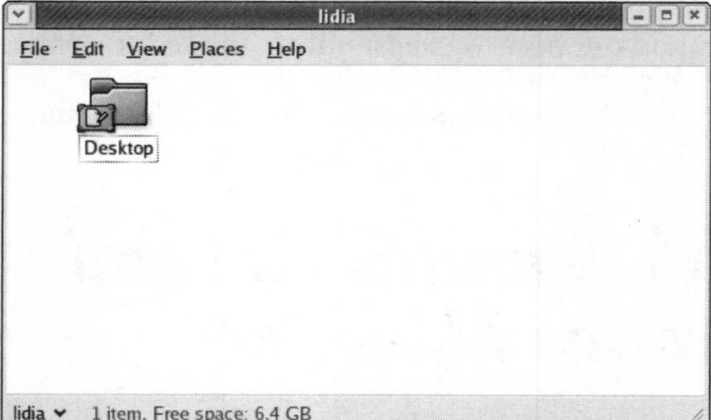

Figure 10-1: The Nautilus file manager.

Moving files and directories

Open a Nautilus window of the directory where your target object (file or directory) lives. Open another window for the destination directory. Moving a file or directory is as simple as clicking and dragging the target object from its current location to its destination directory. Release the button and you have moved your file or directory.

You can also move multiple files by following these steps:

1. **Click and drag the mouse cursor over the files you want to move.**

   The mouse cursor creates a rectangular outline and highlights all files within that box.

2. **Next, click anywhere within the highlighted box and drag the mouse cursor to the directory you want.**

3. **Release the mouse button and the files move to the specified directory.**

Copying files and directories

Copying a file or directory is a bit more complicated than moving one. You can't just simply click and drag an icon someplace. Follow these steps:

1. **Right-click the file or directory icon you want to copy and choose Copy from the menu that opens.**
2. **Enter the directory you want to copy to by double-clicking its icon.**
3. **When the directory opens, right-click anywhere on the background and choose the Paste Files option.**

   The file or directory is copied to the new location.

You can copy multiple files and directories in the same manner as you copied individual ones.

1. **Click and drag the mouse cursor to trace a box around the files or directories you want to copy.**
2. **Right-click any of the blue highlighted icon names (but not the white space around the icons and names) and choose the Copy option.**
3. **Double-click the directory you want to copy to, right-click the background, and choose Paste Files.**
4. **Release the mouse button and the files are copied to the specified directory.**

Deleting files and directories

Deleting files and directories is much the same process as copying them. You right-click the file or directory icon you want and then choose Move to Trash from the menu that opens. The file or directory is moved to the Trash directory.

"Trashed" files and directories aren't immediately deleted. When you use the Move to Trash option to delete a file, for example, the file is moved to the Trash folder. Open the Trash directory by clicking its icon and then right-clicking the file or directory to delete. Choose the Delete from Trash option. The Delete From Trash? warning window opens and prompts you to confirm the deletion. Click the Delete key and the file is erased. Alternatively, erase all files in the Trash by opening the Trash icon, clicking File menu and selecting Empty Trash.

If you have too many files and directories, you can delete a bunch of them. Again, you trace a box by clicking and dragging the mouse cursor. Right-click the blue highlighted icons or icon names (but not the white space around the icon and name). The files or directories are moved to the Trash directory.

Creating files and directories

Right-click anywhere in a Nautilus window and select Create Folder. A new folder (*directory* in Linux terms) is created and named untitled folder. Right-click the new folder, select Rename, and enter any name you want for the directory.

To create a file, right-click in the Nautilus window and select Create Document⇨Empty File. The new file icon appears and you can type in its name.

Viewing files and directories

Files and directories are displayed on-screen as icons by default. The only information an icon shows is the name and whether an item is a file or directory. You can display files and directories as a list by choosing View⇨View as List.

This list describes the differences between views:

- **View as Catalog:** Selecting this option displays thumbnail images of any graphical images stored in the current folder. This option isn't active when no images are stored in the current folder.
- **View as Icons:** The default display option; shows the icon and indicates whether an item is a file or directory. Regular file icons take several forms, but text and configuration files look like pieces of paper with a corner folded. Files containing specific types of data have small subicons overlaid on the file icon. For example, PDF files have a PDF subicon. Links, devices, and other objects take other forms. Directories take the form of a partially open manila folder. Icons are evenly placed across the entire File Manager screen. Icons tend to make distinguishing files and directories easier, but take up more space on-screen.
- **View as List:** Displays the size and time stamp of each file and directory in addition to their names.

You can use Nautilus to create some shortcut icons on your desktop that point to files or applications. In Nautilus, just click and drag any file or application to any blank part of the desktop and then release the mouse button. An icon is placed on the desktop. You can then start the application by double-clicking its icon. If the icon points to a data file (a text file, for example) and Nautilus knows how to handle its MIME type, Nautilus launches the appropriate application to open the file. Otherwise Nautilus prompts you to specify which application to use to open it.

Nautilus is programmed to recognize numerous Multipurpose Internet Mail Extensions (MIME) types, and they define which type of information a file stores — in other words, MIME keeps its own Rolodex, of sorts. Each MIME type is associated with certain file extensions. For example, when you double-click a `.doc` file, Nautilus recognizes that the `.doc` file suffix corresponds to a Word document MIME type and opens the OpenOffice word processor (as described in Chapter 13), which loads the `.doc` file.

Running programs

Nautilus is such a hard worker that it happily launches commands for you. You simply right-click the icon you want to run, which opens a submenu, and then you choose Open. For example, if you click the xclock icon in the `/usr/bin/X11` directory, xclock appears on your desktop. (Double-clicking the icon performs the same function.)

Managers are generally not very smart. But Nautilus is smarter than the average bear, and it knows what to do when it encounters various file types. If you open a non-executable file, such as a PDF file, File Manager knows which program to use in order to view it.

Introducing Fedora Core/GNOME Applications

Numerous applications are installed during the installation process described in Chapter 3. The following sections list each installed application and a short description of their function. Each section corresponds to the submenu you see when you click the GNOME Menu.

Accessories

You'll find miscellaneous applications in this submenu. The following list provides a short description of each application.

- **Calculator.** This is the Gcalctool application. Gcalctool provides three calculator modes: basic, financial, and scientific. It also includes ten storage registers.
- **Dictionary.** This is a network-based client application that looks up word spelling and definition via the MIT dictionary server — dict.org.
- **Text editor.** Gedit provides a simple, effective text editor.

Games

Okay, Linux was initially oriented toward running services, so it may not seem ideal for game players. But indeed, it has lots of games. Open the Games icon and you see many of them. You'll find that you can waste your life with Linux just as easily as with Windows! Ha!

The following list gives a short description of each game:

- **AisleRiot Solitaire.** This game allows you to play several versions of Solitaire.
- **Ataxx.** This is a board game for two players; you play against the computer. The object is to flip discs until your opponent doesn't have any more discs. This game is similar to Reversi.
- **Blackjack.** This game, you guessed it, allows you to play Blackjack.
- **BZFlag.** You get to shoot tanks! Ah, to be 13 again.
- **Five or more.** Theoretically have fun by removing colored balls.
- **Four-in-a-row.** You have to create a line of four marbles. Your opponent, real or computer, has to do the same. First line wins.
- **Freecell Solitaire.** This is another Solitaire game.
- **FreeCiv client and server.** Figure a strategy to destroy other civilizations. You must start the FreeCiv server before starting the game by running a FreeCiv client.
- **Iagno.** This is another disc-flipping game similar to Ataxx.
- **Klotski.** Move a patterned block to accomplish some objective. If you have a lot of time on your hands, you may find this game interesting.
- **Maelstrom.** You fly your spaceship through an asteroid belt to win this game.
- **Mahjongg.** This is a single-player version of the classic Mahjongg Eastern tile game.
- **Mines.** In this game, you need to clear space through a minefield.
- **Nibbles.** You control a snake and try to get it to eat diamonds.
- **Robots.** There are robots out there whose goal is to kill you. Your goal is to — yep, you guessed it — avoid death.
- **Same GNOME.** You get a window full of balls. You must remove as many balls as efficiently as possible.
- **Stones.** In this arcade game, you must pick up as many stones (they're gems) as possible while avoiding falling stones.
- **Tali.** In this game, you roll dice and "create" a poker-like hand.

- **Tetravex.** You must solve a puzzle in this game.
- **Tux Racer.** This is actually a fun and popular game. Tux Racer is actually Tux the Linux Penguin who races down snow-covered mountains.

Graphics

You can view and manipulate graphical images with several utilities. Click the GNOME Menu and then the Graphics menu and you can run applications like The GIMP (an excellent tool for working with and editing images). You can use the Scanning tool to scan images on a scanner and use the digital camera tool to upload pictures from your camera.

- **GIMP Image Viewer.** The GIMP (GNU Image Manipulation Program) is a powerful image program that opens, displays, and manipulates graphical files of numerous formats. There are far too many manipulation functions to list here.
- **PDF Viewer.** The GNOME PDF Viewer opens and displays Portable Document Format (PDF) files.
- **Photo Tool.** This application helps you to download and store photographs from your digital camera.
- **PostScript Viewer.** The Gnome Ghostview displays Postscript files.

Help

This application provides a Nautilus window that contains links to information about the GNOME desktop, applications, and development tools, as well as general and system-info topics.

Internet

Evolution is the new Fedora Core default e-mail client, which is found in this submenu. You also find Mozilla and some other Internet applications here.

- **Evolution Email.** Selecting this menu option starts the Evolution e-mail client. See Chapter 11 for more information on this application.
- **Gaim Internet Messenger.** This is an instant-messaging client. You can use this application to communicate with other instant messengers that use AIM, ICQ, Yahoo!, MSN, Jabber, IRC, Napster, Gadu-Gadu and Zephyr.
- **IM.** This chat client can communicate using several protocols.

- **IRC.** This option starts X-Chat, which is an Internet Relay Chat (IRC) application. With X-Chat you can communicate over numerous IRC networks.
- **Mozilla.** This is a powerful open source web browser. It is the standard of the Linux world.
- **Thunderbird Email.** This is a new e-mail client that is fast and easy to use.
- **Video Conferencing.** GnomeMeeting provides an audio/video conferencing system.
- **Web Browser.** You access either of the two browsers (Epiphany and Mozilla) installed by Fedora Core 3. Epiphany is a GNOME file system browser and is the default. See Chapter 11 for more details.

Office

The open-source OpenOffice.org applications are stored in this submenu. OpenOffice.org provides a word processor, spreadsheet, presentation manager, and drawing tool, all of which you access here (see Chapter 13 for more on OpenOffice). You can also find a diagramming utility here. (The OpenOffice.org icons are also placed on the GNOME Panel by default.)

- **Dia Diagrams.** This is a diagramming program.
- **Evolution.** This is an organizer that provides an e-mail client, calendar, task manager and PDA synchronizer. The e-mail client part is described in Chapter 11.
- **OpenOffice.org Calc.** This is a spreadsheet application capable of reading and writing Excel documents.
- **OpenOffice.org Draw.** This is a drawing program. You draw stuff with it.
- **OpenOffice.org Impress.** This program is similar to PowerPoint. It can read and write PowerPoint slides.
- **OpenOffice.org Math.** You can create mathematical formulas with this application.
- **OpenOffice.org Writer.** This is a full-function word processor capable of reading and writing Word documents. For example, this book was written with OpenOffice.org Writer.
- **Project Planner.** This application helps you to schedule stuff.

Programming

Fedora Core provides a good programming environment. Fedora Core provides links, via this menu, to several programming utilities, such as Emacs, that many people use for editing source code.

- **Bug Report Tool.** Bug Buddy helps you report problems to the GNOME developers.
- **DevHelp.** This program provides an all-in-one reference for numerous GNOME-related manuals. It also provides a search engine.
- **Glade Interface Designer.** This application helps programmers design and create graphical user interfaces.
- **Memory Profiler.** Programmers often encounter the problem of memory leakage. This program helps developers identify and eliminate memory problems.

Sound and Video

Some fun stuff is stored here. You can access applications such as the Rhythmbox, CD player, a music ripper, and other audio applications. In this folder you also find more mundane items, such as the volume control and volume monitor utilities. See Chapter 12 for more details.

- **CD Player.** You can play music CDs with this application.
- **Helix Media Player.** An open source program that plays Ogg formatted files and audio streams.
- **K3b.** This application copies, erases and burns both CD-ROMs and DVDs.
- **Music Player.** This is Rhythmbox, which plays Ogg formatted files and Internet streams.
- **Sound Juicer CD Ripper.** This application allows you to extract music tracks from your CDs.
- **Sound Recorder.** You can record audio with this program.
- **Volume Control.** This application allows you to control numerous volume controls.

System Settings

The applications contained in this submenu provide system administration functions. Please see appendix A for more details.

System Tools

The applications contained in this submenu provide system-administration functions. Please see Appendix A for more details.

Chapter 11

Surfin' the Net and Using E-Mail

In This Chapter

- Brushing up on Web history
- Using Mozilla to surf the Web
- Getting extra help from plug-ins
- Keeping your passwords safe
- Getting your e-mail with Evolution

In this chapter, we introduce the open-source Mozilla Web browser and Evolution e-mail client. Mozilla provides all the capabilities of other popular browsers. We show you how to set up Mozilla for your Fedora Core computer so you can surf the Net. You can use your computer as a multimedia device. After you start working with Mozilla, we describe how to use Evolution as your e-mail system.

Our goal in this chapter is to introduce the basic Mozilla and Evolution features. However, we want you to know that both systems can do far more than we describe in this chapter. For more information about Mozilla and Evolution, check out the features available on the Help menu, such as the Reference Library or Help contents.

Making the World Wide Web Possible

Once upon a time, a company named Netscape created a browser to surf the Internet. The browser was originally named Navigator, and later, Communicator. Millions of people downloaded it from the Internet for free. Netscape put in the hands of millions of people (including us, your authors) the power to access the exploding number of Web servers. Netscape made history and changed the world because it changed the Internet from a medium that served mainly scientists into a tool that anyone can use.

Even though Netscape Communicator is freely distributed to anyone who wants it, it isn't open-source software in the same way that Linux is. Quite simply, Netscape, the company, is a moneymaking venture, and Netscape considers the way the software works to be proprietary.

On the other hand, Netscape recognizes the importance of the open-source dynamic, which is why it released an open-source *version* of Netscape named Mozilla. Now, countless numbers of people are developing and enhancing Mozilla, the default browser for Fedora Core computers.

The DVD that comes with this book includes Mozilla, the open-source brother to Netscape Communicator. Netscape and Mozilla are quite similar, although they have a slightly different look and feel.

Surfin' the Net with Mozilla

If you have ever browsed the Internet (and who hasn't, these days?), the first thing you want to do is to tailor Mozilla to your preferences. You can complete this task without connecting to the Internet. Follow the steps in this section to customize Mozilla to your liking.

1. **Click the GNOME Menu and select Preferences⇨More Preferences⇨Preferred Applications.**

   The Preferred Applications dialog window opens.

   Fedora Core includes three browsers: Mozilla, Mozilla Firefox and Epiphany. Firefox and Epiphany are new, minimalist browsers that are quite fun and easy to use. We still prefer Mozilla for its power and maturity and use it for our examples.

2. **Change the default browser from Firefox to Mozilla by clicking the pull-down Select a Web Browser: pull down menu and select Mozilla.**

3. **Click the Close button.**

Now we'll configure Mozilla.

1. **Start Mozilla by clicking the blue globe icon on the GNOME Panel.**

   The Welcome to Fedora Core screen appears in Mozilla. You can use this page to find out more information about Fedora Core and its products.

   Concentrate on configuring Mozilla; skip over all the Fedora Core information for now (Lots of good information is there, however, so explore its world at your leisure.)

2. **Choose Edit⇨Preferences.**

   On the left side of the Preferences window is a list of categories, which you can think of as a map of where you are in the Preferences window.

3. **Click the plus sign (+) next to the Navigator category to expand it.**

   In this step, you determine which Web page appears when you start Mozilla — and which Web page is loaded when you click the Home button on the Navigation toolbar.

4. **In the Home Page area of the Preferences window, fill in the Location field with the URL of the Web page you want to be your home page.**

   You can also surf to the site of your choice and click the Use Current Page button.

   For example, type **www.linuxworld.com** and you see interesting information about Linux whenever you start up your browser or click the Home button, in the upper-left corner of the Mozilla window.

Mozilla remembers where you have been and lets you select (and go to) a previous location. How long Mozilla remembers (and then how big the list becomes) depends on how many days of history you choose. The History configuration option determines the number of days that the locations you visit are saved. If you're short on disk space, choose a lower History number (such as one or two days). Otherwise leave the default setting alone.

Working with proxies

If your Linux computer is connected to the Internet through a proxy firewall, you need to configure Mozilla to work with the proxy.

1. **Click Edit⇨Preferences in the Mozilla window.**
2. **Click the Plus (+) sign next to the Advanced category.**
3. **Click the Proxies option.**
4. **Click the Manual Proxy configuration radio button and enter the URL of your proxy.**
   - For example, enter **proxy.mynetwork.com** in the HTTP Proxy text box (if that's the name of your firewall) and enter **80** in the Port text box.
   - Optionally, if your LAN uses an automated proxy script, click the option labeled `Automatic proxy configuration URL:` and type in the name of your script.
5. **Click the OK button and you should be able to use Mozilla through your proxy firewall.**

You don't have to perform this configuration process if you're using the Fedora Core default firewall or the packet-filtering firewalls we describe in this book.

Fedora Core 3 introduces the new GNOME Web browser Epiphany. Epiphany is designed to function solely as a browser and to be easy to use. You can launch Epiphany by clicking the GNOME Menu and selecting Internet⇨Web Browser.

Plugging in plug-ins

Mozilla performs the tasks you expect from a browser, like displaying Web pages while going the extra mile to make browsing simple and easy. Unfortunately, Mozilla can't include commercial plug-ins like Flash animation and JavaScript by default.

If you want to go that extra mile, however, Mozilla shows how, by providing URLs to locations where you can download and install most of the plug-in functions you'll ever want or need. You see, many companies allow you *individual* access and use of their proprietary software.

Installing the Shockwave Flash plug-in

To make use of plug-ins, all you need to do is (sorry) plug it in. Adding plug-ins is straightforward process. You obtain the plug-in and place it, or link it to the Mozilla plug-in directory.

You can find, download, and install several popular plug-ins by searching the Mozilla plug-in help page. The following steps show (for example) how to install the popular Macromedia Shockwave Flash and Java plug-ins:

1. **Login as `root`.**
2. **Start up Mozilla and your Internet connection (if necessary).**
3. **Check to see which plug-ins Mozilla are already installed by choosing Help⇨About Plug-ins.**

   Mozilla shows that the only installed plug-in is `libnullplugin.so`.
4. **Click the `plugindoc.mozdev.org` link at the top of the page.**

   You see the Welcome to PluginDoc page, which shows where to find the most popular and useful plug-ins.
5. **Click the Linux (x86) link.**
6. **Click the Macromedia Flash Player link.**
7. **Click the Macromedia Flash Player for x86 Linux link.**

   The Macromedia Flash Player Download Center Linux page opens.
8. **Click the Download Now button.**

   The dialog box labeled `Opening install_flash_player_7_linux.tar.gz` opens.

   Note that the version of this package may change during this book's lifetime. You should be able to use a newer version if and when one becomes available.

9. **Click OK in the dialog box.**

   The Enter name of file to save to dialog opens. The default of this dialog is to save to your home directory. You can change the directory, but the default will work for our purposes.

10. **Click the Save button in the dialog box.**

The Download Manager dialog box opens, showing the progress of the download. You can close the dialog box by clicking on the Close Window button — it looks like an X — at the top, right corner of the window.

Linux provides a utility call File-roller that helps extract files from an archive. File-roller prevents you from having to extract the files manually. The following steps show how to extract and install the Macromedia files from the archive that you just downloaded.

1. **Click your home directory icon on the Desktop.**

   A Nautilus window opens showing the newly downloaded file.

2. **Double-click the icon labeled** `install_flash_player_7_linux.tar.gz`**.**

   A second Nautilus window opens showing a folder named `install_flash_player_7_linux`.

3. **Double-click the folder labeled** `install_flash_player_7_linux` **in the second window.**

   The window displays the contents of the `install_flash_player_7_linux` archive.

4. **Click the Extract button.**

   The Extract dialog opens.

5. **Back in the first Nautilus window, click File⇨Open Location.**

   The Open Location dialog window opens.

6. **Enter** /usr/lib/mozilla/plugins **in the text box and then click Open.**

   Nautilus opens a window labeled `plug-ins`.

7. **Click and hold on the flashplayer.xpt icon, and drag it to the** `plugins` **folder.**

8. **Repeat step 7 to copy the** `libflashplayer.so` **to the** `plugins` **folder.**

9. **Back in your Mozilla browser, click the About Plug-ins from the Help menu and you'll see the new plug-ins displayed, as shown in Figure 11-1.**

   The Mozilla window described in Step 3 opens, displaying the name(s) of the new Flash Player plug-in(s) you just installed.

Your Mozilla browser can now display any Web page that uses Flash content.

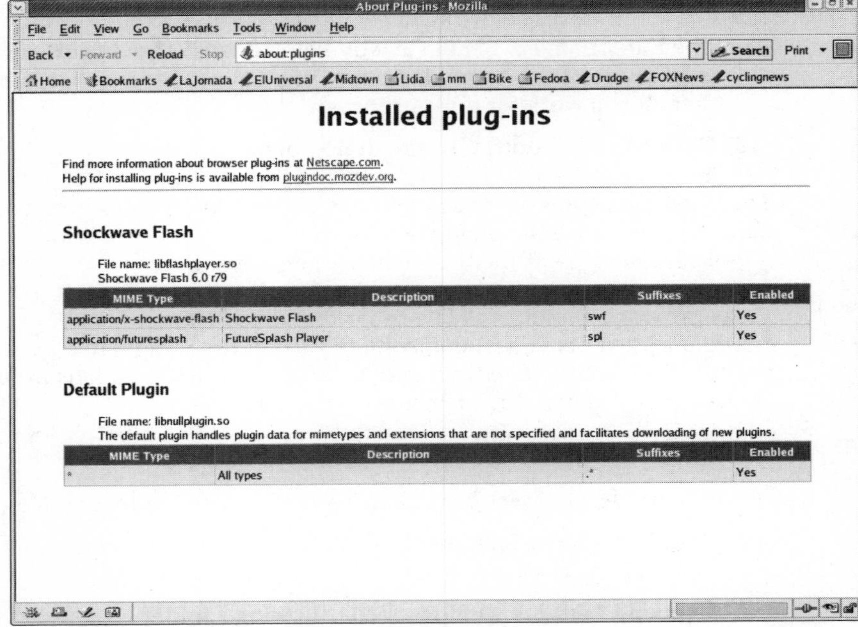

Figure 11-1: The About Plug-ins window, showing the Flash plug-in.

Installing the Macromedia Flash Player plug-in gives you access to a large quantity of multimedia and interesting Web pages. The following section shows how to install another important plug-in.

Installing the Java 2 Runtime Environment

The Java 2 Runtime Environment is another important and useful plug-in. The following instructions show how to obtain and install it:

1. **Login as `root`, start Mozilla and your Internet connection (if necessary).**
2. **Click Help⇨About Plug-ins.**
3. **Click the `plugindoc.mozdev.org` link.**
4. **Click the Linux (x86) link.**
5. **Click the Java Runtime Environment link.**
6. **Click the `Sun JRE 5.0` link.**

   Note that the version number may change by the time this book is published. Use the latest available version.

   The Sun.com Web page opens, telling you that you're not registered yet.
7. **Click the Register Now link on the left side of the page.**

8. **Fill out the registration form as appropriate and click the Register button at the bottom right of the page.**

   The Sun shopping cart page opens.

9. **Click the Check Out button.**

   The License Agreement page opens.

10. **Click the Accept radio button and the Continue button.**
11. **Click the Place Order button when the Verify Order page opens.**

    A JavaScript dialog opens prompting you for a final confirmation.

12. **Click the OK button.**

    The Download page for the Java(TM) 2 Runtime Environment opens.

13. **Click the Linux RPM in self-extracting file link.**

    The dialog box labeled Opening j2re-1_5_0-linux-i586-rpm.bin opens.

14. **Click the OK button.**

    The dialog box labeled `Enter name of file to save to...` opens.

15. **Click the Save button.**

The Download Manager dialog box opens, showing the progress of the file download. You must now extract and link the Java library to Mozilla to make use of them.

1. **Open a GNOME Terminal window by clicking the GNOME Menu and selecting System Tools⇨Terminal.**

   We assume you're still logged in as Root.

2. **In the GNOME Terminal, enter these commands:**

```
chmod +x jre*
./jre*
```

3. **Press the spacebar while you simultaneously read, digest and (presumably) agree with the license agreement.**

   Once again you should probably have your legal team by your side.

4. **Type in** yes **when you finish reading the agreement.**
5. **Enter the following command in the GNOME Terminal:**

```
rpm -ivh j2re*rpm
```

6. **Create a link to the Java plug-in by entering the following (single) command:**

```
ln -s
   /usr/java/j2re1.5.0/plugin/i386/
   ns7/libjavaplugin_oji.so
   /usr/lib/mozilla/plugins/
   libjavaplugin_oji.so
```

Your browser is now Java-capable. Clicking the Help⇨About Plug-ins menu will show the Java plug-ins.

The following list shows some more common plug-ins, available for Linux, that you should consider installing (all can be accessed from the `plugin doc.mozdev.org` page):

- **Acrobat (Adobe):** Reads the Adobe Portable Document Format (PDF) files. Many Web sites provide information via PDF files rather than via HTML or other formats. (Note that you can use the open-source xpdf or gpdf programs to view PDF files.)
- **Java (Sun Microsystems):** A programming language that many Web sites use to provide dynamic content.
- **MPlayer:** Allows Mozilla to play multimedia Internet audio/video streams. See Chapter 12 for a description of the standalone MPlayer (non-plug-in) application.
- **RealPlayer 10 (RealAudio):** Allows you to play the RealNetworks audio and video streams. Many Internet radio stations still use the RealNetworks protocols to stream their content.

  You can also use RealPlayer 10 to listen directly to RealAudio streams.
- **Shockwave (Macromedia):** Provides multimedia, graphics, and game-oriented support.

Protecting your passwords

You can use Mozilla to save passwords that you use when you're browsing the Internet. When you start saving passwords, you should also start encrypting them. Encrypting passwords is optional, but we highly (highly!) recommend it. Encrypting makes finding your passwords much more difficult for someone else. With all the business you may do on the Internet, you must protect your information as much as possible. Follow these steps:

1. **From your Mozilla browser, choose Preferences from the Edit menu.**
2. **Click the plus sign (+) next to the Privacy & Security menu.**

   A submenu opens.
3. **Click the Passwords option.**

   The Passwords dialog box opens.
4. **Click the button labeled Use encryption when storing sensitive data.**
5. **Click OK.**
6. **Click the Edit⇨Preferences menu again.**

7. **Click the Master Passwords option in the Privacy & Security submenu.**
8. **Click the Change Password button.**

   The Change Master Password dialog box opens.
9. **Enter your password in the New password text box.**

   The Password quality meter shows how "good" your password is.
10. **Reenter your password in the New password (again) text box.**

    When both passwords match, the OK button becomes active.
11. **Click the OK button.**

Mozilla will now encrypt any password that you save. You have to enter the master password just once the first time you access a password-protected object. This is a simple and effective security tool.

You can manage passwords whenever you want. Choose Preferences⇨Privacy & Security from the Edit menu. Choose Manage Passwords and the Passwords dialog box opens. You can then remove passwords as desired.

Come the Evolution Revolution

Evolution is a software system that provides a big step in the — sorry — evolution of the Linux desktop. Evolution provides an excellent e-mail-and-calendar client (along with other functions) to create a single, integrated package. Evolution provides these capabilities:

- Calendar
- Contact manager
- E-mail client
- Personal Digital Assistant (PDA) manager
- Task master (to-do list)

The following two sections describe how to configure the Evolution e-mail and PDA functions.

E-mail Evolution

Fedora Core uses Evolution as its default e-mail client. Evolution makes it easy for you to configure one or more e-mail accounts. These steps describe how to configure Evolution to send messages to and receive messages from your ISP e-mail account:

Linux traditionally used the Mozilla e-mail client by default. Mozilla e-mail is still included in the Fedora Core distribution, on your DVD, but is not installed by default.

1. **Click the Evolution Email icon (which looks like an envelope and stamp) on the GNOME Panel.**

   An information dialog box opens, telling you about the state of Evolution.

2. **Click the OK button.**

   The first time you start Evolution — before you configure any e-mail accounts — the Evolution Setup Assistant opens.

3. **Click the Forward button.**

   The Identity window opens.

4. **Enter your name and e-mail address in the appropriate text boxes and click the Forward button.**

   - You can (optionally) enter your organization and *signature file,* a file where you keep personal or business information to be appended to the end of every message you send.
   - Figure 11-2 shows some sample entries in the Identity window.

   The Receiving Mail dialog box opens.

Evolution Setup Assistant
Identity
Please enter your name and email address below. The "optional" fields below do not need to be filled in, unless you wish to include this information in email you send.
Required Information
Full Name: Rod Bush
Email Address: wayofthewheel@yahoo.com
Optional Information
Make this my default account
Reply-To:
Organization:
Cancel Back Forward

Figure 11-2: The Identity dialog box.

5. **Click the Server Type drop-down menu and choose the option that matches your ISP's e-mail system.**
   - Most ISPs use the Internet Message Access Protocol (IMAP) server type.
   - The Receiving Mail window expands so you can enter more information about your ISP's e-mail system.
6. **Enter the host name of your ISP's e-mail server and your ISP user name.**

   Figure 11-3 shows a sample screen in this dialog box.
   - Your ISP provides you with the name of its incoming and outgoing e-mail servers when you first subscribe. You need to enter the incoming server name in the Host text box. For example, your ISP's incoming server may be `mail.myisp.com` or `imap.myisp.com`.
   - Your ISP user name may be different from your user name on your Linux computer. For example, your ISP user name may be based on your first initial and last name — for example, `garagon` — but your home Linux computer user name may be just your first name, as in `gabe`.

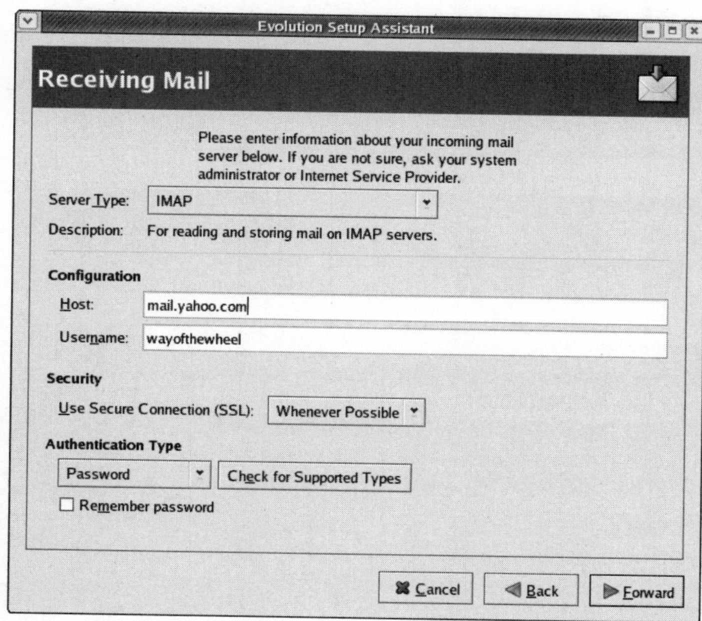

Figure 11-3: The Receiving Mail dialog box.

7. **Click the Forward button.**

   The second Receiving Mail window opens.

   You can change options, such as having Evolution automatically look for incoming messages, by selecting the Automatically check for new mail option.

8. **Make any necessary or optional changes and click the Forward button.**

   The Sending Mail window opens.

9. **Enter your ISP's outgoing mail server name and click the Forward button.**

   Figure 11-4 shows a sample screen in this window.

   - The default outgoing Evolution e-mail protocol is SMTP (which is used frequently by ISPs, so you may not need to change it). Your ISP should supply you with the protocol it uses.
   - A few ISPs may use encrypted Secure Sockets Layer (SSL) connections and require authentication. Again, you need to obtain this information from your ISP and use those options, if necessary.

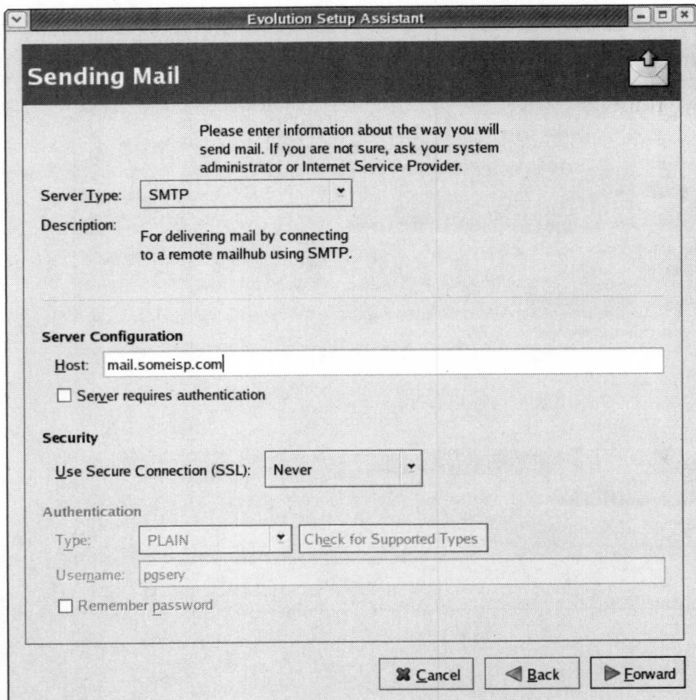

Figure 11-4: The Sending Mail dialog box.

10. **Click the Forward button when the Account Management window opens.**

    Evolution uses your e-mail address as the default name for the account you create. You can change the name if you want, but it's not necessary.

    Your new account is the default account if it's your only one. Otherwise, you can choose to make it the default by selecting the Make This My Default Account option.

11. **The final configuration step requires you to pick your time zone. Click the dot closest to your location on the displayed map.**

    A bigger map appears, which enables you to fine-tune your location, if necessary. It's the same system you use in Chapter 3 to set your computer's time zone.

12. **Click the Forward button.**

    The Done window pops up.

13. **Click the Apply button.**

14. **An informational Evolution dialog window opens. Read the message and click the OK button.**

    An Enter Password dialog window also opens.

15. **Enter your e-mail account password and click the OK button. Optionally, you can click the Remember this password button.**

Evolution opens and displays a Summary window; a separate dialog box also opens and displays information about itself (click the OK button after you finish reading the information in the dialog box). Shortcuts to the Evolution function are on the left side of the window. Click your e-mail account shortcut to see your new e-mail account listed. (You can also access your account by clicking the Summary button, toward the upper-left corner of the window.) Select your account to make it active. You can then send and receive messages. You can also perform any other typical actions on your account, such as sorting, moving, and deleting messages.

Using Evolution with your PDA

You can use the Evolution calendar, to-do manager, and contact manager with your PDA. In this section, we concentrate on showing you how to use Evolution to back up your PDA because that's one of more interesting and fun things you can do (among many). You can find out more about using the calendar by reading the online Evolution documentation (choose Help or visit `www.gnome.org/gnome-office/evolution.shmtl`) or by simply experimenting with it.

You can use the Evolution pilot-link utility to back up your PDA databases to your computer. Follow these steps:

1. **Plug your Pilot cradle into your computer's serial port or USB port, depending on the type of PDA.**

   The cable attached to your cradle has a female 9-pin (a *DB9*) plug attached to it. Most, if not all, modern computers have a 9-pin male plug that connects to a serial-port socket controlled by the `/dev/ttyS0` Linux device file. (In the Windows world, `/dev/ttyS0` is equivalent to COM1, `/dev/ttyS1` is COM2, and so on.)

   If you're using a USB-based cradle, the port is `/dev/ttyUSB0` or `/dev/ttyUSB1`.

2. **Click the Evolution icon on the GNOME panel.**

   The Ximian Evolution application opens.

3. **Click the Contacts button and choose Pilot settings from the Tools menu.**

   The Welcome to GNOME Pilot Wizard window opens.

4. **Click the Forward button and the Gnome Pilot Settings window opens.**

   - You have to tell Evolution where to find your PDA. Open the Port menu and choose the serial device.

   - The device is probably `/dev/ttyS0` or `/dev/ttyS1`. There's no shame in trial and error, so choose each port in order until you find the right one.
   - Don't worry about selecting the speed. The default value is adequate unless you have a very old computer.

5. **Click the Forward button.**

   The Pilot Identification window opens.

6. **Click the No, I've Never Used Sync Software with This Pilot Before button.**

   Your user name is inserted into the User Name text box. (For example, if you're logged in as `paul`, then `paul` is your default Pilot ID.)

7. **Click the Forward button to accept the user name; otherwise, type the name you want to use for your Pilot ID.**

8. **Press the synchronize button (for example, HotSync for a Palm Pilot) on the PDA cradle.**

   The calendar database is copied to your Fedora Core computer.

Chapter 12

Using Audio and Video Applications

In This Chapter

- Introducing Fedora Core multimedia
- Configuring your computer's audio
- Playing your CDs
- Ripping music
- Burning CDs
- Using Rhythmbox
- Introducing and using MPlayer
- Installing the MPLayer plug-in
- Installing and using RealPlayer 10

One of the great innovations of recent times is the use of the Internet to transmit, or *stream,* audio and video programming. Streaming technology gives anyone the capability to create an online radio or TV station — unlimited by geography or governmental approval — inexpensively. Using streaming technology, computer users can listen to or view those broadcasts all around the world.

This chapter describes how to use your Fedora Core machine as a CD player/burner, an Internet radio receiver, and a DVD video player. We use various open-source applications to perform these functions.

Groovin' to Tunes with CD Player

Imagine that you're sitting alone, working at your computer — if you are now, that's not much of a leap — or you could be reading a book that's boring you — say, this one. It's Saturday night, of course. What a drag. Want to go to a party? Have some fun, play some music, watch a video? We can't provide the party, music, video, or instant fun, but we can help get you there — by showing how to use your computer as a multimedia center.

In this chapter, we show you the tools that Fedora Core provides to turn your workstation into a sound-and-video system, including all the necessary applications to play CDs, DVDs, and streaming Internet media. We also show how to connect your PC to a sound card and speakers.

Setting up your sound system

Fedora Core should have automatically configured your computer's sound system during the post-installation process described in Chapter 3. However, you may run into problems — especially on older computers — so Fedora Core provides a sound-card-detection utility.

You can configure and test your sound card at the same time by following these steps:

1. **Log in as any user.**
2. **Click the GNOME Menu button, and choose System Settings⇨Soundcard Detection.**

   Enter the `root` password if prompted.

   The Audio Devices dialog box opens, as shown in Figure 12-1.

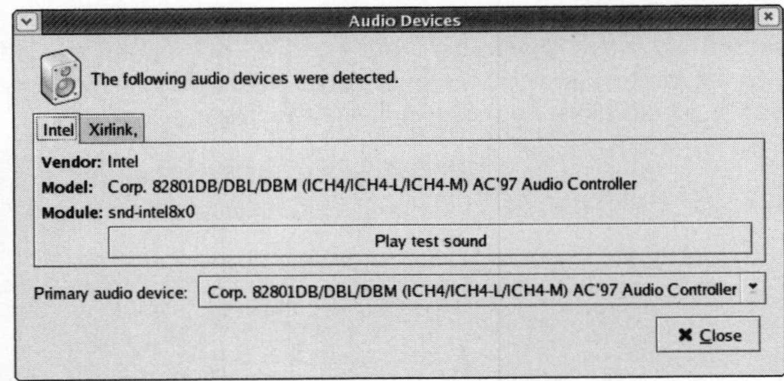

Figure 12-1: A sample Audio Devices dialog box.

3. **Click the Play test sound button.**

   A dialog box opens asking whether you heard the sounds.

4. **Click Yes if you hear the sample guitar — and your computer is ready to rock.**

   If you don't hear the music, click No. Check the following possible causes:

   - Your computer has an old, unrecognizable sound card. In that case, you should purchase and install a new one.
   - You don't have a sound card. You definitely have to purchase a new card and get it put in there.
   - Your speaker connections are faulty. Check your cables and try again.
   - Someone else's stereo is way too loud. Call the cops.

5. **Click OK in the Audio Devices dialog box and you're ready to go.**

Playing CDs

Everyone wants a little music in their lives — but you went ahead and bought a computer instead of that stereo system. (D'oh!) But it's not a problem: As it happens, you did indeed spend your money wisely — because your Fedora Core computer functions well as a stereo system. This section describes how to set up your computer to play music CDs.

Fedora Core bundles several open-source CD players for Linux users: CD Player, XMMS (included in the distribution but not installed by default), and Rhythmbox (we cover Rhythmbox later in this chapter). We describe CD Player in this chapter because it automatically starts whenever you insert a CD in your computer.

The following steps show you how to start playing CDs:

1. **Log in to your computer.**
2. **Pop a CD into the CD-ROM drive.**

   The GNOME CD Player application appears. Depending on how old your audio CD is, you may or may not see the title information displayed in the CD Player window.

3. **Listen as your CD starts playing.**

You can manually start the CD Player by clicking the GNOME Menu button and choosing Sound & Video➪CD Player — there's nothing to it!

The CD Player controls should be familiar territory for anyone born in the twentieth century. Here's a quick refresher for cave people:

- To change the volume, click the vertical slide bar on the right side of the CD Player window. Hold the mouse button while you adjust the volume.
- Click the crossed tools (a screwdriver and wrench) button, toward the middle-left area of the window, to open the Preferences window. You can then select how CD Player reacts when you start and stop it. You can also control the default CD device (the default is `/dev/cdrom`, but you many want to change it to `/dev/cdrom1` or another device, depending on your computer hardware). You can also select the theme of the CD Player skin. A simple help system is available too.
- The remaining music controls are self-explanatory.

As you can see, playing CDs is simple.

Ripping CD Music Files

Are you juiced? If not, Sound Juicer can help you get there. It *rips* — extracts — audio information (the music files) from CDs to files on your hard drive.

These steps show you how to use Sound Juicer to copy music to your hard drive:

1. **Insert your favorite CD in the CD-ROM drive.**
2. **Click the GNOME Menu button and choose Sound & Video⇨Sound Juicer CD Ripper.**

   The Sound Juicer window opens, as shown in Figure 12-2.
3. **By default, all the CD tracks are selected (note the check mark in the Extract column). Click the check mark of any tracks you don't want to extract.**

   Sound Juicer can take some time before it reads and displays the CD tracks.
4. **Click the Extract button in the lower-right corner of the window.**

   The Progress dialog box opens, showing the progress of the track and the overall extraction process. When you're finished, the Information dialog box opens.
5. **Click the Close button.**

Sound Juicer

CD Edit Help

Title: Come Away With Me

Artist: Norah Jones

Duration: 45:29

Extract	Track	Title	Artist	Duration
☑	1	Don't Know Why	Norah Jones	3:08
☑	2	Seven Years	Norah Jones	2:27
☑	3	Cold Cold Heart	Norah Jones	3:40
☑	4	Feelin' the Same Way	Norah Jones	2:59
☑	5	Come Away With Me	Norah Jones	3:20
☑	6	Shoot the Moon	Norah Jones	3:58
☑	7	Turn Me On	Norah Jones	2:36
☑	8	Lonestar	Norah Jones	3:08
☑	9	I've Got to See You Again	Norah Jones	4:15

Re-read Extract

Figure 12-2: The Sound Juicer window shows a CD's tracks.

Sound Juicer stores the music it extracts in Ogg, the up-and-coming open-source audio protocol (it's similar, but technically superior, to MP3). Sound Juicer creates directories with the name of the music CD in your home directory. Each extracted track is stored as an Ogg-formatted file with the name of the song.

After you create the music file, you can listen to it with Rhythmbox (click the GNOME Menu and choose Sound & Audio⇨Music Player).

Burning CDs

Back in the 1980s, when vinyl started to melt away under the invasion of CDs, building the factories to create the CDs cost megabucks; back then, it took a huge effort to make a CD. Now, for the handful of bucks it costs to purchase a CD burner, you can build your own personal CD factory. Amazing!

A one-time writable CD is referred to as a *CD-R;* a rewritable CD is a *CD-RW.* CD burners look like regular read-only drives and are connected with either an IDE or SCSI interface.

But what can you burn? The answer is pretty much whatever you want: data, software, digital photos, or music. We'll start by burning music.

Burning DVDs

The new growisofs utility makes it possible to create DVDs. Because growisofs is still young, its graphical interface is relatively immature. We show you how to use growisofs via a CLI. Follow these steps to copy files to a DVD:

1. **Insert a DVD into your DVD burner.**

   You can use either the "plus" (DVD+RW) or "minus" (DVD-RAM) format DVD burner.

2. **Open a GNOME Terminal emulator window by clicking the GNOME Menu and choosing System Tools⇨Terminal.**

3. **Run the following command to determine which Linux device file corresponds to your DVD writer:**

   ```
   grep -i dvd /var/log/dmesg
   ```

   You should see output similar to the following, where `hdc` is the device file you seek:

   ```
   hdc: Hewlett-Packard DVD
   Writer 200, ATAPI CD/DVD-
   ROM drive
   ```

4. **If you want to burn tracks you ripped via Sound Juicer (in the "Extracting CD Music with Sound Juicer" section), run this command:**

   ```
   growisofs -Z /dev/hdc -l -R
   -J ~/music/*ogg
   ```

   growisofs writes the files to your DVD. Note that `/dev/hdc` corresponds to the information you obtained in Step 3.

5. **You can append more files:**

   ```
   growisofs -M /dev/hdc -l -R
   -J ~/other music/*ogg
   ```

6. **You're not limited to burning only files. You can also write the common ISO-9660-formatted images to a DVD. Run this command to create a DVD using an ISO image:**

   ```
   growisofs -dvd-compat -Z
   /dev/hdc=image.iso
   ```

The easy-to-use growisofs utility allows you to create DVDs, which now store more than 4.5GB of data — much more than CD-ROMs can handle. Future DVD formats will store more than 40GB of data.

The following instructions show how to burn Ogg music files to a writable CD.

1. **Log in as any user and insert a disc (either CD-R or CD-RW) into your CD writer drive.**

2. **Double-click your home-directory icon, in the upper-left corner of your desktop.**

   A Nautilus window opens, showing the contents of your home directory.

3. **Click the Places menu and select CD Creator.**

   The CD Creator window opens.

4. **Back in the first Nautilus window (your home directory), double-click the folder that contains the music files you want to record.**

   For instance, if you follow the directions in the previous section, "Ripping CD Music Files," you save the music in a new directory. The files are saved in Ogg format.

5. **Click any of the files and drag them to the CD Creator window.**

   Repeat this step for each file you want to record.

6. **Click the File menu and select Write to CD.**

   After a little thought, the Write files to a CD recorder dialog box opens.

7. **Click the Write files to CD button.**

   When the CD write is finished, the disc is ejected.

8. **Click the Close button when you're finished.**

9. **Close the CD tray by pushing it back into the drive.**

   A CD Player window opens and plays the music you just recorded.

Using Rhythmbox

The open-source Rhythmbox program is a great tool for listening to audio streams and files. Rhythmbox plays Ogg-formatted audio. The Ogg format — codec — doesn't use any proprietary or patented algorithms. Ogg is free for anyone to use, and people and organizations who don't want to depend on proprietary systems are discovering it; Ogg also produces higher-fidelity audio streams than other popular systems (such as MP3). Why depend on another corporation's whims when you don't have to? (Rhythmbox box doesn't play MP3 formatted music. MPlayer, described later in this chapter, does play MP3s.)

Ogg is the system used to format audio streams; *Vorbis* is used to compress formatted audio streams. Unlike most other technological systems, Ogg/Vorbis isn't an acronym, but rather is named after science fiction characters. For more information about Ogg/Vorbis and similar open-source multimedia systems, go to `www.vorbis.com`.

Now that you have a bit of technological background, you can start using Rhythmbox to listen to Ogg/Vorbis files and streams:

1. **Open Mozilla by clicking the blue globe icon in the GNOME Panel.**

   Alternatively, open Mozilla by clicking the GNOME Menu and selecting Internet⇨Web Browser.

2. **Enter the address** www.vorbis.com/music.psp **in the Mozilla text box and then press Enter.**

3. **Click any of the links.**

   For example, click the first one, `Epoq-Lepidoptera`.

4. **The Opening Epoq-Lepidoptera.ogg dialog box opens. Rhythmbox is the default application for playing Ogg files.**

   Rhythmbox opens, as shown in Figure 12-3, and downloads the music.

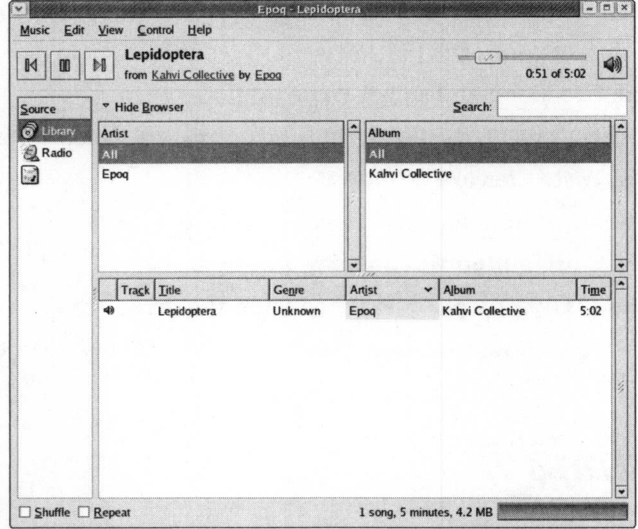

Figure 12-3: The Rhythmbox window.

5. **Next, play an Internet stream.**

   Go to `www.virgin.co.uk/thestation/listen/ogg.html`.

6. **Click any of the Ogg links.**

The Vorbis Web page provides links to other Ogg-capable sources. For example, click the Music Sites Page link, near the top of the `www.vorbis.com/music.psp` page. You see a page with links to other sources. For example, click the WCPE link to go to a Web page that streams classical music.

Introducing the Mighty MPlayer

Whenever a desperate need exists, Superman comes in to . . . er, the open-source movement comes in to save the day. Until recently, you couldn't use any single Linux application to listen to and view most popular streaming formats. Now, MPlayer has burst on the scene and fills that gap.

MPlayer can play most popular (and many obscure) audio and video streaming formats. Although MPlayer is under intense development — it's still technically in the beta phase while its development team fine-tunes its features — it's quite usable, and we think you should consider using it. We do!

This list shows some streaming formats MPlayer can play:

- **MPEG-1/Layer 3 (MP3):** MP3 is a popular but proprietary codec used for both storing and streaming audio.
- **Ogg/Vorbis:** This new, up-and-coming, open-source streaming format is unencumbered by any copyrights or patents (as other formats are).
- **Microsoft Media Server (MMS):** You can listen to radio broadcasts that use the popular MMS format with MPlayer. Previously you had to use the Microsoft client application to listen to MMS streams.
- **Digital Versatile Disc (DVD):** You can play DVDs from your computer with MPlayer.
- **RealAudio:** You have to download, compile, and install the RTSP package to use RealAudio.

Downloading and installing MPlayer

MPlayer is not included in the Fedora Core distribution. We hope that it will be later, but for now, you have to obtain it from its developers. These steps describe how to download, install, and use MPlayer:

1. **Open Mozilla and go to the following Web site:**

   ```
   www.mplayerhq.hu/homepage/design7/dload.html
   ```

2. **Click one of the geographical links next to the MPlayer RPM packages for Red Hat and Fedora header.**

   For example, click the `USA` link. You get redirected to another Web server.

3. **Click the** `Current version ... Recommended` **link.**
4. **Click the Fedora Core 2 link for** `mplayer-common`**. (Click the Fedora Core 3 link if it's available.)**

   A dialog box labeled `Enter name of file to save to` opens.

5. **Click the Save button.**

   The `mplayer-common` file is saved to your home directory.

6. **Repeat Steps 4 and 5 to download the mplayer package.**
7. **Go to** `http://luna.cs.ccsu.edu/dominik/apt/fc1/RPMS.testing`**.**
8. **Click** `lame-libs-3.96-1.i386.rpm` **link.**

   A dialog box labeled `Enter name of file to save to...` opens.

9. **Click the Save button.**

At the time this edition of the book was written, the most recent MPlayer RPM package was version 1.0pre5. You may see — and should use — a more recent version if it's available.

10. **After you have downloaded all the packages, open a GNOME Terminal by clicking GNOME Menu and selecting System Tools➪Terminal.**

    The GNOME Terminal window opens.

11. **Enter the following command to switch to the** `root` **user.**

    ```
    su -
    ```

12. **Enter the following commands to install MPlayer:**

    ```
    rpm -ivh lame-libs*
    rpm -ivh --nodeps mplayer*
    ```

You have the option to change the default caching value to cut the time it takes MPLayer to load streaming media. The default value is 8192 (8MB), which can take a long time to download. Edit the `/etc/mplayer/mplayer.conf` file and change `cache = 8192` to something smaller, such as `cache = 256`.

Playing audio files and Internet streams with MPlayer

You can now use MPlayer to play audio and video. One good source for audio streams is `www.shoutcast.com`. Click any of the Tune In! buttons and Mozilla downloads several playlists and launches MPlayer to play the music via the playlists.

Playlists are files that store the locations of one or more audio and video streams. For example, if you click any of the Shoutcast streams (at `www.shoutcast.com`), Mozilla saves the playlist to the `/tmp` directory, starts MPlayer, and directs it to play the playlists. The playlist MIME type — `x-scpls` — was inserted into Mozilla as a helper application when you installed the MPlayer packages.

You can use MPlayer to play audio files too. The following instructions outline the process.

1. **Use the section "Ripping CD Music Files," to extract music tracks from a CD that you own.**
2. **Open a GNOME Terminal by clicking GNOME Menu and choosing System Tools➪Terminal.**
3. **Enter the following command in the Terminal window to play a file that you've extracted:**

    ```
    mplayer track1.ogg
    ```

4. **You can press the Control key and the C key together (Ctrl+C) to end the session.**

You can also use MPlayer to listen to Internet audio streams. The entire world of Internet radio and (soon, we hope) video broadcasts is open to you. MPlayer will only become more versatile and useful.

1. **Open a GNOME Terminal window by clicking GNOME Menu and selecting System Tools⇨Terminal.**
2. **Enter the following command in the Terminal window:**

   ```
   mplayer http://64.202.98.55:80/wrti
   ```

You'll get to listen to Temple University's (Philadelphia, PA, U.S.A.) jazz and classical station. They use actual human beings to program and play music.

MPlayer plays DVDs too! With MPlayer, your Fedora Core computer becomes a DVD player. The following instructions show how simple the process is:

1. **Pop a DVD into your computer.**
2. **Click the GNOME Menu and select System Tools⇨Terminal.**

   A GNOME Terminal window opens.
3. **Run the following command to determine whether your computer is DVD-capable:**

   ```
   grep -i dvd /var/log/dmesg
   ```

   If you have DVD-capable player, you see output similar to the following text.

   ```
   hdc: Hewlett-Packard DVD Writer 200,
        ATAPI CD/DVD-ROM drive
   hdd: ATAPI CDROM 48X, ATAPI CD/DVD-ROM drive
   hdc: ATAPI 32X DVD-ROM CD-R/RW drive,
        2048kB Cache, UDMA(33)
   ```
4. **Make note of your DVD device file.**

   In this case, the DVD device file is `/dev/hdc`.
5. **Use the information you determined about your DVD to customize the following command:**

   ```
   mplayer dvd:// --dvd-device /dev/hdc
   ```

Your DVD will start playing! You can play bonus tracks by entering the track number after the dvd:// option. For instance, to play track number 2, use the command **mplayer dvd://2 –dvd-device /dev/hdc.** Get your popcorn ready!

You can download a graphical interface to MPlayer called gmplayer. Use the MPlayer download instructions in this chapter to get and install gmplayer.

Installing the MPlayer Plugin

Until now, you'd have had to launch MPlayer manually. In this section, we simplify using MPlayer by installing a plug-in that allows you to play audio streams through Mozilla. Here's the drill:

1. **Click the GNOME Menu and select Internet⇨Web Browser.**
2. **Click the Help menu and select About Plug-ins.**

   The Installed Plug-ins page appears, displaying the currently installed plug-ins.
3. **Click the plugindoc.mozdev.org link at the top of the page.**

   The Welcome to PluginDoc page opens.
4. **Click the Linux(x86) link.**

   The Mozilla Plug-in Support on Linux (x86) page opens.
5. **Click the** `mplayerplug-in` **link.**

   You jump down to the `mplayerplug-in` section.
6. **Click the** `mplayerplug-in Home` **link.**

   You go to another Web server that stores the MPlayer plugin.
7. **Click the Download link in the upper-left corner of the page.**

   You go to the `mplayerplug-in` page at `sourceforge.net`.
8. **Click the Fedora Core link.**

   You go to a Web page that lists download mirrors.
9. **Click the link that's closest to you.**

   A dialog box labeled Opening mplayerplug-in opens.
10. **Click the OK button.**

    A dialog box labeled `Enter name of file to save to...` opens.
11. **Click the Save button and the mplayerplug-in package is saved to your computer.**

Next, you need to install and configure the plug-in. The following instructions show how to install the plug-in RPM package and then play some music with Mozilla.

1. **Double-click your home icon in your GNOME desktop.**

   The Nautilus window opens, showing the contents of your home directory.

2. **Right-click the mplayerplug-in icon and select Open With⇨An Application.**

   The Open with Other Application window opens.

3. **Click the Install Packages option.**
4. **Click the OK button.**
5. **Enter the** `root` **password in the query dialog box if prompted.**

   After thinking for a while, the Completed System Preparation dialog box opens.

6. **Click the Continue button.**

   The plug-in is installed in the `/usr/lib/mozilla/plugins` directory. This is the correct location, and it enables Mozilla to directly play numerous types of multimedia streams.

7. **Click the Mozilla icon in the GNOME Panel.**

   You'll want to browse to any Web page that plays audio streams. For instance, you can go to `www.wrti.org`.

8. **Click the WindowsMedia link under the Listen Live heading in the upper-left corner of the page.**
9. **The mplayerplug-in page opens and plays WRTI's excellent selection of jazz (afternoons and evenings).**

   It may take a while for the mplayerplug-in to connect, buffer, and play the media stream. Please be patient.

You can now use Mozilla to play most of the multimedia streams on the Internet. Enjoy.

Installing and Using RealPlayer 10

We've accounted for almost all of the popular multimedia formats. We've got Ogg/Vorbis and the Microsoft formats covered. However, we need to account for RealAudio's codec.

Use the following instructions to download and install RealPlayer 10:

1. **Open the Mozilla browser.**
2. **Click the Help menu and select About Plug-ins.**
3. **Click the** `plugindoc.mozdev.org` **link.**

4. **Click the Linux (x86) link.**
5. **Click the RealPlayer 10 link.**
6. **Click the Download RealPlayer link.**

   You're redirected to the commercial `www.real.com/linux` Web page.
7. **Click the Download RPM Package link.**

   A dialog box labeled `Opening RealPlayer10GOLD.rpm` opens.
8. **Click the OK button.**

   A dialog box labeled `Enter name of file to save to...` opens.
9. **Click the Save button.**

   The RealPlayer10 package downloads into your home directory.

Now you need to install the RealPlayer 10 package.

1. **Double-click your home-directory icon on your desktop.**

   A Nautilus window opens, showing the `RealPlayer10GOLD.bin` package you just obtained.
2. **Right-click the `RealPlayer10GOLD.bin` package and select Open With⇨An Application.**
3. **Click the Install Packages option.**
4. **Click the OK button.**
5. **Enter the `root` password if prompted.**

   The Completed System Preparation dialog box opens.
6. **Click the Continue button.**

   RealPlayer 10 is installed. (The installation makes Mozilla aware that it can handle Real Audio.)
7. **You can test RealPlayer 10 by opening a GNOME Terminal window and entering a command.**
   - For example, the following command plays an interview that Terri Gross did with Linus Torvalds in June of 2001:

     ```
     realplay rtsp://audio.npr.org/fa/20010604.fa.rm
     ```
   - Alternatively, you can use Mozilla to browse to the following site:

     ```
     www.npr.org/features/feature.php?wfId=1123917
     ```

     There you can click the `Fresh Air Audio` link and you'll be prompted to open the stream with RealPlayer.

Chapter 13

Going to the OpenOffice

In This Chapter

- Introducing OpenOffice
- Using OpenOffice Writer
- Printing from OpenOffice

Fedora Core is a great product that comes with a large base of services and applications. It has always been an outstanding platform for providing services and technical applications. But until recently, you didn't find Fedora Core on many of the world's workday computers; in other words, it lacked a presence on the "desktop."

The Fedora Core problem used to be a lack of a full-blown office suite to work with word-processing documents, spreadsheets, and other documents. Fortunately, desktop productivity suites — such as OpenOffice and its sister application, StarOffice — have moved Linux from the back office to the front.

Opening Your Office

The OpenOffice desktop-productivity suite does nearly everything Microsoft Office does, but for less money. How much less? Well, 100 percent less because it's 100-percent free. Sun Microsystems, Inc. sells the version named StarOffice and also provides an open-source version named — you guessed it — OpenOffice. OpenOffice is licensed under the GPL/LGPL and SIISL licenses. What do all those letters mean? They mean f-r-e-e, and they also mean that Linux can integrate the office-productivity features from OpenOffice (because Linux and OpenOffice share the GPL license). You can find more information about the licenses at

```
www.openoffice.org/project/www/license.html
```

OpenOffice is not only free (did we mention that it's free?), but it's also powerful, providing you with these functions:

- **Word processor:** A full-function, what-you-see-is-what-you-get (WYSIWYG) word processor named Writer comes with the OpenOffice package, complete with many functions you would expect — formatting, cutting and pasting, graphics, spell-checking, and more, as shown in Figure 13-1. It uses its own format and can also read from (and write to) documents in Rich Text Format (RTF); plus, it handles Microsoft Word 6.0, Word 95, Word 97, Word 2000, and Word XP files.

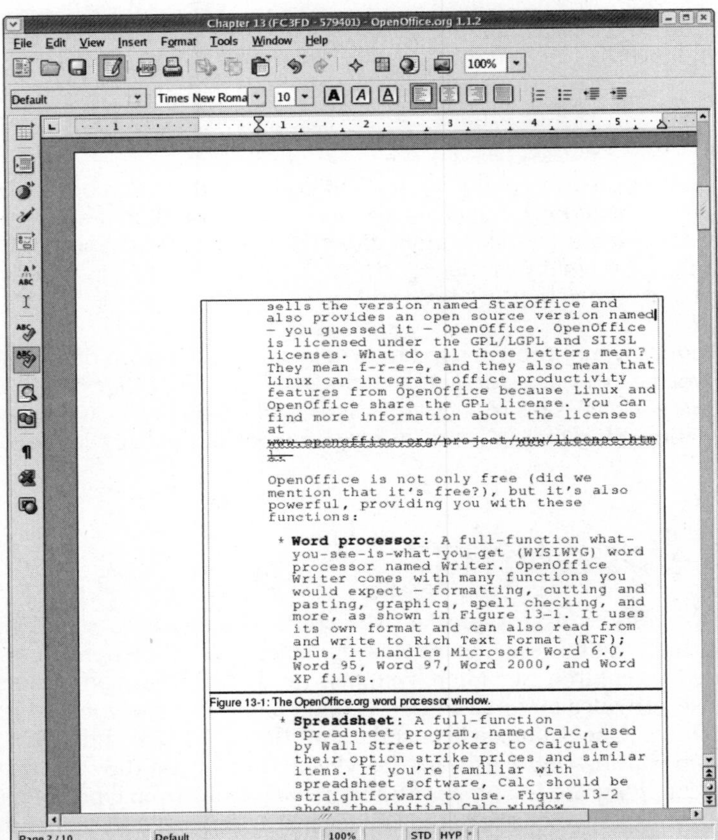

Figure 13-1: The OpenOffice.org word-processor window.

- **Spreadsheet:** A full-function spreadsheet program named Calc, used by Wall Street brokers to calculate their option-strike prices and similar items. If you're familiar with spreadsheet software, Calc should be straightforward to use. Figure 13-2 shows the initial Calc window.
- **Presentation:** A graphics program named Impress, with all the bells and whistles for creating presentations. The first time you start Impress, you're prompted configure the system. Select the default options and you see Impress as shown in Figure 13-3. You can import and export PowerPoint documents with Impress.

Figure 13-2: The OpenOffice.org spreadsheet window.

- **Drawing:** The OpenOffice Draw program has graphics tools for creating anything from a novice drawing to a masterpiece, as shown in Figure 13-4.
- **Miscellaneous:** OpenOffice provides other functions, such as an HTML editor, a math editor for supernerds, and tools for creating labels and business cards. You can also create word-processing templates.

Okay, so OpenOffice has lots of great features. How good are they? Can they get the job done? Well, we wrote this edition of the book using OpenOffice, and we wrote the preceding edition using StarOffice. That's not a bad testimonial to the capabilities of OpenOffice.

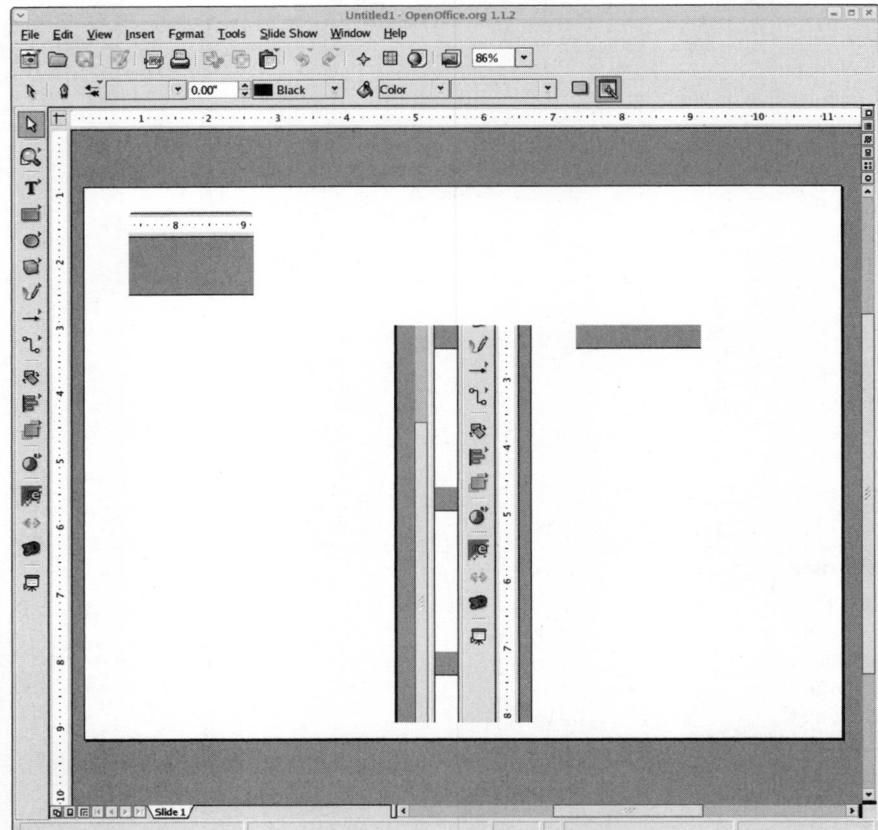

Figure 13-3: The OpenOffice.org Impress window.

Figure 13-4: The OpenOffice.org graphics program, Draw.

Getting to Know OpenOffice

If you're familiar with Microsoft Office, you can find your way around OpenOffice. The look and feel are a little different, but the idea is the same. If you're a wild-eyed power-to-the-people person (who's also thrifty), you may find OpenOffice morally superior to Office because it's free *and* a part of open source. Or maybe you just want to get down to work. Either way, we briefly describe some of the most common OpenOffice functions here.

This section provides only a basic introduction to the things you can do with OpenOffice. No, we're not hopelessly lazy; it's just that it would take too much space to describe it all in detail. Please experiment with your own test documents and consult the online help system for more information.

Firing up and using OpenOffice

Fedora Core provides OpenOffice, and installs it by default. OpenOffice is easy to access. Click the GNOME Menu button and then choose Office⇨OpenOffice.org Writer. You can choose some (but not all) other OpenOffice functions from this menu as well — but you can start the Calc spreadsheet program only from an OpenOffice window. From any window (in Writer or Impress, for example), choose File⇨New⇨Spreadsheet to open Calc.) After thinking about life for a few seconds, the OpenOffice window appears.

The first time you start OpenOffice, it asks whether you want to use the workstation or personal model. The former installs the OpenOffice programs in a central location accessible to all users; the latter option installs a copy of OpenOffice in your home directory. We use the workstation configuration in this section, but you can select the personal model.

When you use OpenOffice for the first time, you're also asked a few questions about importing an address book. (We cancel this operation because we prefer to use the Ximian Evolution address book.)

You can access all OpenOffice functions by clicking the File button, in the upper-left corner of the window, and then clicking the option you want.

The following list introduces the functions; you're probably familiar with the layout and operation of the menu if you have used Microsoft Office:

- **File:** As you may expect, you can open, close, save, and otherwise manipulate OpenOffice documents by using the File menu. Writer files have the `.sxw` extension. You can also read and write other file formats, such as Microsoft Word and HTML, by using the File menu.
- **New:** You can create a new document for any OpenOffice function. When you choose File⇨New, you're given the option to create a new text document, spreadsheet, presentation, or other function.
- **Edit:** This menu provides all the functions you need to modify documents. Functions such as cut, copy, paste, and delete are all there. The functions that are active at any time depend on whether you're editing a document, spreadsheet, or presentation. For example, the cut, copy, and paste options aren't active if you're not editing a document (as when you first start up OpenOffice and haven't opened any files).

You can also track changes, just as you can in Microsoft Word. Choose Edit➪Changes and you can track changes on a character-by-character basis. You can display the changes or keep them hidden from view. When you're satisfied with your edits, you can make the changes permanent and save only the finished document to disk. It's pretty cool.

OpenOffice also provides the Find and Replace function from the Edit menu. The Find and Replace feature enables you to find text strings and either replace them with other strings or delete them. You can use it to search forward or backward through a document, replacing one instance or all instances.

- **Spelling check:** OpenOffice provides a spell checker, of course. You can tell the spell checker to check an entire document by choosing Tools➪Spell Check➪Check. You're prompted to act on each possible spelling error the checker detects.

  Alternatively, you can set the spell checker to operate continuously. Choose Tools➪Spellcheck➪AutoSpellCheck to toggle on the real-time spell checker; when it's activated, a check mark appears next to the menu option. The Continuous option tells OpenOffice Writer to check each word you enter and underline possible misspellings with a squiggly red line. The red line disappears when you successfully correct the mistake.

- **View:** This menu displays or hides the various menu bars. You can display a document's formatting characters and zoom in or out to increase or decrease the size of text displayed on-screen. The zoom function enables you to make smaller fonts more readable without changing the document.

- **Insert:** This menu enables you to insert special characters, objects, files, and macros into your documents. Special characters include various symbols (accents and umlauts, for example) that aren't part of the everyday character set, unless you happen to use words like café frequently. Objects include graphics, symbols, and figures. (You can create your own figures with Draw.) You can also insert macros and hyperlinks into your documents.

  You can insert tables into documents with any number of rows and columns. OpenOffice can automatically adjust the row height, or you can do it manually. Choose Table from the Insert menu and play around with this feature.

- **Tools:** From this menu, you can access the spell checker, thesaurus, various OpenOffice configuration settings, and other functions. Some tools (such as the spell checker) are self-explanatory.

- **Window:** This menu enables you to control the look of your desktop. In addition to enabling you to modify and move windows, the menu provides other manipulation capabilities.

- **Help:** OpenOffice provides pretty good online help services. Many are context-sensitive: If you're editing a text document (for example), click the Help menu to get access to information related to the Writer module.

  For a further illustration, choose Help➪Help Agent and the Help Agent window appears. The Help Agent provides assistance in several areas of interest to new users, including

  - **Introduction to Writer:** Provides an introduction to the word processor
  - **Basic tips text documents:** Tells you all you ever wanted to know about reading, writing, and printing text documents
  - **Advanced tips:** Extends the preceding basic text document tip to more advanced subjects
  - **Menus:** Describes how all the OpenOffice menus work together
  - **Toolbars:** Describes the toolbars that provide information and shortcuts
  - **Shortcuts:** Describes which key combinations can be used to perform various word processing functions
  - **New stuff:** Describes what's new since the last OpenOffice version
  - **Support:** Displays brief information about getting support from Sun Microsystems

Printing with OpenOffice

Printing from OpenOffice is a simple process after you have configured Fedora Core to use a printer. OpenOffice uses the default Linux printer, so all you have to do is configure it. This section first describes how to configure a Fedora Core printer and then shows you how to set up OpenOffice to use it.

Configuring a printer attached to your Fedora Core computer is a simple process. All you have to do is run the `printconf-gui` printer-configuration utility and enter the information about your printer. These steps describe how:

1. **Log in to your Fedora Core computer as `root`.**
2. **Attach a printer to your Linux computer's parallel (printer) or USB port.**

   The *parallel port* is a 25-pin female connector on the back of your computer case. New computers usually label the parallel port with some kind of printer icon (although sometimes it's hard to imagine how they came up with the symbol). If yours isn't marked, there's no harm in finding the appropriate port through trial and error.

3. **Start the printer configuration tool by clicking the GNOME Menu button and choosing System Settings⇨Printing.**

   Enter the `root` password, if you're prompted. The Printer configuration window opens.

4. **To add a printer, click the New button. When the introductory Add a new print queue window opens, click the Forward button.**

   A dialog box labeled `Queue name` opens.

5. **Enter a descriptive queue name (for example,** Epson777**) and, optionally, a description of the queue.**

   You can, of course, use the default name, `printer`, but we prefer to use descriptive names.

6. **Click the Forward button to open the Queue type dialog box.**

   Assuming that your printer is directly connected to your computer, you see the device name `/dev/lp0` in a dialog box labeled `Queue type`.

7. **Select the appropriate device and click the Forward button.**

   A dialog box labeled `Printer model` opens. You can choose from various manufacturers and their printer models.

8. **Click the button labeled** `Generic (click to select manufacturer)`.

   Select your printer's manufacturer from the drop-down list.

9. **Use the vertical slide bar to locate and select your particular model and then click the Forward button.**

   When you finish, a dialog box labeled `Add a new print queue` opens:

10. **Click the Finish button.**

    A Question window opens. You're asked whether you want to print a test page. Click the OK button and a test page is printed. An Information window opens, and you're prompted to check whether the test page printed successfully.

11. **Click the OK button to return to the Printer Configuration window.**

    The GNOME Print Manager window opens, showing an icon for the new print queue you just created. You can create an additional print queue or modify existing ones.

12. **Double-click the new icon.**

    A status window opens, showing current and past print jobs.

Now that you have a printer connected to your Fedora Core computer, you can print from OpenOffice without any further configuration. OpenOffice uses the Fedora Core printer configuration by default. The process is easy:

1. **Open a file you want to print: From the OpenOffice desktop, choose File⇨Print.**
2. **Choose how much of what to print.**

   You can choose to print the entire document, individual pages, or a range of pages.

Chapter 14

The Days of Wine and Windows Applications

In This Chapter

- Introducing Wine
- Using Wine

Linux provides for many, if not most, of your desktop needs. The applications described in the preceding chapters satisfy most of your daily work requirements. All the essential applications, such as OpenOffice, Mozilla, and Evolution, are at your disposal.

Sometimes, however, you need to perform some function that Linux doesn't provide. For example, most games are written for the Microsoft world and aren't available for Linux. At times — such as when you're editing documents with complex macros — you must use Microsoft Word. That's when Wine, Crossover Office, and VMware come to the rescue.

Introducing Wine

Wine doesn't come from the Sonoma Valley, Chile, Australia, or even from the south of France. You can't get tipsy or spend much money on it, either. Wine isn't a beverage, but rather a software system that allows you to run Windows applications on a Linux computer. Wine helps to fill-in the small Linux application gap.

Modern Windows applications are, at their core, written to run on Intel, or Intel-compatible (AMD, for example), Pentium processors. (Some Windows applications are run on Apple Macs; for purposes of this discussion, however, we're talking about only Intel-based PCs.) Linux runs on Pentium-based PCs. However, you can't just load a program like Microsoft Word right onto your Linux computer and expect it to work.

The Microsoft Windows operating system provides a platform for running Microsoft applications, such as Word and Explorer. That platform is a little like an electrical plug that provides the power to run, and a standard way of accessing that power — the electrical outlet, and various appliances — that are analogous to applications. What the Windows "plug" provides is a library of commonly used, low-level functions — referred to as an Application Program Interface (API). Those functions perform tasks common to every application, such as opening a file or talking over a network. Using a common library prevents every application from having to reinvent the wheel. Instead, the applications just plug into the common "outlet" and concentrate on performing their particular functions.

The problem is that the Windows platform (the "plug" in the electrical analogy) has what amounts to square holes while Linux has what amounts to round ones. You cannot plug Word directly into the Linux operating system, for example. That's where Wine comes in: It provides the adapter so you can plug the Windows application into the Linux outlet.

Wine stands for Wine Is Not an Emulator. This typically obscure acronym is the type that Linux and Unix programmers love. It means not only that some people just need to get out more, but also that Wine doesn't do its work by simulating (that is, emulating) the entire Windows environment. Rather, it duplicates one vital part of the environment: the interface between the application and the operating system. In the electrical analogy, Wine isn't trying to be the entire electrical grid (as in Windows) but, rather, the adapter.

Downloading Wine

Come on, now, Fedora Core has to leave a *few* things up to the user. Therefore Wine isn't included in the distribution; you have to download it from the Internet. These steps describe how:

1. **Log in to your Fedora Core computer as any user.**

   You can log in as the superuser (`root`) if you want, but that's not necessary. By not logging in as the superuser, you don't run the risk of unintentionally damaging your computer (for example, deleting all your files).

2. **Open your Mozilla browser by clicking the blue globe on the GNOME Menu.**

   Using Mozilla is described in Chapter 11.

3. **Enter the address** www.winehq.com/site/download **in the text box at the top of the browser and press Enter.**

   Your browser displays the Wine Binary Downloads page. This page contains links to various noncommercial and commercial repositories. (We describe the commercial Wine version in the section "Introducing

CodeWeavers CrossOver Office," later in this chapter.) Just so you know, this section of the chapter describes how to obtain and use the noncommercial version of Wine.

4. **Click the Red Hat link.**

   You're redirected to the SourceForge Web site, which contains Wine packages for Red Hat and Fedora Core. SourceForge is a well-known and popular repository for many Linux systems; it isn't limited to carrying just Wine.

5. **Select the latest Fedora Core RPM.**

   RPM, or Red Hat Package Manager, is used to install and manage software. See Appendix E for information about using RPMs.

   The latest version at the time this book was written was `wine-20040813-1fc2winehq.i686.rpm`. The package was compiled for Fedora Core 2, and also works with Fedora Core 3.

   Select the i386 version if you're not sure which class of Intel (or Intel-compatible) processor your computer uses. Even if your computer uses an i686-class processor, using an i386 version of Wine works — just not as efficiently as an i686.

   The SourceForge.net Download Server page opens and provides you with several geographical locations to download from.

6. **Click the link that's closest to you.**

   A dialog box opens, labeled `Enter name of file to save to....`

7. **Click the Save button.**

   The default location is your current working directory. A progress window opens, showing a progress bar and a time-to-completion estimate.

Installing Wine

You have to install Wine after you download it. These steps describe the installation process:

1. **To install the Wine package, open the Nautilus File Manager by double-clicking the Home icon in the upper-left corner of your desktop.**

   The Home icon is labeled as *`X`*`'s Home`, where *X* is the user name that you're logged in as. For example, if you're logged in as the user `gabe`, the icon reads `gabe's Home`.

2. **Right-click the Wine RPM package file you just downloaded and choose Open With⇨An Application.**

   The Open with Other Application window opens.

3. **Select Install Packages and click OK.**
4. **Enter the** `root` **password in the Query dialog box, if you're prompted.**
   - The package manager checks the current state of your computer and opens the Completed System Preparation window.
   - You can optionally click the Show Details button to see a summary of the Wine package you're about to install.
5. **Click the Continue button and Wine is installed.**

   When the Updating system window closes, your package is installed.

Alternatively, you can "manually" install the package by opening a terminal window, changing to `root` (`su -`) and entering the command **rpm -ivh wine***. See Appendix E for more information about the manual installation process.

Using Wine

Using Wine is straightforward. After you've installed Wine, you simply open your installed Windows application and then run it with Wine — Wine configures itself automatically and starts the application. The following sections provide you with three examples of the type of stuff you can do with Wine. The first example gets you started by showing how to use a built-in Wine text editor that emulates the Windows text editor. The second example shows how to obtain and run a Shareware game that's actually quite fun. The final example shows how to run an actual Windows application.

Starting Simple: Running Notepad

The Wine package you just installed contains several simple Windows applications — *emulated* versions of Windows applications, that is. The Wine contributors have done the work to duplicate the familiar Windows functionality in addition to the look and feel. Hey, we can get behind some immediate gratification.

We can take advantage of the situation by demonstrating a couple of programs. These steps describe how to run the Notepad and file manager programs:

1. **Log in as a regular user (not** `root`**).**
2. **Click the GNOME Menu and select System Tools⇨Terminal**
3. **Type the following command and the Notepad editor opens.**

```
wine notepad.exe
```

Running Wine for the first time creates a `.wine` directory in your home directory. The `.wine` directory contains all the configuration information that the Wine system needs in order to run. The configuration information is in the `config` file. Several additional files, all with the `.reg` suffix, mimic the Windows Registry. The Windows operating system uses the Registry to organize its configuration parameters; Linux on the other hand, uses separate files, such as those in the `/etc`, `/etc/sysconfig`, and `/usr/local/etc` directories, to hold its configuration information.

4. **You can use Notepad to create, modify, and save text files.**
5. **Click File⇨Exit in Notepad to exit.**

Having Fun: Playing games

Now, text editing is great — but when you've been there and done that, you can move on to a more complex application and investigate Wine's true power. Wine is good at running programs that are not yet available in Linux form (a seriously handy capability). In this section, we download and install a Windows-based shareware game.

Shareware is software that the developer lets you test for free; sometimes the software is usable for a limited trial period. If you like the program, you can — and should — send the programmer a small fee.

Wine utilities

Wine provides several useful utilities that help you configure and test it, and we describe some of them here:

wineboot: Simulates the rebooting of a Windows computer. Rebooting is necessary whenever you're installing numerous Windows applications (for example, Microsoft Word), and this utility provides that function.

winedbg: Debugs Wine applications. This utility shows what's going on under the surface, so to speak. You need to use this utility only if you're developing a Wine application.

winecfg: Helps set many Wine configuration options.

clock: Duplicates the simple Windows clock.

regedit: Duplicates the Registry editor.

progman: Functions as a program manager.

You can try running one of the Wine utilities. For example, test the `winefile` utility, which acts as a file manager.

Dull, old guys like us still like dull, old games like PacMan (wow! — even our misspent youth was dull), so we show you how to download a PacMan-like arcade game. The first set of steps describe where to download the software, and the second set of steps cover how to install and run the game (figuring out the heuristics of PacMan is up to you):

1. **Log in as a regular user and open Mozilla.**
2. **Go to** `www.tucows.com`**.**
3. **Enter** winpac **in the search text box and click the Go! button.**
4. **Click the WinPac2 link in the next window.**

   The `WinPac 2_1.03b` page opens.
5. **Click the Win98 option.**

   Mozilla opens a page where you can select a geographical region to download from.

The Wine Web page provides a database of tested applications. Go to `http://appdb.winehq.com/` to browse the applications known to run under Wine.

6. **Select a location close to you.**

   Mozilla displays a mirror location.
7. **Click on a mirror.**

   Another Web page opens giving you various versions to download.
8. **Click on the Win98 version of WinPac2.**

   A dialog box labeled `Opening WinPac2_103b.exe` opens.
9. **Click the OK button.**

   The dialog box labeled `Enter name of file to save to` opens.
10. **Click the Save button.**

    The Download Manager window opens, showing the progress of the download. The WinPac2 installation program is saved to your home directory by default.

The following steps describe how to install and run the game. Most installations should be similar to this one; you start the installation program and then see a graphical user interface (GUI):

1. **Click the GNOME Menu and select System Tools➪Terminal.**

   The GNOME Terminal window opens.
2. **Enter this command in the terminal window:**

```
wine ./WinPac2_103b.exe
```

3. **Read the license when the WinPac2 Setup: License Agreement window opens.**
4. **Click the I Agree button.**

   The WinPac 2 Setup: Installation Options window opens and shows the typical installation options.
5. **Click the Next> button.**

   The WinPac 2 Setup: Installation Direction dialog box opens.
6. **Click the Install button.**

   The WinPac 2 Setup: Completed window shows that the installation is complete.
7. **Click the Close button.**

The `C:` symbol is an alias for the `.wine/c` directory in your home directory. If your home directory is `/home/gabe`, for example, C: corresponds to `/home/gabe/.wine/c`.

You have several ways to start a Wine-based application:

- **Manually, by using a terminal emulator:** Open a terminal emulator window in the usual way and enter this command:

  ```
  wine "C:Program Files/WinPac 2/WinPac2.exe"
  ```
- **By using the GNOME Run utility:** Open the GNOME Run utility and enter this command:

  ```
  wine "C:Program Files/WinPac 2/WinPac2.exe"
  ```
- **By creating and clicking a GNOME icon:** This method is described in the set of steps immediately following. If you want to make the game easier to use (and who needs extra work?), create a GNOME icon. These steps describe the process:

1. **Right-click anywhere on the GNOME Panel and choose Add to Panel⇨Launcher.**

   The Create Launcher window opens.
2. **Enter** WinPac2 **in the Name text box and enter this command in the Command text box:**

   ```
   wine "C:Program Files/WinPac 2/WinPac2.exe"
   ```
3. **Click the Icon button and select an image from the Browse icons windows that opens.**

   For example, select the Apple icon.
4. **Click the OK button and the icon is created on the Panel.**
5. **Click the new WinPac2 icon and the game starts, as shown in Figure 14-1.**

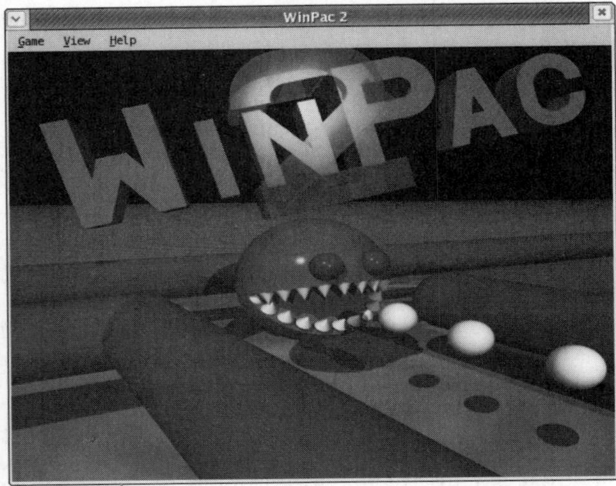

Figure 14-1: The WinPac2 game introduction window.

Oh, yeah: Play the game and if you like it, send $20 to the creators.

Using Something Useful: Microsoft Word 97 Viewer

You can also run useful applications with Wine. For example, you can download Microsoft Word 97/2000 Viewer for free. You might want to see how your OpenOffice.org files (when saved in `.doc` format) look when viewed by Microsoft Word. Microsoft allows you to download their Word97 Viewer for free.

In this section, we show you how to download and install Microsoft Word97 Viewer on your Fedora Core computer.

Wine is continually modified and updated to remain as compatible as possible with Microsoft. Wine occasionally has trouble, however, running such complex applications as Office and Word. If you encounter this type of problem, please consult our help page, at `www.dummies.com/go/rhlfedora3fd` for possible fixes. Commercial Wine wrappers, such as CrossOver Office, do a great job of running applications like those in Microsoft Office. CrossOver Office costs only a few dollars and is described in the following section.

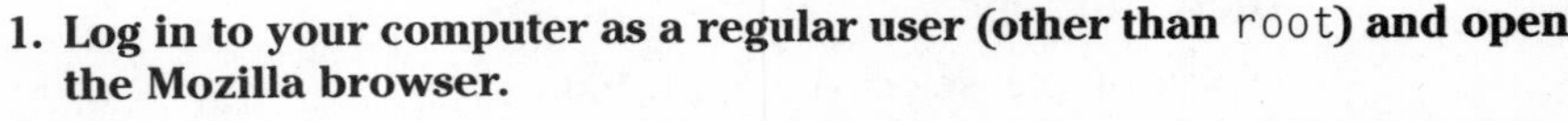

1. **Log in to your computer as a regular user (other than `root`) and open the Mozilla browser.**

   You need to have an Internet connection open and functioning for these instructions to work.

2. **Enter** www.microsoft.com/downloads **in the Mozilla Location text box.**

3. **Enter Word 97 Viewer in the Keywords text box and click the Go button.**
4. **Click the Word 97/2000 Viewer (Windows 95/98/NT) link.**

   The Word 97/2000 Viewer (Windows 95/98/NT/2000) page opens.
5. **Click the Download button.**

   A dialog box labeled `Opening wd97vwr32.exe` opens.
6. **Click the OK button.**

   The software downloads.
7. **Click the GNOME Menu and select System Tools⇨Terminal.**
8. **Enter the following command in the terminal window.**

   ```
   wine wd97vwr32.exe
   ```
9. **Click the Yes button in the Microsoft Word Viewer 97 Setup dialog window.**

   The Microsoft Word Viewer 97 Setup window opens.
10. **Click the Continue button.**
11. **Click the OK button when prompted to save the files.**

    A license agreement dialog box opens.
12. **Read the license and click the Accept button.**

    A dialog box labeled `To start installation...` opens.
13. **Click the Install button.**
14. **Click the OK button if the Microsoft Word Viewer 97 Setup was completed successfully.**

    The Word Viewer 97 Setup window closes.

With the installation complete, you can run the Word Viewer 97 application now. Use the following instructions to start the application.

1. **Click the GNOME Menu and select System Tools⇨Terminal.**
2. **Enter the following command in the Terminal window.**

   ```
   wine "C:\Program Files\WordView\WORDVIEW.EXE"
   ```

   Microsoft Word Viewer 97 opens, as shown in Figure 14-2.
3. **Use the Open Files window, which is opened by default, to find and open a Word file.**
4. **When finished, click File⇨Exit to leave the application.**

You can download and use Wine to run numerous useful and fun applications available from the Microsoft Web site. You can get applications such as Media Player for free. Check it out.

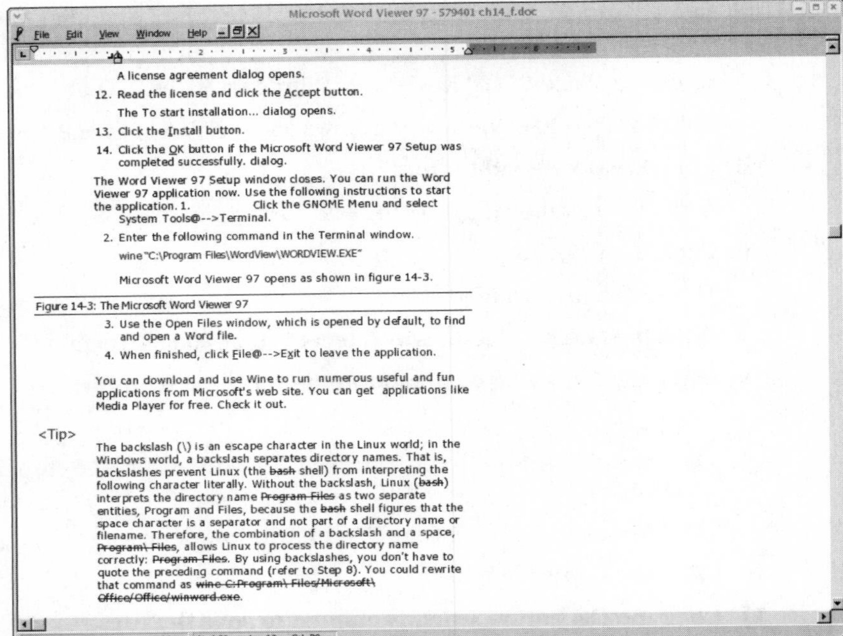
Microsoft Word Viewer 97 - 579401 ch14_f.doc
File Edit View Window Help
A license agreement dialog opens.
12. Read the license and click the Accept button.
The To start installation... dialog opens.
13. Click the Install button.
14. Click the OK button if the Microsoft Word Viewer 97 Setup was completed successfully. dialog.
The Word Viewer 97 Setup window closes. You can run the Word Viewer 97 application now. Use the following instructions to start the application. 1. Click the GNOME Menu and select System Tools@-->Terminal.
2. Enter the following command in the Terminal window.
wine "C:\Program Files\WordView\WORDVIEW.EXE"
Microsoft Word Viewer 97 opens as shown in figure 14-3.
Figure 14-3: The Microsoft Word Viewer 97
3. Use the Open Files window, which is opened by default, to find and open a Word file.
4. When finished, click File@-->Exit to leave the application.
You can download and use Wine to run numerous useful and fun applications from Microsoft's web site. You can get applications like Media Player for free. Check it out.
<Tip>
The backslash (\) is an escape character in the Linux world; in the Windows world, a backslash separates directory names. That is, backslashes prevent Linux (the bash shell) from interpreting the following character literally. Without the backslash, Linux (bash) interprets the directory name Program Files as two separate entities, Program and Files, because the bash shell figures that the space character is a separator and not part of a directory name or filename. Therefore, the combination of a backslash and a space, Program\ Files, allows Linux to process the directory name correctly: Program Files. By using backslashes, you don't have to quote the preceding command (refer to Step 8). You could rewrite that command as wine C:Program\ Files/Microsoft\ Office/Office/winword.exe.
Page 9 Sec 1 9/14 At 4.3" Ln 13 Col 29

Figure 14-2: The Microsoft Word Viewer 97.

TIP

The backslash (\) is an escape character in the Linux world; in the Windows world, a backslash separates directory names. That is, backslashes prevent Linux (the `bash` shell) from interpreting the following character literally. Without the backslash, Linux (`bash`) interprets the directory name `Program Files` as two separate entities, Program and Files, because the `bash` shell figures that the space character is a separator and not part of a directory name or filename. Therefore the combination of a backslash and a space, `Program\ Files`, allows Linux to process the directory name correctly: `Program Files`. By using backslashes, you don't have to quote the preceding command (refer to Step 8). You could rewrite that command as `wine C:Program\ Files/Microsoft\ Office/Office/winword.exe`.

Introducing CodeWeavers CrossOver OfficeWine helps you tap into the resources of the Windows world. Wine is developed under the open-source system, where volunteers provide countless hours of service and innovations to the computing world. The open-source community, however, doesn't limit itself to just the noncommercial world. Software developed under the General Public License (GPL) permits commercial use as long as no restrictions are placed on the original GPL software.

VMware: A Virtual Reality Machine

Sometimes you need to use an application that just doesn't run under Linux, not even with the help of Wine. For example, one of us authors has to use a trouble-ticket system to fix customers' problems. The problem is that the trouble-ticket application doesn't run under Linux, with or without Wine. That author must then install both Windows and Linux on his computer (a *dual-boot* system) or else maintain a separate one for the sole purpose of running the single application.

Nothing is wrong with using a dual-boot computer, of course. But it seems a waste of time if all you need to do is run one or two applications. Dual-boot computers also have to be rebooted whenever you need to switch from operating system to the other. An alternative to dual booting is VMware, a commercial product from VMware, Inc. This program creates a virtual computer within a physical computer. The virtual computer runs as an application, just like OpenOffice or Mozilla.

VMware looks and works just like a real PC. The virtual VMware PC can run an operating system such as Linux or Windows in just the same way any real computer can. The operating system running on the virtual machine behaves just like the real operating system. Any applications that it hosts, therefore, look and work just like the real applications! VMware creates not only virtual computers, but also virtual networks (imagine trying out a network design before you have to hook it up . . .). Each virtual computer that you configure to use bridged networking connects to a virtual switch. If you create two virtual machines on a single host, therefore, each machine can communicate with the other — and the host itself — as though they were connected to an Ethernet hub. This capability allows you to create experimental and production virtual networks. For example, you can use a single powerful PC to create several virtual servers rather than purchase and maintain individual ones.

VMware is (we've found) also good for writing Linux books. Writing techy books like this one requires you to use early beta versions of new software releases while you're writing the initial draft. The old method required installing the beta on your computer and using it for both testing and writing; alternatively, you can use two computers side by side. Both methods are clunky and cause numerous headaches when the beta does some funky thing. VMware solves the problem by allowing you to run the current production version of Fedora Core on your host computer and install the beta on the virtual computer. You can test the beta to your heart's content while writing at the same time in OpenOffice — all on the same virtual computer. Updating from one beta version to another is a snap too.

You can download the VMware Workstation product for free. It requires a license that costs approximately $300 for commercial use and $100 for educational use. It's money well spent.

VMware also offers a 30-day evaluation license for no charge. The temporary license, which isn't limited in any way other than the time limit, is ideal for testing this powerful tool. The steps in the following section describe how to download the product and its temporary license to find out about its power.

The commercial use of open-source software can provide an extra punch in certain circumstances. Open source for profit? Indeed. Companies such as CodeWeavers (`www.codeweavers.com`) and TransGaming (`www.transgaming.com`) deliver just such a punch. Both companies have added features to the basic Wine software to make the installation process simpler. CodeWeavers concentrates on making Wine easier to use on the general desktop; the company makes installing and using Microsoft Office, Internet Explorer, and various plug-ins easy. The TransGaming product WineX, covers the other side of the computing spectrum by providing a gaming-oriented system.

This book is oriented toward using Linux as a useful day-to-day operating system for a workstation. Our work (for example) is tilted toward using word processors and similar programs. We leave it to you to experiment with WineX. Suffice to say that our game-oriented colleagues find WineX useful.

CodeWeavers produces two consumer-level products: CrossOver Office Standard and CrossOver Office Professional. Both Professional and Standard editions provides an installation utility that works with many more Windows applications than does Wine. Crossover Plugin provides internally developed software that helps in using plug-ins. CrossOver Office uses mostly unmodified Wine software, but provides a slick installation system.

CrossOver Office Professional 3.0.1 costs $84.95 while the Standard version is priced at $39.95. (Those prices apply when you download the product from the Internet. The CD versions cost a little more.)

Downloading the CrossOver Office Standard Trial Version

CodeWeavers graciously provides a 30-day evaluation license for CrossOver Office Standard edition. You download the full version of the product but are only limited to 30 days. These steps describe how to download the trial version of CrossOver Plugin:

1. **Log in to your Fedora Core computer as the superuser.**
2. **Open Mozilla and go to the following Web site:**

   ```
   www.codeweavers.com/site/products/download_trial
   ```

3. **Click the Download Trial button.**
4. **Fill out the registration form and click the Request Evaluation button.**

   The Download Trial Version of CrossOver page opens, informing you that instructions for installing CrossOver are being e-mailed to you.

5. **Open the URL listed below (Codeweavers e-mails it to you):**

   ```
   http://crossover.codeweavers.com/download/office-trial
   ```

The CrossOver Secure Download window opens.

6. **In the Access Key and Serial Number text boxes, enter (respectively) your access key (that is, your e-mail address) and the serial number that Codeweavers e-mailed to you.**
7. **Click the Download button.**

   A dialog box labeled `Opening install-crossover-standard-demo-3.0.1.sh` opens. (The version might change after this book is published.)
8. **Click the OK button.**

   The Enter Name of File to Save To dialog box opens.
9. **Click the GNOME Menu and select System Tools➪Terminal.**
10. **Enter the following command in the Terminal window.**

    ```
    chmod u+x install-*.sh
    ./install-crossover-standard-demo*.sh
    ```

    The License Agreement dialog window opens.
11. **Click the OK button and the CrossOver Office Standard Setup window opens.**

Using CrossOver Office Standard

The next phase of the configuration process allows you to choose from numerous popular Windows applications to install. When you select an application, it's automatically downloaded from the Internet for you. No muss, no fuss.

These steps describe how to select and automatically download a Windows plug-in:

1. **Click the Begin Install button in the next CrossOver Office Standard Setup window.**
2. **When the installation completes, click the Configure Now button.**

   A dialog opens prompting you to configure as root.
3. **Click the Next button.**

   A dialog window informs you that a security patch has been installed.
4. **Click the OK button.**

   Another dialog box informs you that the ExecShield system is preventing Crossover Office from working. ExecShield is a system that minimizes the ability of buffer overflow exploits from working on your machine. You must use your judgment whether you want to proceed with these instructions and disable the system.

5. **Click the Disable Exec Shield button.**

   Another dialog box prompts you to finish disabling Exec Shield. It also tells you how to re-enable Exec Shield.

6. **Click the OK button.**

   A window opens prompting you to enter the `root` password.

7. **Enter the `root` password and press the Enter key.**

   The Plugin Setup dialog box opens.

8. **Enter *y* at the next prompt.**
9. **Press the Enter key again.**

   Exec Shield is disabled until you re-enable it. The CrossOver Office Standard Trial dialog box opens.

10. **Click the Register later button.**

    The Welcome window opens.

11. **Click the Next> button.**

    The next window shows where the software will be installed.

12. **Click the Next> button.**
13. **If you're connected to a LAN that uses a proxy firewall, enter the host and port number of the proxy.**
14. **Click the Finish button.**

    The CrossOver Office Standard Demo Setup window opens.

Installing Internet Explorer 6

Crossover Office Standard Demo is installed. You can now install Windows applications. For instance, if you have a Microsoft Office XP Professional license and disc, you can use Crossover Office to install and use it (you can use Wine too, but it's less reliable).

You can also use Crossover Office to do this setup by following these steps:

1. **Click the Install... button in the CrossOver Office Standard Setup window.**

   The CrossOver Installation Wizard dialog box opens.

2. **Click the Internet Explorer 6.0 option in the Install Software window.**
3. **Click the Next> button.**

4. **Click the Next> button in the next Install Software window.**

   The CrossOver Evaluation License window opens.

5. **Click the OK button.**

   The Internet Explorer download starts and you're prompted to accept Internet Explorer license.

6. **Click the I accept the agreement radio button.**

7. **Click the Next> button.**

   The Windows Update: Internet Explorer dialog box gives you two choices: Install with a typical setup or use a custom one. We'll use the default typical installation.

8. **Click the Next> button.**

   The Internet Explorer components are downloaded.

9. **Click the Finish button when the Restart Computer dialog box opens.**

   An Internet Explorer icon is placed on the GNOME Desktop. Click the icon and a full version of Internet Explorer 6 opens, as shown in Figure 14-3!

Microsoft Windows Media Player 6.4 is installed when you install Internet Explorer 6.

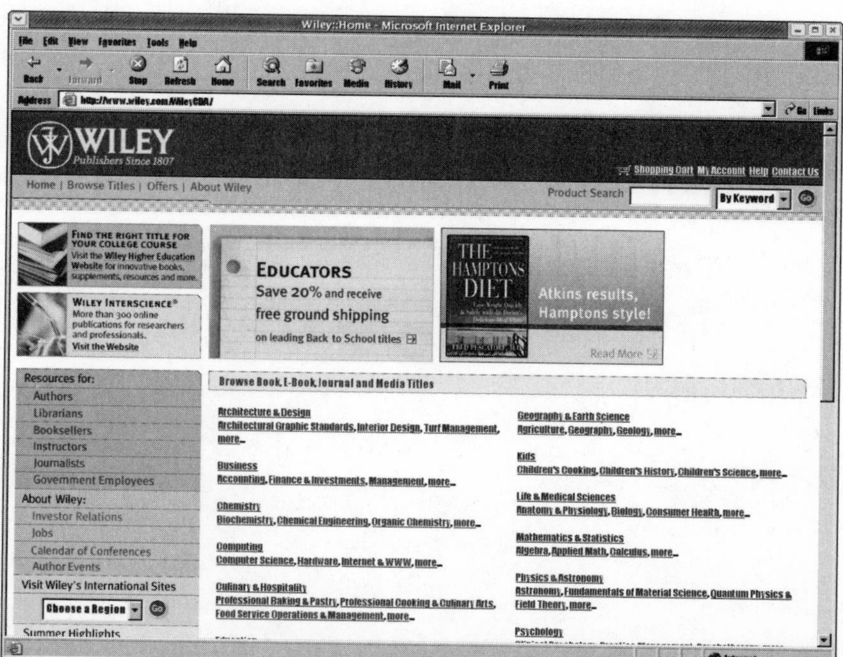

Figure 14-3: Internet Explorer 6, ready for blastoff.

Part IV
Revenge of the Nerds

"I'm not saying I believe in anything. All I know is since it's been there our server is running 50% faster."

In this part . . .

In the great tradition of slackers and procrastinators, we have put off the real work as long as possible. In this part, you find out how to make a server out of your Fedora Core computer. These chapters don't instantly turn you into a Linux guru capable of commanding six-figure consulting fees, but they do introduce you to the technical side of Linux.

We start by describing in Chapter 15 how to build a simple local-area network (LAN). Building a LAN isn't as difficult as it first sounds. You connect your computers, configure them to recognize each other, create an Internet gateway or firewall, and (with any luck) you're off and running.

Chapter 16 shows you how to use your Fedora Core computer as a network server on your newly created network; you can also provide services to the Internet.

We get serious in Chapter 17 and describe how to start securing your Fedora Core servers and private network. You should consider this chapter an introduction to security and plan on learning more.

If (okay, *when*) you need to troubleshoot Fedora Core, check out Chapter 18. It provides some detailed help in fixing computer problems, with a special focus on networking. When you're done with this part, you will be wearing pocket protectors with the best of us!

Chapter 19 returns from the serious world of computer security to have some fun. The chapter describes how to run a streaming audio service. (Yes, you can run your own private-network radio station online.)

Chapter 15

Building Your Own Private Network

In This Chapter

- Designing and creating your private network
- Building an Internet gateway
- Building a private network firewall

A *private network* is made up of two or more computers, interconnected so they can communicate with each other; you can also refer to a private network as a *local-area network* (LAN). The computers are generally in close proximity within a room or building. Unlike the Internet, which is designed to allow the world's computers to communicate with each other, LANs are designed to keep communication local and private. (You can always connect your LAN to the Internet, of course, but we talk about that topic elsewhere in this book.)

Building a private network isn't as difficult as it may sound. First, you have to decide on a general network layout. Second, you have to physically connect the computers with cables and wireless devices. Third, and last, you have to configure each computer's network settings. Design, connect, configure — one, two, three — it's as simple as that.

This chapter shows how to build a simple LAN. If you want to know how to add a Linux computer to an existing network, check out Chapter 7. To find out about adding a firewall to your LAN, check out Chapter 8.

In this chapter, we show you how to wire computers together. You should refer to the Linux network-configuration instructions in Chapter 7 to connect individual computers on your network. The steps in Chapter 7 are also designed to work with any LAN, including the one you're building here.

In this chapter, we describe how to connect computers to form a LAN. However, you can connect many other devices to a network. You can connect a wide range of devices to a network (whether it's wireless or wired); these include broadband (cable and DSL) Internet modems, routers, switches, hubs, network-capable printers, and even some personal digital assistants (PDAs). In the future, we fully expect to be able to connect nearly every electronic device to a LAN. We discuss only computers here because we're focusing on getting your Fedora Core computer connected. However, remember that you're not limited to networking *only* computers.

Designing and Building Your Private Network

Private networks take on many shapes and sizes. As you may expect, the design of a LAN for a large- or medium-size organization is different from what you'd use for a small office or home. Individuals and small organizations generally don't require complex networks unless the work is complex enough to need such a tool. For the purposes of this book, we assume that you want and need a simple network — and Linux excels at networking. We describe how to design a basic LAN that is both powerful and reliable. This network can be used for many small- or medium-size businesses and most households.

This chapter shows you how to design a simple, flat network. *Flat* refers to the fact that all the computers connected to the network communicate over a single *subnetwork* (or *subnet*). Subnets can be combined within a single LAN, but that makes the network more complex to design, build, and maintain.

The network we describe in this section is also designed to use a Fedora Core *Internet gateway* — a computer that acts as a portal, connecting the private network to the Internet. The networked computers in the private network — also referred to as *hosts* or *clients* — are connected via one of two methods:

- **Wired connections:** Hosts are connected to the LAN through a device called an *Ethernet hub* or *Ethernet switch* (or just *hub* or *switch*). Switches are superior to hubs in performance and security, and have become the standard. For your LAN, we suggest that you use an Ethernet switch to connect all the computers (hosts) — including the Internet gateway. Figure 15-1 shows an example of our private network, where the interconnecting fabric is the Ethernet switch. (In recent years, Ethernet switches have become so inexpensive that Ethernet hubs have all but disappeared.) Our example network consists of two computers: Veracruz and Cancun.

- **Wireless connections:** Wireless devices make it possible to build a network without interconnecting cables. Wireless networks can take two forms:
- **An access point:** Using a device called an *access point,* you can connect wireless hosts to a LAN. This design has the hosts connect to the access point via radio frequency (RF) signals. The access point also connects to a wired network, and the wireless hosts communicate with the wired network through that connection.

  Access points have become the most popular system for creating wireless LANs. You can find access point devices in consumer electronics stores for much less than $100.

  - **Ad-hoc mode:** This is an alternative wireless-connection method that doesn't require a separate access point, other than a wireless device for each host (*ad hoc* is the Latin equivalent of "whatever works"). Wireless hosts communicate directly with each other by using ad-hoc mode. (You can read more about ad-hoc mode in the "Wiring without wires" section later in this chapter.)

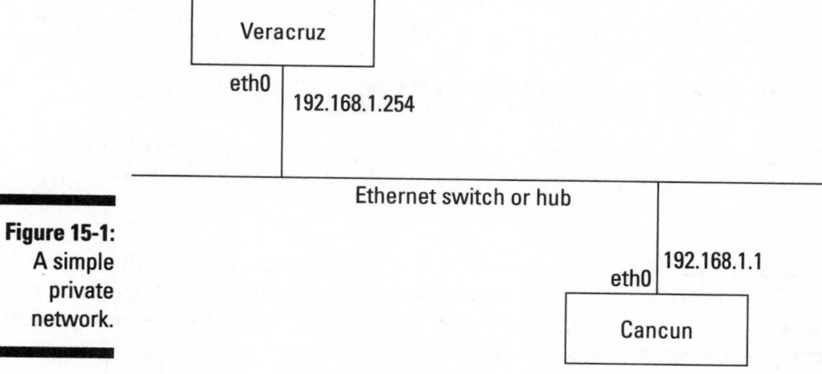

Figure 15-1: A simple private network.

Where did all the wires go?

The RF (radio-frequency) signals used by wireless networks are the same ones you tune in to on your radio — or communicate with on your cell phone — or use to open your garage door. The only differences between the RF signals coming from an AM radio station and a wireless network device are its frequency and strength.

The Federal Communications Commission (FCC) permits anybody to use the 5-gigahertz (GHz) portion of the frequency spectrum — billions of cycles per second — for any purpose as long as the signal strength is low. In effect, radio signals replace the wires in a wireless LAN.

The ABCs of switches and hubs

Switches are better than hubs because switches are more secure and faster. Here's a quick comparison to illustrate the differences.

Suppose your network consists of three machines — A, B, and C — all connected to a switch. When Machine A wants to communicate with Machine B, the switch transmits the network traffic from A directly to B. Machine C is out of the loop. By making sure that C doesn't know what A and B are saying, the switch keeps network communication private. Hubs, on the other hand, broadcast the network traffic from one machine to all machines connected to the hub. When A sends information to B, the hub broadcasts that information to both B and C.

Switches are faster than hubs because network traffic flows only between the machines that are talking to each other. The computers that aren't talking to each other don't use the switch's *bandwidth* (the maximum rate at which information can be transmitted). For example, when Machine A is sending information to Machine B, Machine C doesn't slow up the communication speed by sucking up the bandwidth.

Wiring your network with, yes, wires

This section describes how to build a wired network. You can mix wired and wireless networks, but, for simplicity, we describe how to build a pure wired or wireless network.

Way back in prehistoric times (circa 1996), you had to be technically savvy to wire your own network. Wiring consisted of coaxial cables like those used for cable-TV connections. Coaxial cables are bulky and require you to use special tools to attach the connectors to the cable ends.

Life is easy now. Wiring your network requires that you obtain Cat-5 cables, similar in appearance to telephone cables. *Cat-5* cables are manufactured with telephone-like connectors that are a snap (pardon the pun) to use. No muss, no fuss.

You can buy Cat-5 cables at any electronics store. They come in many colors and sizes. Cat-5 cables aren't cheap, but they're not terribly expensive either. They're reliable and much easier to work with than coaxial cables.

You have to use a network switch or hub in conjunction with Cat-5 cables. Switches and hubs are the glue that holds your network together. Both switches and hubs connect individual computers so they can communicate with each other.

Most, if not all, networking equipment is now based on the Ethernet protocol. Ethernet is inexpensive and readily available. You can purchase it from any consumer-electronics store, mail-order catalog, or online computer seller. You don't need to know any of the technical aspects of Ethernet because it requires no configuration. You need to know only that an Ethernet connector looks similar to a telephone jack. Remember, however, that Ethernet and telephone jacks aren't compatible.

For your network, start by connecting your machines to a central switch. (You can use a hub, if you want.)

Although you can connect as many computers as your switch or hub can handle, to keep the job as simple as possible, these steps describe how to wire two computers, Cancun and Veracruz. The steps assume that you have a switch or hub and at least two Cat-5 cables; here's what to do with them:

1. **On the first computer, plug one end of a Cat-5 cable into the Ethernet network interface connector (NIC) on the back of the machine.**
2. **Plug the other end of the cable into the switch.**

   A green light should appear near the connector you used on the switch. The green light indicates that you have *link status,* indicating that an Ethernet connection has been established: You have an active connection between the computer and the switch.

   If you don't get link status, make sure that both connectors on the cable have been properly inserted. Pull each connector out and firmly press it back in (a procedure called *reseating*).

   If this suggestion doesn't fix the problem, make sure that the cable is working correctly. Check the cable for cracks and cuts, for example. Check the cable's connectors for loose wires. Substitute another cable, if possible; use a cable that you know works. That can help you determine whether the suspect cable is at fault.

   If neither of these options works, you may have a broken switch, cable, or Ethernet NIC, or any combination. You may have to replace either or all of the devices to determine the real problem. Perhaps you can borrow a known good cable and NIC from a working network and use them to narrow down (or eliminate) the problem.

3. **Repeat Steps 1 and 2 for each additional computer.**

After you have successfully connected all your computers to the switch, you can proceed to the section "Building an Internet Gateway," later in this chapter. That section describes how to build an Internet gateway on a Linux computer. The Internet gateway connects your entire private network to the Internet.

Wiring without wires

Life has gotten easier in the past few years. Wireless networking is the best technological advance for home or small-business network users in the past five years, and it's now affordable for consumers.

Going wireless provides the following advantages:

- **Not having to say you're sorry while stringing cables around your house or office.** You don't have to spend money and time pulling wires through walls, ducts, attics, and cellars, for example. (The authors have enjoyed all these activities.) You also save the cost of the cables themselves.
- **Geographical freedom:** You have the freedom to use your computers anywhere, regardless of where your server or Internet gateway or printers are located. Ah, life is easier when you can sit outside on a nice day and clack away at the keyboard.
- **Looking good:** You look high-tech even if you're not. You can impress your friends and family.

However, wireless networking has some drawbacks:

- **Reduced security:** Wireless communications is more vulnerable to hackers. You can partially protect your network by using wireless encryption. You can further increase security by using application-based encryption such as Secure Shell (SSH) and Secure Socket Layers (SSL).
- **Reduced speed:** Wireless networks are generally slower than wired ones. The most commonly available and cheap wireless devices work at a few megabits-per-second (Mbs). Newer devices work at about 10 Mbs. This is slower than the typical wired network operates at 100 Mbs.
- **More complexity:** Configuring a wireless network is a little more complex than wired ones. You have to configure an encryption key and other options to make a wireless network work.

The process of constructing a wireless network is straightforward. You have to decide how to connect your wireless devices to your private network. You can do that in two ways:

- **Use a wireless access point:** A *wireless access point* (WAP) is a device through which wireless devices communicate. An access point provides a single point of contact through which all other devices communicate. If you install and use access points as part of the network structure, you're using *infrastructure mode.*

An access point uses two network connections. One is an Ethernet port that connects to your private LAN through a Cat-5 Ethernet cable, and the other point connects to your wireless devices. The access point serves as a common connection point to your LAN.

The other connection point is the access point's wireless receiver. The wireless "port" communicates with all other wireless devices on your network.

- **Use point-to-point (ad-hoc) communication:** Contrary to popular opinion, you *can* create a wireless network without an access point. Wireless NICs are designed to communicate directly with each other, as well as through an access point. You configure each NIC to know a common network name and a common encryption key, and voilà — the NICs form their own ad-hoc network by communicating directly with each other. We show you how, later in this section.

  Point-to-point communication is referred to as *ad-hoc mode*. The term *ad hoc* is a polite way to say *kludge* — it means putting something together with what you have, in whatever way you can. Using wireless ad-hoc mode means that each wireless device can communicate with the other wireless devices. (Setting up a network with wireless NICs is less expensive than using WAPs.)

You can purchase an access point to construct your wireless LAN (though you may have use the trendy term *Wi-Fi network*, which means the same thing, so the salesperson knows what you're talking about). That's simple and quick, if a little expensive. If you choose that route, we leave it up to you to follow the access point's instructions for connecting other computers to it. You can follow the steps in Chapter 7 for configuring your Fedora Core wireless network-interface card (excuse us, *Wi-Fi NIC*) to an access point.

We describe how to save a few bucks and use a Linux computer to build an ad-hoc network. Building an ad-hoc network requires you to put a Wi-Fi NIC on a Linux gateway. You then configure every computer on your private network to use the same network name and encryption key. The computers can then communicate directly with each other through the Linux gateway to the Internet.

Follow these general steps to create a wireless LAN:

1. **Install both a Wi-Fi and an Ethernet NIC on the Internet gateway computer.**

   Each of your private network's computers can talk to the Internet gateway through the wireless NIC. The Ethernet connects the gateway to the Internet through either a DSL or cable modem; you can substitute a telephone modem for the Ethernet NIC, if necessary.

The next section in this chapter describes how to build an Internet gateway.

2. **Install a Wi-Fi NIC on each of your Linux and Windows computers.**
3. **Configure each Wi-Fi NIC to use the same network name and encryption key.**

   Refer to Chapter 7 to find out how to configure a Wi-Fi NIC; use the network IP addresses, netmasks, and other items described there.
4. **Configure your Internet gateway to forward your private network traffic to the Internet.**
5. **Configure a firewall on your Internet gateway.**

   Refer to the section "Protecting your LAN with a firewall," later in this chapter.

One advantage of using *infrastructure mode* (which is what you have when your network specifically incorporates access points) is that a wireless device can move from access point to access point without reconfiguration. Access points provide mobility and flexibility within the LAN, which can be a good thing if you happen to work on a large, dispersed environment. For example, if your company is spread across several locations, you want to be able to use your computer anywhere. However, if you don't configure your access point correctly — for example, by not using an encryption key — flexibility becomes a security liability. Make sure that you correctly configure all your wireless devices.

Building an Internet Gateway

Okay, you have built your LAN. Woo-hoo! That wasn't too hard. The next question is "What can you do with it?" One answer is that every computer on your private network can communicate with all the others and share information and services. (We describe in Chapter 16 how to share some useful network-based services. You find out how to share files and printers, configure a Domain Name Service — DNS — server, and build a simple Web server.)

One essential network function is to be connected to the Internet. Chapters 5 and 6 show you how to connect a single, stand-alone Linux computer to the Internet. We expand that process a step further and show you how to turn the Internet connection into one that can be used by the entire private network. Any computer connected to your LAN subsequently has Internet access. Sharing is good, and your mom should be pleased.

The remainder of this chapter deals with building an Internet gateway. We assume that you have a working Internet connection, as we describe in Chapters 5 and 6. This connection is the conduit from your LAN to the Internet. You only have to configure a Linux computer to redirect *(route)* Internet-bound traffic from your LAN to the Internet and modify the firewall we describe in Chapter 8 to work with the gateway.

Understanding IP forwarding and network-address translation (NAT)

An Internet gateway requires a Linux computer that has two network connections. You need one Ethernet or wireless NIC to connect to your LAN. The other network connection is used to make the Internet connection; this connection may be a traditional telephone-based modem, a DSL modem, or a cable modem. You use an Ethernet NIC to make the second connection.

Suppose you open Mozilla on the sample Fedora Core computer Cancun (with the IP address `192.168.1.1`) and enter the URL `fedora.redhat.com`. Network packets bound about your LAN and then fly out to the Internet (and back again), and Mozilla ends up displaying the Fedora Core Web page.

Lots of things have to happen to make all these other things happen. Here's a simplified version of how it all works:

1. Mozilla asks Linux to look up the address, via DNS, which translates `fedora.redhat.com` into the numeric IP address `209.132.177.50`.
2. Linux compares the IP address to its internal routing table. The operating system directs network traffic to the default route if the address doesn't match its local networks. (In other words, if the IP address belongs to a machine on the private network, Linux directs its communication to the Ethernet device connected to the LAN. If the IP address is external to the LAN, however, Linux forwards the packets to the appropriate router.)

   In this case, `209.132.177.50` doesn't exist on the LAN, so all traffic for the browsing session is directed to the default route.
3. In the private-network example we describe, the default route of each host points to the Internet gateway Veracruz. For example, all Internet-bound network packets that Cancun produces are sent to Veracruz.
4. The Internet gateway Veracruz receives the outbound packets from Cancun on its internal NIC and forwards them to its external NIC. Packets going through its external NIC are directed to the Internet.

5. Veracruz (internal NIC address `192.168.1.254`) also converts the source address of packets from Cancun (`192.168.1.1`) to the source address of its external NIC. For example, if Veracruz's external NIC (connected to a DSL or cable modem) has the address `192.168.32.254`, the source address of Cancun packets is converted to that same address (`192.168.32.254`); in other words, Cancun's source address `192.168.1.1` is changed to `192.168.32.254`.
6. The packets go to their intended destination. The `fedora.redhat.com` Web server responds to the query and sends back the requested information.
7. Veracruz receives the return packets, converts their destination address back to that of Cancun, and forwards them to the private network.
8. Cancun receives the packets, and the browser displays the information.

Forwarding network traffic through your gateway

This section describes how to configure a Linux computer to work as an Internet gateway. The process requires you to configure the Linux kernel to forward packets from one network interface to another — between the LAN port and the Internet port. Because Fedora Core turns off forwarding by default, the steps in this section describe how to turn on forwarding (you also need a Linux computer with two network connections to construct a gateway):

- One network connection should be an Ethernet or wireless NIC that connects the gateway to the LAN. We refer to it as the *internal network connection.*
- The other connection is either the telephone-based modem or an Ethernet NIC connected to a DSL or cable modem. We refer to it as the *external network connection.*

Figure 15-2 shows the Veracruz computer modified to work as an Internet gateway.

You should turn off your external network connection for now. That's because turning on IP forwarding enables communication between the Internet and your private network. IP forwarding can be a security hazard until you finish the Internet gateway configuration. Temporarily disconnecting your Internet connection removes the insecurity: Unplug your (DSL, cable, or telephone) modem's external (Internet) cable.

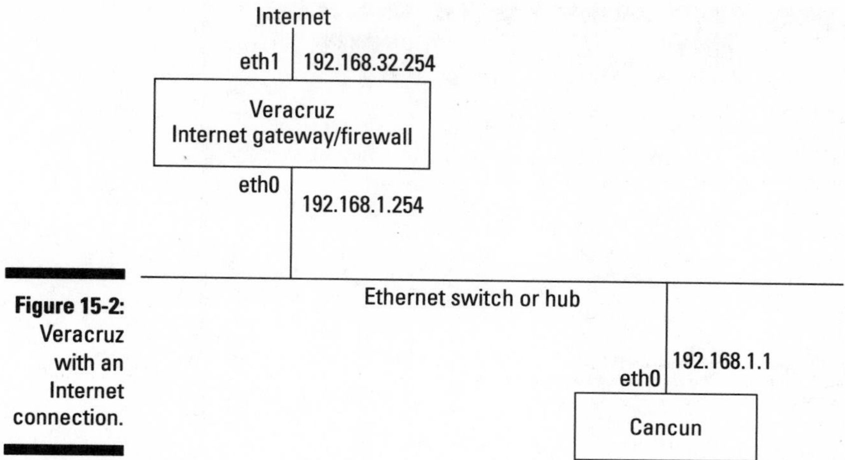

Figure 15-2: Veracruz with an Internet connection.

These steps describe how to configure a Linux computer as the Internet gateway for a LAN:

1. **Add the appropriate internal and external network connections to your intended Internet gateway.**

   For example, the internal network connection is `eth0`, and the external network connection is `eth1`.

2. **Log in to your Internet gateway (in this example,** Veracruz**) as** `root`.
3. **Click the GNOME Menu button, choose System Tools⇨Terminal.**

   The GNOME Terminal window opens.

4. **Type the following command:**

   ```
   gedit /etc/sysctl.oonf
   ```

   The gedit program displays the contents of `sysctl.conf`, as shown in Figure 15-3.

5. **Locate this line (which should be close to the top of the file):**

   ```
   net.ipv4.ip_forward = 0
   ```

6. **Change 0 to 1:**

   ```
   net.ipv4.ip_forward = 1
   ```

7. **Click the Save button and then choose File⇨Quit to close gedit.**

   You can view the change by clicking the Nautilus Refresh button. You have to restart Linux networking for the change to take effect.

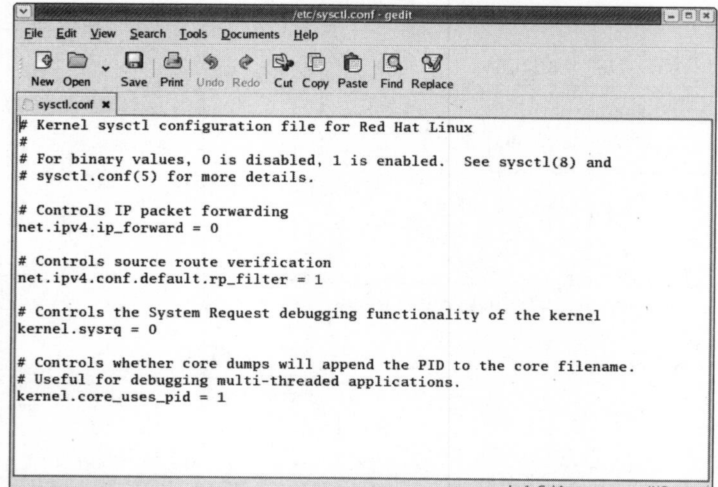
/etc/sysctl.conf - gedit
File Edit View Search Tools Documents Help
New Open Save Print Undo Redo Cut Copy Paste Find Replace
sysctl.conf
Kernel sysctl configuration file for Red Hat Linux
#
# For binary values, 0 is disabled, 1 is enabled. See sysctl(8) and
# sysctl.conf(5) for more details.
# Controls IP packet forwarding
net.ipv4.ip_forward = 0
# Controls source route verification
net.ipv4.conf.default.rp_filter = 1
# Controls the System Request debugging functionality of the kernel
kernel.sysrq = 0
# Controls whether core dumps will append the PID to the core filename.
# Useful for debugging multi-threaded applications.
kernel.core_uses_pid = 1
Ln 1, Col 1
INS

Figure 15-3: The gedit editor opens the sysctl.conf file.

8. **Open the Service Configuration utility by clicking the GNOME Menu button and choosing System Settings⇨Server Settings⇨Services.**
9. **Enter the** `root` **password if you're prompted.**
10. **Locate and click the network service.**
11. **Click the Restart button to turn on IP forwarding.**

    The Information dialog box opens.
12. **Click OK.**

Connecting your Internet gateway

After you configure your Internet gateway to forward network traffic from your private network to your Internet connection (refer to the preceding section), you need to make that connection. In this section, we describe how to use the Internet connections we introduce in Chapters 5 and 6. You build on those instructions to connect your entire network to the Internet through these connections.

TECHNICAL STUFF

From a functional viewpoint, the type of Internet connection you use (telephone, DSL, or cable) doesn't matter because all these Internet connections send and receive the same network traffic. (Practically speaking, of course, the higher throughput and lower latency of broadband make it more desirable than old telephone modems.) For this reason, you can treat as interchangeable the Internet connections you we describe in Chapters 5 and 6.

Configuring your external Internet connection

The forwarding we describe in the preceding section takes care of routing the packets to and from the Internet via your Internet gateway. Follow these steps to configure the Internet gateway:

1. **Install an Ethernet or Wi-Fi NIC on your Fedora Core Internet gateway.**

   You use this NIC to connect your Internet gateway to your private network. We identify this device as the internal NIC (`eth0`).

2. **Install an Ethernet NIC on your Fedora Core Internet gateway; skip this step and the next one if you're using a telephone modem for your Internet connection.**

   You use this NIC to connect to your DSL or cable modem. We identify this device as the external NIC (`eth1`).

3. **Connect the external NIC to the DSL or cable modem with a Cat-5 cable.**

4. **Configure your Internet gateway to allow packet forwarding.**

   (Refer to the section "Forwarding network traffic through your gateway," earlier in this chapter.)

5. **Assign an IP address to each NIC. For example, assign the address** `192.168.1.254` **to your internal NIC (**`eth0`**) and** `192.168.32.254` **to the external NIC (**`eth1`**).**

   Note that when you're using a telephone or cable modem, this action is done automatically for you. Modems connect directly to your gateway and not through an Ethernet NIC; some DSL modems can also plug directly into your computer and don't require an Ethernet connection. For this book, we assume that you're connecting via an Ethernet NIC.

   Check your protocols. Telephone modems use the Point-to-Point Protocol (PPP), whereas cable and some DSL modems use DHCP (Dynamic Host Configuration Protocol), which assigns an IP addresses to their respective interfaces.

6. **Assign a default route that points to the Internet connection device.**

   The PPP and DHCP protocols do this step automatically.

Configuring your internal private network connection

Follow these steps to configure computers or network devices on your private network to connect to the Internet through the gateway:

1. **Configure your computer with its network parameters.**

   In other words, assign an IP address and a netmask (and, optionally, but recommended, a host and network name) to each computer when you're using an Ethernet-based LAN. On a wireless network, you have to assign the IP address, netmask, common network name, and encryption key.

For example, Chapter 7 describes how to set up the sample computer Cancun. You assign it the host name `cancun`; the network name `paunchy.net`; the IP address `192.168.1.1`; and the netmask `255.255.255.0`.

If you use a Wi-Fi NIC on Cancun, you can assign the ESSID (Electronic Service Set Identifier, essentially the network name) `myfi` and specify the encryption key as `iamnotanumber`.

2. **Configure the default route on each device to point to the Internet gateway.**
3. **Rinse and repeat. (Repeat these steps for each computer on your private network.)**

After you have configured your Internet gateway and each additional computer (host) on your private network, you should test whether they can communicate with the Internet. Consult Chapter 18 for pointers on troubleshooting network problems if you encounter difficulties. After you're satisfied that you have your LAN happily connected to the Internet, turn that puppy off. You still need to set up your firewall (as we describe in the following section) because you don't want to stay connected without one.

Protecting your LAN with a firewall

After you have configured your gateway for IP forwarding, you need to protect your network from the bad guys on the Internet. This section describes how to turn your gateway into a firewall. You use the same process and many of the same rules we describe in Chapter 8; however, this firewall is designed to protect your entire network, whereas the one in Chapter 8 is oriented toward protecting individual workstations.

The firewall you're building helps to protect both your computer and your network. The firewall provides the network address translation (NAT) function, which allows the computers on your private network to access the Internet. NAT, you may recall, converts the nonroutable source IP addresses (`192.168.1.1`, for example) into the routable source IP address of your Internet connection.

Network address translation is also referred to as *IP masquerading,* or simply *masquerading.*

The basic configuration of the firewall we describe in Chapter 8 works in the new configuration. The firewall performs these functions:

- **Block all incoming, outgoing, and forwarded packets:** Start by blocking all network traffic by default. This firewall completely protects your private network and also makes it useless! Start with this policy to ensure that the firewall blocks all connections except the ones you explicitly allow.

- **Allow all internal traffic:** You must allow all network traffic on the Internet gateway's internal loopback (lo) interface. The loopback interface is used by the Linux operating system for its own, internal communication. Many internal processes communicate over this virtual network.
- **Allow all internal NIC traffic:** You reap greater convenience if you allow the computers on the private network to communicate with the gateway. For example, you may want to administer the gateway via Secure Shell (SSH). Take a lenient approach and allow any internal machine to communicate with the gateway; this strategy makes constructing the firewall easier. You may decide to limit internal access if your security needs demand it.
- **Allow all outgoing traffic from the firewall:** Allow all outgoing connections from within the firewall. The firewall needs to perform its own internal processes, such as making DNS queries.
- **Forward all traffic from the private network:** A gateway has to pass traffic from one interface to another. You change the forwarding policy to permit communication from the private network to pass through the firewall to the Internet. The downside is that traffic from the Internet can pass right through the firewall to the private network — not a good idea. You fix that problem by adding NAT, which effectively prevents external access through the firewall.

  You can set up specific forwarding rules to provide more protection to your private network. We believe that using NAT to effectively block connections that originate externally is adequate for your needs.
- **Use NAT for outgoing connections:** Create a NAT rule to make all connections originating on the private network appear to be coming from the Internet gateway. All private-network machines have their source addresses and port numbers changed to that of the gateway.

  Network-address translation isn't necessary if your Internet connection device (telephone, DSL, or cable modem) performs NAT. By providing a NAT filtering rule, however, you ensure that your Internet gateway works with any connection device — whether or not it performs NAT. NAT also prevents external access to your private network.
- **Allow incoming SSH connections:** The Secure Shell (SSH) protocol encrypts network connections. SSH provides a reasonably secure system for connecting to your private network from the Internet. We configure the firewall to allow SSH connections into our firewall.

The firewall on the Internet gateway is similar to the firewall we describe in Chapter 8, except you add IP forwarding and NAT. IP forwarding allows packets from the private network to pass outward through the firewall and on to the Internet. In this case, NAT makes all Internet-bound traffic appear to be coming from the firewall or gateway — and prevents incoming packets from being forwarded inward to your private network.

Follow these steps to create your Internet gateway firewall:

1. **Log in to your computer as `root` and open a GNOME Terminal window, by right-clicking any empty portion of the desktop and choosing Open Terminal from the menu.**

   Alternatively, you can click the GNOME Menu and choose System Tools⇨Terminal.

2. **Enter this command to turn off any running firewall:**

   ```
   service iptables stop
   ```

3. **To save the default Fedora Core firewall configuration, type**

   ```
   mv /etc/sysconfig/iptables /etc/sysconfig/iptables.bak
   ```

4. **Start by denying all network traffic on all devices, by entering these commands:**

   ```
   iptables --policy INPUT   DROP
   iptables --policy OUTPUT  DROP
   iptables --policy FORWARD DROP
   ```

5. **To allow all outgoing and incoming traffic on the loopback device, type**

   ```
   iptables -A OUTPUT -j ACCEPT -o lo
   iptables -A INPUT -j ACCEPT -i lo
   ```

6. **Type the following lines to allow all outgoing and incoming traffic on the internal NIC:**

   ```
   iptables -A OUTPUT -j ACCEPT -o eth0
   iptables -A INPUT -j ACCEPT -i eth0
   ```

7. **To allow all outgoing connections from the firewall, enter these commands:**

   ```
   iptables -A OUTPUT -m state
      -state NEW,RELATED,ESTABLISHED -j ACCEPT
   iptables -A INPUT -m state
      -state RELATED,ESTABLISHED -j ACCEPT
   ```

   These rules allow processes running on the firewall computer to connect to the Internet.

8. **To forward all traffic from the internal NIC to the external NIC, type these lines:**

   ```
   iptables -A FORWARD -i eth0 -m state
      --state NEW,ESTABLISHED,RELATED -j ACCEPT
   iptables -A FORWARD -i eth1 -m state
      --state ESTABLISHED,RELATED -j ACCEPT
   ```

   The first rule forwards outgoing traffic via the internal NIC (`eth0`). The second rule forwards the return traffic back into the private network via the external NIC (`eth1`).

Forwarding chains are independent of input and output chains. You could, for example, stop all incoming and outgoing packets to and from the firewall computer Veracruz on the private network, simply by skipping Step 6. You wouldn't be able to communicate with the firewall itself, but Veracruz would still forward packages from the private network to the Internet.

9. **To perform network-address translation on outgoing traffic, type**

```
iptables -A POSTROUTING -t nat -o eth1
   -j SNAT --to 192.168.32.254
```

   All network traffic bound from any private network address to the Internet then appears to be coming from this single address.

10. **Type the following line to allow incoming SSH connections:**

```
iptables -A INPUT -p tcp -m state -state
   NEW,ESTABLISHED -j ACCEPT --dport 22
```

11. **Save the new firewall rules permanently by typing this line:**

```
iptables-save > /etc/sysconfig/iptables
```

12. **To ensure that the firewall runs automatically whenever the Internet gateway is rebooted, enter this command:**

```
chkconfig -level 35 iptables on
```

13. **Reconnect your Internet gateway's external NIC to your DSL or cable modem.**

When the steps are complete, your Internet gateway is protected by a firewall. It also forwards network traffic from your private network to the Internet. Your network is much safer with the firewall than without it. Don't kick back just yet, however — you still have some security work to do. Read Chapters 17 and 21 for more information about how to protect yourself.

Chapter 16

Creating Basic Linux Network Services

In This Chapter

- Preparing a network server
- Building a Linux Web server
- Building a DNS server
- Building a Samba file server
- Building a print server

Linux was built from scratch with networking in mind. Networking is not merely an afterthought, as with other operating systems. Fedora Core comes bundled with software that provides file sharing, printer sharing, and other functions. This is why Linux gained its initial popularity.

In earlier chapters, we show you how to use a Fedora Core computer with an existing network. We also show you how to build a private network using Fedora Core computers as both clients and the Internet gateway, or firewall. In this chapter, we describe how to configure a Linux box to provide some popular services to the private network.

Preparing a Network Server

All examples shown in this chapter can be run from any Linux computer, such as the one set up around the Fedora Core distribution in Chapter 3. Linux doesn't care what your intentions were when you built your computer. Linux eagerly does what it's told and works gracefully as either a workstation or server.

Linux works equally well whether it's running a Web browser or a Web server; the difference between them is just the software used and how it's configured.

For example, you start the Mozilla application when you're using your computer as a Web browser, or you use the Apache program to serve Web pages. You can, of course, run both programs at once and (for example) do word processing while running a Web server.

You can configure the Fedora Core computer from Chapter 3 to provide services to a private network like the one we describe in Chapters 7 and 15. This chapter describes how to make the Apache Web server visible to the Internet. Services such as Samba and printing, however, definitely should be kept private and not shown to the Internet.

We also assume in this chapter that you're connecting to the Internet through a private network, as described in Chapters 7 and 15. (Chapter 15 shows you how to create an Internet gateway/firewall for your private network with a Fedora Core computer.) This chapter assumes that you want to use the same computer to provide services to your private network. This assumption is reasonable for *s*mall-*o*ffice and *h*ome-*o*ffice (SOHO) networks because the demands put on a modern PC by a small network aren't excessive. Using a single computer for multiple purposes greatly simplifies the work you must do and is an efficient way to use your resources.

Using a single Linux computer to act as an Internet gateway *and* provide network services is a cost-effective way of using your limited resources — but this type of configuration is more difficult to secure. Each function you place on a single machine increases the machine's potential number of vulnerabilities. Think of adding functions as similar to adding doors and windows to a house: A house with a single door and no windows is more secure than a house with 5 doors and 15 windows — but who wants to live in a dark house? As with everything else in life, security is a matter of compromise. Consult Part II and Chapters 17 and 21 in this book for ways to increase security.

Building an Apache Web Server

The Web is the Internet, and the Internet is the Web — well, that's not completely true. Although the Internet became immensely popular because of the World Wide Web (WWW), there's more to the Internet — it provides the foundation for widely used functions. E-mail is one such; the Web is another.

The Web isn't as mysterious as it may seem at first. It's composed of essentially all Web servers that are interconnected via the Internet. The Internet itself serves the same function as the world's telephone system: It allows everyone to communicate with each other. You can think of Web servers as the telephones that allow people to contact each other, businesses, and other organizations. Just as you can start a business or organization and let people contact you via your phone, you can also allow people to contact you via your Web server. This section describes how to construct a simple Web server.

Describing how to set up anything more than a simple Web server is beyond the scope of this book. Needless to say, you can configure Apache to provide a whole world (so to speak) of Web services. If you want to utilize the powers of Apache, consult such books as the excellent *Apache Server 2 Bible,* by Mohammed J. Kabir (Wiley).

Installing and starting the Web server

Linux provides the ideal platform for providing Web services. The Apache Web server system — which is bundled with Fedora Core — is easy to set up and use.

Follow these steps to install and configure a basic Apache Web server:

1. **Log in as any user and insert the companion DVD.**

   The Apache software is on the DVD.

2. **Click the Fedora menu and choose System Settings⇨Add/Remove Applications.**

   The Query dialog box opens if you're not already logged in as the superuser (`root`).

3. **Enter the `root` password if you're prompted.**

   The Checking System Status dialog box opens and displays a progress bar while it determines which software is installed on your computer. The Add and Remove Software dialog box opens.

4. **Scroll down and click the Web Server button.**
5. **Click the Update button.**

   The Preparing system update dialog box opens while the package-installation utility prepares to install the software. The window title changes to Completed System Preparation when it finishes.

6. **Click the Continue button.**

   A dialog box labeled `Updating system` shows the installation progress.

7. **Click the OK button.**

   Control returns to the Package Management window.

8. **Click the Quit button.**

If you're connected to the Internet, you can use YUM — the Yellowdog Updater, Modifier (yucky acronym, but, er, yummy functionality) — to install the Apache (or any) package. YUM connects to the Fedora Core project's download server and installs any packages you want; you can also use a Fedora Core mirror. YUM also performs other functions, such as updating your computer. Enter the command **yum -y install httpd** and YUM does all the work for you. YUM "Yummifies" your computer. Stupid puns aside, it's a wonderful system. See Appendix E for more on YUM.

The Apache Web server comes preconfigured to display a sample Web page, which we use for the example in this section. All you have to do is configure your Apache Web server. Fedora Core provides a simple GUI to help you with the configuration.

The following steps describe how to configure your server:

1. **Click the GNOME Menu and choose System Settings⇨Server Settings.**

   A Query dialog box opens if you're not logged in as `root`.

2. **Enter your `root` password if you're prompted.**

   The HTTP dialog box opens.

3. **Enter localhost in the Server Name text box.**

   Alternatively, you can enter the Internet name of your computer (for example, the computer `cancun.paunchy.net` in our example) if you want to share the Web server with your private network.

   You can configure other options by clicking to select the various tabs at the top of the dialog box. A description of those options is beyond the scope of this book; the default settings work fine for your simple Web server.

4. **Click the OK button.**

5. **Click the Yes button when the Question dialog box opens.**

The HTTP window closes and your Web server is configured. You need to start the server to view the sample Web page. Follow these steps to start the server.

1. **Click the GNOME Menu and choose System Settings⇨Server Settings⇨Services.**

2. **Enter the root password if prompted.**

   The Service Configuration dialog box opens.

3. **Scroll down the left submenu and click the box next to the httpd**

4. **Click the Start button to start the Apache Web server.**

   An Information dialog box opens.

5. **Click the OK button.**

Linux uses the term *daemon* when it's referring to a process that runs continually in order to provide a service. The Apache daemon is named `httpd`, which is short for HyperText Transport Protocol Daemon. *HyperText Transport Protocol (HTTP)* is the system used to coordinate the transfer of Web pages between the server and the client (for example, the Mozilla browser). HTTP is the common language that both sides speak.

6. **Start Mozilla.**
7. **Type** http://127.0.0.1 **in Mozilla Location text box and press Enter.**

Figure 16-1 shows that you're now viewing your Web server.

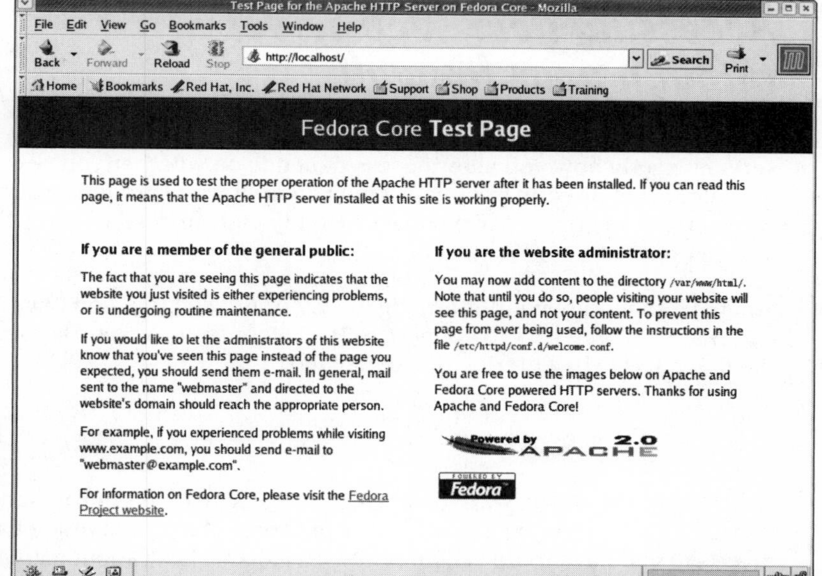

Figure 16-1: Viewing your new Web server.

You can use the `chkconfig` utility to manually configure Linux to automatically start your Web server every time you boot your computer. Enter the following command in a terminal emulator window: **chkconfig –level 35 httpd on**. The `level 35` option configures the Web server to start in either nongraphical mode (Run Level 3) or graphical (Run Level 5) modes. Running the `chkconfig` utility creates *soft links,* which are roughly analogous to a pointer. In this case, the soft link `S85httpd`, found in the `/etc/rc.d/rc3.d` and `/etc/rc.d/rc5.d` directories, is executed automatically whenever you boot your computer.

Your Web server should now be visible on only your workstation. To make it visible to your private network, repeat Step 2 and enter your host name in place of `localhost`. If your computer isn't connected to a LAN (for example, if it's a standalone machine with a telephone, cable, or DSL Internet connection), you can still use your Web server from the machine itself. Of course, keeping your Web server all to yourself isn't much fun. The following section describes how to allow access to your Web server from the Internet.

The Open Office suite has an HTML editor you can use to create Web pages. The editor is simple to use and can produce great-looking documents. Open any Open Office program (Writer or Calc, for example) and choose File⇨New⇨HTML Document. The HTML editor window opens and you can create Web pages.

Accessing your Web server through your firewall

This section describes how to open your firewall to allow access to your Web server. Exactly how you allow access depends on whether you're connecting to the Internet directly from your Linux computer or through a LAN. The steps in this section describe how to modify your firewall to allow the Internet to view your Web page.

You have to modify your Internet gateway or firewall too. You have to allow external Web browsers to connect to Port 80 on your Apache server. Create the firewall rule by entering this command:

```
iptables -A INPUT -p tcp -m state
   --state NEW,ESTABLISHED -j -dport 80
```

Amazons of the world, watch out! Okay, it takes just a bit more than the default Apache Web page to upset the big boys, but you have the basics in place. All you have to do is figure out what to sell. How about a great Linux book?

You probably need to modify your DSL modem to make your Web server visible from the Internet. DSL modems tend to use NAT by default. NAT prevents incoming connections. Cable modems generally don't use NAT, but yours may require modification too. Consult your modem's user manual for instructions about how to allow external connections.

Building a DNS Server

Every device connected to the Internet, including your Fedora Core computer, requires an Internet Protocol (IP) address in order to communicate properly. IP addresses are unique numbers and are therefore difficult for us carbon-based humans to remember and use. The Domain Name System (DNS) solves that problem by converting numbers to names, making it possible to use names like `fedora.redhat.com` rather than `209.132.177.50`. In many ways, DNS makes the Internet usable and therefore popular.

DNS is an interdependent information-sharing system — a distributed database. No centralized servers contain actual addresses, such as `fedora.redhat.com`. Instead, DNS is structured so local servers store local addresses, and a few centralized servers store information about where to go to find local addresses.

DNS makes the Internet possible. The Internet just wouldn't be practical if we had to look up numeric IP addresses from some gigantic phone book. DNS also makes working on smaller private networks more convenient. By building your own DNS server, you avǫid having to remember all the addresses of all your machines. This section describes how to build a simple DNS system to server your network.

Add the name/address pairs to each computer's `/etc/hosts` file if you don't construct a DNS server. Edit `/etc/hosts` and add the IP address, full host name, and, optionally, an alias for every computer on your private network. For example, add `192.168.1.254 veracruz.paunchy.net veracruz` to Cancun's `/etc/host` file. Then add `192.168.1.1 cancun.paunchy.net cancun` to Veracruz's `/etc/host` file. These entries allow each of the two machines in the example to address each other by name.

Introducing DNS componentsOverall, the Domain Name Systemis complex; it contains many components. But because we show you how to build a DNS server for your private network, you can use a simpler system using only a relative handful of DNS components. Building your DNS server requires a good working understanding of the basic DNS components, so here goes:

- **Domains:** You're probably familiar with network domains, whether you realize it or not. *Domains* are the networks you access all the time on the Internet. For example, `redhat.com` is a domain (and `www.redhat.com` is the name of a server within the `redhat.com` domain).
  - Domains can optionally be divided into subdomains. For example, Red Hat has a subdomain, `fedora.redhat.com`, used for the Fedora Core project.
  - Domains themselves are divided into domains. The ubiquitous `.com`, `.edu`, and `.org` are all top-level domains. They organize the Internet into business, educational, and not-for-profit arenas, respectively.
- **Zones:** Domains are divided into zones. DNS servers service zones. A zone can map directly to a domain; multiple zones can service a domain. The DNS server you're building in this section consists of a single domain that services the fictitious `paunchy.net` domain.

- **Authoritative name servers:** Every zone must have an authoritative name server. It holds the information for every host within the zone. You can create primary and secondary authoritative name servers. The secondary name servers back up the primary name servers.
- **Non-authoritative name servers:** To present data that doesn't change much over time, you can create name servers that can load fast but don't have to provide the most up-to-date information.
- **Caching name server:** Name servers can be configured to look up addresses from other name servers and temporarily save, or *cache,* the information. Caching name servers helps spread out the load of servicing large domains.
- `Root` **name servers:** The authorities that control domain-name registrations provide `root` name servers that hold the addresses of name servers for each domain. DNS queries go to `root` name servers to find out where to find authoritative name servers.

The parameters found in DNS configuration and zone files are called resource records (RR). This list describes them:

- **A records:** Address (A) records map IP names to numeric addresses.
- **C records:** Canonical (C) records define aliases for A records.
- **MX records:** Mail-exchange (MX) records specify the mail servers that service a domain.
- **NS records:** Name-server (NS) records specify the name server for a zone.
- **SOA:** The start-of-authority (SOA) parameter creates a section that describes the generic properties of a zone file. The SOA configures parameters that set the serial number and various timeouts, plus the domain name of a zone.

Getting a look at a DNS address request

This section gives you a quick look at the steps your browser takes to find the Fedora Core Web page:

1. **You open your browser and enter any URL, such as** `fedora.redhat.com`.
2. **The browser asks Linux for the Web page's numeric IP address.**
3. **Linux looks in its** `/etc/resolv.conf` **configuration file and finds the address of a name server.**

You can use any available DNS server on the Internet. For example, you can use Albuquerque's finest ISP Southwest Cyberport DNS server, `198.59.115.2`, from anywhere on the Internet. You should use your own ISP's servers because it has fewer router-to-router jumps, or *hops,* to go through, which results in better reliability and higher speed.

4. **Linux requests the IP address for** `fedora.redhat.com` **from the name server.**
5. **If the name server doesn't know the IP address of** `fedora.redhat.com`**, it asks a** `root` **server for the address of an authoritative name server for the** `redhat.com` **domain.**
6. **The root server returns the address of the Red Hat authoritative name server, the first of which is** `ns1.redhat.com` **(**`209.132.177.50`**).**
7. **The name server asks** `ns1.redhat.com` **for the address of** `fedora.redhat.com`**.**
8. **The name server** `ns1.redhat.com` **returns the** `fedora.redhat.com` **address.**
9. **Using the numeric** `fedora.redhat.com` **IP address, your browser starts communicating with the Web server.**

Constructing a DNS server

When you know what you want your DNS server to do, it's time to build one. The steps in this section describe how to build an authoritative name server for your private network. The server provides the addresses for the private, nonroutable network we describe in Chapter 15; you don't have to register the addresses with any authority. The DNS server is authoritative for your private domain, but that information isn't available outside your network.

The steps in this section show you how to install the DNS server software. You use the Fedora Core DNS configuration utility to create the various configuration files. (In the following example, the files are `/etc/named.conf`, `/var/named/local.zone`, `/var/named/paunchy.zone`, and `/var/named/1.168.192.zone` files.)

Installing the DNS software

Start by installing the bind RPM that contains the named server software:

1. **Insert the Fedora Core companion DVD.**
2. **Click the GNOME Menu and choose System Settings➪Add/Remove Applications.**

3. **Enter the** `root` **password if you're prompted.**
4. **Scroll down to the Servers section and click the Details link, next to Server Configuration Tools.**

   The Server Configuration Tools Packages Details window opens.
5. **Click the radio button next to the Red Hat DNS configuration tool package labeled** `system-config-bind-A`**.**
6. **Click the Close button.**

   Control returns to the Package Management window.
7. **Back in the Add and Remove Software window, click the DNS Name Server button.**
8. **Click to select the** `bind`**,** `bind-choot`**, and** `caching-nameserver` **options.**
9. **Click the Update button.**
10. **When the Completed System Preparation dialog box opens, click the Continue button.**

    The Updating System dialog box opens, showing the status of the package installation. The Update Complete dialog box opens when the package installation completes.
11. **Click the OK button.**

    Control returns to the Add or Remove Packages window.
12. **Click Quit.**

Creating the DNS configuration file

If you have followed the steps in the preceding section, you have to create a DNS configuration file, `/etc/named.conf`. Follow these steps to create a basic `named.conf` file:

1. **Log out and log back in.**
2. **Click the GNOME Menu and choose System Settings⇨Server Settings⇨Domain Name System.**

   At the time of this writing, the Domain Name System configuration utility doesn't automatically appear in the Server Settings menu until you log out and log back in. With any luck, this problem will be fixed by the time this book is published.
3. **Enter the root password, if you're prompted.**

   The Domain Name Service window opens.
4. **Click the New button and the Select a Zone Type dialog box opens.**

5. **Enter the name of your domain in the Domain name text box and click the OK button.**

   As in all our examples, we use the domain `paunchy.net`.

   The Name to IP Translations dialog box opens.

6. **Enter the name of your domain in the Primary Nameserver (SOA): text box and click the OK button.**

   For example, enter the name `paunchy` followed immediately by a period. In this example, we entered `paunchy.` into the text box.

7. **Click the Add Record button.**

   The Add Record dialog box opens.

8. **Enter the host name and IP addresses in the appropriate text boxes and click the OK button.**

   For example, type **veracruz** and **192.168.1.254**.

9. **Click the Add Record button and then click to select the Alias tab in the dialog box labeled (in this case)** `Add Record to paunchy.net`**.**

10. **Enter an alias in the Alias: text box.**

    You can enter aliases for host names to help remember what machines are used for. For example, enter **ns** in the Alias: text box and choose `veracruz.paunchy.net` from the Host name: menu.

11. **Click the OK button.**

12. **Repeat Steps 6 through 10 to add host names and their IP addresses and aliases to your DNS server.**

    For example, enter the name of another one of our machines, **cancun**, with the address **192.168.1.1** and the alias **gateway**.

13. **Click the Save button and then close the utility by choosing File⇨Quit.**

Starting your DNS server

After you have created the DNS configuration and zone files, you can start your server. Here's the drill:

1. **Click the GNOME Menu and choose System Settings⇨Server Settings⇨ Services.**

2. **Enter the** `root` **password if prompted.**

3. **Locate the named service and click its radio button.**

   This step selects the server to be started at boot time.

4. **Click the Restart button.**

5. **Click the OK button in the Information window that pops up.**

   You now have a DNS server.

Alternatively, you can start the DNS server by running the following command as `root`:

```
service named restart
```

Configuring your DNS clients

To use your new DNS server, you have to configure the hosts on your LAN and modify the `/etc/resolv.conf` file on your Linux computers. (You also have to modify the network settings on your Windows machines.)

Modify the `resolv.conf` file on Linux computers to look like this:

```
search paunchy.net
nameserver 192.168.1.254
```

Your private network DNS server answers local and external queries. It provides the IP addresses for machines on your LAN. It also goes out to the Internet and finds IP addresses. You get answers when you ask for Cancun's address as well as any external one, such as `wiley.com`.

You can specify as many as three name servers, so you may add a backup DNS server, if you have one, or your ISP's name servers.

Open a GNOME Terminal window and run this command:

```
host cancun
```

You see this result:

```
cancun.paunchy.net has address 192.168.1.1
```

The host command provides numerous options that provide more information about your query. For example, you can see information about where the host command gets its information. Add the verbose (`-v`) option to the preceding example and you see information similar to this output:

```
Trying "cancun.paunchy.net"
;; ->HEADER<<- opcode: QUERY, status: NOERROR, id: 18016
;; flags: qr aa rd ra; QUERY: 1, ANSWER: 1,
   AUTHORITY: 1, ADDITIONAL: 0

;; QUESTION SECTION:
```

```
;cancun.paunchy.net.            IN      A

;; ANSWER SECTION:
cancun.paunchy.net.  86400   IN    A    192.168.1.1

;; AUTHORITY SECTION:
paunchy.net.         86400   IN    NS   ns.paunchy.net.1
Received 69 bytes from 192.168.1.120#53 in 263 ms
```

This list describes what the various sections in the preceding output mean:

- **Question section:** You see in the Question section that the query is `cancun.paunchy.net`. Note that we ask for only the address of `cancun`, but that the search parameter in the `resolv.conf` file specifies that the `paunchy.net` domain be appended to `cancun`. You also see that an A record is part of the query — you're asking for an IP address.
- **Answer section:** This section shows you the answer to your query. The answer includes the host name and domain — `cancun.paunchy.net` — and its numeric IP address. The Answer section also includes the time-to-live (TTL) value.
- **Authority section:** The data in this section shows where the information was found in the preceding Answer section. You got the answer from the name server — `192.168.1.254` — that you just built.

All the computers on your network can use your DNS server. Your DNS server supplies addresses for all internal machines. The server forwards requests for external addresses as necessary.

Building a Samba Server

Early in the game, Linux gained much popularity by acting as a file server for both Windows and Linux computers. It did that by dancing the Samba. Samba is more than just a dance they do in Brazil: It's a suite of programs that speaks the same file-sharing language (the *protocol*) as Microsoft Windows. Using Samba produces a way to share the Linux file system on a network.

This section describes how to install and configure Samba on your Fedora Core computer. Samba comes bundled with Fedora Core, of course, so installation is a breeze. Samba is also configured to automatically share the ubiquitous `/home` directory, so configuration is also easy.

Samba is based on the client-server model in which a computer (server) provides services to one or more computers (clients). Samba uses the term *share* (which comes from the Microsoft Windows world) to refer to any object it exports to a network. An object can be a directory or a printer.

Samba consists of several programs, configuration files, and documentation files. The complete Samba package consists of four RPM files that come bundled on the DVD accompanying this book. The following list describes the purpose of each RPM file:

- **samba-client:** This package contains the utility and other supporting software to connect a Linux computer to a Samba server. You can use the interactive utility `smbclient` to connect to a Samba share. The default Fedora Core installation installs this package by default.
- **samba:** The Samba server software is included in this package. All the programs for sharing files, directories, and printers are included here; the two essential daemons are `smbd` and `nmbd`; the essential configuration file is `smb.conf`. The utilities for controlling the daemons are also included.
- **samba-swat:** You can manually configure the Samba configuration file, `smb.conf`, if you're an expert. However, Samba provides a Web-based system that is much easier to use and produces clean and readable configuration files.
- **samba-common:** All the software required by the other three packages is included in this file. This package is also installed by default.

Samba was originally designed and coded by Andrew Tridgell, of Australia. Samba instantly became popular worldwide — and became too much work for a few people to handle — so the Samba Project was started to take care of further development and promotion. You can find more information about Samba at `www.samba.org`.

Installing Samba

We start by showing you how to install all the Samba software on your computer. Follow these steps:

1. **Log in as any user.**
2. **Insert the Fedora Core companion DVD into the DVD/CD-ROM drive.**
3. **Click the GNOME Menu and choose System Settings⇨Add/Remove Applications.**

   If you're not logged in as `root`, the Query window opens.
4. **Enter the `root` password if you're prompted.**

   The Add and Remove Software window opens.
5. **Scroll down to the Servers section and click the Windows File Server button.**

6. **Click the Update button.**

   The Completed System Preparation dialog box opens.

7. **Click the Continue.**

   The packages are installed.

8. **Click the OK button.**

   Control returns to the Package Management window.

9. **Click the Quit button.**

Configuring Samba

When you've finished installing Samba and its configuration utility, we show you how to configure it. The process requires you to first activate SWAT and second to configure Samba.

Linux uses a general-purpose daemon called `xinetd` to handle numerous Internet service requests. When `xinetd` receives a request for a particular service, it reads the service's configuration file in the `/etc/xinetd.d` directory and starts the service (assuming all conditions are satisfied).

We must configure the SWAT `xinetd` configuration before using SWAT to configure Samba. The following steps describe how to configure `xinetd` to start SWAT:

1. **Click the GNOME Menu and select System Tools⇨Terminal.**

2. **Enter the following command to switch to the** `root` **user account:**

   ```
   su -
   ```

   (That's short for "superuser." Red cape optional.)

3. **Edit the Samba Swat** `xinetd` **configuration file by entering the following command:**

   ```
   gedit /etc/xinetd.d/swat
   ```

4. **Change** `disable = yes` **to** `disable = no`**.**

5. **Click the Save button.**

6. **Click the File⇨Quit button.**

7. **Restart the** `xinetd` **daemon with this command:**

   ```
   service xinetd restart
   ```

With `xinetd` configured, it's time to configure Samba. The following steps show how to set Samba to share your CD-ROM/DVD drive with your private network. We start by connecting to the SWAT configuration utility with Mozilla.

1. **Open the Mozilla browser by clicking the blue globe in the GNOME Panel.**
2. **Enter** http://127.0.0.1:901 **in the location text box and press Enter.**

   The Prompt dialog window opens.
3. **Enter** root **in the User Name: text box.**
4. **Enter the** `root` **password in the Password: text box.**
5. **Click the OK button.**

   The Samba configuration page opens.
6. **Click the GLOBALS link at the top of the page.**

   The Global Parameters page opens.
7. **Change the workgroup name if you use one different from the default (MYGROUP).**
8. **Optionally, change the server string to a descriptive one.**
9. **Change the security value from** `USER` **to** `SHARE`**.**

The following steps show how to configure the global Samba parameters.

1. **Click the** `SHARES` **link at the top of the page.**

   The Share Parameters page opens.
2. **Click the Choose Share pull-down menu and select** `homes`**.**
3. **Click the Delete button.**

   We remove the `homes` share because we're using share authentication — which means essentially no authentication. Without authentication, we don't want to share our home directory with the world!
4. **Enter** cdrom **in the Create Share text box.**
5. **Click the Create Share button.**

   The Share parameters page expands.
6. **Enter** /media/cdrom **in the Path text box.**
7. **Enter a comment of your choosing in the comment text box.**
8. **Click the Commit Changes button.**

   Your Samba server is now set up to share your CD-ROM with your network.

Use the following instructions to restart the Samba daemons and make your changes visible to your network.

1. **Click the STATUS button.**
2. **Click the Start All button.**

   The Samba daemons — `smbd` and `nmbd` — start. You can restart these daemons by clicking the Restart All button.

   Share authentication essentially leaves your Samba server open to anyone who wants to browse it. In this case, however, you're still safe because you're exporting the DVD/CD-ROM drive — which is read-only. Nobody can modify your file

Using the Share authentication option makes sharing objects a breeze — but use it carefully. This option also increases your security risks because there's no password protection. This risk is generally acceptable when sharing read-only objects such as printers and CD-ROMs (although you do risk unauthorized reading of what's on your read-only media). However, if you start exporting read-write shares, such as your home directory, you should switch to User Authentication mode and add user names with passwords to your Samba configuration. In that case, you have to authenticate from your Windows computer and specify a user name and password before you can print.

Building a Print Server

Fedora Core easily works with many, if not most, makes and models of printers. All you have to do is connect your computer to the printer, run the printer-configuration utility, and you're done.

Most consumer-level printers must be physically connected to a computer to work; physical connections use either USB (Universal Serial Bus) or parallel-port cables. Many business-type printers, however, use either physical or network connections. Although Fedora Core computers can connect to either type, we focus on those that use physical connections.

You can, of course, use your Fedora Core computer as a print server for your network.

The following section describes how to physically connect your Fedora Core computer to a printer. The subsequent two sections show how to configure a network print server for both Linux and Windows computers.

Connecting your computer to a printer

You have two types of printers to choose between when you're creating a print server:

- **Networked printers:** Printers that can be connected directly to a LAN are networked printers. They have their own Ethernet (and, in the future, wireless) NICs. Networked printers are divided between those that can act as their own print servers (also called *print spoolers*) and the ones that need to be connected to print servers.
- **Non-networked, locally connected printers:** Local printers must be connected to a computer through the traditional parallel port or Universal Serial Bus (USB) connector. The computer and printer must be close enough to each other to connect via parallel or USB cables.

Non-networked, locally connected printers outnumber networked printers because they cost less. But locally connected printers are less flexible because they must be connected directly to a computer; networked printers can be located anywhere that a network connection exists.

This section describes how to use non-networked computers because they're so common. The process is simple: You connect your printer to the Linux print server via the USB or parallel port. After you're connected, the Linux computer can be configured to send print jobs to the printer.

Using a parallel port requires no configuration of the Linux operating system. The USB connection, however, requires that Linux load a USB *kernel module* (essentially a driver, in Windows terminology — a small program that tells the computer how to run the device). Loading the kernel module is automatic.

Configuring a local printer

After you connect a printer, you have to configure Linux to act as a print server. Fedora Core provides an excellent print-configuration utility that we'll use later to configure our printer.

Fedora Core can handle five printer types. The printer-configuration utility allows you to configure each type. This list describes the printer types:

- **Locally connected:** Use this type if your printer is physically connected to your computer through a USB or parallel port. We use this type of configuration in the steps in this section to show you how to connect a printer to the Fedora Core print server.

- **Networked CUPS (IPP):** The Common Unix Printing System (CUPS) is the new de facto Linux and Unix printing standard. CUPS uses the Internet Printing Protocol (IPP) and is easy to use. Windows computers cannot print through CUPS. We use CUPS for the Linux-to-Linux networked print server that we describe in the following section.
- **Networked Unix (LPD):** The Line Printing Daemon (LPD) is the older printing protocol used by Linux and Unix. You can use this system if you're creating a print server that only other Linux and Unix computers use. Windows computers cannot print through LPD.
- **Networked Windows (SMB):** Use this printer type if you're printing to a Windows print server. Samba makes the print server look like a Windows print server; the clients on the private network use this setting.
- **Networked Novell:** Use this printer type if you're printing to a Novell print server.
- **Networked JetDirect:** Use this printer type if you're printing to a Hewlett-Packard (HP) JetDirect printer. The HP JetDirect interface is built into many HP and other printers. You can also purchase JetDirect print server devices that connect to non-networked, traditional printers. JetDirect print servers convert traditional printers into networked printers.

The configuration utility works with many different types of printers. The following instructions show you how to configure an Epson Stylist printer because it's a good, inexpensive, and common inkjet printer:

1. **Connect your printer to your computer by plugging in the appropriate (USB or parallel port) cable.**
2. **Click the GNOME Menu button and choose System Settings⇨Printing.**

   The Query dialog box opens if you're not logged in as `root`.
3. **Enter the `root` password, if you're prompted to do so.**

   The Printer configuration window opens.
4. **Click the New button.**

   A dialog box labeled `Add a new print queue` opens.
5. **Click the Forward button.**

   The Queue Name dialog box opens, and you're prompted to enter a name for the queue (plus an optional short description of the printer).
6. **Enter the name of the printer queue in the Name text box (the default is `printer`).**

You can use any name you want for the queue name. For example, `Epson777` clearly indicates that you're accessing an Epson Stylus 777 printer.

7. **Click the Forward button and the Queue Type dialog box opens.**

   The printer-configuration utility should detect the printer attached to either the USB or parallel port.

   You can also configure a networked printer here, if you have one. For example, if you have a high-end HP LaserJet with a JetDirect interface, select `Networked Jet-Direct` rather than `Locally-connected`.

   Linux parallel (printer) ports correspond to Windows printer ports. Linux `lp0` is equivalent to LPT1, and `/dev/lp1` is equivalent to LPT2.

8. **Click the printer device (typically, it should be listed as `/dev/lp0` or `/dev/lp1`) and then click the Forward button.**

   The Printer model window pops up.

9. **Click the Generic (click to select manufacturer) pull-down menu and select your printer's manufacturer.**

   For example, select Epson. The manufacturer's model list appears.

10. **Scroll down the model list and select your printer model.**

    For example, select Stylus Color 777.

11. **Click the Forward button and then the Finish button.**

    The Question dialog box opens.

12. **Click the Yes button to print a test page.**

    The printer utility prints a test page and opens a dialog box.

13. **Click the Yes button, assuming that the test page was printed successfully.**

    Clicking the No button displays the print queue log file in a dialog box.

    Control returns to the Printer Configuration window.

14. **Click the Apply button to save your new printer configuration and then close the configuration utility by choosing Action⇨Quit.**

    The printer-configuration utility closes and you have yourself a functioning printer.

Now you can print from your Fedora Core computer to your printer. That's great — and many people find this simple configuration is all they need. However, you can configure your computer to function as a network print server.

Sharing your printer to your private network

This section describes how to set up another Fedora Core or Linux computer to print through your print server. The first step requires you to share your printer on your network. The following steps show you how to create a printer queue to service your network:

1. **Select the print queue you just created, in the Printer configuration window.**
2. **Click the Edit button.**

   A dialog box labeled `Edit a printer queue` opens.
3. **Click the Sharing button at the bottom of the window.**

   A dialog box labeled `Sharing properties` opens.
4. **Click the radio button labeled** `This queue is available to other computers`.
5. **Click the Edit button.**

   A window labeled `Edit allowed hosts printer` opens.
6. **Click the radio button labeled** `Network address`.
7. **Enter your private network address in the text box. For example, enter** 192.168.1.0 **if you're using the network address example we use throughout his book.**

   This step is optional and you can leave the default `All hosts` option in effect. However, limiting the sharing of your printer to your private network is safer if you're connected to the Internet (or using wireless networks).
8. **Click the OK button (note that your net mask is automatically selected).**

   Control returns to the dialog box labeled `Sharing properties`.
9. **Click the OK button.**

   You return to the window labeled `Edit a print queue`.
10. **Click the OK button.**

    Control returns to the Printer Configuration window.
11. **Click the Apply button.**

Your Fedora Core computer is now ready to share its printer with other Linux computers on your private network.

Printing from Networked Linux clients

You can configure any Linux or Unix computer that uses CUPS to print through the print server that you find out how to configure in the preceding section.

These steps show you how to configure a Fedora Core computer as a print client:

1. **Log in as any user to your Fedora Core client.**
2. **Click the GNOME Menu and choose System Settings⇨Printing.**

   The Printer configuration utility opens.
3. **Click the New button.**

   A dialog box labeled `Add a new print queue` opens.
4. **Click the Forward button.**

   A dialog box labeled `Queue name` opens.
5. **Enter the name of your local queue in the Name text box.**

   The name is arbitrary and can be the same as or different from the print server queue name.

   Entering a description is optional.

   The window labeled `Queue type` opens.
6. **Click the Locally-connected pull-down menu and choose the Networked CUPS (IPP) option.**
7. **Enter the host name of the print server in the Server text box.**
8. **Change** `queue1` **in** `/printers/queue1` **to the queue name of the print server.**

   Refer to the section "Sharing your printer to your private network," earlier in this chapter for details. For example, if the queue name on the print server is Epson, you enter **/printers/Epson**.
9. **Click the Forward button.**
10. **Select the printer manufacturer by clicking the pull-down message labeled** `Generic (click to select manufacturer)`.
11. **Find and select your printer model.**

12. **Click the Forward button.**
13. **Click the Finish button in the window labeled** `Finish and create the new print queue.`
14. **Click the Yes button the Question window that opens to print a test page via your Fedora Core print server.**
15. **Click the Yes button in the Information window that opens.**

    If your print job doesn't work, click the No button, review the log information, and repeat the steps in this section or the preceding section, as appropriate.

You now have a Linux client that can send print jobs to a Linux server. The next section describes how to configure your print server for Windows clients.

Network Printing from Windows computers

Samba makes sharing a printer to Windows computers possible. The Samba configuration that we describe in the section "Building a Samba Server," earlier in this chapter, can also be used to share your printer with Windows computers. The following instructions describe how to configure Samba to allow Windows printing:

1. **Open Mozilla and enter** http://127.0.0.1:901.
2. **Enter the** `root` **user name and password when prompted.**
3. **Click the PRINTERS button.**
4. **Type the name of your printer queue in the Create Printer text box.**
5. **Click the Create Printer button.**

   The Printer Parameters page opens.
6. **Optionally enter a descriptive comment in the comment text box.**
7. **Click the pull down menu labeled** `guest ok` **and select Yes.**
8. **Click the Commit Changes button.**

   The printer configuration is saved to the `/etc/samba/smb.conf` file.
9. **Click the Status button at the top of the page.**
10. **Click the Restart All button and your printer becomes visible to your network.**

You can configure a Linux computer to print through the Linux/Samba print server. The CUPS printer driver that we show you how to install on your Fedora Core print server doesn't "understand" Windows printer drivers. You cannot use the printer drivers that come with your Windows computer. CUPS does understand the nearly universal PostScript printer language, however. Just download a generic PostScript driver to your Windows computer and use the driver to communicate with your Fedora Core print server.

The following steps describe how to download and install the Adobe PostScript print driver on a Windows XP computer:

1. **Open Internet Explorer (IE) on your Windows computer and go to** `www.adobe.com/support/downloads/main.html`.
2. **Click the Windows link under the** `PostScript printer drivers` **heading in the middle of the page.**
3. **Select on the next page the most recent driver that meets your language requirements.**

   For example, select `Adobe Universal PostScript Windows Driver Installer 1.0.6-English`.
4. **Bring your lawyers in, read the license agreement together, and collectively click the red download button.**

   The File Download dialog box opens.
5. **Click the Open button.**

   The file downloads and the Adobe PostScript Driver Installer window opens.
6. **Click the Next button.**

   The End User License Agreement window opens.
7. **Pay your lawyers more money and click the ACCEPT button.**

   The Printer Connection Type dialog box opens.

Now you get to configure the print driver you just downloaded (the hits keep right on comin'):

1. **Click the button labeled** `It is connected to your network (Network Printer)` **and then click the Next button.**

   The Windows computer should automatically see the printer share on your Linux server and display it in the text box.
2. **If your printer is detected, click the Next button.**

If no printer is detected, click the Browse button and search your private network for your computer and printer. Although a description of how to browse from a Windows computer is beyond the scope of this book, the process is generally straightforward.

An Error window pops up, but don't worry. The driver installation utility assumes that you may not want to install a generic PostScript driver.

3. **You want to install the driver, so click the Yes button.**

   The Select Printer Model dialog box opens, showing you the Generic PostScript Printer option.

4. **Click the Next button and the Printer Information dialog box opens.**
5. **You may or may not want to use this new printer as your default, so click the appropriate button.**

   Leave the Yes (Recommended) option selected so you can print a test page when you're finished.

6. **Click the Next button.**
7. **Click the Install button in the Setup Information dialog box and the driver is installed.**
8. **When the Printer Configuration dialog box opens, click the Next button.**
9. **Click the OK button when the Generic PostScript Printer Properties dialog box opens.**
10. **Click the OK button.**

    The Setup Complete dialog box shows that you're almost done.

11. **Click the Finish button and you're finished.**

Your test page should print! You can now print from your Windows *and* Linux computers through the Fedora Core print server.

If you cannot browse your Linux print server, you can configure it manually. For example, if your print server uses the IP address `192.168.1.254` and the print queue `Epson`, enter **\\192.168.1.254\Epson** in the appropriate configuration utility.

Chapter 17

Securing Your Future

In This Chapter

- Thinking security
- Preventing intruders
- Updating Fedora Core packages
- Deactivating services
- Using the Secure Shell client
- Configuring a Secure Shell server
- Securing your Web server with SSL
- Reading logs
- Introducing Security-enhanced Linux
- Understanding the security process

Protecting your computers and private network is an essential task in today's insecure world. Unfortunately, computer and network security is a big, complex job. It's still more of an art than a science.

This chapter describes several security methods and utilities that will help make the job more manageable. We have chosen the tools and systems that should give you the most bang for your buck. This chapter provides a starting point for making your computers and network safer. We encourage you to continue learning and evolving your security system.

Thinking Security

Computer security is best thought of as an imperfect and ongoing process. No single method, tool, or system can magically protect you from the Wild-West Internet. There is no silver bullet! Security, like exercise and diet, is just plain hard work.

Because no silver bullet exists, you have to use the method of *defense in depth,* which uses layers of security measures. Each layer helps to protect each other. When one layer fails, you fall back on the other. You can also add and remove layers as necessary.

Layered security systems and measures fall into four categories:

- **Prevention:** You can use security-oriented tools, utilities, and methods effectively to prevent any attacks from succeeding. Setting up firewalls and updating software fall under this heading.
- **Detection:** Not all attacks can be prevented, so detecting them, if possible, is essential. However, using an intrusion-detection system (IDS) is still more of an art than a science.
- **Eradication:** If you ever get hacked, you must be able to eradicate all traces of the compromise. Be ready to reinstall your Fedora Core operating system if you cannot identify and remove the software the hacker puts on your computer.
- **Process:** Most computer users would prefer to construct a security system and then sit back and forget about it. However, the hacker world changes as fast as the rest of the world, and the systems that work now won't necessarily work tomorrow. Therefore you must keep learning and use that knowledge to improve your security.

An Ounce of Protection: Preventing Intruders

We start by describing how to minimize your chances of being hacked. The following sections describe systems that increase your security:

- **Updating software:** The Fedora Core up2date and YUM utilities help keep your computer's software up-to-date, which eliminates vulnerabilities as they are discovered.
- **Removing services:** Hackers cannot take advantage of vulnerable software if you don't use it. Turning off unnecessary services reduces your exposure. You may also want to remove software, such as compilers, on your servers. Removing the software prevents a hacker from using it.
- **OpenSSH and SSL:** Except when you're viewing garden-variety, nonsecure Web pages, you should never communicate over the Internet (or wireless LANs) without using encryption. The open-source SecureShell (SSH) and Secure Sockets Layer (SSL) provide effective encryption for your communications.

We describe each system in this section.

Updating software to remove vulnerabilities

Standard hacker operating procedure is simple: Find and then exploit vulnerabilities. The method, simple but effective, works like this: Joe Hacker walks around the Internet, rattling doorknobs and occasionally finding one that's open. When no door is unlocked, the hacker looks for easier locks to pick. Your job is to make sure that your doors and windows are locked and reasonably safe.

Running firewalls, shutting down unnecessary services, and using good passwords ensures that you don't leave anything unlocked. Making sure that your locks aren't easily defeated requires constant supervision and maintenance. Software is getting ever more powerful, but also complex. Complexity breeds bugs, and with bugs come vulnerabilities. Because the only certainties in life are death, taxes, and buggy software, the bugs have to be fixed whenever possible. Everyone needs to continually update software whenever errors are found and corrected.

The new Linux 2.6 kernel (used by Fedora Core 3) uses the Exec-shield system to minimize the danger from buffer overflows. Hackers have long used vulnerabilities found in stack queues (buffers) to execute their own malicious programs; operating systems such as Linux use queues for their internal bookkeeping. ExecShield removes many, if not most, of those vulnerabilities.

Fedora Core uses an excellent method for updating its software: The Yellowdog Updater Modified (YUM) can be configured to automatically detect new software and install it for you. Fedora Core installs YUM by default. Next to using good passwords and firewalls, it's probably the most effective security system you can run. Fedora Core uses the YUM system too.

Follow these steps to run YUM:

1. **Log in as** `root` **and connect your Fedora Core computer to the Internet.**

   See Chapters 5, 6, and 7 for information about connecting to the Internet.

2. **Configure YUM to run automatically at boot time.**

   ```
   chkconfig --level 35 yum on
   ```

3. **If your computer is connected to the Internet through a proxy firewall, add the following line to** `/etc/cron.daily/yum.cron`**:**

   ```
   export http_proxy=http://abc.xyz:port
   ```

You'll have to change the fictitious proxy address and port (`abc.xyz:port`) to match your network's proxy.

4. **Start YUM update service via `cron`, using this command:**

```
service yum start
```

You can manually update your computer, by logging in as `root` and running the command: **yum -y update**. Removing the `-y` option forces you to verify that you want to run the updates once they've been detected.

Regularly updating your computer is an essential security measure that's easy to do. Many break-ins occur because of out-of-date software. With the help of up2date, you eliminate most vulnerabilities as they occur.

Reducing your exposure: Removing and reducing services

Hackers look for computer vulnerabilities by probing for vulnerable network services. Network services — such as Apache, Samba, and DHCP — are, of course, designed to respond to network queries. Therefore hackers can readily find out which services you run — and then figure out which, if any, attacks to use.

We describe elsewhere how keeping software updated minimizes your vulnerability. However, you can go one step further and make a service invulnerable by turning it off. One simple security rule is "Keep it simple." The simple fact is that if you don't need to run a service, you shouldn't.

We describe in this section how to eliminate or reduce both network and non-network services. These steps describe how to use the `chkconfig` utility to change the startup scripts that control when, how, and whether a network services starts at boot time:

1. **Click the GNOME Menu and choose System Settings⇨Server Settings⇨Services. Enter the `root` password if you're prompted.**

   The Service Configuration dialog box opens.

2. **Select an unnecessary service and shut it off by clicking the Stop button.**
3. **Click the OK button when the confirmation dialog box appears.**
4. **Click the check mark to the left of the service to remove the check mark.**

   Removing the check mark prevents the service from starting automatically at boot time.

5. **Repeat Steps 2 through 4 for each unnecessary service.**
6. **When you have turned off each unnecessary service, click the Save button.**
7. **Choose Quit from the File menu.**

Which services you turn off depends on your needs, of course. For example, if you're unintentionally running a Web server, turn off the `httpd` service. You generally should be able to turn off these services:

- **The Advanced Power Management Daemon (APMD):** APMD is useful if you, like most people, regularly power-off your personal workstation or laptop. However, APMD is generally unnecessary on servers that run continuously. You want to keep APMD in the former case (workstation or laptop) and remove it in the latter (server).
- **GPM:** This service allows you to use a mouse when you're running in nongraphical mode. You're running in graphical mode, so turn it off.
- **The job-queue daemon:** The `atd` daemon is used to schedule one-time cron-like jobs. If you need `atd`, you know it. Otherwise, turn it off.
- **Network File Sharing (NFS):** You need only services such as `nfs`, `nfslock`, `portmap`, and `autofs` when you're running an NFS server or client. The last thing you want to do is share files to the Internet, for example.
- **Print services:** Many people don't run the printer daemon on servers. Turn off CUPS (Common UNIX Printing System) or lpd whenever you don't need to print.
- **Samba:** As with NFS, you should turn off Samba if you don't need it.

The rest is up to you. Terminate hackers with a vengeance.

Using chkconfig

You can use the CLI-based `chkconfig` utility to set services to start automatically or not. Open a GNOME Terminal session and log in as `root` (type **su -**). This list shows your options:

- List the services by running the **chkconfig - - list** command.
- List an individual service by specifying the service after the `-list` option: **chkconfig - - list** ***apmd***.
- Stop a service with the `- - add` option: **chkconfig - - add** ***apmd***.
- Delete a service with the `- - del` option: **chkconfig - - del** ***apmd***.

Using a Secure Shell client

You may be most familiar with graphical network communication applications, such as the Mozilla Web browser and Evolution e-mail clients. However, a world of text-based tools is available, such as Secure Shell, Telnet, and FTP. Those applications provide an interactive method for connecting to other computers across networks and the Internet by using a command-line interface (CLI); refer to Chapter 4 for more information about CLIs.

Interactive communication is effective for performing tasks on remote machines. For example, the primary way to work on Linux machines originally was via the CLI. The CLI is often the best way to perform remote tasks.

CLI-based communication used to be carried out primarily over the insecure Telnet, FTP, and `rsh` connections. All services used unencrypted connections, and passwords were readily detected. The `rsh` service also used a system of intermachine trust. That trust allowed hackers (such as the infamous Kevin Mitnik) to "own" a network by breaking into one machine and then logging in to additional ones without authentication.

Open Secure Shell (OpenSSH) provides an encrypted channel to perform all those tasks. Fedora Core bundles OpenSSH by default. We describe (first) how to use the OpenSSH client to communicate with other machines and (second) create an OpenSSH server.

You should (dare we say *must*?) use encrypted channels when you're communicating over the Internet and wireless networks. Both the Internet and Wi-Fi connections are inherently insecure, and you have to protect your communications.

Connecting to a Secure Shell server

Start by using OpenSSH as a client. Suppose you want to log in to your ISP server, `ssh.myisp.com`, with OpenSSH. Here's the drill:

1. **Open a GNOME Terminal session.**
2. **Enter this command:**

   ```
   ssh ssh.myisp.com
   ```

   Your mileage may vary, of course. You may have to use the `-l` option if, for example, your ISP user account name is different from your local computer. If your user name on your local machine is `rod`, but it's `wayofthewheel` at your ISP, enter this line:

   ```
   ssh -l wayofthewheel ssh.myisp.com
   ```

   The first time you connect to a remote server, you're prompted to accept the remote server's fingerprint.

3. **Enter** yes **when you're prompted.**

4. **Enter your password when you're prompted, and you're logged in.**

   For example, you can now use a text-based e-mail client, such as `pine`, to read your messages. This program is useful if you want to read your e-mail securely but cannot connect to your ISP with an SSL-enabled Mozilla or Evolution e-mail client.

Tunneling X across a network

That was a simple and useful way to use OpenSSH, but you can do more. The Red Hat OpenSSH client is automatically configured to forward X-based graphics across its secure connection. While logged on to your ISP, you can run X Window client software and view it on your local machine:

1. **Log in to your ISP (or any machine running a Secure Shell server), as just described.**

2. **Run an X Window application, such as xclock.**

   The simple xclock window is displayed on your desktop.

   OpenSSH also bundles the file-transfer applications Secure Copy (scp) and Secure FTP (sftp). Secure Copy is non-interactive and copies files to and from a remote machine. Secure FTP is a secure version of FTP and is also interactive. This list describes how to copy files between two machines:

   - **Copy from a local machine to a remote one:** To transfer files from your local computer to a remote one, use Secure Copy (`scp`):

```
scp abc myacct@remote.myisp.com
```

     This command copies the filename `abc` from the directory you're working to the `myacct.myisp.com` home directory on the remote machine. You can specify either or both of the local and remote directories. For example, the following command copies the file `abc` from the */tmp* directory on the local machine to the */var/tmp* directory on the remote machine and renames it to *xyz*:

```
scp myaccount@remote.myisp.com:/tmp/abc /var/tmp/xyz
```

     The `scp` syntax is important. If you leave out the colon (`:`), your file isn't copied to the remote machine but rather is simply copied to a file named `myacct@remote.myisp.com` in your local directory.

   - **Copy from a remote to local machine:** Reverse the order of the parameters to copy from a remote machine. The following example copies the file `abc` from your home directory on the remote machine to your current working directory on the local machine:

```
scp myacct@remote:abc
```

The `sftp` program works like the old standby FTP, but uses encryption, of course. Follow these steps to perform simple file transfers with `sftp`:

1. **Open a GNOME Terminal session.**
2. **Enter this command:**

   ```
   sftp ssh.myisp.com
   ```

3. **Enter your user name and password.**
4. **Enter the help command at the `sftp` prompt.**

   You see a list of `sftp` commands. The ones you use most are `cd`, `lcd`, `dir`, `ls`, `get`, and `put`. These commands work in a similar fashion to their Linux equivalents.

   Using `sftp` is self-explanatory. Use `get` to transfer a file, files, or a directory from the remote machine to a local machine; `put` transfers stuff from local to remote.

Another cool feature of OpenSSH is its ability to tunnel any protocol. You can potentially display an entire X Window from a remote machine via X, for example. Consult the OpenSSH documentation for more information.

Configuring an OpenSSH server

Configuring an OpenSSH server is straightforward. You only have to modify the `/etc/ssh/sshd_config` file and run the command **service sshd restart** to restart the OpenSSH server daemon. Take a look at the configuration file, the important parts of which are listed here:

- **Remove the older and faulty protocol version 1:** Version 1 is broken and should not be used (change the parameter Protocol 2,1 to Protocol 2, as shown in this example):

  ```
  Port 22
  Protocol 2
  # HostKeys for protocol version 2
  HostKey /etc/ssh/ssh_host_rsa_key
  HostKey /etc/ssh/ssh_host_dsa_key
  ```

- **Remove the comment from in front of the login grace-time parameter:** This action sets a limit on the length of time from when you start a login and the time you complete it:

  ```
  LoginGraceTime 600
  ```

- **Disallow** `root` **logins:** You should prevent users, including yourself, from logging in directly as `root`. Forcing users to first log in as a regular user and then "`su`-ing" to `root` provides an audit trail that can be used to see who did what as the `root` user; it also forces everyone to jump through two hoops before anyone can become the all-powerful `root` user:

```
PermitRootLogin yes
StrictModes yes
```

- **Uncomment the following parameters to allow the various authentication modes:**

```
# rhosts authentication should not be used
RhostsAuthentication no
# Don't read the user's ~/.rhosts and ~/.shosts files
IgnoreRhosts yes
# For this to work you will also need host
  keys in /etc/ssh/ssh_known_hosts
RhostsRSAAuthentication no
# similar for protocol version 2
HostbasedAuthentication no
# Change to yes if you don't trust ~/.ssh/known_hosts for
 RhostsRSAAuthentication and HostbasedAuthentication
IgnoreUserKnownHosts no
```

- **Allow people to use password authentication, but don't allow unauthenticated access:**

```
# To disable tunneled clear text passwords,
   change to no here!
PasswordAuthentication yes
PermitEmptyPasswords no
```

To start the OpenSSH daemon, follow these steps:

1. **Make the changes and restart the Secure Shell daemon:**

```
service sshd restart
```

2. **If you're running a firewall, add this rule to your** `iptables`**-based firewall:**

```
iptables -A INPUT  -p tcp --dport 22
    -m state --state NEW,ESTABLISHED -j ACCEPT
```

3. **Save your new firewall:**

```
iptables-save > /etc/sysconfig/iptables
```

4. **Restart the firewall:service:**

```
iptables restart
```

Now you can use the OpenSSH client and server to communicate to and from your Linux computer. Using the OpenSSH client, you can interactively log in to other computers, copy data between computers, and piggyback an arbitrary communication stream (such as X Window) with this puppy. You can reverse that process and communicate with your host Fedora Core computer. OpenSSH encrypts all your communication and prevents the exposure of your passwords and data to prying eyes.

Exchanging keys makes your life easier

You use OpenSSH by default to log in to a remote user account by using traditional passwords. However, OpenSSH can use a second authentication method that takes a little work to get started but saves work in the long run.

OpenSSH provides an authentication method named *public-key cryptography*. This system uses one public and one private key. You install the public key on the remote system and keep the private key on your computer. The public key can be shared with anyone — hey, it's public. The private key must be kept secret at all costs. In fact, OpenSSH encrypts the private key by default. You must use a pass phrase (essentially a password with spaces) to decrypt the private key before using it.

Whenever you want to log in or communicate with the remote computer, the keys are used to negotiate the process. The public-private key system guarantees that your user account is authenticated and is also the initiating host; passwords authenticate only your login account, not the computer you're connecting from.

Setting up for a public-key cryptographic key exchange

To set up the key exchange, follow these steps:

1. **Log in to your user account on the local computer.**

   For example, log in as the user `rod` on `cancun`.

2. **Open a GNOME Terminal session.**

3. **Run this command:**

   ```
   ssh-keygen -t dsa
   ```

   This step starts the program that generates your public and private keys. Several encryption methods exist: DSA (Digital Signature Standard) and RSA (named after Ron *R*ivest, Adi *S*hamir, and Len *A*dleman) are the most popular. DSA is a nonproprietary algorithm, whereas RSA was until recently patented. Even though RSA is available for public use, we recommend using DSA.

   The program thinks for a moment and returns this output:

   ```
   Enter file in which to save the key
         (/home/rod/.ssh/id_dsa):
   ```

The keys are saved to the `.ssh` directory in your home directory. The default should be okay, so press the Enter key.

4. **The `ssh-keygen` program asks you to enter a pass phrase, which it uses to encrypt your private key:**

```
Enter passphrase (empty for no passphrase):
```

5. **Enter your pass phrase and `ssh-keygen` generates the keys.**

   Use a phrase peppered with numbers and other characters. For example, you may try a pass phrase like this (no, not this exact one, but you knew that):

```
Giv3 m3 @ bre@k!
```

6. **Verify the phrase by entering it a second time.**

The `ssh-keygen` program generates your public and private keys. Those keys are stored by default in the `.ssh` directory. The `.ssh` directory is stored by default in your home directory; `ssh-keygen` creates the `.ssh` directory, if necessary.

Copying your public key to the remote computer

You have to copy the public key to the computer you securely communicate with. These steps describe how to copy and configure them:

1. **Log in to your user account on the local computer.**

   For example, log in as the user `rod` on `cancun`.

2. **Open a GNOME Terminal window by clicking the GNOME Menu button and choosing System Tools⇨Terminal.**

3. **Copy your public key to your account on the remote computer. For example, if your account on the remote computer `cancun` is `rod`, you can use Secure Copy (`scp`):**

```
scp .ssh/id_dsa.pub rod@cancun:
```

   In this example, you're connecting to the same computer you're already logged in to. This technique is the simplest way to test the OpenSSH server you're experimenting with. No other machines, or even a network, are needed.

4. **Enter your account password when you're prompted, and the DSA public key is copied to your home directory on Cancun.**

5. **Log in to the remote machine. For example, use `ssh`:**

```
ssh cancun
```

6. **Enter your password when you're prompted.**

OpenSSH looks for public keys by default in the `authorized_keys` file in the `.ssh` directory (in your home directory).

7. **Use these commands to copy the public key into the `authorized_keys` file (remember that you should still be in your home directory):**

```
cat id_dsa.pub > .ssh/authorized_keys
```

   The `cat` command "concatenates" the contents of `id_dsa.pub` to the Linux standard output (that's generally your console, which is the GNOME Terminal, in this case). The double greater-than symbols (>) append the standard output to the `authorized_keys` file in the `.ssh` directory. No preexisting keys are disturbed.

   The `authorized_keys` file must have the right permissions. (See Appendix C for more information about file permissions.) In this case, loose permissions sink ships, and OpenSSH doesn't work with, for example, `read/-write/-execute` group permissions.

8. **Ensure the correct permissions:**

```
chmod 644 .ssh/authorized_keys
```

9. **Make sure that the OpenSSH server configuration allows key exchange. These options should be set in the `/etc/ssh/sshd_config` file:**

```
RSAAuthentication yes
PubkeyAuthentication yes
AuthorizedKeysFile      .ssh/authorized_keys
```

10. **Restart the `sshd` daemon if you make any changes to the `sshd_config` file:**

```
service sshd restart
```

Connecting to the remote computer by using key exchange

Ready to use the key exchange authentication system? From the host (local) computer, try these steps:

1. **Log in to your user account on the local computer.**

   For example, log in as the user `rod` on `cancun`.

2. **Open a GNOME Terminal session.**
3. **Log in to the remote machine:**

```
ssh cancun
```

4. **Enter the pass phrase you used to encrypt your private key.**

The remote computer authenticates you and your host computer. Voilà! You're in.

Making life even easier with ssh-agent

Red Hat automatically starts a system named `ssh-agent`. With `ssh-agent`, you enter your pass phrase and `ssh-agent` remembers it. You have to enter the pass phrase only once while logged in to your account. From then on, `ssh-agent` provides the OpenSSH clients with the pass phrase and you no longer have to enter a password or pass phrase. Life is easy.

Setting up `ssh-agent` is simple. Follow these steps:

1. **Log in to your user account on the local computer.**

   For example, log in as the user `rod` on `cancun`.

2. **Open a GNOME terminal by clicking the GNOME Menu and choosing System Tools⇨Terminal.**
3. **Enter this command:**

   ```
   ssh-add
   ```

4. **Enter your pass phrase when you're prompted.**
5. **Connect to the remote machine — for example, Cancun:**

   ```
   ssh cancun
   ```

You get logged in to your account on the remote machine without having to enter a password or pass phrase. This system works great.

Introducing encryption and security

Running a simple Web server, such as the one we introduce in Chapter 16, shouldn't require you to make heroic security measures. Serving up static text and graphics doesn't pique the interest of many hackers. However, when you start using the Web to do business or process sensitive information, you want to bump up your security. You build on the basic Web server and create a secure Web server.

Use the Secure Sockets Layer (SSL) protocol to construct a secure Web server. SSL provides a mechanism that allows your Web server to provide protected and authenticated connections. Using SSL with Apache allows the Web server to prevent eavesdropping by encrypting the network communications to and from the Web server and to identify itself to the client browser.

SSL provides encryption and ensures identification, as described in the following two sections.

Encryption

The mathematical process *encryption* essentially garbles information so only those with authorization can ungarble (and read) it; encryption prevents those you don't want to read your communication from reading it. The process of encryption and decryption requires the combination of the mathematical process named *encryption algorithm* and the mathematical entity *cryptographic keys* (*keys,* for short). A *key* is basically a very long number that the encryption algorithm uses to hide your message, information, or files from unauthorized people.

A description of the mathematical process of encryption is beyond the scope of this book, but suffice it to say that you need a key to encrypt information and a key to decrypt it. SSL uses a type of encryption named *public-key* encryption. Public-key encryption works by having the server keep a secret key and the client use a public key. The public key can be known and used by anyone and everyone; the private key must be kept secret and known only to the server.

Public-key encryption has an advantage over other encryption types because distributing public keys across a medium such as the Internet is easy. It sounds counterintuitive, but public-key encryption does work.

Identification

All the encryption in the world is useless if you're tricked into connecting to the wrong Web server. Suppose that you want to purchase a book from Amazon.com. You fire up Mozilla, connect to `www.amazon.com`, and happily enter your credit card number, expecting to receive your book the next day. It never comes.

In this scenario, some clever hacker has injected false DNS information into the Internet, and your browser has connected to `www.hackazon.com`. (Your Web browser looked up the numeric IP address of Amazon.com, but was deceived and received the address of the hacker's fraudulent Web server.) In this case, encryption worked just as it was supposed to, and prevented *other* hackers from intercepting your credit card. However, it didn't ensure that the Web server was the one you thought it was, and now the hacker is enjoying a wonderful vacation in Cancun — the real one — thanks to your credit card. (D'oh!)

SSL identification is based on the concept of a certificate. *Certificates* contain the public key you need in order to set up an encrypted connection and additional information used to verify the identity of the Web server. The certificate also comes with information about who created it, when it was created, and how it was created. After you obtain a certificate from the Web server you're connecting to, you're ready to safely conduct business. (Huh? What good does that do if you're connecting to the hacker's Web server? The certificate just ensures that you connect *securely* to the bad-boy site.)

The problem is solved by using a go-between called a *certificate authority (CA)*. When you connect to a secure Web server, it sends you its certificate. The Web server also subscribes to a CA. The CA has investigated the subscribing Web server and — if satisfied with its authenticity — vouches for its identity. If the CA is on your list of known CAs, you accept the certificate and use the public key to verify the server's identity and set up the encrypted connection.

Protecting your Web server with SSL

A secure Web server requires a *certificate* — a special code used to verify the Web server to its clients. The steps in this section describe how to create the certificate and work with a certificate authority (CA).

You can view a list of all the CAs your browser knows about. Follow these steps to view the CA list:

1. **Choose Mozilla Edit⇨Preferences.**

   The Preferences dialog box opens.

2. **Expand the Privacy & Security menu by clicking the plus (+) sign immediately to the left of the menu option.**

3. **Click the Certificates menu.**

   The Certificates subwindow opens.

4. **Click the Manage Certificates button.**

   The Certificate Manager window opens behind the Preferences window.

5. **Click the upper margin of the Preferences window and move it so you can see the Certificate Manager window.**

6. **Click to select the Authorities tab and you see a list of all CAs that your browser knows about.**

Your browser automatically accepts the certificate from any secure Web page you visit that subscribes to one of these CAs.

It costs time and money to subscribe to a CA, of course. However, you don't necessarily need to spend the money if you intend to use your secure Web server for personal use (or just to experiment). We show you how to construct a certificate and then use it without registering with a CA.

These steps outline the general process of creating a certificate:

1. **Install the SSL software.**

2. **Create your Web server's private key.**

3. **Create your Web server's certificate.**

   You can optionally register your certificate with a CA. For example, VeriSign, Inc., is one of the most widely known CAs. Go to `www.verisign.com` and click the SSL Certificates link to find out more about its service.

4. **Connect to the secure Web server and accept the certificate; accepting the certificate is automatic if the server subscribes to a CA; otherwise you have to accept the certificate manually.**

   As with Apache, the SSL software is included in the Fedora Core distribution. The following sections describe how to install, configure, and use SSL to create a secure Web server.

Installing the SSL package

Follow these steps to install the SSL module package (we assume that you have already installed the Apache Web server, as described in Chapter 16):

1. **Log in as `root` and open the GNOME Terminal session by clicking the GNOME Menu button and choosing System Tools⇨Terminal.**

   Apache needs an additional RPM package to provide SSL connections.

2. **Insert the companion DVD in the DVD or CD-ROM drive.**
3. **Enter the following command to install the SSL package:**

```
rpm -ivh /media/cdrom/Fedora/RPMS/mod_ssl*
```

Creating a private key

You may recall that public-key encryption requires that the server use a private key. (Your Web browser, the client, uses the public key.) We describe in this section how to generate a private key.

Generate your Web server's private key by following these steps. Installing the `Mod_ssl` package created several directories in `/etc/httpd/conf` that contain generic keys and certificates. You have to remove those "dummy" files (pardon the expression) before you can create your own:

1. **Enter these commands to remove the generic key and certificate:**

```
cd /etc/httpd/conf/ssl.key
rm server.key ../ssl.crt/server.crt
```

2. **Press** Y **each time you're prompted to remove the files.**
3. **Change to this directory, where the makefile certificate is located:**

```
cd /usr/share/ssl/certs
```

4. **The makefile contains instructions for making the certificate. All you have to do is "run" the makefile and specify the action to take:**

```
make genkey
```

This text is printed:

```
umask 77 ; \
/usr/bin/openssl genrsa -des3 1024 >
   /etc/httpd/conf/ssl.key/server.key
Generating RSA private key, 1024 bit long modulus
......................++++++
...................++++++
e is 65537 (0x10001)
Enter pass phrase:
```

Remember your pass phrase! You're asked to enter the pass phrase whenever you start your secure Web server. You also have to start the Web server manually, entering the pass phrase to start it.

5. **Enter a pass phrase.**

   Like a password, a pass phrase protects your private key on the Web server. Enter a good pass phrase — for example, something like this:

   ```
   hack me no more
   ```

   Note that spaces are allowed — and are, in fact, encouraged.

6. **Enter the same phrase a second time when you're prompted.**

The Apache Web server's private key is now in place. The key is readable by only the `root` user. Protect this key at all costs.

Certify yourself: Creating your own certificate

Although the secure Web server uses the private key, your Web browser uses a public one. The browser uses the public key to verify the authenticity of the server; the server uses the public and private keys to create the encrypted connection. (Public keys are contained within a certificate.)

You need a public key to use with the private one, and here's where you generate it; follow these steps to create your own certificate:

1. **Change to the directory where the certificate-generating `makefile` is located:**

   ```
   cd /usr/share/ssl/certs
   ```

2. **Make the new certificate by entering this command:**

   ```
   make testcert
   ```

3. **When you're prompted for the pass phrase created in the preceding section, enter the pass phrase.**

   You're prompted to enter information about your location and IP address and other information that can help identify your certificate as valid. These steps outline the questions and what you need to enter.

4. **You're prompted to enter your country code.**

   For example, enter **US** if you live in the United States, **GB** for Great Britain, or **MX** for Mexico.

5. **Enter your state (for the United States) or province name. (Don't abbreviate the name.)**

   For example, enter **New Mexico**.

6. **Enter your city name.**

   In this example, enter **Albuquerque**.

7. **Enter your organization or company name, if you have one.**

   - For example, enter **Paunchy Heavy Industries, Ltd.**
   - Optionally, you can enter your suborganization if you have one.

8. **Enter the full name of your Web server.**

   For example, the Web server in the example is named `veracruz`, and the network name is `paunchy.net`. Therefore, you enter **veracruz.paunchy.net**.

   The name of your server must match its DNS name (if you run your own DNS server). If the two don't match, you're prompted to access or reject the certificate every time you connect to the Web server.

9. **Enter your e-mail address:**

   ```
   paul@paunchy.net
   ```

   Your certificate is constructed.

10. **Restart your Web server with this command:**

    ```
    service httpd restart
    ```

11. **Enter the pass phrase when you're prompted.**

    Your secure Web server starts.

Connecting to your secure Web server

After you have created the private key and certificate, you're ready to connect to your secure Web server.

These steps describe how the process of obtaining the server's certificate works:

1. **Log in to your Fedora Core computer and open Mozilla.**
2. **Click the GNOME Menu and choose Internet⇨Mozilla Web Browser.**
3. **Enter the URL of your secure Web server.**

   For example, enter **https://cancun.paunchy.net** if that's where you installed the server. The `https`, which stands for HyperText Transport Protocol Secure, is used for secure browsing.

Unless you have paid a CA to certify you, you're asked to accept the certificate. Every time you connect to a nonsubscribed (CA) secure Web server from a browser for the first time, you're prompted to accept or reject the certificate. Because this secure Web server is your own, you can accept the certificate and know that you're securely and authentically connected.

A dialog box named Website Certified By an Unknown Authority opens.

4. **Click the Examine Certificate button and another dialog box opens.**

   The new window shows all the information you entered while creating the certificate.

5. **Click the Close button and you return to the preceding dialog box.**

   You're given three options: Accept the certificate temporarily, permanently, or not at all.

6. **Select the option that makes the most sense to you and click OK.**

   For example, click the button labeled `Accept This Certificate Temporarily for This Session`, and you're allowed to view and interact with the secure Web server. (You have to accept the certificate again the next time, however.)

7. **Right-click anywhere on the Web page and choose View Page Info.**

   Another dialog box, labeled `Page Info`, opens. Click to select the Security tab. Information about your Web site is displayed.

8. **Click the View button and you see the information about your certificate.**

9. **Click the Close button to leave the dialog box and return to viewing your Web page.**

After you have accepted the certificate, your browser coordinates with the Web server and sets up an encrypted connection — also referred to as a *channel.* All your communication is hidden from eavesdropping.

You can view the certificate you just accepted by opening the Manage Certificate window from the Mozilla Preferences dialog box, as described earlier in this chapter.

Go to this site to find out how to create and register a certificate with a Certificate Authority (CA):

```
www.redhat.com/docs/manuals/linux/
   RHL-9-Manual/custom-guide/
      s1-secureserver-generatingkey.html
```

Danger, Will Robinson! Detecting intruders

Everybody needs a loyal, vigilant robot to sound the alert when aliens, monsters, Dr. Smith, and hackers come at you. You cannot have literal robots (or can you?), but you can have an intrusion-detection system (IDS).

Intrusion detection is the flip side of intrusion prevention. You cannot depend on *not* getting hacked unless you turn off your computer and lock it in your panic room. Remember that no silver bullet exists in the world of computer security. You have to take measures to detect whether — and when — you get compromised.

Intrusion detection requires more ongoing work than any of the security systems we discuss in this book. The other systems, such as firewalls and password protection, require some upfront work and then run without much additional work. An IDS, however, requires some initial installation and configuration and then continual review. You have to monitor an IDS daily if you want it to be of any use to you.

Many IDSs (far too many to describe here) can give you extra security. We suggest two mature and relatively easy-to-use systems that provide good bang for your buck: Snort and Tripwire.

Snort is a network-based IDS. It looks for patterns in your network traffic that indicate hacker probes and break-in attempts. Snort isn't perfect and does report false positive alerts. You have to spend time identifying and eliminating false positives if you want to use Snort — but that time is well spent, because system administrators and security professionals consider Snort an excellent IDS. Go to `www.snort.org` to find more information. Wiley publishes *Snort For Dummies* by Charlie Scott, Paul Wolfe, and Bert Hayes.

Tripwire works by securely recording the fingerprints of files and directories and then comparing them to subsequent ones. Any differences between the current and original fingerprint indicate the file has changed and may have been compromised. The fingerprints, or *checksums*, are unique mathematical values calculated from the contents of a file or directory. You can find Tripwire at `www.tripwire.com`.

Modifying your firewall to allow SSL

You have to modify your Internet gateway or firewall to allow secure connections. You have to allow external Web browsers to connect to Port 443 on your Apache server. The following rule allows SSL connections:

```
iptables -A INPUT -p tcp -m state
   --state NEW,ESTABLISHED -j -dport 443
```

If you're using a DSL modem such as the one we describe in Chapter 6, you must modify the modem's network address translation (NAT) configuration. Many DSL modems are now on the market; describing how to configure them individually is beyond the scope of this book. Consult your modem's manual for configuration instructions: You have to allow external connections to Port 443.

Reading your logs

You are ultimately your own best intrusion-detection system (IDS). Log files store information about nearly every one of your Fedora Core systems. Reading your logs lets you discover what has been happening on your computer — and it's one way to detect intrusions.

Unfortunately, exploring log files is somewhat akin to reading tea leaves. No mechanical method exists for sifting through log-files. You have to look for unusual and suspicious occurrences. As you read more, you realize what is usual and, of course, unusual. Experience counts for a great deal when you're an IDS.

Red Hat provides two good systems for viewing log files. The e-mail-based *Logwatch* log-alert system sifts through the log files in `/var/log` and e-mails the root user any alerts or errors. You can configure the Logwatch operational parameters to better fit your operation. However, the default works well at alerting you to the happenings on your computer. The Red Hat *Logviewer* graphical utility provides one-stop shopping for all standard log files. This manual tool helps you to remember which log files to look at.

Using Logwatch

Logwatch, installed by default during the Red Hat installation process, is a Perl script that's run nightly by `cron`. It reads through every log file in the `/var/log` directory and picks out items that it thinks are interesting.

The Logwatch Perl script is in `/etc/log.d/scripts/logwatch.pl`. The soft link, `00-logwatch`, in the `/etc/cron.daily` directory, directs the cron system to run the script nightly.

Logwatch is controlled by the `/etc/log.d/conf/logwatch.conf` file. This file controls such options as who is e-mailed the results. The `logwatch` configuration file is self-documented and simple to configure.

Using Logviewer

Logviewer is a simple utility designed to display any of the standard Fedora Core log files in the `/var/log` directory. Logviewer displays by default the raw log information and leaves sifting out suspicious entries to your eyes.

Nothing is special about Logviewer, except it helps you access common log files and look at their data. Don't underestimate the value of that simple assistance. Although our busy lives make reading log files a difficult task, it's one of those mind-numbing but necessary jobs — boring but essential!

Fending off modular rootkits

A *rootkit* is a software program that a hacker installs on your machine and then uses against you and others; the software also includes tools to hide itself from you. Garden-variety rootkits run as regular applications and can be detected with standard tools. Many rootkits (nearly 60 at the time we wrote this book) can be detected with the easy-to-use `chkrootkit` system. Go to `www.chkrootkit.org` and download the software by clicking the Latest Source Tarball link (about a page down under "Download").

One of the newer and more insidious threats is the *modular* rootkit. Modular rootkits insert themselves into your Linux kernel and then control everything on your computer. Because they live in your kernel, you cannot depend on any standard detection tools to ferret them out.

After you employ the good security techniques discussed in this chapter and this book, the best way to avoid modular rootkits is to prevent kernel modules from being loaded. You can download the Linux kernel source code from `kernel.org` and compile it as a *monolithic kernel* — that is, compile modules directly into the kernel. Describing how to compile monolithic kernels is beyond the scope of this book, but an alternative method is quite easy to use.

Here's the alternative: You can take advantage of a feature in the 2.6 Linux kernel that Fedora Core 3 uses. The 2.6 kernel and its modules include cryptographic signatures that can be used to prevent non-signed modules from loading. Using this feature greatly reduces the danger of getting infected with modular rootkits.

To prevent unsigned module loading add the `enforcemodulesig` option to the kernel configuration in `/boot/grub/grub.conf`. For instance, your `grub.conf` file should look like the following:

```
title Fedora Core (2.6.8-1.541)
    root (hd0,0)
    kernel /vmlinuz-2.6.8-1.541 ro
        root=LABEL=/ rhgb quiet enforcemodulesig
    initrd /initrd-2.6.8-1.541.img
```

This option will take effect the next time you reboot your computer.

Introducing SELinux

The new and powerful Security-Enhanced Linux (SELinux) was designed by the National Security Agency (NSA) to increase computer security (see `www.nsa.gov/selinux/`). SELinux has recently been added to the Linux kernel. (Adding new functions to the kernel is a difficult process. Only the very best software gets added.)

SELinux is based on the Linux Security Module (LSM), which is a general-purpose and powerful mechanism for adding security software to Linux. SELinux provides the framework to make Linux more secure. Please go to `http://lsm.immunix.org/` for more information.

Introducing access-control types

Linux uses a Discretionary Access Control (DAC) model to control file access; see Appendix C for more information about file permissions. If used correctly, the DAC model provides some security. However, when used incorrectly, or misused, it can cause problems. For instance, if you own a file or directory, you can make it world-readable and world-writable. Owning a file gives you nearly unlimited power over its use. This can create security holes, especially if you're the root user. (For instance, making /etc/shadow file world-writable is a very bad idea because that makes it possible for a hacker to change your user passwords.)

SELinux adds Mandatory Access Control (MAC) capability to the Linux kernel. You configure the SELinux policy before starting the computer so users, root included, and processes can't arbitrarily allow access to other objects (files, directories, and sockets) they own. This model also helps minimize the access that buggy software provides hackers. SELinux isolates processes, files, and users from each other to create a more secure environment.

SELinux can't allow access to an object if the Linux operating system doesn't. Even if SE Linux's MAC allows access to a file or directory, you're prevented access if denied by Linux's DAC. Linux takes precedence over SELinux.

Introducing security contexts

SELinux uses the concept of *security context* (SC) and policy to control access to resources such as files, directories and objects; such resources are referred to as objects. When viewed from 40,000 (virtual) feet, this system is very simple: Every Linux resource has a security context. A predefined policy determines whether one SC (the source) can access another SC (the target).

The details of how SC and policy work together, however, is more complicated. The rules that define policy and the security context for every object take many thousands of lines. Fortunately, Fedora Core 3 configures all this for you.

Defining individual rules to account for every possible SC combination would be impossibly complex and rigid because a Fedora Core computer has thousands of files, directories, and so on.

Therefore, SELinux uses role-based access control (RBAC) to simplify policy definitions. RBAC defines what SC users and programs can enter.

The security context for an object — a file, directory, socket, and so on — consists of a security identity (SID), role and type. A process SC is made up of a SID, a role, and a domain. An object gets tagged with a type and a process belongs to a domain.

The following list describes the components of an SC:

- **Domain.** Processes belong to domains. Domains define the object type that a process can access. Domains are the flip side of Types.
- **SELinux Identity.** Every process has a SELinux Identity (`sid`). SELinux uses the SID to track users and processes — that isn't possible with plain Linux. The SID is different from the Linux user identity (UID).
- **Role.** Roles determine the domains that users and processes can access.
- **Type.** Objects are assigned types. An object Type defines the domains that can access it.

Introducing SELinux policy options

Fedora Core 3 installs and configures SELinux by default. The installation includes two security policies: `Targeted` and `Strict`.

The `Strict` policy creates a separate Domain for every daemon, the `root` user, and for nonprivileged users. Using the `Strict` policy creates a very safe system, but one that is difficult to modify (thus inflexible). You generally have to manually configure the SELinux SC for third-party software and that can be a difficult process. Only experienced SELinux administrators should use the Strict policy.

Fortunately, the Fedora Core development team created the `Targeted` policy as a compromise between the traditional Linux DAC and SELinux with a `Strict` policy.

The `Targeted` policy creates separate domains for a handful of service daemons such as Apache; Apache daemons belong to the HTTP domain (`httpd_t`), for instance. These domains are restricted from accessing all other domains. They're isolated islands that can access the bare minimum of resources.

On the other hand, every user, process, and object belongs to the Unconditional (`unconditional_t`) domain. No access limitations are placed on members of the unconditional domain. Unconditional domain members effectively operate as if they were under control of the standard Linux DAC system.

The `Targeted` policy compromise makes sense. If you use your Fedora Core computer as a workstation protected by a firewall and the methods and systems described in this chapter, then you have relatively little security exposure. However, if you start running network services such as Apache, then your risk accelerates. Protecting network-based services with SELinux provides a big step up in security.

Describing more about the inner workings of SELinux is beyond the scope of this book. Using the `Targeted` policy should be adequate for most people's needs. However, you can read more about SELinux from the following mailing list and Web sites:

- `http://fedora.redhat.com/mailman/listinfo/fedora-selinux-list`
- `www.lurking-grue.org/gettingstarted_newselinuxHOWTO.html`
- `www.crypt.gen.nz/selinux/faq.html#WWW.1`
- `www.samag.com/documents/s=7835/sam0303a/0303a.htm`
- `www.crypt.gen.nz/selinux/faq.html`

Understanding the Security Process

The best way to look at security is as a process. The more you think about it and the more you study it, the safer you are. You should use the security systems described in this chapter as the foundation for your security process. However, you should continue to build your security process to meet the needs of your own computer system and network.

This section outlines some additional building blocks you may consider adding to your process:

- **Making backups:** Backups are part of the security process? Yes! Backups are an essential security tool in the sense that you can never eliminate the possibility of getting hacked. When your security is breached, you may lose all sorts of information and configurations. For example, all the information on your computer may be completely erased or, worse, you may not know which files are good or bad. You must ensure your ability to recover from these types of catastrophes.

  One good backup method is to use the GnomeToaster application, as we describe in Chapter 11. You can store your user account and configuration files on a CD-R/RW or DVD+/-RW. This method is reliable, and the discs should last forever. The only limitation is the CD's ability to store only 700MB to 800MB of data (although you can store more data with compression).

- **Security education:** Keeping up with security trends and topics helps you avoid getting bitten by new hacks. Knowing your adversaries and their techniques is essential.

  These URLs provide good security-based information; see Chapter 21 for some current top security holes:

  - `www.linuxsecurity.com`
  - `www.sans.org`
  - `www.nmap.org`
  - `www.securitytracker.com`
  - `www.counterhack.net`
  - `www.infosyssec.com`
  - `www.cert.org`

- **Physical security:** We focus on discussing network-based security in this book. We assume that your Fedora Core computer is running on your home network, in which case you have to worry mostly about Internet bad guys. In an office environment, however, you have to worry about physical security.

  Physical security involves preventing people from walking up and gaining unauthorized access to your computer. You should set a BIOS password to prevent anyone else from booting your computer into single-user mode (which would totally avoid your Linux passwords). You should lock your computer in your office, if possible, to prevent anyone from stealing your hard drive. Don't, under any circumstances, write your passwords in any accessible place (such as on your desk or computer).

  You should also set the GNOME (or KDE) screen lock unless you want to log out every time you leave your desk. Choose GNOME Menu⇨Preferences⇨Screensaver and then select the Lock Screen After option. Select the amount of time to wait before locking your screen and then click the Close button.

- **Boring consistency:** Good long-term security depends on consistency. Making backups, reading security logs, and performing other, similar tasks all depend on your maintaining interest. It's like staying in shape: You cannot be good for a while and then forget about your routine.

Chapter 18

Bringing In the Fedora Core Repairman

In This Chapter

- Understanding the art of troubleshooting
- Gardening with the fault tree
- Diagnosing network problems

This book is perfect, and there's no way that anything we have written can ever go wrong — never, ever. You may be as lonely as the Maytag repairman if you expect trouble. As the Pop Will Eat Itself tune goes: The trouble is, trouble never happens. Errata (corrections) are as outdated as a brick-and-mortar bookstore. This book makes setting up computers and networks so easy that you may wonder why other people have so many problems! Blah, blah, blah.

Yeah, right. The problem is that this guy named Murphy (as in Murphy's Law) hangs out in both virtual and real bookstores, and visits all things mechanical and electronic. He's always jumping in just when things are starting to go well. The guy just cannot keep his nose out of other people's business. This chapter is meant to smooth things out between you and Murphy in case he catches up with you.

One common problem involves getting your Fedora Core computer to work on a network. Sometimes, the best-laid plans go a little awry and Murphy comes to visit. This chapter is designed to help when networking problems pop up.

The Fix Is In: Troubleshooting Your Network

Your Fedora Core machine is the foundation of your network and must be set up correctly for anything to run. If it isn't working or if you have an unusual setup (or if Murphy is in a bad mood), you can check for several different causes.

We use a Fedora Core computer connected to a private network as the troubleshooting example in this chapter. The Fedora Core network is one of the more difficult things to set up correctly because it depends on not only your Linux computer but also other computers. Suppose that your Fedora Core computer isn't working within your private network. If that's the case, use this chapter to help troubleshoot your network.

See Part V for insights into other problems. Chapter 20 describes how to find information about common problems with your Fedora Core computer. Chapter 21 describes several security fixes.

Introducing Fault Trees

As with a surprising number or technical pursuits, troubleshooting is more of an art than a science. Sometimes, you can easily see what the problem is and how to fix it. At other times, that's not so easy. The degree of difficulty you have in fixing a problem depends on how complex the problem is and how well you know your stuff. Obviously, the better acquainted you are with computers and Linux, the better you are at troubleshooting.

Every problem has a solution. Computers are cause-and-effect-based machines. When something breaks or doesn't work, there's always a reason. The reason or reasons may not be easy to find, but they exist.

How do you find the cause? That's a million-dollar question. Getting a million bucks isn't easy unless you're willing to grind your teeth, plot against your fellow contestants for weeks on a remote island, purchase 10 million PowerBall tickets, or — believe it or not — work hard and work smart. Some people are willing to eat rats for the chance at a million bucks or are lucky enough to win the lottery; most just have to work hard. Oh, well.

Working hard is conceptually easy, but how do you work smart? This concept is where the idea of the fault tree comes into play. (You mean faults grow on trees? Not exactly . . . .) The *fault tree* is a conceptual aid that helps you to eliminate all but the real cause of your problem. The fault tree looks like an upside-down tree, where the trunk of the tree represents the fault, or problem. The ends, or leaves, of the branches represent all the possible causes. After that's done, solving the problem is virtually guaranteed.

For example, Figure 18-1 shows part of a fault tree that points out which major subsystems you should examine. To find the solution to a problem, you have to systematically identify what's working. You work your way to what's not working and then when you find it, you usually solve your problem. The fault tree simply helps to formalize the process of problem solving.

Here are some possible faults:

- **The first branch on the left involves problems with the physical connection.** Do you have a malfunctioning network adapter or switch/hub? Is the cable not connected properly to the adapter? In that case, jiggle the cable or fuss with the connector. Do you have a break in the cable or a loose connector?
- **The second branch deals with the network interface configuration.** Have you correctly configured the IP address for your Ethernet adapter (NIC)?
- **The third branch helps you to decide whether the problem exists with the network routing.** Can your network packets be directed toward the correct network?

The fault tree helps you to break down any big problem into several simpler ones. By eliminating each simple problem one by one, you should eventually locate the root cause.

The blind leading the blind

A colleague of ours, Ken Hatfield, once said, "One of the side benefits from lots of troubleshooting comes from what I call 'the value of blind alleys.' Most often in troubleshooting, you go down blind alleys or, in your tree example, the wrong branches of the solution tree. But in doing so, you learn something. In the future, when you encounter a different problem, that previous blind alley may be the road to the solution." Well said.

Here's an example: we recently had a server that was having lots of problems. The `/var` file system had filled up, which caused some programs to fail. When space on `/var` was freed up, most of the programs started to do their jobs again. But one program didn't work. Paul spent a long time trying to figure out why it didn't work even after the problem was fixed. As it turned out, this particular program's real problem was that its license had expired. He had not only walked down a blind alley but also bumped into a wall and kept trying to go forward. (D'oh!)

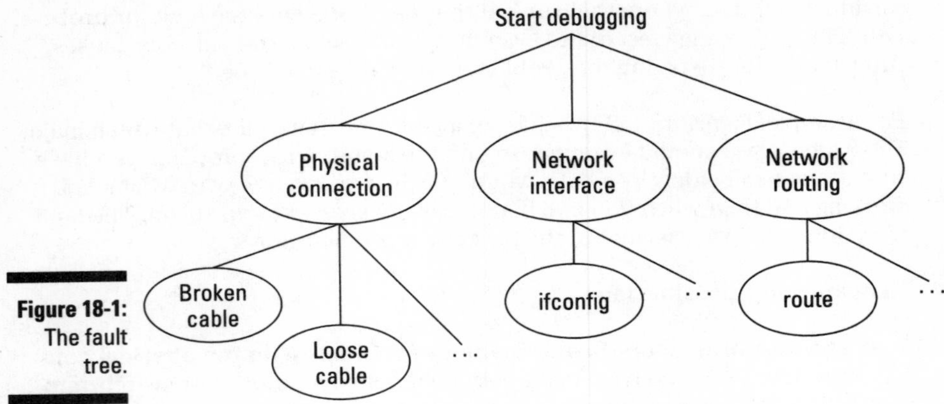

Figure 18-1: The fault tree.

Ticking Through Your Linux Networking Checklist

We describe in this section some common network problems and symptoms. We start with simpler network problems and move on to more complex ones. After cataloging the problems, we look at one of the branches of the fault tree to solve a problem.

Is the power turned on?

First, verify that you turned on the power. It sounds simple, but, hey, sometimes the simplest things go wrong.

Is your network cable loose or broken?

Make sure that your network cables aren't broken or cut. Check the connectors to make sure that they're okay. You should also make sure that you're using the correct network cable, which should be Category 5 (8-wire) straight-through cable.

Is your Ethernet hub or switch working?

Your Ethernet hub or switch should also be turned on. Ensure that the network cables are also connected securely.

"I is an enganeer"

An experienced electrical engineer and Linux author once got really angry with a cable TV company. His cable service went dead in the middle of a Philadelphia Eagles game. It didn't matter that the Eagles were losing — he wanted to see the game because the Eagles don't appear on TV often in Albuquerque. The engineer called the cable company immediately. "Blah! Blah! Blah! My connection — Blah! Blah!" The nice support person guided the poor engineer step-by-step through his own fault tree. Step 1: Is your VCR or TV turned on? "Yes, of course." Step 2: Is the VCR button on your VCR toggled on? "Of course — ah, whoops, no, it isn't. Ah, yes, it works now, thank you very much. Goodbye." D'oh! What was five years of electrical engineering school good for? (Well, okay, maybe they didn't cover On switches.)

The *link status* lights should be lit for every cable that's connected to the hub or switch. You should also see lights for active connections flash on and off as network communication occurs. If you don't see any lights, ensure that the cable is plugged in snugly.

Is your Ethernet adapter inserted correctly?

You have to have an Ethernet adapter to be connected to an Ethernet network. Make sure that your Ethernet adapter is plugged in to your computer's motherboard — snugly. Sometimes you have to pull out the adapter and then reinsert it (carefully, of course); this process is called *reseating*.

Is your network adapter configured correctly?

Sometimes a startup script is misconfigured, which causes the startup screen to go by without you seeing an error message. If that happens, log in as `root` and from the shell prompt and type this command:

```
ifconfig
```

You see a listing of two different interfaces, as shown in the following code, or three interfaces if you have PPP configured. The `ifconfig` command tells the

Linux kernel that you have a network adapter and gives it an IP address and a network mask. This step is the first in connecting your Linux computer to your network:

```
eth0    Link encap:10Mbps Ethernet  HWaddr 00:A0:24:2F:30:69
          inet addr:192.168.1.1 Bcast:192.168.1.255
                        Mask:255.255.255.0
          UP BROADCAST RUNNING MULTICAST  MTU:1500  Metric:1
          RX packets:16010 errors:18 dropped:18 overruns:23
          TX packets:7075 errors:0 dropped:0 overruns:0
          Interrupt:10 Base address:0x300

lo        Link encap:Local Loopback
          inet addr:127.0.0.1  Bcast:127.255.255.255
                        Mask:255.0.0.0
          UP BROADCAST LOOPBACK RUNNING  MTU:3584  Metric:1
          RX packets:115 errors:0 dropped:0 overruns:0
          TX packets:115 errors:0 dropped:0 overruns:0
```

Checking your wireless NIC

Linux provides several tools to work with Wi-Fi network interfaces. Fedora Core installs the wireless-tools RPM package by default. The tools include `iwconfig`, `iwspy`, and other utilities. We describe how to use `iwconfig` to examine your Wi-Fi interface configuration.

Log in as `root`, open a GNOME Terminal window (refer to Chapter 4 for more information), and run the `iwconfig` command. If your NIC is configured correctly, you see output similar to this example:

```
lo        no wireless extensions.

eth0     IEEE 802.11-DS  ESSID:"linky" Nickname:"..."
            Mode:Ad-Hoc  Frequency:2.437GHz  Cell: "..."Bit
            Rate:11Mb/s   Tx-Power=15 dBm   Sensitivity:1/3
         Retry limit:4   RTS thr:off   Fragment thr:off
         Encryption key:A654-6277-43D6-ACC3-E6ED-1C12-98
         Power Management:off
         Link Quality:0  Signal level:0  Noise level:0
         Rx invalid nwid:0  Rx invalid crypt:0  Rx invalid ...
         Tx excessive retries:0  Invalid misc:0   Missed ...
```

These options are the important ones to examine:

- **Mode:** You have to set this value to `Ad-Hoc` when you're connecting to an ad-hoc network. (Refer to Chapter 7 for more information about this method.) You can use the value `Any` when you're connecting to an infrastructure network. The `Any` value can work for an ad-hoc network in some cases; however, a description of those cases is beyond the scope of this book, so use ad-hoc mode whenever necessary.

- **ESSID:** You have to use the same value on every machine connected to an ad hoc LAN. For example, every machine on the network is given the ESSID `linky`.
- **Encryption key:** You must use the same encryption key on every machine connected to a wireless network. The key comes in two flavors: 40-bit and 128-bit. The 40-bit key is effectively useless; it can be readily cracked by hackers, using widely available software. The 128-bit key can also be cracked, but takes more time, so it's better than no key at all.

Your wireless network should work as long as you set these parameters correctly and your computer is within range of the other devices on your LAN. The other parameters are either self-generating or unimportant in getting the card to work.

Maybe the physical connections aren't set up right

If you don't see the line containing `lo`, which is the loopback interface, or `eth0`, which is your network adapter, your physical network connections aren't set up right. The loopback interface isn't a physical device; it's used for the network software's internal workings. The loopback interface must be present for the network adapter to be configured.

If the loopback interface isn't present, type this command:

```
ifup lo
```

If the loopback still isn't configured, run this command:

```
ifconfig lo 127.0.0.1
```

If the network adapter (generally, an Ethernet card) isn't present, type

```
ifup eth0
```

If that doesn't work, run this command:

```
ifconfig eth0 192.168.1.1
```

Because this address is a class C network address, `ifconfig` automatically defaults to the `255.255.255.0` netmask. If you suspect that the netmask isn't being set — for example, you're using a Class B address, such as `10.0.0.1` on a Class C network — type this command:

```
ifconfig eth0 10.0.0.1 netmask 255.255.255.0
```

Type **ifconfig** and your network adapter should be displayed correctly. If it's not, examine the manual page on `ifconfig`. You display this manual page by typing this command and then pressing Enter:

```
man ifconfig
```

You can page through the document in several ways: Press Enter to go line by line, press the spacebar to go forward one page at a time, press Ctrl+B to page backward, or press **Q** to exit. The `ifconfig manual` page (man page) shows a great deal of information about what `ifconfig` is and how it works. (Linux provides man pages for most of its programs, libraries, etc.) If you're still having problems, look at the Linux startup information by running this command:

```
dmesg | more
```

You *pipe* (route by using the `|` symbol) the output from `dmesg` to the `more` command. Linux pipes transmit the output of one command to the input of another. After you run the preceding command, you see the information that was displayed during the boot process. The `more` command shows one page of information at a time; press the spacebar to display each subsequent page.

Maybe you have a hardware problem

If you don't see your Ethernet adapter, you may have a hardware problem. Check your adapter. *Reseat* it (take it out and put it back in) and see whether it works. If not, you probably need a new NIC. If you see the NIC, look inside the Linux kernel and see which devices it has. Type the following command to change to a special directory named `/proc`, where process information is located:

```
cat /proc/devices
```

You should see a line with your network adapter listed. If you don't, Linux doesn't know that it exists.

Try to run your Ethernet NIC again. If it still doesn't run, you have to find out more information.

Maybe you have an interrupt or address conflict

You may have an interrupt or address conflict. Look at the list of interrupts and then the I/O addresses of all devices that the kernel knows about, by typing these commands:

```
cat /proc/interrupts
cat /proc/ioports
```

The I/O address is the location in memory where the device, such as the network adapter, is accessed by the microprocessor (for example, your Pentium chip). The interrupt communicates to the microprocessor that it should stop whatever it's doing and process the information that has arrived at the device that's sending the interrupt.

When your Ethernet adapter receives a packet, it sends an interrupt to the microprocessor to signal that an event has occurred. Your Pentium stops what it's doing and processes the new information. The microprocessor even interacts with Linux to do the processing.

Type **cat /proc/interrupts** to show both the interrupts and the I/O addresses with which Fedora Core is familiar. The output should look like this example:

```
 0:     378425   timer
 1:       1120   keyboard
 2:          0   cascade
10:      16077   3c509
13:          1   math error
14:      63652 + ide0
```

This listing shows that Linux knows that the Ethernet NIC (3c509) exists.

Typing `cat /proc/ioports` shows the input-output ports used by Fedora Core to interact with the computer's devices. This output shows the I/O ports used on this computer:

```
0000-001f : dma1
0020-003f : pic1
0040-005f : timer
0060-006f : keyboard
```

Look for your network adapter. In this case, it's `3c509`. If the adapter is working, you shouldn't have any conflicts. If the I/O ports of two devices overlap, a conflict exists and you have to reconfigure the adapter. Run your Ethernet NIC configuration program and set the adapter's parameters in its EEPROM. Older adapters may have jumpers or little switches, called *DIP switches,* to set. If you think that you have to do this, remember to write down all the other devices' interrupts and I/O addresses so you don't end up conflicting with something else.

Perhaps you're missing the correct module

You also may be missing the correct module. This situation is virtually impossible with Fedora Core because the Linux kernel automatically loads networking, and other modules, on demand (it's mature technology). Go ahead and look at these files to gain an understanding of how Linux works. Display the networking devices by typing this command:

```
cat /proc/net/dev
```

If you don't see the Ethernet interface, you may have an unsupported network adapter or a defective or misconfigured one. The Fedora Core kernel, by default, automatically loads modules as they're needed. You can look back at the results of your boot process by using the `dmesg` command. Look for a message that says `delaying eth0 configuration`. This message probably means that Linux couldn't load the network adapter module or that the adapter isn't working.

Display the information about your devices by using the `cat /proc/net/dev` command.

The next step is to ensure that your network routing is configured correctly. This area is one where you can easily get confused. You don't have to set up routing outside your LAN yet, but Linux needs to know where to send packets on its own network. Look at your routing table by typing this command:

```
netstat -nr
```

You see a listing of your routing table. In this abbreviated example, some options that aren't important have been removed:

```
Kernel IP routing table
Destination Gateway  Genmask        Flags  Iface
192.168.1.0 0.0.0.0  255.255.255.0 U      eth0
169.254.0.0 0.0.0.0  255.255.0.0   U      eth0
127.0.0.0   0.0.0.0  255.0.0.0     U      lo
0.0.0.0   192.168.1.254 0.0.0.0    UG     eth0
```

This list briefly describes what's in the fields in the routing table:

- **Destination:** The location, or IP address, where you want to send packets. For example, the address `192.168.1.0` refers to your local network.
- **Gateway:** The address (computer or router) where the packets have to be sent so they can find their way to their destination. When the destination is the local network, the address `0.0.0.0` means no gateway.
- **Genmask:** Used to separate from the host number the parts of the IP address used for the network address.
- **Flags:** Indicates various interface information, such as *U* for *up* and *G* for *gateway.* The metric is used as a measure of how far a packet must travel to its destination (a number greater than 32 is considered infinite; packets live in a small universe). The next two flags, Ref and Use, aren't important here.

- **Iface:** Shows which network interface is being used. (etho refers to an Internet adapter, and lo refers to the loopback interface. The loopback interface is used internally by the Linux kernel, and you shouldn't have any need to use it directly.)

The 169.254.0.0 entry is an IPV6 (the next-generation Internet Protocol Version 6) connection. We don't use IPV6 in this book.

The information about each interface — the routing table — is displayed below the headings. For example, the first line tells Linux to send packets destined for the addresses 192.168.1.0 through 192.168.1.255 to the Ethernet adapter (eth0). The second line deals with the kernel's internal loopback interface. The third and last line, with the address 0.0.0.0, is the default route. It defines where to send all packets not covered by a specific route.

If your table deviates from the example, you may have a routing problem. For example, if you don't have the default route, 0.0.0.0, you cannot communicate with any machines on your LAN or the Internet. If you lack a loopback — 127.0.0.1 — route, many internal processes are doomed to fail.

Defining a route to the loopback interface

You must have a route to the loopback interface (also referred to as lo), which is the 127.0.0.0 address. If you're missing either or both parameters, you must set them. To set the loopback device, which must be set for the network adapter to work, type this command:

```
route add -net 127.0.0.0
```

To set the route for the network adapter and your local network, type

```
route add 192.168.1.0 dev eth0
```

This route is assigned automatically to your network adapter. You can assign the route to another NIC, if necessary. Here's an example:

```
route add 192.168.1.0 dev eth1
```

Type **netstat -rn** to see your routing table. You should see entries for the loopback and Ethernet. If you don't see a route to your network interface, try repeating the steps. You may have to delete a route. To delete a route, type

```
route del 192.168.1.0 dev eth0
```

Note that you use the network address rather than a host address here. The zero (0) designates the Class-C network address 192.168.1.

Doing the ping thing

If the network adapter is configured correctly and the routing is correct, check the network. The best way to do it is to `ping` the loopback interface first and then the other computer. Type the following command, let it run for a few seconds (one ping occurs per second), and stop it by pressing Ctrl+C:

```
ping 127.0.0.1
```

You should see a response like this one:

```
PING 127.0.0.1 (127.0.0.1) 56(84) bytes of data.
64 bytes from 127.0.0.1: icmp_seq=0 ttl=64 time=0.079 ms
64 bytes from 127.0.0.1: icmp_seq=1 ttl=64 time=0.039 ms
```

Each line shows the number of bytes returned from the loopback interface, the sequence, and the round-trip time. The last lines comprise the summary, which shows whether any packets didn't make the trip. This is a working system, but if you don't see any returned packet, something is wrong with your setup and you should check your network connections and configuration.

Next, try `ping`ing your Ethernet interface by typing this command:

```
ping 192.168.1.1
```

You should see a response similar to this bit of code:

```
PING 192.168.1.1 (198.168.1.1): 56 data bytes
64 bytes from 198.168.1.1: icmp_seq=0 ttl=64 time=2.0 ms
64 bytes from 198.168.1.1: icmp_seq=1 ttl=64 time=1.2 ms

--- 198.168.1.1 ping statistics ---
4 packets transmitted, 4 packets received, 0% packet loss
            round-trip min/avg/max = 1.1/1.8/4.6 ms
```

"Can I talk to another computer or device?"

Try to `ping` another computer, if one exists, on your network. Type the following command, let it run for 10 to 15 seconds, and stop it by pressing Ctrl+C:

```
ping 192.168.1.254
```

This example assumes that another computer has the IP address 192.168.1.254. Adjust the address you use to work with your network. You should see a response similar to what's shown in this bit of code:

```
PING 192.168.1.2 (192.168.1.2): 56 data bytes
64 bytes from 192.168.1.254: icmp_seq=0 ttl=32 time=3.1 ms
64 bytes from 192.168.1.254: icmp_seq=1 ttl=32 time=2.3 ms

--- 192.168.1.2 ping statistics ---
4 packets transmitted, 4 packets received, 0% packet loss
round-trip min/avg/max = 2.3/2.5/3.1 ms
```

If you see a continuous stream of returned packets and the packet loss is 0 or near it, your network is working. If not, the problem may be in the other machine. Review the troubleshooting steps in this chapter. Note that the ICMP is taking about 1 full millisecond (ms) longer to travel to the external computer than to the loopback device. The reason is that the loopback is completely internal to the Linux computer.

Chapter 19

Building a Streaming Audio Server

In This Chapter

- Introducing Ices2 and Icecast2 streaming audio servers
- Creating a music source
- Installing and configuring Ices2 and Icecast2
- Streaming audio to your private network

All work and no play makes Linux a dull boy. So forget the workaday world of word processors and network services for a while and have some fun. This chapter describes how to configure your Fedora Core computer as an audio-streaming server for your private network.

We show you in Chapter 12 how to use Linux applications, such as MPlayer, and to listen to Internet audio streams. In this chapter, we switch sides and show you how to serve up these types of streams. It's pretty cool when you think about it: you can carry your laptop computer around your home and listen to your music.

Introducing Ices2 and Icecast2

Once again, the open-source movement fills the bill with Ices2 and Icecast2. Ices2 and Icecast2 are designed to serve up audio streams.

You're most likely to know how audio streaming works from the user's perspective. Chapter 12, for instance, shows how to use Rhythmbox and MPlayer to listen to Internet audio streams. However, most of us aren't familiar with how multimedia streams (audio, video, and slide shows) are created. To create networked audio stream, you feed content such as a music track from a CD to the multimedia server Ices2. Ices2 converts the audio stream to Ogg format and feeds it to Icecast2. (Shoutcast and RealServer, which are commercial servers, operate in a manner similar to Icecast2.) Ices2 in turn streams the content to a private network or the Internet. You then use a multimedia client such as Rhythmbox to listen to the audio stream.

Be careful where you get the audio content. You must abide by copyright law. Of course you're free to broadcast content that you create or for which you obtain permission to use on the Internet. You can also use music that you purchase for your own. That's why we describe how to create a private network streaming system. The system that we create is just a glorified cd player.

The original Icecast worked with MP3 streams. Icecast is still available, but is no longer being developed or supported. Because of possible copyright problems, Icecast has essentially been abandoned in favor of Icecast2, which works with the open-source Ogg/Vorbis format.

This list provides more detail on each component in the system:

- **Multimedia client:** The client connects to the multimedia server and plays the feed. For example, you use Rhythmbox to connect to Icecast2.
- **Multimedia server:** The server is responsible for accepting requests from a client and then streaming multimedia information to the client. The server also converts the original multimedia content into Internet Protocol (IP) packets in order to route it across a private network or the Internet.
- **Multimedia content:** Your multimedia server isn't very useful without a content source. Your source may be a music CD or a DJ — you, for example. Sources are either fixed or dynamic. For example, a music CD is a fixed source. The Ices2 application reads from a fixed source and feeds it to Icecast2.

Creating a Music Source

Before you create your server, you have to create something to play. This section describes how to create an Ogg/Vorbis file to play. We assume that you want to create a file from a commercial music CD. This practice is legal, and does not violate copyright law because you don't create a server that is broadcast on the Internet. Instead, you're creating a server that is broadcast to a private network (yours). As far as we know, you're still allowed to listen to your own CDs.

The Ogg/Vorbis audio formatting system is similar in function to MP3. However, Ogg/Vorbis (or just Ogg) is an open-source format (also known as a codec) and — unlike MP3, doesn't use any proprietary algorithms or protocols. Ogg also provides higher fidelity than other formats. Ogg/Vorbis is really two separate entities: Ogg is an audio compression format, and Vorbis is an encoding system.

Use the following steps to create an Ogg-Vorbis-formatted music file:

1. **Log in as the Root user and insert an audio CD.**
2. **Click the GNOME Menu button and choose Sound & Video➪Sound Juicer CD Ripper.**

   The Sound Juicer window opens, displaying the CD's tracks. All tracks are automatically selected for extraction (you see check marks in the Extract column check boxes). Unselect unwanted tracks by clicking the check boxes.
3. **Click the Extract button in the subwindow.**

   A progress dialog box opens. Sound Juicer extracts the music from the CD to files on your computer. The files are stored in a subdirectory named after the album title, which itself is stored in a subdirectory with the name of the artist. For example, if the artist is Norah Jones and the album is *Come Away with Me,* the music tracks live in the directory `Norah Jones/Come Away with Me` (in your home directory).
4. **When the music is extracted an Information dialog box opens and you can click the Close button.**

   Ices2 and Icecast2 use what's called a Playlist to determine what media to stream. The following steps show how to create a simple playlist from the music you just extracted.
5. **Copy the first Ogg file you just created to the `/tmp` directory and rename as `example1.ogg`.**

   We're copying to the `/tmp` directory and renaming, just to keep the configuration files as simple as possible. Here's what that looks like:

   ```
   cp 01*ogg /tmp/example1.ogg
   ```
6. **Create the `playlist.txt` file that points to the Ogg music file, like this:**

   ```
   echo "/tmp/example1.ogg" > /usr/local/etc/playlist.txt
   ```

Your simple Playlist is now created and ready to be played.

You can convert from Wave to Ogg format by running this command in a terminal emulator: `oggenc *wav`. You can play Ogg-encoded files: `ogg123 xyz.wav`.

You now have one or more Ogg-Vorbis-formatted audio files. You have to install and configure Icecast2 and Ices2 to broadcast music to yourself.

Installing Ices2 and Icecast2

In this section, we break from our self-imposed rule of using only pre-compiled software in package form. First, even though Icecast2 comes packaged in RPM format, it requires a library package not included with Fedora Core 3. Second, Ices2 does not come in package form yet. Third, we need to install a library that's also not yet packaged. We'll show how to download and build Libshout, Ices2 and Icecast2 from source code.

Compiling code like Icec2 and Icecast2 is the reason we recommended installing the Workstation class of Fedora Core in Chapter 3. Using the Workstation class installs the compilers and associated utilities needed to compile from source code.

In the Linux world, building from source code requires that you follow these general steps:

1. **Configure.** The first step requires configuring the software. The configuration process builds dependency files. Several Linux systems that do this are available. Icecast2 and Ices2 use a configure script.
2. **Compile.** After the software is configured, you have to compile it. *Compiling* is a universal computer process that changes source code into executable code. Source code is readable by human beings — well, at least the class of humans known as nerds. Compiling source code changes it into a form that computers can understand. All applications are compiled from source code.
3. **Install.** After the result is compiled, it must be installed. Linux uses default directories such as `/usr/bin`, `/usr/sbin`, `/usr/local/bin`, and `/usr/local/sbin` to store executable files (applications and services). Most software systems need to be placed in these types of locations to work correctly.

Downloading Libshout, Icecast2 and Ices2

Before you can build your streaming-audio server, you have to get the Icecast2 and Ices2 software plus the Libshout library. This section describes how to download the software.

By now, you know that Linux uses many names and acronyms, many of which are cryptic at best. So you probably didn't raise an eyebrow when you encountered the name Ogg/Vorbis, Icecast2, or xiph.com. Ogg/Vorbis is a science-fiction character that its developers like. Icecast2 is a variation on the name *Shoutcast*, and Xiph is short for *Xiphophorus helleri,* a small swordtail fish that's popular in small aquariums.

These steps help you prepare your Fedora Core computer to start building the multimedia server:

1. **Log in to your computer as any user.**
2. **Open Mozilla, go to** `www.icecast.org`**, and click the Download link at the top of the page.**

   Now you have to download the Icecast2 and Ices2 software from the Internet.
3. **Click the icecast-2.0.2.tar.gz link.**

   A dialog box labeled `Opening icecast-2.0.2.tar.gz` opens.
4. **Click the Save it to disk option and then click the OK button.**

   A dialog box labeled Enter name of file to save to... opens.
5. **Click the Save button.**

   The file is downloaded to your computer.
6. **Back in your browser, scroll down the page and click the libshout-2.0.tar.gz link.**

   The Enter name of file to save to... dialog opens.
7. **Click the Save button and the libshout archive file is downloaded to your computer.**
8. **Once again, back in the www.icecast.org Web page, click the Ices link at the top, right of the page.**

   The Ices download page opens. Now it's time to download the Ices2 source code.
9. **Click the ices-2.0.0.tar.gz link.**

   A dialog box labeled Enter name of file to save to... opens.
10. **Click the Save button.**

    The Ices2 file is downloaded into your current directory.

Note that in this section, we break our unstated rule of installing only precompiled software from RPM packages. Although Icecast2 is available in RPM format, Ices2 is not. We could use the Icecast2 package, but it requires a *library* (software that's shared between many programs) that's difficult to find. Therefore, compiling Icecast2 and Ices2 from scratch turns out to be easier. (It's also fun to know how we nerds spend our Saturday nights!)

Before installing Icecast2 and Ices2, we have to install the libshout libraries:

1. **Open a terminal window by clicking the GNOME Menu and choosing System Tools⇨Terminal.**

   These instructions assume that you're working from your home directory.

2. **Change to become the `root` user:**

```
su
```

Note that we don't use the `su -` command. Using the dash (-) tells the substitute user (su) command to adopt the new user's environment and change to the new user's home directory. That would include changing to the user home directory and complicate this process.

3. **Unpack the libshout archive and change to the new libshout directory.**

```
tar xzf libshout*
cd libshout-2.0
```

4. **Run the following command to set up the compilation process:**

```
./configure
```

5. **Compile and link the software by running the `make` command:**

```
make
```

6. **Install the software:**

```
make install
```

The libshout library is installed into /usr/local/lib. The following instructions show how to configure, compile and install Ices2 multimedia server.

1. **Go back up one level to your home directory:**

```
cd ..
```

2. **Unpack the Ices2 archive:**

```
tar xzf ices-2*
```

The asterisk matches any characters after the major version number — 2. We use it here just in case the Ices2 version number has changed.

3. **Change to the Ices2 directory that you created with the `tar` command in Step 2:**

```
cd ices-2*
```

4. **Run the following command to set up the compilation process:**

```
./configure
```

5. **Compile and link the software by running the `make` command:**

```
make
```

6. **Install the software:**

```
make install
```

The Ices2 software is installed in the /usr/local directories.

7. **Copy the sample configuration file to its working location and move up one level:**

```
cp conf/ices*.xml /usr/local/etc
cd ..
```

Next, use the following to configure, compile and install Icecast2.

1. **Unpack the Icecast2 archive:**

```
tar xzf icecast*
```

2. **Change to the newly created Icecast2 directory:**

```
cd icecast*
```

3. **Configure Icecast2 for compilation:**

```
./configure
```

4. **Compile the source code:**

```
make
```

5. **Install the code:**

```
make install
```

   The Icecast2 software is installed in the /usr/local directories.

6. **Copy the sample configuration file to its working location:**

```
cp conf/icecast*dist
   /usr/local/etc/icecast.conf
```

Your Ices2 and Icecast2 servers are now ready for prime time. The following section describes how to configure both systems. After they're configured, you can serve up multimedia streams.

Configuring Icecast2

Ices2 gets its multimedia content from static files, such as music formatted in Ogg/Vorbis. Ices2 then feeds the audio streams to the Icecast2 server. You can then connect to the Icecast2 serves with your client application to listen to the music. All these connections are made over IP networks.

Ices2 and Icecast2 use the loopback (`127.0.0.1`) interface to communicate. (The *loopback interface* is an internal network interface that doesn't use any physical device.) Using the loopback interface provides a simple method for testing your configuration.

Icecast2 uses Port 8000 to communicate with its stream source and Port 8001 for administration.

You begin by configuring Icecast2:

1. **Create the icecast user.**

```
useradd -m -d /var/log/icecast icecast
```

This user will be run the icecast server, but will not function as a login account because we don't set a password.

2. **Change to the /usr/local/etc directory.**
3. **Open the Icecast2 configuration file, like this:**

```
gedit icecast.xml
```

Now, you have to make some minor modifications to the configuration file to set up your simple streaming server.

4. **Find the part of the configuration file that defines the port number and bind address — 127.0.0.1. Remove the comments from those parameters.**

Comments encapsulate the configuration parameters with these character strings: `<!--` and `-->`.

5. **Remove the comments and the code should look like this:**

```
  <!-- You can use these two if you only want a single
        listener -->
    <port>8000</port>
    <bind-address>127.0.0.1</bind-address>
```

These parameters tell the Icecast2 server which port number and IP address to listen to. They also define the master server as the same machine.

6. **Find the Master Server section of the configuration and remove the comments. The configuration should look like this:**

```
<master-server>127.0.0.1</master-server>
<master-server-port>8001</master-server-port>
<master-update-interval>120</master-update-interval>
<master-password>hackme</master-password>
```

7. **Find the** `<logdir>` **parameter and change it to this:**

```
<logdir>/var/log/icecast</logdir>
```

This location is where all the information about the running Icecast2 server is kept (in logs). Information about Icecast2 problems is placed there too.

8. **Find the** `<security>` **section and change the user and group to** `icecast`**:**

```
<security>
  <chroot>0</chroot>
  <!--
  <changeowner>
      <user>nobody</user>
      <group>nogroup</group>
  </changeowner>
   -->
</security>
```

Running the server as nobody reduces the security risk — breaking into your Icecast2 server doesn't provide a hacker with superuser privileges.

9. **Remove the comments from before the** <changeowner> **parameter and after the** </changeowner> **parameter:**

```
<security>
  <chroot>0</chroot>

  <changeowner>
      <user>icecast</user>
      <group>icecast</group>
  </changeowner>

</security>
```

Removing the comments allows the <user> and <group> directives to become active and force Icecast2 to run as user and group nobody. If you don't remove the comments, Icecast2 runs as the user and group of the process that starts it. Because you're logged in as root, Icecast2 runs as the root user.

Running any service as root can compromise your computer's security.

10. **Save your changes by clicking the Save button.**

11. **Quit Gedit by selecting File➪Quit.**

You just started your multimedia server, but aren't transmitting anything. You have dead air now. Because you don't want to run afoul of the FCC, the next section describes how to configure and start the Ices2 server so you can feed content to the Icecast2 server.

Configuring Ices2

Configuring Ices2 is similar to configuring Icecast2. Follow these steps to configure Ices2 and then feed an audio stream to Icecast2:

1. **Open the Gedit text editor running the following command:**

```
gedit /usr/local/etc/ices-playlist.xml
```

Ices2 can handle both static and live audio streams. The `ices-live.xml` configuration file deals with live streams, and the `ices-playlist.xml` configures static streams. However, providing live streams is more than we have space to describe in this book, so we leave it up to you to investigate that subject.

2. **Change the <logpath> directive to the following:**

```
<logpath>/var/log/icecast</logpath>
```

3. **Modify Ices2 to work with Ogg audio file, that you just extracted. Find the `<input>` module and modify the file parameter to point to your newly created `playlist` file:**

```
<input>
   <module>playlist</module>
   <param name="type">basic</param>
   <param name="file">
      /usr/local/etc/playlist.txt
   </param>
   <param name="random">0</param>
   <param name="restart-after-reread">
      0
   </param>
   <param name="once">0</param>
</input>
```

The `<input>` and `</input>` delimiters tell Ices2 that these parameters are used to define the playlist:

   - ***<module>* and *</module>*:** These delimiters define the playlist boundary.
   - **Type:** This parameter defines the type of playlist you're using. In this case, it's a basic system.
   - **File:** The name of the file that contains the playlist is defined here.
   - **Random:** If this option is set to `1`, the playlist tracks are played randomly.
   - **Once:** If this parameter is set to `1`, it tells Ices2 to play each track only once.

4. **Save your changes by clicking the Save button.**

5. **Choose File⇨Quit and the Gedit window closes.**

Ices2 uses a configuration file (that is, a *playlist*) to provide static streams to Icecast2. Playlists define which audio files Ices2 provides to Icecast2.

Ices2 starts streaming to the Icecast2 server the Ogg/Vorbis file you created. You can start listening to your private streaming server. We describe how to do just that in the following section.

Putting It All Together: Streaming Music to Your Private Network

You can use a multimedia player such as Rhythmbox to connect to and listen to an audio stream. The following steps describe how to do it (they assume you're still logged in as Root):

1. **Start your Icecast2 server:**

   ```
   icecast -c /usr/local/etc/icecast.xml &
   ```

2. **Start the Ices2 server:**

   ```
   ices /usr/local/etc/ices-playlist.xml &
   ```

3. **Start Rhythmbox or MPlayer to play the stream. For instance, use MPlayer as follows:**

   ```
   mplayer http://127.0.0.1:8000/example1.ogg.
   ```

That's it! You hear whatever music you ripped from your music CD.

It's common to restart Ices2 multiple times while trying to get it working. In that case, you may tie up the loopback port that Ices2 and Icecast2 use to communicate. In that case, you'll see a warning in the `/var/log/ices/ices.log` file, saying that it can't connect to port `127.0.0.1:8000`. You can solve that problem by running the following command as root: **service network restart.**

You have little to gain by using Icecast2 to serve up music streams locally on your PC. Using the CD player described in Chapter 12 is much easier. However, listening to your multimedia-streaming server is useful and interesting when it's done across a network.

Streaming on Your Private Network

The preceding section describes how to broadcast music on and to the computer you're sitting at. If you've created Jukebox, now's the time to expand Jukebox into a private-network radio station.

These steps describe how to configure your Icecast2 server to broadcast over your private network:

1. **Log in as root and open the Gedit text editor by clicking the GNOME Menu and choosing Accessories⇨Text Editor.**
2. **In the Gedit window, choose File⇨Open.**
3. **Select** /usr/local/etc/icecast.xml **and click OK.**
4. **Change the loopback address,** 127.0.0.1**, to the IP address of your Icecast2 server.**

   For example, if your server's IP address is 192.168.1.1, modify the file as shown here; change the host name as appropriate too:

   ```
   <hostname>cancun</hostname>
   <!-- You can use these two if you only want a
       single listener -->
   <port>8000</port>
   <bind-address>127.0.0.1</bind-address>

   <!-- You may have multiple <listener> elements -->
       <listen-socket>
           <port>8000</port>
           <bind-address>192.168.1.1
           </bind-address>
       </listen-socket>
   ```

   Note that the port number doesn't change.
5. **Change the source password from its default value. Otherwise, anyone who downloads the Icecast2 package can determine your password:**

   ```
   <source-password>
     givememusic
   </source-password>
   ```
6. **Modify the e-mail and location information to match your network.**

   This step gives any listeners an idea of who you are and where you're coming from.

   ```
   <location>Hi-Fi Paunchy</location>
   <admin>olgomez@paunchy.net</admin>
   ```
7. **Save your changes by clicking the Save button.**
8. **Open the Ices2 configuration file —** /usr/local/etc/ices-playlist.xml **— in Gedit.**

Understanding URLs

Have you ever wondered what the various parts of a URL mean? Using a URL such as `http://localhost:8000/track1.ogg` to access a streaming-audio server, we thought that we should dissect what the various parts mean and do. This list describes the function of each URL element:

- **Protocol:** Icecast2 uses HyperText Transport Protocol, or HTTP, packets to encapsulate audio streams. HTTP is a good choice because it's easy to configure your firewalls to allow HTTP connections.
- **Address:** The Icecast2 server's IP address can be either a domain name or in numeric form. For example, you could replace `localhost` with its numeric address, `127.0.0.1`.
- **Port:** Icecast2 lists connection requests on a TCP port and uses port 8000 by default. You can easily change the port by modifying the Icecast2 configuration file.
- **MountPoint:** This component specifies the Icecast2 stream to connect to. Icecast2 is capable of playing two streams. In this example, you use the content file `track1.ogg`, which you can create by following the steps in the preceding section.

9. **Modify the file so Ices2 contacts the Icecast2 server:**

```
<hostname>veracruz</hostname>
<port>8000</port>
<password>givememusic</password>
<mount>/example1.ogg</mount>
```

10. **Save your changes and close the Gedit window.**

    You can run the following two steps from the Fedora Core computer running `Icecast2/Ices2` or any Linux computer on your private network.

    You can easily expand your music selection by adding tracks to your playlist. For example, if you have a few tracks in another location, just add a line for each one in `/usr/local/etc/playlist.txt`.

11. **Open a GNOME Terminal window and start the server (after stopping any old versions):**

```
killall -9 icecast ices
icecast -c /usr/local/etc/icecast.xml &
ices /usr/local/etc/ices-playlist.xml &
```

12. **Enter this command to start Rhythmbox and connect to the newly configured Icecast2 stream:**

```
rhythmbox http://192.168.1.1:8000/example1.ogg
```

    You can also use MPlayer to listen to the stream, if you want:

```
mplayer http://192.168.1.1:8000/example1.ogg
```

You have yourself an Internet radio station. The firewall you find out about in Chapter 8 prevents anyone from connecting to the audio stream from the Internet, so you shouldn't be violating any copyright laws — you're still allowed to listen to your own CDs. You can listen to your radio from any computer on your private network, including wireless laptops. That's pretty cool. Sometime soon, we hope, you may see Ogg-capable music players similar to the Apple iPod and listen to our station, just as we would on a portable radio.

Part V
The Part of Tens

"When we started the company, we weren't going to call it 'Red Hat'. But eventually we decided it sounded better than 'Beard of Bees Linux'."

In this part . . .

Ah, the part you find in every *For Dummies* book: The Part of Tens. Here we get to rummage around and come up with ten of this and ten of that.

In Chapter 20, we list some frequently encountered problems (and their solutions).

Unfortunately, the world is still a dangerous place. Chapter 21 outlines ten computer-security threats. We describe how to be a little safer in the Wild West, otherwise known as the Internet.

Chapter 20

Ten Problem Areas and Solutions

In This Chapter

- Finding information about Linux
- "I forgot my password"
- "I forgot my `root` password"
- "I need to break into my own computer!"
- "I want to change the GRUB boot order"
- "When I boot into Windows, I get the recovery process"
- "My network is working, yet not working"
- "I want to make an emergency boot floppy disk"
- "I can't boot from my DVD"
- "Linux can't find a shell script (or a program)"
- "I don't know how to make the X Window System start at boot-time"

In any technical situation, people end up having problems and issues they need help with. This chapter is designed to help answer the most common problems you may encounter when you're using Fedora Core.

"Help! I Need Some Help!"

Before this chapter gets into showing you how to solve specific problems, it first describes several sources of information. Because we cannot cover more than a few of the most common problems, we first point you in the direction toward more information and help.

Books and more books

When we were working with computers during the Jurassic era, the number of books about computers could fill little more than one bookshelf, and they were mostly about the electronics of the hardware itself. Networking books concentrated on such subjects as the probability of two Ethernet packets colliding and not on how to build simple networks. You could hardly ever find any computer operating-system books in the popular bookstores. The immensely popular book *DOS For Dummies,* by Dan Gookin (Wiley), was, in fact, one of the first operating-system books — and launched the *For Dummies* series.

Thousands of books about computers are available now; most describe the software and its interactions, with the hardware taking a back seat. Books such as the ones in the *For Dummies* series aren't just for bookstores any more. You can also find them in mass-market venues, such as your local electronics superstore.

One great source for information about *For Dummies* books is the television series *The Simpsons.* That show loves and greatly respects *For Dummies* authors in particular and provides an amazingly accurate portrait of us. (D'oh!)

Perhaps you looked at other books before you bought this one and were intimidated by their use of technical terms. Or maybe you thought the other books were too general for what you want to do, and you want something more task-oriented. You may want to look over those books again (especially technical books from Wiley) because your knowledge level should be higher if you read this book. TCP/IP networking, compiler design, operating-system theory, formal language theory, computer graphics, and system-administration training are all topics you can study in greater depth when you have a Linux computer at your disposal.

Many books specifically about the Unix operating system are partially or completely applicable to Linux, such as books about Perl, a comprehensive interpreter. By getting one book (or more) about Perl and sitting down with your Linux system, you gain both a new tool for doing your work and a new appreciation for a complete programming language. If you want to find out how to write Perl code, you can just view the source code.

Fedora Core and Linux documentation

Fedora Core includes lots of information about its components on your local disk drive. Look in the `/usr/share/doc` directory for manuals, `HOWTOs`, and other documents about nearly every software package on your computer. For example, open Mozilla and choose File⇨Open File. When the Open File dialog box opens, type `/usr/share/doc/cups-1.1.21/index.html` in the File Name text box and click OK. (The CUPS version may change by the time this book is published. You can find the location of the manual by entering the command **cups -ql cups | grep index**.) The Common Unix Printing System Web (CUPS) page opens. Use Mozilla to browse the `/usr/share/doc` directory and obtain information about systems such as CUPS.

You can find lots of information about Linux from the Linux Documentation Project (LDP). LDP documents are published under a *copyleft,* which is essentially the same as a copyright and simply means that you can print and use them. You can find LDP documents at `www.tldp.org`. You can also find the Fedora Core release notes locally, at

```
file:///usr/share/doc/HTML/index.html
```

Red Hat provides online versions of the manuals you get when you purchase its full distribution. Look at `www.redhat.com/docs/manuals/linux/RHL-9-Manual` for information about nearly every aspect of Red Hat. Fedora Core is a direct descendant of Red Hat Linux 9, and these manuals are still valuable.

School days

Another way to find out more information about Unix and Linux is to take a course, perhaps at a local community college. Many colleges offer courses in Unix, and some have started using Linux to teach their Unix courses. You can do your homework on your system at home, or, if you have a notebook (laptop computer), you can work anywhere. (Jon typed text for the first edition of this book in a hotel in Auckland, New Zealand, and updated text for the second edition in the United Airlines lounge in Chicago.) What we would have given during our college years for the chance to do computer projects while sitting in the comfort of our own pub, er, dorm rooms. Instead, we had to sit in a room with a bunch of punch-card machines — well, never mind. We would have been much more comfortable and productive with a Linux system. Sometimes progress *is* real.

In the news

You can obtain additional information about the Linux operating system from mailing lists and newsgroups on the Internet. In fact, one of the first popular uses of the Internet was the Usenet information-sharing system. Usenet is similar to the World Wide Web in that it uses a set of protocols to perform a special type of communication over the general-purpose Internet. Usenet provides the capability to let people participate in discussions via e-mail. People post messages to a specific interest group that anyone can view and respond to.

Newsgroups and mailing lists are dedicated to specific topics: technological and any topic in which two or more people are interested. Dozens of newsgroups and mailing lists are devoted to Linux topics. Searching these groups often provides laser-like answers to your questions because someone else is quite likely to have encountered your problem and found a solution to it. You can also post your questions to newsgroups when necessary.

Check out the Fedora Core mailing lists at

```
http://fedora.redhat.com/participate/communicate
```

This Web page provides access to all the Fedora Core lists.

You can search for newsgroups at, for example, `www.dejanews.com` and `www.mailgate.org`. Google also provides an excellent mechanism to search groups, named Google Groups, at `www.google.com/advanced_group_search`.

User groups

User groups are springing up all over the world. Some are more active than others, but most hold meetings at least once a month. Some groups are Linux only; others are connected to a larger computer group, either Unix or a more general computer users' association. User groups offer a great opportunity to ask questions. User groups also tend to stimulate new ideas and ways of doing tasks.

You can find out whether a Linux user group is in your area by checking with GLUE (Groups of Linux Users Everywhere), a service run by Specialized Systems Consultants, Inc. (SSC), which publishes *Linux Journal*. You can find GLUE, an automated map of user groups, at `www.ssc.com`.

When you arrive at the site, click the Resources link, which takes you to the *Linux Journal* site. Then check out the Resources area there, to find out where the user group closest to you meets.

No user group in your area? Post a message at your local university or community college saying that you want to start a group; other people in your area may decide to join you. Terrified at the thought of trying to start a user group? User-group leaders often aren't the most technically knowledgeable members, but are simply good planners. They organize the meeting space, find (or hound) speakers, send out meeting notices, locate sponsors, arrange refreshments (usually beer), and perform other organizational tasks. Sometimes, being the leader seems a thankless job, but when a meeting goes really well, it makes all the work worthwhile. So take heart: As a newbie to Linux, you may not know a `grep` from an `awk` (yet) but you still may make a good chairperson.

Fixing Common Problems

This section describes how to fix several common problems. Each of the following sections outlines the problem and then describes the solution.

"I forgot my password"

Problem: You have to remember a zillion passwords at work and home. Unfortunately, you cannot remember your Linux password.

Solution: The solution is simple if you have forgotten a user account password but still remember the root password. In that case, simply log in as root and reset the user password. For example, if your user name is `rod`, run the command **passwd rod** and enter the new password — for example, **likes coffee.**

The solution is more difficult when you forget the root password. You have to become a hacker and break in to your computer to fix the problem. Fortunately, Red Hat provides two possible solutions: Either boot into single-user mode via GRUB or boot from the first Red Hat installation disc.

"I forgot my root password!"

Problem: You cannot reset a regular user's password if you cannot log in as `root` (superuser). However, you can easily circumvent having to log in as the `root` user by booting your Fedora Core computer into single-user mode.

Solution: Turn on or restart your computer and press the cursor keys to select the Linux operation system when the GRUB boot screen appears; Linux is selected automatically if you're not using a dual-boot system (you installed only Linux). Next, press the **e** key to edit the GRUB configuration. You see three lines, the middle of which starts with the word *kernel.* Use the cursor keys to select the `kernel` line when the three-line menu appears. Press the **e** key again, press the spacebar, and then enter the number **1** at the end of the line. Press the Enter key and you return to the original GRUB window. Finally, press the **b** key to boot your system into single-user mode.

You can tell Linux to boot into nongraphical, rather than single-user, mode by substituting **3** for `1` when you're editing the GRUB boot mechanism.

"I need to break into my own computer!"

Power-on or reset your computer. Change your BIOS to boot from CD-ROM, if necessary. Before your computer starts the GRUB boot system, insert the companion DVD into the DVD or CD-ROM drive. When the Red Hat installation process begins, type **linux rescue** at the `boot:` prompt.

Red Hat boots into single-user mode and mounts your Linux partitions. You can access and use your computer's `root` file system by entering the following command:

```
chroot /mnt/sysimage
```

You now have complete control over your computer. For example, you can reset the `root` password:

```
passwd
```

Enter the new password when you're prompted — and note that anyone who has physical access to your computer can use this method to break into it! If you use your computer in public or semipublic places, you should set your BIOS password. Setting a BIOS password doesn't make using this method of breaking in impossible, but it does make it harder.

"I want to change the GRUB boot order"

Problem: You created a dual-boot computer with Fedora Core and Windows, and you want to change which one boots by default.

Solution: Modify the `/etc/grub/grub.conf` file on your Linux computer. The `grub.conf` should look similar to this example:

```
default=0
timeout=10
splashimage=(hd0,2)/grub/splash.xpm.gz
title Fedora Core (2.6.3-2.1.253.2.1)
        root (hd0,2)
        kernel /vmlinuz-2.6.3-2.1.253.2.1
           ro root=LABEL=/ rhgb
        initrd /initrd-2.6.3-2.1.253.2.1.img
title Other
        rootnoverify (hd0,1)
        chainloader +1
```

In this case, Linux is the operating system that boots by default, unless you select otherwise; `default = 0` corresponds to the first operating system on the list — the first Title line. To change the order, simply change the default value from `0` to `1`. Here's what that looks like:

```
default=1
timeout=10
splashimage=(hd0,0)/grub/splash.xpm.gz
title Fedora Core (2.6.3-2.1.253.2.1)
      root (hd0,2)
      kernel /vmlinuz-2.6.3-2.1.253.2.1 ro root=LABEL=/ rhgb
```

```
     initrd /initrd-2.6.3-2.1.253.2.1.img
title Other
     rootnoverify (hd0,1)
     chainloader +1
```

The next time you boot your computer, your Windows operating system (the DOS line) automatically boots.

"When I boot into Windows, I get the recovery process"

Problem: You have a dual-boot computer with Microsoft Windows as the alternative operating system. When you boot into Windows, you see the Windows recovery screen. "What happened? Help, I'm scared!"

Solution: Relax — you almost certainly haven't lost your mind or your Windows partition. What happened is that the Fedora Core installation process mistakenly selected the Windows recovery partition from which to boot Windows. Most computers now come with a preinstalled Windows recovery partition (rather than a recovery CD-ROM), so Fedora Core sees at least two Windows partitions when it's configuring GRUB, and it made the wrong choice. For example, you have `hda1` and `hda2`, and GRUB thinks `hda1` is the Windows partition — but `hda1` is actually the recovery partition, and `hda2` is Drive C in Windows.

You have to reconfigure GRUB to point to the correct Windows partition to make it work correctly. For example, you may have this `/etc/grub/grub.conf` file:

```
default=0
timeout=10
splashimage=(hd0,2)/grub/splash.xpm.gz
title Fedora Core (2.6.3-2.1.253.2.1)
     root (hd0,2)
     kernel /vmlinuz-2.6.3-2.1.253.2.1 ro root=LABEL=/ rhgb
     initrd /initrd-2.6.3-2.1.253.2.1.img
title Other
     rootnoverify (hd0,0)
     chainloader +1
```

Change the `rootnoverify (hd0,0)` parameter to `rootnoverify (hd0,1)` and reboot your computer. Alternatively, if your recovery partition is set to `rootnoverify (hd0,1)`, change it to `rootnoverify (hd0,0)`. This technique should fix your problem.

"My network is working, yet not working"

Problem: You have configured and checked your network connection and it appears to be okay. But you cannot connect to some or all of the machines or network services you want. You're perplexed.

Solution: Check your Iptables-based firewall. Red Hat configures two different levels of firewalls during the installation. This book describes several different Iptables firewall configurations too. If your firewall isn't configured correctly, it prevents some or all network communications. Even if your firewall is configured correctly, it may be designed, in many cases, to block the type of communications you want.

Turn off your firewall with this command:

```
/etc/init.d/iptables stop
```

If your network connection instantly works, your firewall was most likely the culprit. In that case, you have to modify your firewall to make it work for your needs. Turn the firewall back on as soon as you fix the problem:

```
/etc/init.d/iptables start
```

A description of how to customize an Iptables firewall is beyond the scope of this book. However, the firewalls we show you how to construct in this book may work for you and also be easier to understand and modify. Refer to Chapter 8 for more information about Iptables-based firewalls.

"I want to make an emergency boot floppy disk"

Problem: You skipped making an emergency boot disk when you installed Fedora Core and want one now.

Solution: All is not lost if you read Chapter 3 and skipped making a boot disk; it's easy, in fact, to make one. Log in to your computer as `root` and insert a blank floppy disk — or one that has information you don't mind deleting (losing everything on that disk). Then run this command:

```
uname -r
```

This command returns information about the version of Linux you're running. The output looks similar to this:

```
2.6.3-2.1.253.2.1
```

Use that number to run this command:

```
mkbootdisk 2.6.3-2.1.253.2.1
```

You have a Fedora Core boot floppy disk when the process finishes writing to the disk. Restart your computer and press the Enter key at the `boot:` prompt. Your computer then starts Fedora Core.

"I can't boot from my DVD"

Problem: You get a DVD (or CD-ROM) disc that you cannot boot from. The disc may otherwise be good, but it just doesn't work for booting.

Solution: You can get around this problem by using the boot image supplied with the companion DVD in the back of this book to create a bootable floppy disk. (This disc is different from the emergency-boot floppy disk you have the option to create in Chapter 3.)

Log in to your Fedora Core computer as root and mount the companion DVD, using the following command:

```
mount /media/cdrom
```

Change to the `images` directory on the CD-ROM:

```
cd /media/cdrom/images
```

Insert a disk into the floppy drive and run this command:

```
dd if=bootdisk.img of=/dev/fd0
```

A boot image is written to the disk, from which you can boot your computer.

You can also create a bootable CD-ROM if you have a CD-R drive. Insert a writable CD-ROM (CD-R or CD-R/W) and run this command:

```
cdrecord -isosize boot.iso
```

"Linux can't find a shell script (or program)"

Problem: You type a command name, but Linux cannot find the command, even if it's in the current directory.

Solution: When you type a shell or binary command name, Linux looks for the name in specific places and in a specific order. To find out which directories Linux looks in — and in which order — type the command `echo $PATH`.

You see a stream similar to this one:

```
/bin:/usr/bin:/usr/local/bin
```

Linux looks at these directories to find the command, program, or shell you want to execute. You may see more directories, depending on your distribution or how your system administrator (if you have one) set up your system.

Suppose you create a shell or program named `bark` and want to execute it (assuming that you have set the permission bits to make `bark` executable by you). You have a couple of choices (you actually have more than two choices, but we list just the safest ones). One choice is to type this command on the command line:

```
./bark
```

This line tells Linux to look in the directory you're in (`./`) and execute `bark`. Your second choice is to move `bark` to one of the directories shown in the PATH variable, such as `/usr/local/bin`, and enter **bark** at the prompt again.

"I don't know how to make the X Window System start at boot time"

Problem: You don't want to log in to command-line mode (such as in DOS) and type `startx`. Instead, you want to log in through the X Window System.

Solution: If you like to see a graphical interface from the beginning, change the following line in the `/etc/inittab` file:

```
id:3:initdefault:
```

to

```
id:5:initdefault:
```

Save your changes and reboot. The X Window System starts at the end of the boot process, and you can then log in through the graphical interface. To go back to the old way of booting, change the line in the `/etc/inittab` file back to the following and reboot your machine:

```
id:3:initdefault:
```

Chapter 21

Ten Security Vulnerabilities and Their Fixes

In This Chapter

- Simplifying your system
- Encrypting your communications
- Using firewalls
- Updating your software
- Backing up your data
- Introducing buffer overflows
- Getting social
- Using good passwords
- Scanning the horizon
- Keeping track of your logs

They're here! The monster is under the bed. That big wooden horse is full of Greeks, er, geeks. He-e-e-ere's Johnny! Come into the light. And so on and so on. However you say it, one thing's for sure: The computer world is getting more dangerous.

Do you want the good news or the bad news first? The good news is that the Internet has changed the world for the better and continues to do so in more (and unforeseen) ways. And the speed of change will only accelerate. The bad news is that because the Internet is constantly changing, the number of ways that someone can use the Internet to hurt you is always growing. This chapter outlines some of the more dangerous spooks who lurk out on that poorly lit electronic street.

Our purpose in this chapter is to point you in the right direction so you can gain a general awareness of computer security. Computer security is, unfortunately, a complex subject. Because of the complexity of the topic of security, we cannot hope to do any more here than touch on some important aspects. We just try to give you the most bang for your buck by adding a few simple but effective security measures to your new Fedora Core computer.

This chapter introduces ten important security topics. You can use them as a good starting point to increase your computer security.

How Many Daemons Can Dance on the Head of the Linux Process Table?

Every software company wants to make its operating systems easy to install and use. Operating systems are inherently complex animals, and Linux is no exception. (Of course, we're not biased when we say that Linux is, overall, a simpler system than Windows, whether you measure simplicity by the number of lines of code or the transparency — the open-source concept — of its design.) Companies walk the tightrope of making systems easy to use and also making them reasonably secure — they sell more copies when they make it simple — but buy your wrath when you get hacked.

Ease of use and security often don't get along. Your operating system is much easier to use, for example, if you install and activate every software package and option. On the other hand, running every software package means that you have more potential vulnerabilities. Entering your own house is a breeze if you install 10 doors and 20 windows, but the convenience also provides burglars with juicy opportunities. The same logic applies to your computer's operating system: The more software you install, the more chances someone has of breaking into your computer.

We don't know of a cure-all for this dilemma. The best answer from a security viewpoint is to not provide intruders with any openings: Place your computer in a locked room with no network or external connections, and turn it off. You then have a truly safe system whose only job is to hold the floor down.

As with most things in life, the best answer is to learn the security basics and then use your best judgment to balance security with convenience. Run only the services you need. For example, don't run the Samba file system service if you don't want to use your Fedora Core computer as a (Windows) file system server. Don't run the text-based `gpm` mouse program if you use the graphical X Window mode on your computer. The list is endless — and beyond the scope of this book to discuss in detail. You can find more info from these sources:

- **Web sites:** Both `www.sans.org` and `www.usenix.org` deal with security issues.

- **HOWTOs:** Go to `www.fedora.redhat.com/docs` or `www.fedoranews.org` and search for security articles. You can also go to `www.redhat.com/docs/manuals/linux/RHL-9-Manual` and open the *Customization Guide* and *Reference* documents to access security advice. Red Hat Linux 9 and Fedora Core 3 share a common heritage, and the Red Hat 9 manuals can provide you with valuable insights.
- **Books covering security:** Browse through your local bookstore to find Linux books that discuss how to reduce services. Some good books are *Red Hat Linux Security and Optimization,* by Mohammed J. Kabir, and *Linux Security Toolkit,* by David A. Bandel (both published by Wiley). Although these books don't specifically cover Fedora Core, they provide general Linux security information.

Hide Your Communications with OpenSSH

You may find it difficult to trust communication media that you don't completely control — such as university LANs, wireless home networks, and the Internet. Our (and Agent Mulder's) point: Trust no one!

The *Secure Shell (SSH)* protocol is used to conduct encrypted CLI (command-line interface) terminal sessions and file transfers. Fedora Core bundles OpenSSH with its distributions. When you install Fedora Core, you automatically get the OpenSSH client. You can use OpenSSH from a terminal session by entering the command `ssh` *`destination`*. The destination is the computer you want to communicate with. You can get information about OpenSSH from `www.openssh.org`.

Using encryption is essential when you use wireless networking. Wi-Fi (also known as 802.11b or 802.11g) wireless networks can use built-in encryption based on the WEP (Wired Equivalent Protocol). WEP does have some significant security vulnerabilities, though. The only long-term answer is either to wait until the next standard comes along to fix the problem, or use OpenSSH to provide your own encryption. You're much safer if you use OpenSSH and SSL for as much of your communication as possible.

Aha! No Firewall — Oh Boy!

Broadband connections give you a quantum leap in speed and convenience when you're connecting to the Internet. The two most popular choices for a broadband connection are DSL and cable modem. After you start using them, you may never go back to slow, Stone Age telephone-based modems.

But every silver lining implies a dark cloud. Broadband connections give you not only fast Internet connections but also continuous ones. When you're talking about a telephone-based modem, a *hacker* refers to someone who invents and creates technological devices that can attack your home computer and private network only while you're connected to the Internet. Using a 24/7 broadband connection means that every hacker on the Internet (that means every hacker in the world) can constantly bang on your computer and private network. That's a lot of vulnerability.

Firewalls provide your number-one protection from Internet-based attacks. The modern Netfilter/Iptables packet-filtering firewall system gives you excellent protection when it's properly configured. The Fedora Core installation process installs a good Iptables-based firewall by default, and Chapter 8 describes how to configure an even better one. You should never, ever, connect to the Internet without first configuring your personal firewall.

We don't mean to imply that you're invulnerable to attack if you use a telephone-based modem to connect to the Internet. Traditional modem connections are just as vulnerable as continuous broadband connections *when they're active.* What we mean is that an unconnected modem is a safe modem.

Keeping Up with the Software Joneses

Nobody's perfect, and that goes for operating-system vendors too. Even open-source Linux developers make mistakes. Vulnerabilities are found in software systems all the time and have to be fixed.

Fedora Core provides a way to keep up-to-date with current problem and security fixes through its Web site. Go to `fedora.redhat.com/download/updates.html` to find the newest and safest versions of all your system's RPM packages. Refer to Chapter 17 for information about updating your computer.

"Backups? I Don't Need No Stinking Backups!"

If you don't regularly make backups of your computer's contents, then you face a security vulnerability, plain and simple. You may lose some or all of your valuable information if your computer is compromised. You should back up your data as frequently as possible.

You can choose from many techniques and software programs for making backups, but that's a topic we couldn't possibly begin to cover in this book. We wouldn't be able to cover Fedora Core if we even began to go into detail. One great book that covers Fedora Core in great detail is *Red Hat Linux Bible: Fedora and Enterprise Edition,* by Christopher Negus (Wiley).

For example, the following commands use the ubiquitous Linux *t*ape *ar*chive (`tar`) command to create an archive of your home directory. You can then use the OpenSSH `scp` command to securely copy the archive to another location, such as your ISP account or another computer you have access to.

Follow these steps to create an archive of your home directory:

1. **Log in to your user account.**
2. **Run this `tar` command:**

   ```
   tar czf mybackup.tgz
   ```

   In this case, the `c` option means to use tar to create a new archive. The `z` option tells `tar` to compress the data. The `f` option defines the text that follows it, *`mybackup`*`.tgz`, as the file to copy the files to. The single dot (`.`) says to copy to the archive all files in the current working directory.
3. **Use OpenSSH to copy the `tar` archive to another location:**

   ```
   scp mybackup.tgz myloginaccount@myisp.com
   ```

   This command securely copies the `tar` archive to the account *`mylogin account`* at the ISP *`myisp.com`*.

My Buffer Overfloweth

Beneath the surface, computer programs — applications — are made up of many subprograms known as subroutines. *Subroutines* allow programmers to divide into many smaller tasks the task a program is to perform. Designing big or small programs without subroutines would be impossible.

Whenever a program calls a subroutine, or a subroutine calls a subroutine, information can be passed between the two via the stack. A *stack* is like a can of tennis balls: The first ball pushed into the can is the last one taken out. This type of stack is called *first-in-last-out.* (Other variations are possible, such as first-in-first-out.) Stacks turn out to be quite efficient for transferring information: Memory is consumed when transferring information to a subroutine and then automatically released when the subroutine finishes. Stacks are also referred to as *buffers* and *queues*.

Although stacks make programming with subroutines efficient, they're vulnerable to a hacking technique called *buffer overflows* (or *stack-smashing*). Overflowing a buffer is one of the most popular methods hackers use to break into computers. The idea is to feed seemingly crazy streams of code, in binary form, to a program in order to make them behave in ways their designers never intended.

Here's how buffer overflows work:

1. The character stream overflows the intended boundaries of the subroutine's buffer.
2. When the subroutine finishes, it reads the return address of the calling program or subroutine off the stack.
3. But the false return address executes the malicious hacker code — and you have been hacked!

A little more has to happen for the hacker to be successful, but you get the idea. When a hacker finds and exploits a vulnerable program, he gains access to your computer. Sometimes that access comes in the form of superuser (`root`) access! Yikes!

Here are some simple techniques you can use to minimize buffer overflows:

- **Your first line of defense is simply to minimize the number of services you run.** You run zero risk of compromise from a buffer-overflow vulnerability in any particular service *if you don't run that service.*

  For example, the Lion worm wreaked havoc in Spring 2001. Lion took advantage of a vulnerability in the Linux `sendmail` and `Lpd` printer services. Computers that didn't run those services weren't vulnerable to the Lion worm.

- **Your second defense is to update your Fedora Core computer as often as possible.** Fedora Core posts package updates (as they become available) that fix vulnerabilities. Buffer overflow fixes comprise many of the package updates. Updating your system fixes many buffer overflow vulnerabilities.

  Click the red exclamation button on the GNOME Panel to start the up2date service. You can also run the command **yum update** to accomplish the same function.

- **Your last defense is the new stack-protection system named ExecShield.** ExecShield places a canary in the stack. A *canary* is a number that, if overwritten by a buffer overflow, creates an invalid state for the calling software. The software that called the compromised subroutine sees the invalid state, and can decide to exit before any damage is done.

ExecShield is included in the Fedora Core kernel. When ExecShield is enabled, it prevents sections of a program, including its stack, from executing code or other programs. Some sections of a program (such as data) shouldn't be executable — and that includes the stack, of course.

ExecShield provides three modes of operation:

- **Disabled:** ExecShield is disabled and doesn't affect your computer's operation.

  You manually configure Linux to disable ExecShield by logging in as root, starting the GNOME Terminal, and running this command:

  ```
  echo 0 > /proc/sys/kernel/exec-shield
  ```

  Alternatively, you can add the following option to the `/etc/sysctl.conf` configuration file to turn ExecShield off at boot time:

  ```
  kernel.exec-shield = 0
  ```

- **Enabled for marked binaries only:** This mode, the default, enables only enabled programs — binaries — to work with ExecShield. You may want to use this mode with, for example, a Web server. You would protect your most vulnerable services with ExecShield and not worry about, for example, your Mozilla browser.

  This mode of operation is the default for ExecShield. However, if you have changed to another mode, you can reset this mode by logging in as root, starting the GNOME Terminal, and running this command:

  ```
  echo 1 > /proc/sys/kernel/exec-shield
  ```

- **Enabled for all binaries:** In this mode, all programs on your computer use ExecShield. Because ExecShield is relatively new, we recommend this mode only for experimenting.

  You can manually configure Linux to use this higher level of security by logging in as root, starting the GNOME Terminal, and running the command **echo 2 > /proc/sys/kernel/exec-shield**. Alternatively, you can add the option **kernel.exec-shield = 2** to the `/etc/sysctl.conf` configuration file to set ExecShield to its maximum level at boot time.

You can find out whether a program is compatible with ExecShield. Use the program `execstack` to query and set programs to use ExecShield. For example, enter the command **execstack -q / sbin/*** and you see that a few files, such as GRUB, are compatible; the capital *X* in the first column indicates that the file has been compiled with the ExecShield hooks. You can set GRUB to use ExecShield by typing **execstack -s /sbin/grub**. You should eventually see more programs become ExecShield-compatible.

ExecShield can also randomize the location where programs are loaded into your computer's virtual memory. A hacker can exploit the knowledge of where a program is loaded into your computer's memory. Linux loads programs at fairly predictable locations, but ExecShield mostly fixes the problem.

ExecShield randomizes Linux memory by default. Woo-hoo! You can manually configure the ExecShield random function: Log in as `root`, start the GNOME Terminal, and run the command **echo 1 > /proc/sys/kernel/exec-shield-randomize**. Alternatively, you can add the line `kernel.exec-shield-randomize = 1` (or `0`) to `/etc/sysctl.conf` to automate the process at boot time.

Social Engineering 1010101010

Hackers don't have to discover supertechnical tricks to break into your computer. Many smart hackers aren't deterred when they encounter a well-protected computer or network. What does a poor hacker in these security-aware times have to do to break into your system? Not all that much.

Some hacker techniques don't rely on technological means. One such technique is *social engineering,* which is a fancy way of saying "I plan to trick you or your associates into giving me information that I will use against you."

Social engineering can be as simple as a hacker calling you to see whether you're at home or in the office. If you're not physically present, the hacker can drop by, or break in, and simply steal your computer or its disks. A hacker who's not that bold may be able to gain access to a computer by tricking a help desk technician into resetting a password. The idea is to gain access or control of your computer or network in unexpected ways.

Another social-engineering technique hackers employ is to call a corporation's help desk and pretend to be a VIP. The poor minimum-wage employee can often be bullied or cajoled into giving out a password or other important information.

The moral of the story is to exercise good security hygiene and be careful of strangers. Don't give out information unless it's essential and you can verify the authenticity of the request.

Bad Passwords

The vulnerability that's probably the easiest to avoid, and most often abused, is poor or non-existent passwords. Passwords are your first line of defense. If your password is easily guessed or — even worse — blank, someone will break in.

Bad passwords are easy to fix. Start by assigning a password to every account you create — *especially* `root`. Then make it a habit to use "good" passwords. Passwords can be cracked by brute force because computers have become very fast. Because you connect to the Internet, hackers can steal your /etc/passwd file, which contains the encrypted version of your text-based passwords, and then use a computer to crack them.

Don't use any password found in a dictionary. Simple words of any language are easy to crack. For example, don't use the password *fedora*. Instead, using the words *fedora* and *rocks,* you can change *e* to *3* and *o* to *0* and then combine them into the good password f3doraR0cks!, which means that the cracking software has to use brute force, which takes longer, rather than a mere dictionary search, to discover it.

Scan Me

Information is king when it comes to people hacking into systems and keeping them out. Hackers use knowledge about your computer and network to break into your systems. One common and powerful tool for gaining information about which type of operating system you have and the services it runs is nmap. This port-scanning tool can discover a wealth of information about individual computers and networks.

nmap is included in the Fedora Core distribution. To install it, log in as root, mount the DVD (insert it in to the drive), and enter the following command:

```
rpm -ivh /media/cdrom/Fedora/RPMS/nmap*
```

You can then scan yourself, or any computer on your private network (if you have one). If you're logged in to cancun, for example, you can run the nmap localhost command.

The nmap command probes your internal loopback network interface — lo, for example — and returns a list of services you're running. This list shows a sample result:

```
Starting nmap 3.48 ( www.insecure.org/nmap/ ) at 2004-10-19

Interesting ports on localhost.localdomain (127.0.0.1):
(The ports scanned but not shown below are in state: closed)
Port        State       Service
22/tcp      open        ssh
25/tcp      open        smtp
80/tcp      open        http
111/tcp     open        rpcbind
631/tcp     open        ipp
6000/tcp    open        http-alt

Nmap run completed -- 1 IP address (1 host up) scanned
```

If you're a hacker, this is good stuff. By knowing that the machine is running certain services, you can try to find vulnerabilities to exploit. Lots of hackers do.

Another good test is to log in to your ISP account and scan the Internet connection to which your computer or private network is attached. If your firewall is running correctly, the scan shows little or nothing. That's good. If the scan displays information about your computer and network, your firewall either isn't running correctly or isn't running at all.

You can use that information to your advantage. Seeing what the hackers see gives you the ability to plug your security holes.

I Know Where You Logged In Last Summer

Linux is good at keeping a diary. Fedora Core is configured during installation to keep logs of every user login and other technical information. Examining logs is more of an art than a science, however. (We don't have any explicit techniques for determining whether your system is presently being attacked or has been broken into. There are, however, some good intrusion-detection products out there — Snort, for example — and we do know of a book that can help you: Wiley publishes *Snort For Dummies* by Charlie Scott, Paul Wolfe, and Bert Hayes. Check it out.)

Experience counts for a great deal when you're examining logs for discrepancies. The more you keep track of your system, the more you recognize its idiosyncrasies and general behavior. Fedora Core stores its general-purpose logs in the `/var/log` directory.

Naturally, Fedora Core provides a useful graphical log-checking utility. To run it, follow these steps:

1. **Click the GNOME Menu and choose System Tools⇨System Logs.**
2. **Enter the root password, if you're prompted.**

   The System Log window opens.
3. **Choose any of the log groups on the left submenu to see the selected information.**

The moral of the story is "Check your logs frequently!"

Part VI
Appendixes

"It's called Linux Poker. Everyone gets to see everyone else's cards, everything's wild, you can play off your opponents' hands, and everyone wins except Bill Gates, whose face appears on the jokers."

In this part . . .

This part is the area of every book where you find things that just didn't fit into the flow of the chapters: the fun and exciting *appendixes*. This book has six of 'em.

Appendix A outlines the Fedora Core systems administration utilities. Appendix B shows how to figure out what stuff your computer is made of. Appendixes C and D describe the Linux file system and how to use it. In Appendix E, you find out about RPM (the Red Hat Package Manager) and YUM (the Yellowdog Updater, Modifier). As a final bit of preparation, Appendix F describes the contents of this book's companion DVD.

Appendix A

Fedora Core Administration Utilities

In This Appendix

- The Fedora Core system settings
- The Fedora Core server settings
- The Fedora Core system tools

Among Linux distributions, Fedora Core tries to set itself apart from the pack by creating utilities to make your life easier. For example, it provides numerous system-administration utilities that are integrated, easy to use, and quite powerful. These utilities are one reason that Fedora Core wins the market-share competition. This appendix outlines the Fedora Core administration utilities.

You should be able to perform most system-administration tasks by using the utilities described in the lists throughout this appendix. The available utilities are organized according to the menus on which you find them; the lists given here should help you locate the ones you need to manage your Fedora Core computer.

Not all utilities listed in this appendix are installed by default. Many are installed only if you install their respective services. For example, you can use the Apache configuration utility only if you install the Apache Web server package. We tell you when a utility isn't installed as part of the Workstation installation type that we recommend you install in Chapter 3.

System Settings

The system setting utilities are on the GNOME System Settings menu, which you find by using the GNOME Menu or the Start Here window:

- **Add/Remove Applications:** Adds and deletes RPM packages. See Appendix E for more information.

- **Authentication:** Deals with all forms of Linux user account authentication. The default settings should satisfy most people's needs.
- **Date & Time:** Sets the date, time, and time zone of your Linux computer. You can also configure the automatic time synchronizer — the Network Time Protocol (NTP) — daemon.
- **Display:** Allows you to configure both your video driver and monitor. Chapter 4 provides more information about how to use this utility.
- **Keyboard:** Lets you choose the nationality of your keyboard.
- **Language:** Helps you choose the default language your computer uses.
- **Login Screen:** Lets you configure the look and feel, and other aspects, of your login screen.
- **Network:** Configures your network interfaces. You can also use it to turn network devices on and off. Refer to Chapters 5, 6, and 7 for examples of how to use this tool.
- **Printing:** Configures a printer. Chapter 16 provides an example that uses this utility.
- **Red Hat Network Configuration:** Updates your Fedora Core software. Use this utility to configure your RHN configuration.
- **Root Password:** Resets the `root` password.
- **Security Level:** Enable/disable and configure your workstation's firewall (using iptables) with this utility. As we discuss in Chapter 3, the Fedora Core installation process allows you to enable/disable a firewall and also provides options to allow certain external connections such as SSH. The installation also allowed you to enable/disable SELinux. This tool allows you to reconfigure those options.
- **Server Settings:** See the next section, "Server Settings."
- **Soundcard Detection:** Detects and configures your sound card. Chapter 12 has more instructions.
- **Users and Groups:** Creates new users and groups. You can also modify existing ones. Chapter 4 shows how to use this utility.

Server Settings

You display the Server Settings menu by choosing the GNOME Menu⇨System Settings menu and selecting Server Settings. It contains, by default, only the Services configuration utility. This list describes the various utilities (beyond the Service Configuration) that you can install optionally:

- **Apache Configuration:** Create and modify your Apache Web server. Refer to Chapter 16 for an introduction to Apache.

- **Domain Name System:** Create and modify your DNS server's configuration. DNS converts Internet names to numeric addresses.
- **NFS:** The Network File System (NFS) allows a computer to share its file system with other computers. NFS, which predates Samba, is simpler to configure and use but doesn't provide as much security as Samba.
- **Network Booting Service:** Use this system to boot your computer from a network.
- **Samba Server Configuration:** Creates and modifies your Samba server. Samba shares files, directories, and printers with other computers on your network. Those computers can run Windows, Linux, or Unix; Linux and Unix computers, however, must run the Samba client software to connect to a Samba server.
- **Services:** Controls all the services that your Fedora Core computer can run. You can start, stop, or restart any server as well as set a service to start, or not start, at boot time.

System Tools

Click the GNOME Menu and choose System Tools to find these tools:

- **Archive Manager:** Starts the File Roller utility used to create, modify, and unpack various archive files. You find the tape archive (`TAR`) system used most often on Linux and Unix computers. This utility also works with ZIP, ARJ, and other protocols.
- **Configuration Editor:** Starts the GConf editor. GConf edits the GNOME configuration, its utilities, and other general application-oriented applications and utilities.
- **Disk Management:** Mounts, dismounts, and formats specific file systems and devices.
- **Floppy Formatter:** Formats floppy disks.
- **Hardware Browser:** Displays information about your computer's hardware subsystems. Appendix B has more information about this tool.
- **Internet Configuration Wizard:** Lets you create network interfaces. Refer to Chapters 5, 6, and 7 for examples of how to work with this tool.
- **Kickstart:** Helps you automate and customize Fedora Core installations. Use it to record and customize the settings that created your current Fedora Core installation and use that template to create new installations.
- **Network Device Control:** Turns your network devices on and off.
- **Red Hat Network:** Starts the RHN up2date utility.

- **Red Hat Network Alert icon:** Indicates that an RHN update is available.
- **System Logs:** Shows the contents of your system logs.
- **System Monitor:** Displays information about your computer's running processes. This utility also shows the recent history of your computer's processor and memory use.
- **Terminal:** Starts the GNOME Terminal. You can use the Terminal to interact with your computer minus the fancy on-screen graphics. Refer to Chapter 4 for information about using the Terminal.

Appendix B

Discovering Your Hardware's True Identity

In This Appendix

- PC hardware subsystems
- Hard-drive controllers
- Computer memory
- Hardware identification on Windows 9*x* and Windows Me computers
- Hardware identification on Windows NT, Windows 2000, and Windows XP computers

You should know as much about your computer as possible before installing Fedora Core. This appendix introduces the basic systems that make up a computer. We also show you how to discover information about those parts.

Knowing your hardware can be useful at parties: "My processor is faster than your processor!" In addition to letting you brag at parties, this knowledge can be helpful if you have problems installing Fedora Core 3 as described in Chapter 3. Understanding the bits and pieces that comprise your computer also lets you know better what your new Linux computer is capable of. This appendix helps you get started on your path to self-discovery.

Linux runs on Intel processors from the venerable 386 on up to the Digital Equipment Corporation (DEC) Alpha, Sun SPARC, and other systems. However, the version of Fedora Core included with this book works on only Intel 386-, 486-, and Pentium-based computers. That shouldn't be a problem because it seems 99.9 percent (well, maybe not *quite* that many) of the world's computers use Intel.

Breaking Down Your Computer

No, we don't want you to break your computer. But we do want to describe the computer subsystems. Computers may seem mysterious when you first use them, but the truth is that they're not terribly complex. When you look at the parts that make up a PC, you see that each one performs a specific task. The sum of the parts equals a computer. This list outlines the subsystems that comprise a computer:

- **Central processing unit (CPU):** The CPU, or microprocessor, is often referred to as the brains of a computer because the CPU controls, in minute detail, everything the computer does. CPUs are controlled by software that is essentially a recipe for doing tasks as simple as detecting keyboard input or as complex as communicating across networks to display pictures in a Web browser.

  The most common CPUs running current PCs are now Intel Pentiums; chances are you have one in your PC. Generally, the faster the CPU, the faster your computer. CPU speed is measured in *megahertz* (MHz), which means millions of cycles per second. To perform complex tasks, such as sending e-mail, a CPU has to perform many simple tasks, or *instructions,* to complete the larger one. Although the simplest instructions require a single CPU cycle, most require several cycles. By and large, however, the MHz measurement is a reasonably good measure of how fast a microprocessor runs.

- **Hard drives:** Hard drives, also referred to as hard disks, store all the permanent information on a computer. The actual disks are metal platters that store bits and bytes in tiny magnetic domains (spots). The disk spins, and a magnetic head that floats on a cushion of air reads and writes from the disk. The spinning disk allows gives the head quick access to any location on the disk and also creates the air cushion.

- **Disk controllers:** The disk controller connects the drive to the computer's microprocessor. Several types of controllers are commonly used: IDE, USB, FireWire, and SCSI. Most PCs come with IDE internal hard drives. However, high-performance computers tend to use SCSI–based drives because they're faster (and more expensive). IDE controllers can connect as many as four drives.

- **CD-ROM:** CD-ROMs store information in much the same way as hard drives do, but use light rather than magnetic fields to write the data. Most PCs use IDE-based CD-ROMs. SCSI CD-ROMs are faster (as are SCSI hard disks). Because the prices of USB and FireWire CD-ROMS are dropping fast, they're becoming more common.

- **RAM, or Random-Access Memory:** Working in RAM is much faster than from hard disks and CD-ROMs . Because RAM is used to store temporary information, programs, data, and other types of information are stored in RAM — it "forgets" everything when power to the computer is turned off. RAM is measured in megabytes (MB). A *megabyte* is roughly one million bytes.

- **Mouse:** Not all mice are created equal. Which type of mouse do you have — bus, PS/2, or serial? How many buttons does it have? If you have a serial mouse, which COM port is it attached to and which protocol (Microsoft or Logitech) does it use?

- **Monitor/flat-panel display:** What are the make and model of the monitor or flat-panel display? What are its vertical and horizontal refresh rates? You need this information only if you plan to use the X Window System, the graphical portion of Linux. Monitors and flat-panel displays perform exactly the same function, but with different technologies. Monitors are the ubiquitous, heavy, television-like, glass vacuum-tube devices that are quickly being replaced by flat-panel displays. These screens use liquid crystal display (LCD) technology, which uses less power and space.
- **Video card:** What are the make and model number of the video card or video chip set, and what is the amount of video RAM?
- **Network interface card (NIC):** If you have a network connection, what are the make and model number of the network interface card?

That's the rundown of computer subsystems. Each one performs a specific function; buttoned up inside a computer *chassis* (whether a desktop box or laptop); they work together to create the computer you're familiar with. The next two sections describe hard drives and memory in more detail.

Understanding Hard-Drive Controllers

The two main types of hard drives are IDE and SCSI, and each type has its own controller. IDE is more common in PCs; newer PCs usually have two IDE controllers rather than one. For each IDE controller, your system can have only two hard drives: a master and a slave. Therefore a PC with two IDE controllers can have as many as four hard drives. You should know which hard drive is which. Also, if you have a Windows system that you want to preserve, you should know on which hard drive it resides. The following list shows a normal configuration on a Windows system:

- The first controller's master drive is named C.
- The next hard drive, named D, is the slave drive on the first controller.
- The next hard drive, E, is the master drive on the second controller.
- The last hard drive, F, is the slave drive on the second controller.

Windows is normally located on drive C, and your data is on your other drives. This lettering scheme is one possibility; your hard drives may be set up differently and may include CD-ROMs as drives on your IDE controllers.

Some high-end PCs have SCSI controllers on their motherboards or on separate SCSI controller boards, either in addition to or instead of the IDE controllers. Older SCSI controllers can have as many as eight devices on them, numbered from 0 to 7, including the controller. Newer SCSI controllers (known as *wide controllers*) can have as many as 16 devices, including the controller itself.

If all you have is a SCSI hard drive, Drive 0 or Drive 1 is usually your drive C, and others follow in order.

If you have a mixture of IDE and SCSI controllers, your drive C could be on any of them. The sections "Discovering Your Windows 9*x* or Windows Me Hardware" and "Discovering Your Windows NT, Windows 2000, or Windows XP Hardware," later in this appendix, show you how to identify how many hard drives you have, which type(s) they are, and which controllers they're attached to.

Consider putting Fedora Core on a separate hard drive, away from any Windows operating system, for a couple of reasons. First, you can now find 80GB hard drives for well under $100 (U.S.). Second, it's a pretty daunting task (at worst, nearly impossible) to shrink MS-DOS and Windows till they're small enough to allow Fedora Core to reside in its full glory on an existing hard drive. Also, although technically you can split the Fedora Core distribution and put it on several hard drives, doing so makes updating the distribution difficult later.

A Bit About Memory Bytes

Memory is the most important factor in determining how fast your computer runs. Computers use Random-Access Memory (RAM) to store and access the operating system, programs, and data. The Intel processor usually has the following amounts of RAM (main memory):

- Linux can run on a surprisingly small amount of memory. With some work and no graphics, you can squeeze Linux onto an old PC with only 16MB of memory; 32MB makes life much easier and your computer significantly faster.

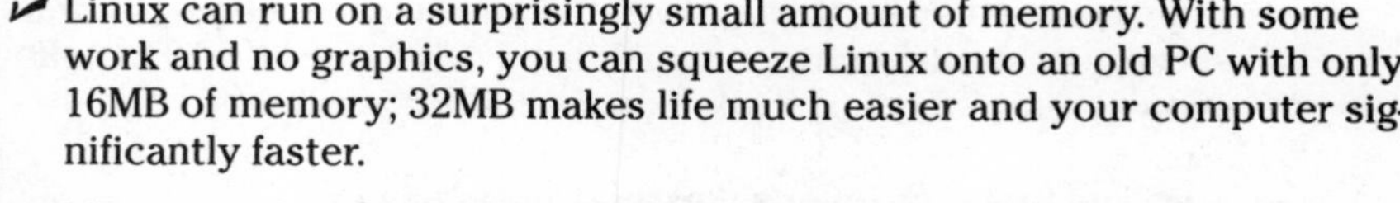

  Many people use suitable old PCs with small amounts of memory as simple network servers.
- If you want to run Linux with graphics, however, you need 64MB.
- With 128MB, Fedora Core runs multiple graphical programs (such as OpenOffice.org) with ease.
- You need 256MB or more (many PCs now come standard with 512MB) for hard-core computing. Using big applications, such as VMware, makes having enough memory essential.

VMware virtual computers need their own RAM to operate at a reasonable speed; for example, you should allocate a minimum of 128MB of memory to run a Windows 2000 virtual computer. Plan to use 512MB if you want to run multiple instances of VMware virtual computers.

You can install Fedora Core on most laptop computers by using the notebook's built-in CD-ROM drive, or a PCMCIA, USB, or proprietary CD-ROM drive. If you don't have any of these items, you can try to get a PCMCIA Ethernet controller and do a network installation, as long as another Linux system on the network has a CD-ROM drive installed. If that's the course you take, consult the Fedora Core installation documentation at `www.redhat.com/support`. You also need a video card that Fedora Core understands. Fedora Core supports most video cards, and usually the only problems result from bleeding-edge notebook computers that use the latest and greatest video hardware. You can use the generic VGA, XGA, or SVGA drivers that Fedora Core supplies if you cannot find the specific driver.

Discovering Your Windows 9x or Windows Me Hardware

You don't have to go to Hollywood to be discovered — provided you're a piece of computer hardware. Windows provides the tools to discover your bits and pieces right at home. This section describes how to use Windows 9*x* or Windows Me (which Microsoft will still support for a while yet) for the discovery process.

If you have a Windows 9*x* or Windows Me computer, use this section to discover and display information about your computer. We use the ubiquitous Control Panel. Start your Windows computer and follow these instructions:

1. **Click the Start button and choose Settings⇨Control Panel. Double-click the System icon and select the Device Manager tab.**
2. **At the top of the screen, select View Devices by Connection. This step shows you all components and how they relate to each other.**
3. **On the Device Manager tab (from the Control Panel) in the System Properties dialog box, select the View Devices by Type option.**

   On the list, notice how a plus (+) or minus (–) sign precedes some icons. A plus sign indicates that the entry is collapsed. A minus sign indicates that the entry is expanded to show all subentries.
4. **Click the plus (+) sign to expand the list.**

   Expanding the list shows each computer subsystem. Every device that makes up your computer is shown. Right-click a device and choose the Properties option to display information about a particular device.

You can use the Web to find out about your computer. Computer companies provide detailed information about their products on their Web sites. Go to the manufacturer's Web page and look up your computer's model number. When you get to your page, look for the Specification (or Specs) link.

Discovering Your Windows NT, Windows 2000, or Windows XP Hardware

Discovering information about a system running Windows NT, Windows 2000, and Windows XP is similar to making the same discovery on a Windows 9*x* or Windows Me system. The process is the same, although getting there is a little different:

On Windows NT and Windows 2000 computers, follow these steps:

1. **Click the Start button and choose Settings⇨Control Panel. Then, double-click the System icon in the Control Panel window.**
2. **Click the Hardware tab when the Systems Properties window opens. Then, click the Device Manager button to open the Device Manager window.**
3. **Click the plus (+) sign of any hardware subsystem you want to examine.**

   A submenu opens, showing you all the devices of a particular type.
4. **Right-click any hardware subsystem and choose Properties.**

   The Properties option shows you information about that particular device.

On Windows XP computers, follow these steps:

1. **Click the Start button and choose the My Computer option.**
2. **Double-click the Control Panel icon.**
3. **Double-click the System icon, select the Hardware tab, and then double-click the Device Manager button.**

   The Device Manager window opens.
4. **Click the plus (+) sign to display the devices within a subsystem.**
5. **Right-click a device to open a menu from which you can choose the Properties option.**

   The Properties window opens and shows information about the device.

Appendix C

Filing Your Life Away

In This Appendix

- Finding out all about Linux files and directories
- Navigating the Linux file system
- Creating, moving, copying, and destroying directories and files
- Changing file ownership and permissions

In this appendix, you step boldly through the Linux file and directory structure. Don't worry: Linux may live a structured life, but it's still flexible. With a little bit of introduction, you can quickly get the hang of the Linux way of life.

We also introduce you to file types, subdirectories, paths, and the `root` directory. You're also shown the way home — to your home directory. After you're oriented to the Linux files-and-directories structure, we show you how to make some changes, such as how to copy and move files and directories and how to — eeek! — destroy them.

Getting Linux File Facts Straight

Linux files are similar to Unix, DOS, Windows, and Macintosh files. All operating systems use files to store information. Files allow you to organize your stuff and separate your information. For example, the text that makes up this appendix is stored in a file — as is every other chapter, each in its own file. Follow the bouncing prompt as we make short work of long files.

Storing files

We assume that you know that a *file* is a discrete collection of information identified by a filename — and that Linux can store multiple files in directories, as long as the files have different names. (Linux stores any files with the same name in different directories.)

Wonderful or not, Linux filenames can be as long as 256 characters. The filenames can contain uppercase and lowercase letters (also known as *mixed case*), numbers, and special characters, such as underscores (_), dots (.), and hyphens (-) and spaces. Because filenames can be composed of mixed-case names, and because each name is distinct, these names are *case sensitive*. For example, the names `FILENAME`, `filename`, and `FiLeNaMe` are unique filenames of different files, although they're made up of the same letters.

Although filenames technically can contain wildcard characters, such as asterisks (*) and question marks (?), using them isn't a good idea. Various command interpreters, or *shells,* use wildcards to match several filenames at once. If your filenames contain wildcard characters, you have trouble specifying *only* those files. We recommend that you create filenames that don't contain spaces or other characters that have specific meanings to shells. That's one way Linux filenames are different from DOS and Windows filenames.

Sorting through file types

Linux files can contain all sorts of information. In fact, Linux sees every device — disk drives, monitor, mouse, or keyboard, for example — as a file; the only exception is a network interface. These five file categories eventually become the most familiar to you:

- **User data files:** These contain information you create. User data files, sometimes known as *flat files,* usually contain the simplest data, consisting of plain text and numbers. More complex user data files, such as graphics or spreadsheet files, must be interpreted and used by special programs. These files are mostly illegible if you look at them with a text editor because their content isn't always ASCII text. Changing these files generally affects only the user who owns the files.
- **System data files:** These are used by the system to keep track of users on the system, logins, and passwords, for example. As system administrator, you may be required to view or edit these files. As a regular user, you need not be concerned with system data files (except, perhaps, the ones you use as examples for your own, private startup files).
- **Directory files:** These hold the names of files — and other directories — that belong to them. These files and directories are called *children.* Directories in Linux (and Unix) are just another type of file. If you're in a directory, the directory above it is the *parent.* Isn't that homey?

  When you list files with the `ls -l` command, it displays a list of files and directories. Directory files (for example) begin with the letter *d,* so they're easy to spot in this example:

  ```
  [lidia@cancun lidia]$ ls -l
  drwxr-xr-x 5 lidia lidia 1024 Aug 3  2004 Desktop
  drwx------ 2 lidia lidia 1024 Aug 10 2004 nsmail
  ```

- **Special files:** These represent either hardware devices (such as disk drives, tape drives, or keyboards) or some type of placeholder that the operating system uses. The `/dev` directory holds many of these special files. You can see this directory by running this command at a command prompt:

```
ls -l /dev
```

- **Executable files:** These contain instructions (usually called *programs* or *shell scripts*) for your computer. When you type the name of one of these files, you're telling the operating system to *execute* the instructions. Some executable files look like gibberish, and others look like long lists of computer commands. Many of these executable files are located in `/bin`, `/usr/bin`, `/sbin`, and `/usr/sbin`.

Understanding files and directories

If you live in the Windows world, you can think of a Linux file system as one huge file folder that contains files and other file folders, which in turn contain files and other file folders, which in turn contain files and — well, you get the point. In fact, the Linux file system is generally organized in this way. One big directory contains files and other directories, and all the other directories in turn contain files and directories.

Directories and subdirectories

A directory contained, or *nested,* in another directory is a *subdirectory.* For example, the directory named `/mother` may contain a subdirectory named `/child`. The relationship between the two (even if they don't have such family-derived filenames) is referred to as *parent-and-child.* The full name of the subdirectory is `/mother/child`, which would make a good place to keep a file named `/mother/child/reunion` that contains information about a family reunion.

The root directory

In the tree directory structure of Linux, DOS, and Unix, the big directory at the bottom of the tree is the *`root` directory.* The `root` directory is the parent of all other directories (the poor guy must be exhausted) and is represented by a single `/` symbol (pronounced "slash"). From the `root` directory, the whole directory structure grows like a tree, with directories and subdirectories branching off like limbs.

If you could turn the tree over so that the trunk is in the air and the branches are toward the ground, you would have an *inverted tree* — which is how the Linux file system is normally drawn and represented (with the tree's root at the top). If we were talking about Mother Nature, you would soon have a dead tree. Because the subject is computer technology, however, you have something that looks like an ever-growing, upside-down tree.

What's in a name?

You name directories in the same way as you name files, following the same rules. Almost the only way you can tell whether a name is a filename or a directory name is the way the slash character (/) is used to show directories nested in other directories. For example, `usr/local` means that `local` is in the `usr` directory. You know that `usr` is a directory because the trailing slash character tells you so; however, you don't know whether `local` is a file or a directory.

If you issue the `ls` command with the `-f` option, Linux lists directories with a slash character at the end, as in `local/`, so you know that `local` is a directory.

The simplest way to tell whether the slash character indicates the `root` directory, other separate directories, or directories and files, is to see whether anything appears before the slash character in the *directory-path specification* (a string that shows exactly which directories and subdirectories you have to go through to get to the file). If nothing appears before the slash, you have the `root` directory. For example, you know that `/usr` is a subdirectory or a file in the `root` directory because it has only a single slash character in front of it.

Home again

Linux systems have a directory named `/home`, which contains the user's home directory, where she can

- Store files
- Create more subdirectories
- Move, delete, and modify subdirectories and files

Linux system files and files belonging to other users are never in a user's `/home` directory. Linux decides where the `/home` directory is placed, and that location can be changed only by a superuser (`root`), and not by general users. Linux is dictatorial because it has to maintain order and keep a handle on security.

Moving Around the File System

You can navigate the Linux file system without a map or GPS (Global Positioning System). All you need to know are two commands: `pwd` and `cd`. (You run these commands from the command line.) However, you also need to know where to start — hence the usefulness of the next section.

Figuring out where you are

Log in to your Fedora Core computer and open a GNOME Terminal session. In this case, as an example, you log in as the user `lidia`. To find out where you are in the Linux file system, simply type **pwd** at the command prompt:

```
[lidia@cancun lidia]$
```

You receive this response:

```
/home/lidia
```

This response indicates that you're logged in as `lidia` and are in the `/home/lidia` directory. Unless your alter ego is out there, you should be logged in as *yourself* and be in the `/home/`*`yourself`* directory, where *yourself* is your login name.

The `pwd` command stands for *p*rint *w*orking *d*irectory. Your *working directory* is the default directory where Linux commands perform their actions; the working directory is where you are in the file system when you type a command. When you type the `ls(1)` command, for example, Linux shows you the files in your working directory. Any file actions on your part occur in your working directory unless you're the `root` user. For security reasons that we don't go into here, the `root` user isn't configured by default to be able to work on the current working directory. You can change this setting, but the `root` user generally must explicitly specify the working directory. For example, if you are `root` and are in the `/etc` directory and you want to indicate the `hosts` file, you must type **cat ./hosts** rather than just **cat hosts.**

If you use this command:

```
ls -la
```

you see only the files in your working directory. If you want to specify a file that isn't in your working directory, you have to specify the name of the directory that contains the file in addition to the name of the file. For example, this command lists the `passwd` file in the `/etc` directory:

```
ls -la /etc/passwd
```

Specifying the directory path

If the file you want to read is in a subdirectory of the directory you're in, you can reach the file by typing a relative filename. *Relative paths* specify the location of files relative to where you are.

In addition to what we discuss earlier in this appendix about specifying directory paths, you need to know these three rules:

- One dot (.) always stands for your current directory.
- Two dots (..) specify the parent directory of the directory you're in.
- All directory paths that include (.) or (..) are relative directory paths.

You can see these files by using the `-a` option of the `ls(1)` command. Without the `-a` option, the `ls(1)` command doesn't bother to list the . or .. files, or any filename beginning with a period. This statement may seem strange, but the creators of Unix thought that having some files normally hidden keeps the directory structure cleaner. Therefore, filenames that are always present (. and ..) and special-purpose files are hidden. The types of files that should be hidden are those a user normally doesn't need to see in every listing of the directory structure (for example, files used to tailor applications to the user's preferences).

Specify a path relative to where you are. Here's an example:

```
cd /etc
ls -la ../etc/passwd
```

The first command moves you to the `/etc` directory, where the `passwd` file resides; the command uses an absolute path (`/etc`) in this case. The second command redundantly starts one directory up (..) and then looks in the `/etc` directory for the `passwd` file. You move up one directory level and then back down to `/etc`; this demonstrates the use of relative paths (`../etc/passwd`).

If you want to see the login accounts on your system, you can issue this command from your home directory:

```
ls -la ..
```

This command lists the parent directory. Because the parent directory (`/home`) has all the login directories of the people on your system, this command shows the names of their login directories.

You have been looking at relative pathnames, which are relative to where you are in the file system. Filenames that are valid from anywhere in the file system are *absolute paths.* These filenames always begin with the slash character (/), which signifies the `root` directory. Here's an example with two:

```
ls -la /etc/passwd
```

Changing your working directory

You occasionally (often?) want to change your working directory. Why? We're glad you asked — because changing it enables you to work with shorter relative pathnames. To do so, you simply use the `cd` (for *c*hange *d*irectory) command.

To change from your working directory to the `/usr` directory, for example, type this command:

```
cd /usr
```

Going home

If you type **cd** by itself, without any directory name, you return to your home directory. Just knowing that you can easily get back to familiar territory is comforting. There's no place like home.

You can also use `cd` with a *relative* specification, like this:

```
cd ..
```

If you're in the directory `/usr/bin` and type the preceding command, Linux takes you to the parent directory named `/usr`:

```
cd /usr/bin
cd ..
```

Here are a couple of tricks: If you type **cd ~**, you go to your home directory (the tilde symbol (~) is synonymous with `/home/username`). If you type **cd ~<*username*>**, you can go to that user's home directory. On very large systems, this command is useful because it eliminates the need for you to remember — and type — large directory specifications.

This list describes the shell redirection symbols:

- > is known as *redirect standard output.* When you use it, you tell the computer "Capture the information that normally goes to the screen, create a file, and put the information in it."
- > is known as *append standard output.* When you use this symbol, you tell the computer "Capture the information that would normally go to the screen and append the information to an existing file. If the file doesn't exist, create it."

- < tells the computer, "Feed the information from the specified file to *standard in* (also known as *standard input*), acting as though the information is coming from the keyboard."

Manipulating Files and Directories

Linux has many ways to create, move, copy, and delete files and directories. Some features are so easy to use that you need to be careful: Unlike other operating systems, Linux doesn't tell you that you're about to overwrite a file — it just follows your orders and overwrites!

We have said it elsewhere in this book, and we'll say it again: Make sure that you're *not* logged in as the `root` user when you read through these sections. You can unintentionally harm your computer when you're logged in as `root`. As `root`, or the superuser, you can erase any file or directory — regardless of which permissions are set. Be careful!

Creating directories

To create a new directory in Linux, you use the `mkdir` command (there's an identical command in MS-DOS). It looks like this:

```
mkdir newdirectory
```

This command creates a subdirectory under your current or working directory. If you want the subdirectory under another directory, change to that directory first and then create the new subdirectory.

Create a new directory named `cancun`. Go ahead — do it:

```
mkdir cancun
```

(Can you tell where we would rather be right now?)

Create another directory named `veracruz`:

```
mkdir veracruz
```

Then change the directory to put yourself in the `cancun` directory:

```
cd cancun
```

Now, verify that you're in the directory `cancun`:

```
pwd
```

Moving and copying files and directories

The commands for moving and copying directories and files are `mv` for move and `cp` for copy. If you want to rename a file, you can use the `mv` command. No, you're not really moving the file, but the Linux (and Unix) developers realized that renaming something was much like moving it. The format of the move command is

```
mv source destination
```

Create a file that you can practice moving. The `touch` command updates the time stamp on an existing file or creates an empty file if it doesn't exist. In this case, the file `test` doesn't exist and is created by `touch`:

```
touch go
```

Move the new file:

```
mv go to
```

This command leaves the file in the same directory and changes its name to `to`. The file wasn't really moved — just renamed.

Try moving the `to` file to the `veracruz` directory. To do that, you have to first move the file up and then move it into the `veracruz` directory. You can do it with one command:

```
mv to ../veracruz
```

The destination file uses the double-dot (..) designation; every directory contains a double-dot directory that points to the parent directory. This command tells Linux to go up one directory level and look for a directory named `veracruz` and then put the file into that directory with the name `newgoto` because you didn't specify any other name. If you do this instead:

```
mv go ../veracruz/now
```

the `go` file moves to the `veracruz` directory named `now`. Note that in both cases (with the file maintaining its name, `go`, or taking the new name `now`), your current directory is still `cancun` and all your filenames are relative to that directory.

Strictly speaking, the file still hasn't really moved. The data bits are still on the same part of the disk as they were originally. The *file specification* (the directory path plus the filename) you use to talk about the file is different, so it appears to have moved.

Removing files and directories

The command for removing, or deleting, a file is `rm`. Using `rm` is straightforward. For example, create a dummy file to erase:

```
touch junk
```

You can delete the file with this command:

```
rm junk
```

You have removed the dummy file from the current directory. To remove a file from another directory, you need to provide a relative filename or an absolute filename. For example, if you want to expunge `now` from the `veracruz` directory, you type this line:

```
rm ../veracruz/now
```

You can use metacharacters (similar in many ways to Windows wildcards) with `rm`, but *be very careful* if you do so! When files are removed in Linux, they're gone forever — kaput, vanished — and cannot be recovered.

The following command removes *everything* in the current directory and all the directories under it that you have permission to remove:

```
rm -r *
```

Do *not* give this command as root (the superuser)! You should always be careful when you're running any command as `root`, but be especially careful with commands that can erase entire directories and file systems.

To decrease the danger of removing lots of files inadvertently when you use metacharacters, be sure to use the `-i` option with `rm`, `cp`, `mv`, and various other commands. The `-i` option, which means *interactive,* lists each filename to be removed (with the `rm` command) or overwritten (with the `mv` or `cp` command). If you answer either **y** or **Y** to the question, the file is removed or overwritten, respectively. If you answer anything else, Linux leaves the file alone.

You can remove not only files but also directories. Suppose that you have an old directory, `/tmp/junk`, that you don't need any more. You can remove it and all its contents by typing this:

```
rm -rf /tmp/junk
```

Giving the `rm` command these options (`r` and `f`) removes the `/tmp/junk` directory and all files and directories under it. The `r` option means to remove *recursively;* in recursion, the command works through every subdirectory in the parent directory. The `f` option issues the command *forcefully.* No prompts are given.

Changing File Ownership and Granting Permissions

All Linux files and directories have owners and are assigned a list of permissions. This system of *ownership* and *permissions* forms the basis for restricting and allowing users' access to files. File permissions can also be used to specify whether a file is executable as a command and to determine who can use the file or command.

Files and directories are owned by user accounts. User accounts are defined in the `/etc/passwd` file. For example, you created the `root` (superuser) user account when you installed Fedora Core in Chapter 3, and the installation system created the superuser home directory, `/root`, plus several configuration files (for example, `.bashrc`). The `root` user owns all those files and directories. If you created a regular user account — for example, `lidia` — that user's home directory and configuration files are all owned by user `lidia`. Users can access and modify any files or directories they own.

Files and directories all have group ownership in addition to user ownership. Groups are defined by the `/etc/group` file and provide a secondary level of access. For example, you can assign group ownership to files you own and allow other users who belong to the group to access those files.

Files and directories are assigned permissions that permit or deny read, write, and execute access. Permissions are assigned to the owner, group, or non-owner of the file or directory. Any non-owner is referred to as *other*. Permissions for the owner, for the group, and for any others are independent of each other.

Using the `ls` command with the `-l` option allows you to see the file's permissions along with other relevant information, such as who owns the file, which group of people have permission to access or modify the file, the size of the file or directory, the last time the file was modified, and its name.

First, create a file and then list it:

```
touch gotowork
ls -l gotowork
```

You get this response:

```
-rw-rw-r-- owner group 0 Jul 26  16:00 gotowork
```

The `-rw-rw-r--` characters are the permissions for the `gotowork` file: The owner is you, and the group (though it's probably you) may be someone or something else, depending on how your system is set up and administered.

You may be wondering how you can become an owner of a file. You're automatically the owner of any file you create, which makes sense. As the owner, you can change the default file permissions — and even the ownership. If you change the file ownership, however, *you* lose ownership privileges.

To change the ownership of a file or a directory, use the `chown` (*ch*ange *own*ership) command. You generally have to be the `root` to do this.

Suppose that you have decided to settle down and lead a more contemplative life, one more in line with a new profession of haiku writing. Someone else will have to plan the weekend sprees and all-night bashes. You give up ownership of the `gotowork` file:

```
chown root gotowork
```

This command changes the ownership of `gotowork` to the root. To change it back, you can use the `chown` command, but you have to do it as `root`.

Files and users all belong to *groups*. In the `gotowork` example, the group consists of users. Having groups enables you to give large numbers of users — but not all users — access to files. Group permissions and ownership are handy for making sure that the members of a special project or workgroup have access to files needed by the entire group.

To see which groups are available to you on your system, look at the file `/etc/group`. Use the `more` command and you see a file something like this:

```
root:x:0:root
bin:x:1:root,bin,daemon
...
nobody:x:99:
users:x:100:
floppy:x:19:
.....
your_user_name:x:500:your_user_name
```

where *`your_user_name`* is the login name you use for your account. Remember that the file doesn't look exactly like this — just similar. The names at the beginning of the line are the group names. The names at the end of the line (such as `root`, `bin`, and `daemon`) are `user-group` names that can belong to the `user-group` list.

To change the group the file belongs to, log in as `root` and use the `chgrp` command. Its syntax is the same as that of the `chown` command. For example, to change the group that `gotowork` belongs to, you issue this command:

```
chgrp newgroupname gotowork
```

Fedora Core assigns a unique group to each user. For example, when you add the first user to your system, that user gets the user ID and group ID of 500. The next user receives the user ID and group ID of 501, and so on. This system gives you lots of control over who gets what access to your files.

Making Your Own Rules

You, as the owner of a file, can specify permissions for reading, writing to, or executing a file. You can also determine who (yourself, a group of people, or everyone in general) can do these actions on a file. What do these permissions mean? Read on (you have our permission):

- **Read permission:** You can read the file. For a directory, read permission allows the `ls` command to list the names of the files in the directory. You must also have execute permission for the directory name to use the `-l` option of the `ls` command or to change to that directory.
- **Write permission:** You can modify the file. For a directory, you can create or delete files inside that directory.
- **Execute permission:** You can type the name of the file and execute it. You cannot view or copy the file unless you also have read permission. Files containing executable Linux commands, called *shell scripts,* must therefore be both executable and readable by the person executing them. Programs written in a compiled language, such as C, however, must have only executable permissions, to protect them from being copied where they shouldn't be copied.

  For a directory, execute permission means that you can change to that directory (with `cd`). Unless you also have read permission for the directory, `ls -l` doesn't work. You can list directories and files in that directory, but you cannot see additional information about the files or directories by using just an `ls -l` command. Although this arrangement may seem strange, it's useful for security.

The first character of a file permission is a hyphen (`-`) if it's a file; the first character of a directory permission is `d`. The nine other characters are read, write, and execute positions for each of the three categories of file permissions:

- Owner (also known as the user)
- Group
- Others

Your `gotowork` file, for example, may show the following permissions when it's listed with the `ls -l gotowork` command:

```
-rw-rw-r--
```

The hyphen (`-`) in the first position indicates that it's a regular file (not a directory or other special file). The next characters (`rw-`) are the owner's permissions. The owner can read and write to the file, but cannot execute it. The next three characters (`rw-`) are the group's permissions. The group also has read-write access to the file. The last three characters (`r--`) are the others' permissions, which are read-only.

`[-][rw-][rw-][r--]` illustrates the four parts of the permissions: the file type followed by three sets of triplets, indicating the read, write, and execute permissions for the owner, group, and *other* users (meaning *everyone else*).

You can specify most file permissions by using only six letters:

- **ugo** stands for — no, not a funky 1980s car — *u*ser (that is, owner), *g*roup, and *o*ther.
- **rwx** stands for *r*ead, *w*rite, and e*x*ecute.

These six letters, and some symbols — such as the equal sign (=) and commas — are put together into a specification of how you want to set the file's permissions.

The command for changing permissions is `chmod`. Here's its syntax:

```
chmod specification filename
```

Change the mode of `gotowork` to give users the ability to read, write, and execute a file:

```
chmod u=rwx gotowork
```

That was easy enough. What if you want to give the group permission to only read and execute the file? You execute the following command:

```
chmod g=rx gotowork
```

This command doesn't affect the permissions for owner or other — just the group's permissions. You can set the permission bits in other ways. But because this way is so simple, why use any other?

Appendix D

Becoming a Suit: Managing the Linux File System

In This Appendix

- Mounting and unmounting a file system
- Increasing disk space with a new drive or memory stick

Managing the Linux file system isn't a complex job, but it's an important one. You have the responsibility of managing the Linux file system and ensuring that users (even if you're the only user) have access to secure, uncorrupted data. You're the manager (yes, — gag — a suit) of your file system.

This appendix introduces you to managing your Linux file system. Consider yourself a management trainee. When you're done reading this appendix, feel free to take a nice, long, expensive lunch.

Mounting and Unmounting a File System

Fedora Core and other Unix-like operating systems use files in different ways from MS-DOS, Windows, and Macintosh operating systems. In Linux, *everything* is stored as files in predictable locations in the directory structure; Linux even stores commands as files. Like other modern operating systems, it has a tree-structured, hierarchical directory organization: the *file system.*

All user-available disk space is combined in a single directory tree. The base of this system is the *root directory* (not to be confused with the root user), designated with a slash (/). A file system's contents are made available to Linux by using the mounting process. *Mounting* a file system is setting it up to make Linux aware of the files and directories it contains. This process is just like mounting a horse — except no horse is involved, and anyway you'd *dis*mount from a horse. Maybe we'd better forget the horse.

Unlike in the Windows world, all Linux file systems except for `/root` must be explicitly *mounted* or *unmounted,* which means that file systems can be (respectively) connected to or disconnected from the directory tree.

Mounting Windows files from a floppy disk

The process of mounting and unmounting a file system provides a good example of the difference between Linux and Windows. If you use a floppy disk or CD with Windows, you just insert it into the drive and you have immediate access to what's on it. With Linux, you must insert the floppy disk into the drive and then explicitly mount it. Sound complicated? Not really.

You can mount a Windows hard-drive partition or floppy-disk drive on your Linux computer. You can read and write to FAT or FAT32, but can only read from NTFS file systems. Here's how to mount a Windows floppy disk:

1. **Insert a Windows MS-DOS-formatted floppy disk into the drive, click the GNOME Menu button, and choose System Tools⇨Disk Management. Enter the `root` password if it's requested.**
2. **Select the floppy disk and click the Mount button.**

   You know that the floppy disk has been mounted successfully when a floppy-disk icon shows up on the left side of the screen.

   You can now read and write to the floppy disk (unless the read-only tab on your disk is set).
3. **Click the Close button to close the utility.**

Fedora Core and GNOME are configured to automatically start the process that mounts your floppy disk or CD when you insert it into the drive. We use the manual method here to show you how the process works. To mount the floppy disk manually from the command-line interface, log in as `root`, open the terminal window, and run the following command:

```
mount '-t msdos /dev/fd0 /mnt/floppy
```

Unmounting file systems

Unmounting a Linux file system is a little simpler than mounting one. Because the file system is already mounted, you don't have to specify any options or other information. You just have to tell the Red Hat disk management druid to unmount the file system. Follow these steps:

1. **Click the Main Menu button and choose System Tools⇨Disk Management. Enter the root password, if you're prompted.**
2. **When the User Mount Tool window appears, click the button of the file system in which you're interested.**

The button indicates whether the file system is mounted or unmounted. After a few seconds, the button label changes from `Unmount` to `Mount` to show that the file system has been unmounted.

3. **Click the Close button to exit the utility.**

   The file system is unmounted. If the file system is a removable type, such as a floppy disk or CD, you can remove it. Otherwise, the file system is simply not available for use until you remount it.

You can run the `eject` command from a `bash` shell to eject a CD. You have to unmount the CD first and then enter the `eject` command. Otherwise, to eject a CD, you must unmount it and then press the eject button on the CD-ROM drive. In either case, you cannot eject the CD until you have unmounted it.

Adding a Disk Drive

Sooner or later, life catches up with you, and you're likely to need or want a bigger house or car or a diamond in your tooth, or whatever. The same goes for disk space, in which case you want to add another disk drive.

The first step to increasing your drive space is to add a new storage device. It can be a hard drive (IDE or SCSI) or a USB or FireWire memory stick. These steps describe the general process of adding a storage device and then formatting and mounting it:

1. **Install the hard drive or insert the USB or FireWire device.**

   If the device is an IDE or SCSI hard drive, turn off the power to your computer and monitor. Unplug the power cable and open the computer case. (Don't cut yourself on the sometimes-sharp metal edges when you're reaching into the computer.) Use the antistatic strap that comes with the hard drive; follow the instructions included with the strap.

   Most PCs use IDE controllers. SCSI-based PCs are more expensive and aren't commonly owned by consumers; these SCSI types are more common in the commercial realm. IDE-based PCs have two IDE controllers. Each device can control as many as two IDE devices. Ribbon cables connect the controller to the devices.

   You have to configure your new disk to function as a slave device if it's connected to a ribbon cable or IDE controller that already has another device (hard drive or CD-ROM) attached.

   If the device is a USB or FireWire memory stick, skip to Step 3.

2. **Reboot your computer and run the `dmesg` command from a GNOME Terminal window.**

If you added an IDE drive, look for the mention of an `hdx` device, where *x* is replaced with the letter *b, c, d,* or *e.* This information tells you that your kernel "saw" the new hard drive as it booted:

```
hdb: HITACHI_DK227A-50, 4789MB w/512KB
        Cache,CHS=610/255/63
```

If you added a SCSI drive, the general device type is `sdx`.

3. **Partition the new drive.**

   Run the `fdisk /dev/hdb` command for an IDE drive.

   Use the command `fdisk /dev/sda` for a USB or FireWire memory stick. The memory stick appears as a SCSI device, such as `/dev/sda`, `/dev/sdb`, or `/dev/sdc`, depending on your computer's configuration.

4. **Create a file system on the new partition (change the devices as appropriate).**

   When you're using an IDE or SCSI drive, for example, enter the following command:

   ```
   mkfs /dev/hdb
   ```

   For a USB memory stick (long, linear chip), enter this command:

   ```
   mkfs /dev/sdc
   ```

5. **Create a new directory in which to mount the new device:**

   ```
   mkdir /space
   ```

6. **Mount the newly formatted drive by using the appropriate command:**

   ```
   mount /dev/hdb /space
   ```

   or

   ```
   mount /dev/sdc /space
   ```

   Your drive has been physically added to your system and partitioned, and you have added file systems. The drive is ready to join the rest of the file system.

Appendix E

Revving Up with RPM and YUM

In This Appendix

- Introducing RPM
- Using RPM
- Introducing and using YUM

This appendix introduces you to the Red Hat Package Manager (RPM) and the Yellowdog Updater, Modifier (YUM). Red Hat, Inc., developed RPM in conjunction with another Linux distributor, Caldera Systems. Duke University gave us the wonderful YUM.

RPM is the meat-and-potatoes of much of the Linux world. Its purpose is to reduce the amount of work you have to do when you install, remove, and manage software. RPM partially automates the installation, updating, and removal of software. Without RPM, Linux would never have become as popular as it is because installing and managing a computer would have been too difficult.

Although other Package Managers are available, RPM has become the most popular system for installing, modifying, and transporting Linux software. This handy-dandy tool is a big reason that Red Hat is the *de facto* Linux distribution leader. Motor through this chapter to find out everything you need to know about RPM.

YUM is a new entry into the world of software installation and maintenance. Working at a higher level than RPM, YUM manages RPM packages, taking care of installing, updating, querying, and removing them. YUM simply makes life with a computer easier.

Introducing the Red Hat Package Manager

One of the primary reasons that the Red Hat Linux (and, subsequently, Fedora Core) distributions became so popular was that Red Hat, Inc., added value for its customers with technologies such as RPM.

All the software that was installed during the Fedora Core installation process is stored in RPM's format, called packages. A *package* is a collection of individual software (applications, libraries, and documentation, for example) contained in one file.

The package-management concept has been around for quite a while. The major Unix vendors supply their own systems. The idea is to distribute, in a single file, some software that performs a particular function — and have a Package Manager do the work of installing, removing, and managing the individual files. The Linux world has benefited greatly from this system, which simplifies the distribution and use of software.

You *can* install software without RPM, but we're not sure why you would want to — the RPM package contains everything you need to install and run an application. For example, if you didn't have the RPM package, installing Mozilla would work a little something like this: You would have to install the individual pieces that make up the Mozilla system, which can require dozens of steps. You can also install, update, or uninstall RPM software (see the following section for details).

We remember, back in the day, when we used the Linux operating system for the first time. We had to install all the software using the dreaded *tape archive* system (TAR) . . . from dozens of floppies! Trust us: Installing, maintaining, and upgrading Linux with tar was a difficult task. RPM has made life easier for those of us who used to walk uphill both ways in the snow to school and back.

The `/Fedora/RPMS` directory on the companion DVD contains all the Fedora Core RPM packages.

RPM performs three basic functions: It installs, upgrades, and removes packages. In addition to these functions, it can find out all sorts of information about installed and yet-to-be-installed packages. (All this, and it washes windows too.) Here's a brief rundown of each function:

- **Installing packages:** RPM installs software. Software systems, such as Mozilla, have files of all types that must be put into certain locations in order to work properly. For example, under Red Hat, some (but not all) Mozilla files need to go into the `/usr/bin` directory. RPM performs this organizational stuff automatically, without any fuss or muss.

RPM not only installs files in their proper directories, but also performs tasks such as creating the directories and running scripts to do the things that need to be done. (It's such a tidy and organized little scamp.)

- **Upgrading packages:** Gone are the days when updating a system was worse than going to the dentist. RPM acts like the personal Linux assistant that we all wish we'd had, by updating existing software packages for you. RPM also keeps track (in its own database) of all the packages you have installed. When you upgrade a package, RPM does all the bookkeeping chores and replaces only the files that need to be replaced. It also saves the configuration files it replaces.
- **Removing packages:** The package database the RPM keeps is also useful in removing packages. To put it simply, RPM takes out the trash. (Housekeeping was never so easy.) RPM goes to each file and uninstalls it. Directories belonging to the package are also removed when no files from other packages occupy them.
- **Querying packages and files:** RPM can also give you a great deal of information about a package and its files. You can use the query function to find out the function of a package and which files belong to it. RPM can also work on the RPM packages themselves, regardless of whether they have been installed.
- **Verifying packages:** RPM can validate an installed package against a `checksum` (a computer fingerprint) to see whether and how it has been changed. This feature is useful for security reasons. If you suspect that a file or system has been hacked, you can use RPM to find out how it has changed.

RPM packages often include configuration files as part of their installation. If you erase an RPM package, those configuration files are *not* deleted but rather are renamed by appending the suffix `.rpmsave` to the end of the original filename. For example, removing the Kerberos package, `krbafs`, saves the configuration file by renaming `/etc/krb.conf` to `/etc/krb.conf.rpmsave`.

When you remove a package, RPM removes the associated files and directories. RPM cleans up after itself — what Martha Stewart (when she's not on laundry detail) would definitely call "a good thing."

Using the Red Hat Package Manager

Fedora Core provides a tool named Red Hat Package Manager for working with RPM packages. The Package Manager graphical tool provides all the functions for managing RPMs. It's like putting an automatic transmission on a car: The Package Manager does the shifting for you — okay, but you still have to drive it.

The Package Manager provides easy access to RPM functions; you can install, upgrade, remove, query, and verify. This section describes how to use the Package Manager to rev up your RPM.

To start the Package Manager, click the GNOME Menu button and choose System Settings⇨Add/Remove Applications. If you aren't logged in as the `root` user, type the `root` password in the Input window when you're prompted. A progress window appears briefly while the Package Manager determines which packages you have installed. After "thinking," the Package Management window appears.

The Package Manager displays all the Red Hat package groups that are installed by default on your system. Individual packages are organized into groups, such as the X Window System and GNOME. When the check box to the left of a group is active — as designated by a check mark — one or more packages from that group is installed. The number to the right of the Package group shows how many packages of the total number in the group are installed.

Clicking the Details option opens the GNOME Desktop Package Details window, which shows all the base and optional packages in the group; short, one-line descriptions of each package are also displayed next to each package. Standard Packages are always installed with a package group. Extra packages are, well, optionally installed.

Installing an RPM package from the DVD

When you install your Fedora Core system, all the software that is copied to your hard drive from the DVD comes from RPM packages. When you want to add software from the companion DVD or an RPM repository, such as `www.freshmeat.net`, or from Red Hat, at `www.redhat.com`, you can do so by using the Install button. To install an RPM package from a CD-ROM, follow these steps:

1. **Start the Package Manager: Choose System Tools⇨Add/Remove Packages.**

   Enter the `root` password in the Information window, if you're prompted.

2. **When the Add and Remove Software window opens, select the package group you want to install.**

   For example, if you want to install the Mozilla e-mail client, you have to do some exploring first. Scroll down to the Graphical Internet package group. The short description next to the package group says "This group includes graphical e-mail, Web, and chat clients," which indicates that you're on the right path.

3. **Click the Details button to find out the details of the package you're installing.**

   For example, select the Graphical Internet group and the Graphical Internet Package Details window opens. You see that the Mozilla mail client is included.

4. **Select the check box next to the menu option.**
5. **Click the Close button to return to the Package Management window.**
6. **Click the Update button and the Preparing Systems Update window opens.**

   The Package Manager determines which additional packages are needed by the package you're installing. After the dependencies are determined, the Completed System Preparation window displays the number of packages to be installed and how much disk space they require.

7. **Click the Continue button.**

   The Information window opens and you're prompted to insert the DVD.

8. **Insert the CD and click OK.**

   The System Update Progress Installing window shows a progress meter.

9. **Insert additional CDs, if you're prompted, and click the OK button in the Information window.**

   After the installation process is finished, the System Update Process window shows the Update Complete message.

10. **Click the OK button to return to the Add and Remove Software window.**

Until the advent of the RPM (and the Debian Package Manager on Debian Linux systems), Linux software was distributed only by `tar` archives, which are sometimes referred to as *tarballs* or (more descriptively) *hairballs.* The `tar` file-storage mechanism stores one or more files in a single file in a `tar` format. A `tar` file has the `.tar` file suffix; if the `tar` file is compressed, it has a suffix like `.tgz` or `.tar.gz`. Using the `tar`-based distribution system is sufficient if your software doesn't change often and you're young. But when you need to upgrade or change software or work with complex software systems, `tar` becomes quite difficult to work with. Rather than spend your life spitting up hairballs, use systems such as RPM to greatly simplify your life.

Removing an RPM package

You can remove Red Hat packages as easily as you install them. Use the RPM erase (`-e`) function, which is the opposite of the install (`-i`) function. The

Package Manager removes a package when you unselect an installed package. These steps describe how to remove a package:

1. **Click the GNOME Menu button and choose System Settings⇨Add/Remove Applications.**
2. **Enter the `root` password in the Information window, if you're prompted.**

   The Package Management window opens.
3. **Click the Details button next to the package group that contains the package you want to remove.**

   For instance, if you click the details button for the Development Tools group, the Development Tools Package Details window opens.
4. **Click the check-box to the left of the package you want to remove.**

   The check mark disappears.
5. **Click the Close button.**

   Control returns to the Package Management window.
6. **Click the Update button.**

   The Preparing System Update dialog box opens briefly, and you return to the Completed System Preparation window.
7. **Click the Continue button.**

   The package (or packages) is removed.
8. **Click the OK button in the Update Complete window.**
9. **Back in the Package Management window, click the OK button.**

Be sure that you really want to get rid of the package because when you remove a package, it's gone — as in *gone.* Okay, okay, maybe we're being a little dramatic. You can always go online to a site such as `www.freshmeat.net` or `www.redhat.com` and download more packages to install. We recommend that you do so. Some new tool is always coming out that can help optimize your Fedora Core computing experience.

Manual Shifting with RPM

The first part of this chapter concentrates on showing you how to use Red Hat Package Manager to install and remove packages. You also have the option of using the `rpm` command. It provides additional features for installation and removal functions. You can use `rpm` to install, update, remove, and query packages. This section provides examples of how to use the manual `rpm` command.

Manually installing and upgrading packages

The RPM -i parameter indicates that an installation will take place. You can add Verbose mode (which provides additional information) by using the -v option. (You can combine options into a single group; for example, -i -v can become -iv.) Follow these instructions to install and upgrade packages:

1. **Log in as** root**.**
2. **Open a terminal emulator window by clicking the terminal icon in the GNOME Panel (refer to Chapter 4 for instructions).**

   The GNOME Terminal emulator window opens.
3. **To add the package, type the following command from a terminal window:**

   ```
   rpm -iv /media/cdrom/Fedora/RPMS/mozilla-mail*
   ```

Alternatively, you can upgrade a package that has already been installed on your system. Substitute the RPM upgrade option, -U, in place of the install option, -i. For example, the following command updates the Mozilla e-mail client package:

```
rpm -Uv /media/cdrom/Fedora/RPMS/mozilla-mail*
```

The files that constitute the newer Mozilla-mail package overwrite the older version. Existing configurations, however, are saved by adding the .rpmsave suffix to the configuration file.

Manually removing packages

RPM packages are good residents on your computer because they lend themselves to easy removal. The rpm command permits you to remove packages via the erase (-e) function.

Suppose you're not so fond of the Mozilla e-mail client because you like the Evolution client better. No problem: You can remove the Mozilla mail package. To remove an RPM package, follow these steps:

1. **Log in as** root **and open a terminal emulator window.**

   The GNOME Terminal window opens.
2. **Enter the following command to find the name of the package to remove:**

   ```
   rpm -qa | grep mozilla
   ```

You should see these results:

```
mozilla-nss-1.0.1-10
mozilla-1.0.1-10
mozilla-nspr-1.0.1-10
mozilla-psm-1.0.1-10
mozilla-mail-1.0.1-10
```

You need to know the name of the package before you can remove it. We use this step to display all installed Mozilla packages to find the name of the package.

3. **You can also find out about the package by using the following command:**

```
rpm -qi mozilla-mail
```

Alternatively, you can display a list of all installed packages by using the `rpm -qa` command. Run the `man rpm` command to find query options.

4. **Enter the following command to remove the Mozilla e-mail client:**

```
rpm -e mozilla-mail
```

Introducing YUM

The Yellowdog Updater, Manager (YUM) is, simply put, a wonderful system. YUM takes software installation and management to the next level by providing three functions that RPM doesn't:

- **Takes over the task of finding and obtaining software packages:** YUM can download packages from the Internet (or a private network), a DVD or CD-ROM, or your local hard disk.
- **Computes package dependencies:** If you want to install an RPM package that happens to require the installation of other packages, you usually have to determine what those packages are, find them, and install them manually.
- **Updates your computer:** YUM can update your entire Fedora Core computer as well as install and remove individual packages or package groups. RPM can update individual packages, but not your entire system. The YUM update option performs the same function as the Red Hat up2date system.

YUM is easy to configure, and can access multiple software repositories (mirrors). Here's the default YUM configuration, `/etc/yum.conf`:

```
cachedir=/var/cache/yum
debuglevel=2
logfile=/var/log/yum.log
pkgpolicy=newest
```

```
distroverpkg=fedora-release
tolerant=1
exactarch=1
exclude=

[base]
name=Fedora Core $releasever - $basearch - Base
baseurl=http://fedora.redhat.com/releases/fedora-core-
          $releasever

[updates-released]
name=Fedora Core $releasever - $basearch - Released Updates
baseurl=http://fedora.redhat.com/updates/released/fedora-
          core-$releasever

#[updates-testing]
#name=Fedora Core $releasever - $basearch - Unreleased
          Updates
#baseurl=http://mirrors.kernel.org/fedora/core/test/1.90/$bas
          earch/os
```

The YUM configuration options are shown in this list:

- `cachedir`: This option sets the location where YUM stores RPM packages and their headers (storing the files and other information about the package). YUM downloads the RPM packages (and headers) before installing or updating them. The default is the `/var/cache/yum` directory.
- `debuglevel`: This option sets the detail level of information that is transmitted to the log file. The range is from 0 to 10, where 0 is no information and 10 is way too much information. The default is 2.
- `logfile`: The location of the log file. Not surprisingly, the default location is `/var/log/yum.log`; `/var/log` is the default location for most, if not all, Linux log files.
- `pkgpolicy`: There are two options: `newest` and `last`. The newest option tells YUM to install the most recent version of a package. The last option selects the package found on the last server in an alphabetical list of servers. We can think of no reason to use the last option.
- `distroverpkg`: Your Fedora Core computer contains an RPM package named `fedora-release`. This package contains information about the version of your installation. (Red Hat Linux computers contain a package named `redhat-release` that contains the same type of information.) Because YUM is platform independent (it works on multiple Linux distributions), this option tells YUM where to look for the distribution name and version number. The default is `fedora-release`.
- `tolerant`: YUM can be strict or not so strict. When `tolerant` is set to `1` (the default), YUM ignores minor errors that occur during its operation.

- `exactarch`: YUM can also be strict about the architecture of the packages it installs. When YUM is set to its default of `1`, it doesn't install an i386 if the installed package is i686.
- `exclude`: You can tell YUM not to install certain packages. For example, if you don't want YUM to automatically update your Linux kernel, set `exclude=kernel*`.

The remaining contents of `/etc/yum.conf` contain the Server sections. These sections tell YUM where to look for RPM packages. The Server sections also let YUM know the general purpose of the packages. The following list describes each Server section option in more detail:

- `[serverid]`: The server identification (`serverid`) field tells YUM which type of software repository it controls (known as a *channel* by the Red Hat up2date system). Fedora Core is configured to work with the following types: `base`, `updates-released`, `updates-testing`, and `development`. The base repository contents are identical to what's on your companion DVD — it includes the "base" Fedora Core 2 distribution. The `updates-released` repository includes all the officially tested and blessed updates to the base installation; the `updates-testing` type includes pending updates not officially released yet. The `development` type includes packages intended for the next Fedora Core version. It's essentially the beta version of the next release.

  By the time you read this book, the Development repository will include the software destined to become Fedora Core 4 (or beyond, depending on when you read this book). You can participate in the Fedora Core test cycle by downloading and installing the Fedora Core 3 Test distribution. Alternatively, you can use YUM to update your computer from the Development repository. That's what we did while writing this book.

- `name`: This option sets a description for the `serverid` that's displayed when you run YUM.
- `baseurl`: This option points to the `serverid` repository URL. You can use the `base`, `updates-released`, `updates-testing`, and `development` repository types. The default URL is `fedora.redhat.com`, but you can add one or more mirrors.

  For example, you can change the base server ID to

  ```
  baseurl=
     http://fedora.redhat.com/releases/
        fedora-core-$releasever\
     http://mirrors.kernel.org/fedora/core/
     $releasever/i386
  ```

  This example provides YUM with two repositories to use (in sequence); if one is unavailable, the second is used. Note that each mirror is likely to use slightly different directory structures to store its repository. The Fedora Core project's default repository `download.redora.redhat.com` uses `/fedora/linux/core/3/i386/os` as its base directory, but `mirrors.kernel.org` uses `/fedora/core/3/i386/os`. YUM works as long as `baseurl` points to the location in the repository where the headers directory is found. For example, if you browse the mirror site `limestone.uoregon.edu`, you find the headers directory at `/fedora/3/i386/os`, although `/fedora/core/3/i386/os` contains the headers at `mirrors.kernel.org`.

YUM functions

YUM provides capabilities to perform the following tasks:

- **Clean.** Use this option to remove accumulated files from the YUM cache directory.
- **Install.** You can use this option to install one or more packages; you can use this function to install entire groups too. Let's say that you want to use the XMMS multimedia player that's included on the Fedora Core 3 distribution but not installed by default. But your DVD is in another room and you don't want to get up and get it. (We're revealing too much of our lazy habits.) No problem. Assuming you're connected to the Internet, run the **yum install xmms** command and you don't have to get up.
- **Info.** This option provides a summary of the package(s). Run the **yum info mozilla** command and YUM goes out and provides the Mozilla package information summary.
- **List.** This option provides information about packages installed on your computer. Enter the **yum list mozilla** command to find out the information about the Mozilla package installed on your computer.
- **Provides.** You use this option plus a character string, and wildcard, to find what feature or files a package provides.
- **Remove.** Use this option to remove one or more packages and any dependencies.
- **Search.** Use this option to find packages that match the text string you provide. For instance, if you enter **yum search moz**, you'll get a list of Mozilla packages.
- **Update** and **check-update.** Use the update option to, yes, update individual packages or your entire computer; the updating process removes the older version and then installs the newer one. If you run the command yum update, your entire computer will be updated. Specifying a single package (for instance, **yum update mozilla**), updates that package.

  You can display which, if any, packages can be updated. Enter the **yum check-update** command and all the available package updates for your computer will be displayed.
- **Upgrade.** This option is no longer used and will be removed in the future. Use the Update option.

Appendix F

About the DVD

The DVD that comes with this book contains the full Fedora Core 3 distribution. Wiley has pioneered the use of DVDs in place of CD-ROMs because they're easier to use and, we hope, will make using Fedora Core more enjoyable.

This appendix describes the minimum computer configuration you need in order to install Fedora Core and also some of what you get on the companion DVD.

If your computer isn't capable of reading DVDs, you can get the Fedora Core 3 distribution on CD-ROMs by sending in the coupon in the back of this book.

Although the DVD contains the Linux kernel and supporting GNU programs and applications, it doesn't carry some applications described in this book. You must download applications such as Wine, VMware, MPlayer, and Icecast2/Ices2 from the Internet. We describe where and how to download all the applications we discuss in this book that aren't on the companion DVD.

System Requirements

Make sure that your computer meets (or exceeds) the minimum system requirements listed here and in Chapter 3. More resources are needed for a graphical workstation. If your computer doesn't match up to most of these requirements, you may have problems installing and running Fedora Core:

- A Pentium-class PC with a 400MHz or faster processor is recommended for graphical mode (that's what most people use). Use a 200MHz Pentium-class PC to run your computer in text mode. Many people run their Fedora Core computers in text mode when they're providing simple network services (such as Apache Web or a LAN firewall). You can make great use of old machines!
- For reasonable performance using the graphical X Window System, we recommend at least 256MB, but you can get away with only 192MB of main memory. You can never have too much memory, and we recommend that you increase your computer's memory, if possible.

- You can run Fedora Core in text mode with less than 64MB of memory.
- Fedora Core provides several installation classes that install different bundles of software. The various classes take up different amounts of space, of course. The default class, Personal Desktop, requires 2.3GB of disk space. The Workstation class we use throughout this book (refer to Chapter 3) requires 3GB. The server class can live with 1.1GB, and the minimal Custom installation reduces that number to 620MB. Using the Custom (Everything) installation option requires at least 6.9GB.

  We recommend that your computer have at least 5GB (not such a big requirement anymore) when you're using the Workstation installation so that you have some room to work with after you install Linux.
- You should also have a DVD drive (and, optionally, a 3¼-inch floppy disk drive plus a blank 3¼-inch disk), a multisync monitor, an internal IDE or SCSI hard drive, a keyboard, and a mouse.

The instructions for installing the Fedora Core operating system from the DVD are detailed in Part I. After you install the software, return the DVD to its plastic jacket, or another appropriate place, for safekeeping.

What You Find

You can view much of the documentation on this DVD through an HTML viewer, such as Mozilla, which is also included on the DVD; or, you can print it. You can also view most of the documentation from other operating systems, such as DOS, Windows, or Unix.

Because the DVD has a full implementation of Linux, to list all the accompanying tools and utilities would take too much room. The DVD includes, briefly, most of the software so that you can

- Access the Internet
- Write programs in several computer languages
- Create and manipulate images
- Create, manipulate, and play back sounds (if you have a sound card)
- Play certain games
- Work with electrical design

If You Have Problems with Your DVD

We tried our best to test various computers with the minimum system requirements. Alas, computers can be cranky, and Linux may not install or work as stated.

The two likeliest problems are that you don't have enough RAM for the programs you want to use or you have some hardware that Linux doesn't support. Luckily, the latter problem occurs less frequently each day as more hardware becomes supported by Linux.

You may also have one or more FireWire, USB, or SCSI hard drives that use a driver (called a *kernel module* in Linux parlance) not supported by Linux — or a controller that is simply too new for the Linux development team to have given it the proper support at the time the DVD was recorded.

If you have trouble with the DVD, call the Wiley Product Technical Support phone number: 800-762-2974. Outside the United States, call 1-317-572-3994. You can also contact Wiley Product Technical support on the Internet, at `www.wiley.com/techsupport`. Wiley Publishing, Inc., provides technical support for only installation and other general quality-control items; for technical support for the applications themselves, consult the program's vendor or author.

To place additional orders or to request information about other Wiley products, call 800-225-5945.

Index

• Symbols and Numerics •

• A •

• B •

• C •

• D •

• M •

• N •

• Q •

• R •

• S •

• T •

• Z •

ISO Distribution: This book includes an ISO copy of Fedora Core 3 Linux from the Fedora Project, which you may use in accordance with the license agreements accompanying the software. For more information, see the Fedora Project Web site (`http://fedora.redhat.com/`). Red Hat does not provide support services for Fedora Core. You may purchase Red Hat® Enterprise Linux® and technical support from Red Hat through its Web site (`www.redhat.com`) or its toll-free number (1-888-2REDHAT).

Limited Warranty: (a) WPI warrants that the Software and Software Media are free from defects in materials and workmanship under normal use for a period of sixty (60) days from the date of purchase of this Book. If WPI receives notification within the warranty period of defects in materials or workmanship, WPI will replace the defective Software Media. (b) WPI AND THE AUTHOR(S) OF THE BOOK DISCLAIM ALL OTHER WARRANTIES, EXPRESS OR IMPLIED, INCLUDING WITHOUT LIMITATION IMPLIED WARRANTIES OF MERCHANTABILITY AND FITNESS FOR A PARTICULAR PURPOSE, WITH RESPECT TO THE SOFTWARE, THE PROGRAMS, THE SOURCE CODE CONTAINED THEREIN, AND/OR THE TECHNIQUES DESCRIBED IN THIS BOOK. WPI DOES NOT WARRANT THAT THE FUNCTIONS CONTAINED IN THE SOFTWARE WILL MEET YOUR REQUIREMENTS OR THAT THE OPERATION OF THE SOFTWARE WILL BE ERROR FREE. © This limited warranty gives you specific legal rights, and you may have other rights that vary from jurisdiction to jurisdiction.

Wiley Publishing, Inc.
Fedora™ Core 3 Linux® CD-ROM Offer

If you do not have access to a PC with a DVD drive, we are offering the complete set on CD-ROMs for a nominal shipping-and-materials fee. If you'd like the CDs sent to you, please follow the instructions below to order by phone, online or coupon.

For each ordering method, please use ISBN: 0764588214 and Promo Code FL3FD when prompted. The cost is $11.00 (USD) plus shipping.

Terms: Void where prohibited or restricted by law. Allow 2-4 weeks for delivery.

To order by phone:

1. Call toll free in the United States – 1-877-762-2974. International customers, dial 1-317-572-3994.
2. Give the operator the appropriate ISBN and Promo Code. Please have your credit card ready.

To order online:

1. Go to `http://www.wiley.com/`.
2. Use the Product Search feature to search for RHFLinux 3 Multipack or 0764588214.
3. Place the item in the shopping cart and use the Promo Code (FL3FD) when prompted.

To order by coupon:

1. Complete the coupon below.
2. The cost is $11.00 (USD) plus shipping. To find out the shipping costs, call 1-877-762-2974 in the US or 1-317-572-3994 for international customers.
3. Send it to us at the address listed at the bottom of the coupon.

Name ______________________________

Company ______________________________

Address ______________________________

City __________ **State** __________ **Postal Code** __________ **Country** __________

E-mail ______________________ **Telephone** ______________________

Place where book was purchased ______________________________

❑ Check here to find out what we're up to by joining our e-mail list—a convenient way to receive news about our products and events as well as about special discount offers.

Return this coupon with the appropriate U.S. funds to:
Wiley Publishing, Inc.
Customer Care
RHFLinux 3 Multipack, 0764588214 Promo: FL3FD
10475 Crosspoint Blvd.
Indianapolis, IN 46256

Terms: Wiley is not responsible for lost, stolen, late, or illegible orders. For questions regarding this fulfillment offer, please call us at 1-877-762-2974 or 1-317-572-3994.

GNU General Public License

Version 2, June 1991

Preamble

The licenses for most software are designed to take away your freedom to share and change it. By contrast, the GNU General Public License is intended to guarantee your freedom to share and change free software — to make sure the software is free for all its users. This General Public License applies to most of the Free Software Foundation's software and to any other program whose authors commit to using it. (Some other Free Software Foundation software is covered by the GNU Library General Public License instead.) You can apply it to your programs, too.

When we speak of free software, we are referring to freedom, not price. Our General Public Licenses are designed to make sure that you have the freedom to distribute copies of free software (and charge for this service if you wish), that you receive source code or can get it if you want it, that you can change the software or use pieces of it in new free programs; and that you know you can do these things.

To protect your rights, we need to make restrictions that forbid anyone to deny you these rights or to ask you to surrender the rights. These restrictions translate to certain responsibilities for you if you distribute copies of the software, or if you modify it.

For example, if you distribute copies of such a program, whether gratis or for a fee, you must give the recipients all the rights that you have. You must make sure that they, too, receive or can get the source code. And you must show them these terms so they know their rights.

We protect your rights with two steps: (1) copyright the software, and (2) offer you this license which gives you legal permission to copy, distribute and/or modify the software.

Also, for each author's protection and ours, we want to make certain that everyone understands that there is no warranty for this free software. If the software is modified by someone else and passed on, we want its recipients to know that what they have is not the original, so that any problems introduced by others will not reflect on the original authors' reputations.

Finally, any free program is threatened constantly by software patents. We wish to avoid the danger that redistributors of a free program will individually obtain patent licenses, in effect making the program proprietary. To prevent this, we have made it clear that any patent must be licensed for everyone's free use or not licensed at all.

The precise terms and conditions for copying, distribution and modification follow.

Terms and Conditions for Copying, Distribution, and Modification

0. This License applies to any program or other work which contains a notice placed by the copyright holder saying it may be distributed under the terms of this General Public License. The "Program", below, refers to any such program or work, and a "work based on the Program" means either the Program or any derivative work under copyright law: that is to say, a work containing the Program or a portion of it, either verbatim or with modifications and/or translated into another language. (Hereinafter, translation is included without limitation in the term "modification".) Each licensee is addressed as "you".

   Activities other than copying, distribution and modification are not covered by this License; they are outside its scope. The act of running the Program is not restricted, and the output from the Program is covered only if its contents constitute a work based on the Program (independent of having been made by running the Program). Whether that is true depends on what the Program does.

1. You may copy and distribute verbatim copies of the Program's source code as you receive it, in any medium, provided that you conspicuously and appropriately publish on each copy an appropriate copyright notice and disclaimer of warranty; keep intact all the notices that refer to this License and to the absence of any warranty; and give any other recipients of the Program a copy of this License along with the Program.

   You may charge a fee for the physical act of transferring a copy, and you may at your option offer warranty protection in exchange for a fee.

2. You may modify your copy or copies of the Program or any portion of it, thus forming a work based on the Program, and copy and distribute such modifications or work under the terms of Section 1 above, provided that you also meet all of these conditions:

   a) You must cause the modified files to carry prominent notices stating that you changed the files and the date of any change.

   b) You must cause any work that you distribute or publish, that in whole or in part contains or is derived from the Program or any part thereof, to be licensed as a whole at no charge to all third parties under the terms of this License.

   c) If the modified program normally reads commands interactively when run, you must cause it, when started running for such interactive use in the most ordinary way, to print or display an announcement including an appropriate copyright notice and a notice that there is no warranty (or else, saying that you provide a warranty) and that users may redistribute the program under these conditions, and telling the user how to view a copy of this License. (Exception: if the Program itself is interactive but does not normally print such an announcement, your work based on the Program is not required to print an announcement.)

These requirements apply to the modified work as a whole. If identifiable sections of that work are not derived from the Program, and can be reasonably considered independent and separate works in themselves, then this License, and its terms, do not apply to those sections when you distribute them as separate works. But when you distribute the same sections as part of a whole which is a work based on the Program, the distribution of the whole must be on the terms of this License, whose permissions for other licensees extend to the entire whole, and thus to each and every part regardless of who wrote it.

Thus, it is not the intent of this section to claim rights or contest your rights to work written entirely by you; rather, the intent is to exercise the right to control the distribution of derivative or collective works based on the Program.

In addition, mere aggregation of another work not based on the Program with the Program (or with a work based on the Program) on a volume of a storage or distribution medium does not bring the other work under the scope of this License.

3. You may copy and distribute the Program (or a work based on it, under Section 2) in object code or executable form under the terms of Sections 1 and 2 above provided that you also do one of the following:

   a) Accompany it with the complete corresponding machine-readable source code, which must be distributed under the terms of Sections 1 and 2 above on a medium customarily used for software interchange; or,

   b) Accompany it with a written offer, valid for at least three years, to give any third party, for a charge no more than your cost of physically performing source distribution, a complete machine-readable copy of the corresponding source code, to be distributed under the terms of Sections 1 and 2 above on a medium customarily used for software interchange; or,

   c) Accompany it with the information you received as to the offer to distribute corresponding source code. (This alternative is allowed only for noncommercial distribution and only if you received the program in object code or executable form with such an offer, in accord with Subsection b above.)

   The source code for a work means the preferred form of the work for making modifications to it. For an executable work, complete source code means all the source code for all modules it contains, plus any associated interface definition files, plus the scripts used to control compilation and installation of the executable. However, as a special exception, the source code distributed need not include anything that is normally distributed (in either source or binary form) with the major components (compiler, kernel, and so on) of the operating system on which the executable runs, unless that component itself accompanies the executable.

   If distribution of executable or object code is made by offering access to copy from a designated place, then offering equivalent access to copy the source code from the same place counts as distribution of the source code, even though third parties are not compelled to copy the source along with the object code.

4. You may not copy, modify, sublicense, or distribute the Program except as expressly provided under this License. Any attempt otherwise to copy, modify, sublicense or distribute the Program is void, and will automatically terminate your rights under this License. However, parties who have received copies, or rights, from you under this License will not have their licenses terminated so long as such parties remain in full compliance.

5. You are not required to accept this License, since you have not signed it. However, nothing else grants you permission to modify or distribute the Program or its derivative works. These actions are prohibited by law if you do not accept this License. Therefore, by modifying or distributing the Program (or any work based on the Program), you indicate your acceptance of this License to do so, and all its terms and conditions for copying, distributing or modifying the Program or works based on it.

6. Each time you redistribute the Program (or any work based on the Program), the recipient automatically receives a license from the original licensor to copy, distribute or modify the Program subject to these terms and conditions. You may not impose any further restrictions on the recipients' exercise of the rights granted herein. You are not responsible for enforcing compliance by third parties to this License.

7. If, as a consequence of a court judgment or allegation of patent infringement or for any other reason (not limited to patent issues), conditions are imposed on you (whether by court order, agreement or otherwise) that contradict the conditions of this License, they do not excuse you from the conditions of this License. If you cannot distribute so as to satisfy simultaneously your obligations under this License and any other pertinent obligations, then as a consequence you may not distribute the Program at all. For example, if a patent license would not permit royalty-free redistribution of the Program by all those who receive copies directly or indirectly through you, then the only way you could satisfy both it and this License would be to refrain entirely from distribution of the Program.

   If any portion of this section is held invalid or unenforceable under any particular circumstance, the balance of the section is intended to apply and the section as a whole is intended to apply in other circumstances.

   It is not the purpose of this section to induce you to infringe any patents or other property right claims or to contest validity of any such claims; this section has the sole purpose of protecting the integrity of the free software distribution system, which is implemented by public license practices. Many people have made generous contributions to the wide range of software distributed through that system in reliance on consistent application of that system; it is up to the author/donor to decide if he or she is willing to distribute software through any other system and a licensee cannot impose that choice.

   This section is intended to make thoroughly clear what is believed to be a consequence of the rest of this License.

8. If the distribution and/or use of the Program is restricted in certain countries either by patents or by copyrighted interfaces, the original copyright holder who places the Program under this License may add an explicit geographical distribution limitation excluding those countries, so that distribution is permitted only in or among countries not thus excluded. In such case, this License incorporates the limitation as if written in the body of this License.

9. The Free Software Foundation may publish revised and/or new versions of the General Public License from time to time. Such new versions will be similar in spirit to the present version, but may differ in detail to address new problems or concerns.

   Each version is given a distinguishing version number. If the Program specifies a version number of this License which applies to it and "any later version", you have the option of following the terms and conditions either of that version or of any later version published by the Free Software Foundation. If the Program does not specify a version number of this License, you may choose any version ever published by the Free Software Foundation.

10. If you wish to incorporate parts of the Program into other free programs whose distribution conditions are different, write to the author to ask for permission. For software which is copyrighted by the Free Software Foundation, write to the Free Software Foundation; we sometimes make exceptions for this. Our decision will be guided by the two goals of preserving the free status of all derivatives of our free software and of promoting the sharing and reuse of software generally.

NO WARRANTY

11. BECAUSE THE PROGRAM IS LICENSED FREE OF CHARGE, THERE IS NO WARRANTY FOR THE PROGRAM, TO THE EXTENT PERMITTED BY APPLICABLE LAW. EXCEPT WHEN OTHERWISE STATED IN WRITING THE COPYRIGHT HOLDERS AND/OR OTHER PARTIES PROVIDE THE PROGRAM "AS IS" WITHOUT WARRANTY OF ANY KIND, EITHER EXPRESSED OR IMPLIED, INCLUDING, BUT NOT LIMITED TO, THE IMPLIED WARRANTIES OF MERCHANTABILITY AND FITNESS FOR A PARTICULAR PURPOSE. THE ENTIRE RISK AS TO THE QUALITY AND PERFORMANCE OF THE PROGRAM IS WITH YOU. SHOULD THE PROGRAM PROVE DEFECTIVE, YOU ASSUME THE COST OF ALL NECESSARY SERVICING, REPAIR OR CORRECTION.

12. IN NO EVENT UNLESS REQUIRED BY APPLICABLE LAW OR AGREED TO IN WRITING WILL ANY COPYRIGHT HOLDER, OR ANY OTHER PARTY WHO MAY MODIFY AND/OR REDISTRIBUTE THE PROGRAM AS PERMITTED ABOVE, BE LIABLE TO YOU FOR DAMAGES, INCLUDING ANY GENERAL, SPECIAL, INCIDENTAL OR CONSEQUENTIAL DAMAGES ARISING OUT OF THE USE OR INABILITY TO USE THE PROGRAM (INCLUDING BUT NOT LIMITED TO LOSS OF DATA OR DATA BEING RENDERED INACCURATE OR LOSSES SUSTAINED BY YOU OR THIRD PARTIES OR A FAILURE OF THE PROGRAM TO OPERATE WITH ANY OTHER PROGRAMS), EVEN IF SUCH HOLDER OR OTHER PARTY HAS BEEN ADVISED OF THE POSSIBILITY OF SUCH DAMAGES.

END OF TERMS AND CONDITIONS

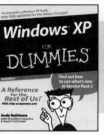

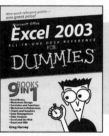

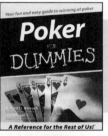

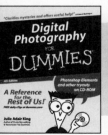

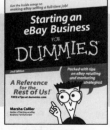

SPORTS, FITNESS, PARENTING, RELIGION & SPIRITUALITY

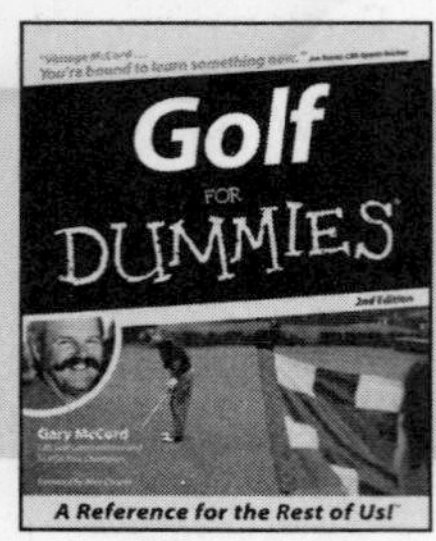

0-7645-5146-9

0-7645-5418-2

Also available:

- Adoption For Dummies 0-7645-5488-3
- Basketball For Dummies 0-7645-5248-1
- The Bible For Dummies 0-7645-5296-1
- Buddhism For Dummies 0-7645-5359-3
- Catholicism For Dummies 0-7645-5391-7
- Hockey For Dummies 0-7645-5228-7
- Judaism For Dummies 0-7645-5299-6
- Martial Arts For Dummies 0-7645-5358-5
- Pilates For Dummies 0-7645-5397-6
- Religion For Dummies 0-7645-5264-3
- Teaching Kids to Read For Dummies 0-7645-4043-2
- Weight Training For Dummies 0-7645-5168-X
- Yoga For Dummies 0-7645-5117-5

TRAVEL

0-7645-5438-7

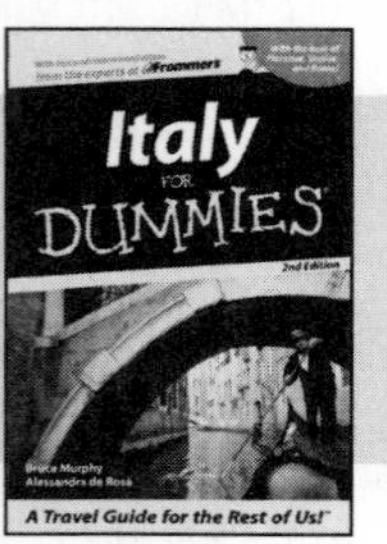

0-7645-5453-0

Also available:

- Alaska For Dummies 0-7645-1761-9
- Arizona For Dummies 0-7645-6938-4
- Cancún and the Yucatán For Dummies 0-7645-2437-2
- Cruise Vacations For Dummies 0-7645-6941-4
- Europe For Dummies 0-7645-5456-5
- Ireland For Dummies 0-7645-5455-7
- Las Vegas For Dummies 0-7645-5448-4
- London For Dummies 0-7645-4277-X
- New York City For Dummies 0-7645-6945-7
- Paris For Dummies 0-7645-5494-8
- RV Vacations For Dummies 0-7645-5443-3
- Walt Disney World & Orlando For Dummie 0-7645-6943-0

GRAPHICS, DESIGN & WEB DEVELOPMENT

0-7645-4345-8

0-7645-5589-8

Also available:

- Adobe Acrobat 6 PDF For Dummies 0-7645-3760-1
- Building a Web Site For Dummies 0-7645-7144-3
- Dreamweaver MX 2004 For Dummies 0-7645-4342-3
- FrontPage 2003 For Dummies 0-7645-3882-9
- HTML 4 For Dummies 0-7645-1995-6
- Illustrator CS For Dummies 0-7645-4084-X
- Macromedia Flash MX 2004 For Dummie 0-7645-4358-X
- Photoshop 7 All-in-One Desk Reference For Dummies 0-7645-1667-1
- Photoshop CS Timesaving Techniques For Dummies 0-7645-6782-9
- PHP 5 For Dummies 0-7645-4166-8
- PowerPoint 2003 For Dummies 0-7645-3908-6
- QuarkXPress 6 For Dummies 0-7645-2593-X

NETWORKING, SECURITY, PROGRAMMING & DATABASES

0-7645-6852-3

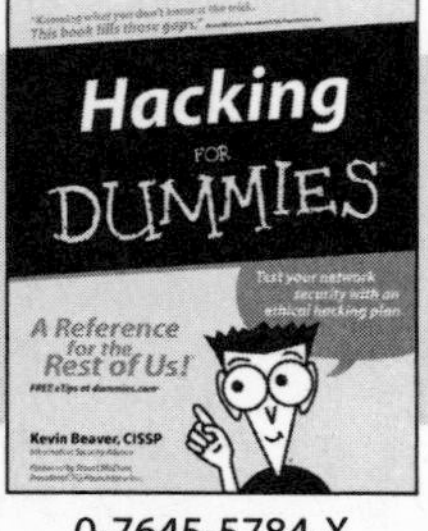

0-7645-5784-X

Also available:

- A+ Certification For Dummies 0-7645-4187-0
- Access 2003 All-in-One Desk Reference For Dummies 0-7645-3988-4
- Beginning Programming For Dummies 0-7645-4997-9
- C For Dummies 0-7645-7068-4
- Firewalls For Dummies 0-7645-4048-3
- Home Networking For Dummies 0-7645-42796
- Network Security For Dummies 0-7645-1679-5
- Networking For Dummies 0-7645-1677-9
- TCP/IP For Dummies 0-7645-1760-0
- VBA For Dummies 0-7645-3989-2
- Wireless All In-One Desk Reference For Dummies 0-7645-7496-5
- Wireless Home Networking For Dummie 0-7645-3910-8

HEALTH & SELF-HELP

0-7645-6820-5 *†

0-7645-2566-2

Also available:

- Alzheimer's For Dummies 0-7645-3899-3
- Asthma For Dummies 0-7645-4233-8
- Controlling Cholesterol For Dummies 0-7645-5440-9
- Depression For Dummies 0-7645-3900-0
- Dieting For Dummies 0-7645-4149-8
- Fertility For Dummies 0-7645-2549-2
- Fibromyalgia For Dummies 0-7645-5441-7
- Improving Your Memory For Dummies 0-7645-5435-2
- Pregnancy For Dummies † 0-7645-4483-7
- Quitting Smoking For Dummies 0-7645-2629-4
- Relationships For Dummies 0-7645-5384-4
- Thyroid For Dummies 0-7645-5385-2

EDUCATION, HISTORY, REFERENCE & TEST PREPARATION

0-7645-5194-9

0-7645-4186-2

Also available:

- Algebra For Dummies 0-7645-5325-9
- British History For Dummies 0-7645-7021-8
- Calculus For Dummies 0-7645-2498-4
- English Grammar For Dummies 0-7645-5322-4
- Forensics For Dummies 0-7645-5580-4
- The GMAT for Dummies 0-7645-5251-1
- Inglés Para Dummies 0-7645-5427-1
- Italian For Dummies 0-7645-5196-5
- Latin For Dummies 0-7645-5431-X
- Lewis & Clark For Dummies 0-7645-2545-X
- Research Papers For Dummies 0-7645-5426-3
- The SAT I For Dummies 0-7645-7193-1
- Science Fair Projects For Dummies 0-7645-5460-3
- U.S. History For Dummies 0-7645-5249-X

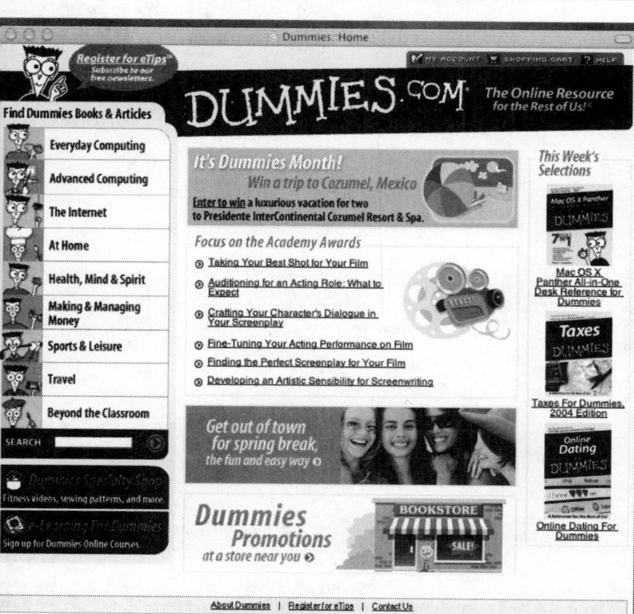

Get smart @ dummies.com®

- **Find a full list of Dummies titles**
- **Look into loads of FREE on-site articles**
- **Sign up for FREE eTips e-mailed to you weekly**
- **See what other products carry the Dummies name**
- **Shop directly from the Dummies bookstore**
- **Enter to win new prizes every month!**

***Separate Canadian edition also available**
†Separate U.K. edition also available

Available wherever books are sold. For more information or to order direct: U.S. customers visit www.dummies.com or call 1-877-762-2974. U.K. customers visit www.wileyeurope.com or call 0800 243407. Canadian customers visit www.wiley.ca or call 1-800-567-4797.